WORLD WIDE WEB JOURNAL

XML

Principles, Tools, and Techniques

O'REILLY™

WORLD WIDE WEB JOURNAL

XML: PRINCIPLES, TOOLS, AND TECHNIQUES **Volume 2, Issue 4, Fall 1997**

Publisher: Dale Dougherty

Guest Editor: Dan Connolly

Series Editor: Rohit Khare

Managing Editor: Donna Woonteiler

News Editor: D.C. Denison

Production Editor: Nancy Crumpton

Technical Illustrator: Robert Romano

Software Tools Specialist: Mike Sierra

Quality Assurance: Ellie Fountain Maden

Cover Design: Hanna Dyer

Text Design: Nancy Priest, Marcia Ciro

Subscription Administrator: Marianne Cooke

Photos: Flint Born

This book is printed on acid-free paper with 85% recycled content, 15% post-consumer waste. O'Reilly & Associates is committed to using paper with the highest recycled content available consistent with high quality.

ISSN: 1085-2301

ISBN: 1-56592-349-9 10/2/97

W3C GLOBAL TEAM

W3C Administration

Jean-François Abramatic
W3C Chairman and Associate Director, MIT Laboratory for Computer Science
jfa@w3.org

Tim Berners-Lee
Director of the W3C
timbl@w3.org

Vincent Quint
Deputy Director for Europe
quint@w3.org

Nobuo Saito
W3C Associate Chairman and Dean, Keio University
nobuo.saito@w3.org

Alan Kotok
W3C Associate Chairman
kotok@w3.org

Tatsuya Hagino
Deputy Director for Asia
hagino@w3.org

User Interface

Vincent Quint
Domain Leader
quint@w3.org

Bert Bos
bert@w3.org

Ramzi Guetari
guetari@w3.org

Arnaud Le Hors
lehors@w3.org

Håkon Lie
howcome@w3.org

Chris Lilley
chris@w3.org

Masayasu "Mimasa" Ishikawa
mimasa@w3.org

Dave Raggett
dsr@w3.org

Irène Vatton
vatton@w3.org

Technology and Society

Jim Miller
Domain Leader
jmiller@w3.org

Eui-Suk Chung
euisuk@w3.org

Daniel Dardailler
danield@w3.org

Philip DesAutels
philipd@w3.org

Josef Dietl
jdietl@w3.org

Joseph Reagle
reagle@w3.org

Ralph Swick
swick@w3.org

Architecture

Dan Connolly
Domain Leader
connolly@w3.org

Jim Gettys
jg@w3.org

Philipp Hoschka
hoschka@w3.org

Youichirou Koga
y-koga@w3.org

Yves Lafon
lafon@w3.org

Ora Lassila
lassila@w3.org

Henrik Frystyk Nielsen
frystyk@w3.org

Daniel Veillard
veillard@w3.org

Cross Areas and Technical Support

Janet Bertot
bertot@w3.org

Stephane Boyera
boyera@w3.org

Daicho Funato
daichi@w3.org

Tom Greene
tjg@w3.org

José Kahan
kahan@w3.org

Sally Khudairi
khudairi@w3.org

Stéphan Montigaud
montigaud@w3.org

Gerald Oskoboiny
gerald@w3.org

Luc Ottavj
ottavj@w3.org

Pierre Fillault
fillault@w3.org

Takeshi "Yamachan" Yamane
yamachan@w3.org

Administrative Support

Pamela Ahern
pam@w3.org

Susan Hardy
susan@w3.org

Marie-Line Ramfos
ramfos@w3.org

Josiane Roberts
roberts@inria.fr

Nancy Ryan
ryan@w3.org

Yukari Mitsuhashi
yukari@w3.org

W3C MEMBERS

ABN-AMRO Bank
Access Company Limited
Adobe Systems Inc.
Aérospatiale
AGF.SI
Agfa Division, Bayer Corp.
Agranat Systems, Inc.
Alcatel Alsthom Recherche
Alfa-Omega Foundation
Alis Technologies, Inc.
America Online, Inc.
American International Group Data Center, Inc. (AIG)
American Internet Corporation
Apple Computer, Inc.
ArborText, Inc.
Architecture Projects Management Ltd.
ArrowPoint Communications
Art Technology Group
Asymetrix Corporation
AT&T
Attachmate Corporation
BackWeb Technologies, Inc.
BELGACOM
Bellcore
Bitstream, Inc.
British Telecommunications Laboratories
Bull S.A.
Canal +
Canon, Inc.
Cap Gemini Innovation
Center for Democracy and Technology
Center for Mathematics and Computer Science (CWI)
CERN
CIRAD
CNET—The Computer Network
CNR—Instituto Elaborazione dell'Informazione
CNRS
Commissariat a L'Énergie Atomique (CEA)
CompuServe, Inc.
Computer Answer Line
Corporation for National Research Initiatives (CNRI)
CosmosBay
Council for the Central Laboratory of the Research Councils (CCL)
CyberCash, Inc.
Cygnus Support
Daewoo Electronics Company
Dassault Aviation
Data Channel
Data Research Associates, Inc.
Defense Information Systems Agency (DISA)
Deutsche Telekom—Online Pro Dienste GmbH & Co. KG (T-Online)
Digital Equipment Corporation
Digital Vision Laboratories Corporation
DigitalStyle Corporation
Direct Marketing Association, Inc.
DoubleClick
Eastman Kodak Company
École Nationale Supérieure d'Informatique et de Mathématiques Appliquées (ENSIMAG)
EDF
EEIG/ERCIM
ENEL
Engage Technologies
ENN Corporation
Enterprise Integration Technology
Entrust Technologies, Inc.
ERICSSON
Ernst & Young LLP
ETNOTEAM S.p.A.
Firefly Network, Inc.
First Virtual Holdings, Inc.
FirstFloor Software, Inc.
Folio Corporation
Foundation for Research and Technology (FORTH)
France Telecom
Fujitsu Limited
Fulcrum Technologies, Inc.
GCTECH S.A.
GEMPLUS
General Magic, Inc.
Geoworks
GMD Institute FIT
Graphic Communications Association
Grenoble Network Initiative
GRIF S.A.
Groupe ESC Grenoble
Harlequin Inc.
HAVAS
Hewlett Packard Laboratories, Bristol
Hitachi, Ltd.
@Home Network
Hong Kong Jockey Club
Hummingbird Communications Ltd.
IBERDROLA S.A.
IBM Corporation
ILOG, S.A.
InContext Systems
Industrial Technology Research Institute
Infopartners
INRETS
Inso Corporation, Providence
Institut Franco-Russe A.M. Liapunov
Institute for Information Industry
Intel Corporation
Intermind
Internet Profiles Corporation
Intraspect Software, Inc.
Joint Info. Systems Comm. of the UK Higher Ed. Funding Council
Justsystem Corporation
K2Net, Inc.
KnowledgeCite
Kumamoto Institute of Computer Software, Inc.
Lexmark International, Inc.
Los Alamos National Laboratory
Lotus Development Corporation
Lucent Technologies
Mainspring Communications, Inc.
Marimba, Inc.
Matra Hachette
MBED Software
MCI Telecommunications
Metrowerks Corporation
Michelin
Microsoft Corp.
Microsystems Software, Inc.
MITRE Corporation
Mitsubishi Electric Corporation
MTA SZTAKI
Narrowline
National Center for Supercomputing Applications (NCSA)
National Security Agency (NSA)
National University of Singapore
NCR
NEC Corporation
Netscape Communications
NHS (National Health Service, UK)
Nippon Telegraph & Telephone Corp. (NTT)
NOKIA Corporation
Novell, Inc.
NTT Data Communications Systems Corp.
Nynex Science & Technology, Inc.
O'Reilly & Associates, Inc.
Object Management Group, Inc. (OMG)
Object Services and Consulting, Inc.

W3C MEMBERS

OCLC (Online Computer Library Center, Inc.)
Omron Corporation
Open Market, Inc.
Open Sesame
Open Software Associates, Inc.
Open Software Foundation
Open Text Corporation
Oracle Corp.
ORSTOM
Pacifitech Corporation
Partners HealthCare System, Inc.
Pencom Web Works
Philips Electronic N.V.
Poet Software Corporation
PointCast Incorporated
Pretty Good Privacy, Inc.
Prodigy Services Corporation
Progressive Networks
Public IP Exchange, Ltd. (PIPEX)
Qualcomm Inc.
Raptor Systems, Inc.
Reed-Elsevier
Reuters Limited
Rice University for Nat'l HCPP Software
Riverland Holding NV/SA
Royal Melbourne Institute of Technology
Security Dynamics Technologies, Inc.
Sema Group
Sharp Corporation
SICS
Siemens-Nixdorf
Silicon Graphics, Inc.
SLIGOS
SoftQuad. Inc.
Software Publishers Association (SPA)
Sony Corporation
Spyglass, Inc.
Strategic Interactive Group
Sun Microsystems Corporation
SURFnet bv
Swedish Institute for Systems Development (SISU)
Syracuse University
Tandem Computers Inc.
Technische Universitat Graz
Teknema Corporation
Telecom Italia
Telequip Corporation
Terisa Systems, Inc.
Texcel Group
The Productivity Works, Inc.
Thomson-CSF
TIAA-CREF
Toshiba Corporation
TriTeal Corporation
TRUSTe
UKERNA
Unwired Planet
USWeb Corporation
VeriSign, Inc.
Verity, Inc.
Vignette Corporation
VTT Information Technology
webMethods, Inc.
WebTV Networks Inc.
Wolfram Research, Inc.
WWW. Consult Pty Ltd.
WWW—KR
Xerox Corporation
Xionics Document Technologies, Inc.

CONTENTS

This issue's cover image was photographed by Kevin Thomas and manipulated in Adobe Photoshop 4.0 by Edie Freedman.

CONTENTS

W3C REPORTS 27

TECHNICAL PAPERS 95

CONTENTS

EDITORIAL

IN THE ORIGINAL HTML DOCUMENTATION from 1991, Tim Berners-Lee wrote:

> *The hypertext markup language is an SGML format.*

The result of that design decision is something of a collision between the World Wide Web development community and the SGML community—between the quick-and-dirty software community and the formal ISO standards community. It also creates a collision between the interactive, online hypermedia technology and the bulk, batch print publications technology.

XML: Principles, Tools, and Techniques heralds the appearance of Extensible Markup Language (XML), a simple, powerful subset of Standard General Markup Language (SGML). In this issue of the World Wide Web Journal you'll find the complete technical specifications, primers, implementation case studies, applications, and even historical and philosophical reflections on the emerging role of XML.

A Splendid Inheritance

SGML is a complex, mature, stable technology. The international standard, ISO 8879: 1986, is over ten years old, and GML-based systems were established years earlier still. On the other hand, HTML is a relatively simple, new, and rapidly evolving technology.

When Tim Berners-Lee designed HTML, he chose to base it on SGML because SGML was an open, extensible technology that facilitated sound information management techniques. He knew extensibility was crucial because data formats on the Web would have to evolve as the system grew and changed. And openness was critical because he didn't want any single company or group to be able to prevent good ideas from other places from taking off.

Anyone who is familiar with HTML knows that its evolution has been far from graceful. What Tim didn't realize was that SGML was so complex and obscure that developers would guess what the standard said rather than looking it up—and they wouldn't always guess right.

The result is that our hard-won interoperability is not based on an open specification, but by the costly, primitive black art of reverse-engineering.

Another result is that today's Web software does not benefit from the extensibility of SGML: the market is full of specialized tools and applications that add tags to HTML for specific purposes—but the Web infrastructure as a whole does not accommodate these extensions.

XML is destined to remedy all that. It is a clean, simple dialect of SGML that developers can understand and implement consistently, and it provides extensibility—room to grow—beyond the centrally maintained set of HTML tags.

"Make the easy things easy and the hard things possible," is an established maxim in computer language design. HTML is successful in making the easy things easy, but if you have something that can't be done with the existing idioms in HTML, you might have to develop a completely new browser from scratch. Component technologies like plug-ins and Java are lowering the bar somewhat, true. But with the deployment of XML and stylesheets, the option of developing your own look and even your own document structures makes it easy enough to appeal to just about any information provider who is willing to tinker around.

Punctuated Equilibrium

XML is the product of careful evolution. Contradictory as that may seem, that is W3C's mission: "Leading the Evolution of the Web." Unlike the invisible hand of Nature, red in tooth and claw, W3C's technical staff takes an active role in cultivating the garden of Web technologies. Years spent nurturing the idea of Generic SGML are about to pay off in an explosion of new species of documents and unleash new applications to roam the Earth. But will this punctuation in the equilibrium of Web evolution drive its predecessors to extinction?

Beyond the engineering details of new Web technology, you can look to the *Web Journal* to provide context about the community behind the ideas and the broader role of standards bodies and industrial developments. In the first section of this book, we present a round table interview with members of the W3C design committees behind XML and lively first-person argument from David Siegel on the virtues of structured information. In "W3C Reports," you'll also hear about Mathematical Markup Language, a flagship XML application, as well as the Document Object Model's hooks for client-side scripting to animate those elements.

In "Technical Papers," several contributors posit how XML is a natural complement to Java and Web automation technologies. In the same way that URLs are shared technology for pointing to and accessing resources in distributed applications, XML provides an interchange format with extremely broad appeal. Each time a common programming task is institutionalized as shared technology, it lowers the cost of applications development and increases efficiency and innovation.

This is not to say that HTML will fade away: not everyone wants to develop a new document structure, stylesheet, or Java applet just to put up a Web page. HTML will always be there making the easy things easy. But with XML, if you want to go beyond the boundaries of HTML, it will be straightforward to do just that.

Kudos

The XML specification developers have taken on quite a challenge, and delivered specifications that work. But even they will tell you that the specification by itself is not sufficient to establish shared understanding in the community. Most of them are probably at a trade show or conference right now, teaching the basics or the nuances of XML to a few more people. They know well that another critical step to shared understanding is running code that developers can see, touch, run, use, and generally get their heads around. Some of their code is in this issue. Shared understanding in the community also involves an appreciation for the motivation, history, and rationale for the technology. I think we've captured some of that here too.

We'd like to thank those that made it possible for so many in the Web community—ourselves included—to study SGML and structured documents via the Internet by releasing software and documentation, maintaining ftp archives, hypertext bibliographies, and answering countless questions in USENET forums: Robin Cover, Erik Naggum, Dave Hollander, Conleth O'Connell, Darrell Raymond, Eliot Kimber, Lou Burnard, C.M. Sperberg-McQueen, and James Clark. And of course, a tip o' the hat to the dedicated O'Reilly staff for riding this bronco. ■

Dan Connolly, Austin, TX
Rohit Khare, Ellicott City, MD
September 19, 1997

XML BACKGROUND

The Road to XML

ADAPTING SGML TO THE WEB

Many computer scientists have talked about simplifying SGML. The W3C's XML Editorial Review Board has been working at it since July '96. So far, their efforts have received almost universal acclaim. Recently D.C. Denison canvassed a group of Editorial Review Board (ERB) members, and asked them to look back on how the XML project got off the ground, and where they think it's going from here.

XML wasn't the only acronym in the running when W3C's Working Group began to consider a name for what they hoped to create: specifications for a subset of SGML that was optimized for the Web.

"There were several acronyms that we considered," **Tim Bray** remembers. "I believe there was MGML, for Minimal Generalized Markup Language, and something called SIMPL for Simple Internet Markup Protocol, or something like that. Eventually we voted, and XML—for Extensible Markup Language—won out. It was short and sweet, and people liked it."

"Marketing XML to the HTML user was one of our prime goals," **Jean Paoli** adds. "We thought that putting the spin on the 'Extensibility' part of the language would attract the HTML user."

Choosing a name for the project was trivial, of course, compared to some of the other challenges that faced the group when they first started working together in July, 1996. Many other efforts to simplify SGML had run out of steam long before reaching the proposal stage. Somehow, however, this group managed to pull it off, publishing a working draft that's received wide acceptance in both the SGML and Web communities. How did they do it?

Let's Go Back a Few Years

A slimmed-down SGML is not a new concept. Many members of the XML team have been discussing the idea for years.

"Most computer scientists who have worked with SGML have proposed simplifications; specifically, keeping all the structural flexibility but losing many syntax options," ERB member **Steve DeRose** says. "I've heard of about a dozen proposals over the years."

Some of the XML authors, in fact, were already using a sort of proto-XML.

"I think it's important to understand that I and some other people had actually been doing XML for years," Tim Bray says. "A lot of people who are in the business were actually using SGML data in the case of open text searching and displaying. In the case of electronic book technology, there was a similar kind of story: we had long observed the fact that if they sent you some nicely-tagged text you could do any number, any amount of useful things with it without worrying about the minutiae of the standard and without having to have a DTD. So what XML in effect is has been around for a long time."

"Everyone who uses HTML for very long discovers that they want 'just one more tag.'"

Dave Hollander was another XML author who had already jumped the gun, so to speak.

"I developed a simplified SGML language while working on HP's LaserROM program in the early '90s," he recalls. "That evolved into the language used in our HP-UX help systems."

The rise of the Web, and HTML, pressed other members of the ERB to approach XML from the other direction.

"Everyone who uses HTML for very long discovers that they want 'just one more tag,'" according to Steve DeRose. "If you're doing catalogs you need a <PRICE> tag; for repair manuals you need <PARTNUM>; for ancient manuscripts you need <LACUNA> and <SIC>. Having been through this enough times, I want to be able to create new information structures any time my data justifies them, and do it easily. This is why C++ lets you make your own classes (imagine a development environment that didn't!), and it's why XML is absolutely necessary. To do generalized processing, retrieval, etc., I have to be able to say what things in documents *are*. I can do that with XML, but I can't do it with any one particular fixed tag set."

Jean Paoli was also well aware of HTML's shortcomings. "I discovered that a lot of Web content providers were using what they called 'structured comments' to hide information in their HTML," he says. "I was convinced that they needed a simple way to extend HTML, and I always thought that it could be a kind of simplified SGML that my SGML customers were all already using."

Jon Bosak was similarly inspired.

"XML arose from the realization that HTML is insufficient for certain kinds of Web applications," he says. "I was one of the people who came to this realization early because I was working in a field—online technical documentation—where the requirements are well understood and it's clear that HTML can't meet them. I was putting this complex material in online browsers used by millions of people before anyone had heard of HTML or the Web, and I knew from experience that HTML wasn't going to work for that kind of publishing. I knew that it wouldn't work well for any kind of large-scale content production. So I could see a time coming when large content providers would have to turn from HTML to something more powerful. The question was, what would they provide?

"I could see only two possibilities: either the big software companies would offer proprietary and probably binary-coded formats or we could get them to adopt a single, standard, human-readable format. The only standard solution that I knew could do the job was SGML."

Bosak's solution: "I started a working group in the W3C to provide specifications that could put SGML on the Web. What came out of that activity was XML—a subset of SGML designed for Web use."

Working and Evangelizing

The official W3C group, originally called the SGML ERB, began working together in July 1996; the larger mailing list discussions, the SGML Working Group, started the following September. Work proceeded quietly through most of 1996 and early 1997, via teleconferences, email, and the occasional conference. (In July '97, the SGML ERB became the XML WG and the SGML WG became the XML SIG.)

Meanwhile interest was growing, as the XML authors discussed the project with their colleagues. Perhaps it was an early indication of XML's flexibility that some authors, like Tim Bray, found that they could tailor their descriptions of XML to their audience.

"If I was talking to people to whom search and retrieval is very important, I would point out that when you invent your own tags, you can use them to drive searches and that's a lot better," he recalls.

"When I was talking to people to whom Java and that whole type of thing is important, I would point out that HTML is fine but it doesn't give Java much to chew on. And XML does. And if was talking to people who are in the publishing business and are irritated at HTML's fairly primitive page make-up facilities, I would point out that one solution to that is to de-couple the markup syntax and the formatting semantics, and XML does that.

When ERB member **C.M. Sperberg-McQueen** spoke to colleagues about XML, he promoted "the ability to use your own tags, rather than the rather eccentric and constricted vocabulary of HTML," he recalls. "That's easily the most important aspect of XML from the point of view of academic research. The ability to write an XML parser that fits in 30 Kb of memory also captured the attention of a lot of programmers and tool developers."

Eve Maler found that the XML applications that generated the most excitement were "the ones that blur the distinction between information delivery and transacting business, such as ordering a new part by clicking on a part number in an online service bulletin. And the idea of using XML as an exchange protocol for purely transaction-oriented applications is also pretty popular, as we've seen by the quick promotion of XML-based EDI initiatives.

"Of course, for many people who have had exposure only to HTML, they're most impressed simply by the notion that tags can have *meaning*," Maler continues. "Many of the business and technical requirements they've conceived to date could be addressed with this one innovation!"

Soon, a certain software company began to show an interest in XML. Jean Paoli, of Microsoft, a member of the original SGML Editorial Review Board, had been aggressively evangelizing XML to the company's Explorer product teams.

"When I talked about XML to the people here at Microsoft," Paoli remembers, "I always stressed its ability to encode data, not documents. Nobody at Microsoft understood why you would want to use XML for things that HTML is good for. But data? Yes. And describing customers and orders? Yes. Financial information? Yes. So I always sold XML to the database people, the people who understood the value of structuring data."

"Adam Bosworth (who designed Microsoft Access) and Thomas Reardon helped me a lot selling this idea."

"But, even more important, it was the Channel Definition Format (CDF) that helped sell the whole XML story to Microsoft," Paoli continues. "At that moment (February '97), the push battle was terrible between Netscape and Microsoft, and the Internet Explorer team was searching for a good data file format to represent Webcasting information. It was evident that XML was a good choice. I presented XML to the managers of the Microsoft Internet Push team and we modeled their Webcasting data in ten minutes! It took only a few days to decide to use XML. The first XML application (CDF) by Microsoft gave Microsoft a big win. This was the beginning of a lot of PR around XML. Starting XML with a winning application was a great thing for XML!"

In March '97, Microsoft officially announced that they were going to base their new Channel Definition Format on XML. This generated a fair amount of interest in XML among programmers and Internet professionals.

Breakthroughs

As late '96 turned into early '97, two events brought a new level of attention to the XML project. The first was the SGML '96 conference, held in November 1996.

"The SGML '96 conference was a watershed," Steve DeRose remembers, "because it was not clear whether the SGML community would see XML as SGML writ large, or as some kind of competitor. Since SGML software already supports tag extensibility, variant delimiters, etc., and the SGML market has huge amounts of high-value data, this community is important.

The SGML community saw the benefits of simplicity and ease of adoption and jumped on board. The Web community has done the same, though for different reasons: extensibility and validation. The beauty of XML is that it gets you the best of both worlds; but any technology like that overlaps partly with both of the things it draws on; the reception in both communities is therefore crucial. As soon as I saw the major SGML vendors *and* the major Web vendors all diving in, I knew we were in good shape."

The WWW6 Conference, held early in 1997 in Santa Clara, California, was another milestone.

"We put on a major PR blitz at that conference, and I think it went over pretty well," Tim Bray recalls. "I think XML was one of the hot stories of that conference. By May 1 of '97 it was pretty obvious we were onto something that was going to be significant. And it's grown since then."

"Microsoft announced CDF based on XML a few weeks before the WWW6 conference, on purpose, in order to boost the interest in XML," Paoli remembers. "I took a bunch of Microsoft people who were involved in XML to the conference, and we made as much noise as possible in all the XML sessions."

"The SGML people got it as soon as they saw XML," Jon Bosak recalls, "because they all come from industries that had to solve this problem a long time ago. The HTML people only got it this year; that's when they started hitting the wall in large numbers, in terms of having to deal with significant levels of content. At the WWW5 Conference in Paris a year earlier, not many people knew what I was talking about. But when we presented the XML draft at the WWW6 Conference in April '97, about half the faces in the audience lit up. Those were content providers and Web site administrators who'd finally hit that wall. They knew that they had a problem, they just didn't know what to do about it. As soon as they saw XML, they knew."

Microsoft versus Netscape

Soon Netscape joined Microsoft in agreeing to support the new standard. Tim Bray began working with Netscape as a consultant. Articles on XML began showing up in a variety of print magazines and online publications. Predictably, many media stories played up the Microsoft-versus-Netscape angle.

"The SGML people got it as soon as they saw XML because they all come from industries that had to solve this problem a long time ago."

Many ERB members tend to downplay the importance of the competition between Microsoft and Netscape, but they all agree it will have an impact.

"Looking at this purely from the industry point of view," Jon Bosak says, "the competition can only do us good by accelerating the acceptance of a truly open, human-readable data format."

"The participation of both Microsoft and Netscape has been very beneficial," C.M. Sperberg-McQueen adds. "They bring a particular technical perspective to the discussions: the view of the world from a large programming shop with enormous numbers of current users is rather different from the view of the world from an academic institution or from a smaller commercial organization. In that sense, the Microsoft and Netscape viewpoints have been more similar than different, in my view."

Steve DeRose believes that competitive issues will not intrude on the creation of the XML specification.

"The competition between Microsoft and Netscape would be almost a non-issue if not for a few over-excited articles," he says. "All the representatives on the XML Working Group are deeply committed to doing the right thing, and to a consensus process. Neither Netscape nor Microsoft has tried to dominate the process or to foist any self-serving proposals on the [XML working] group. Also, I think both companies realize they have better places to compete than over syntax. Let them and everyone else compete on user interface quality, reliability, performance, and functionality—not on who can dream up new tag names or punctuation marks faster!"

Details, Details

Although XML has met with an enthusiastic reception, the ERB members are well aware of the work that remains. First and foremost, they have to finish the specification.

"It would be nice if we could finish XML 1.0 and get it snapshotted," Tim Bray says. "We should get it blessed by W3C as a recommendation, and maybe even get it blessed by another standards organization as well, just so that we have a line in the sand and can say, 'Okay, this phase is done.' I think we need to do that simply because there are so many implementations happening so fast that just to be fair to the people who believed in what we've done we have to stop changing it. We have to stop and say, 'Okay, here's what it is. Maybe it's not perfect yet, it could be improved still further, but here's 1.0 and that's what 1.0 is.' I think clearly by the end of the year we must have 1.0 finished, blessed, and canonized. There will still be lots of other things to work on. The 1.0 version won't have a solution to the style sheet problem, it won't have a solution for lots of other things, but the base language has to be frozen."

Jon Bosak, for one, is hopeful that the big issues are behind them.

"I may be whistling in the dark," he says. "But aside from the political issues we're going to have to deal with as a result of competition, I don't think that XML really faces any major problems once we get the specification for 1.0 finished. It's been designed to be easy to implement, and outside of all the last-minute internationalization details, it hasn't really changed much for a while. The basics have been in place since last November '96, and most of the finer points were settled by April '97."

Still there are details on top of details.

"In addition to the greater complexity of XML itself," Bosak says, "we're dealing with all kinds of issues that were never confronted directly in HTML—how to handle whitespace, for example, or whether to make stuff like tag names case-sensitive or not, or whether the Japanese character for an ideographic space is really a space or not. Lots of nitty but mind-bogglingly complex problems that finally can't be sidestepped any more. And there was a big policy question, which was what to do about error-handling—but we're past that now."

"The real action," Bosak continues, "shifts now to the other two pieces of the puzzle, the linking piece and the style sheet piece. We call them XLL, for extensible linking language, and XSL, for extensible style sheet language. XML itself is just about syntax. With XLL and XSL we get into semantics, and that's where the real competition is going to be: how you actually *do* stuff."

"The hardest thing, in general," Steve DeRose says, "is to look far enough ahead to make sure that the language will scale up smoothly and accommodate later extensions without getting kludgy. The broadstroke picture is very clear, but if you don't pin all the details down well enough, systems won't interoperate and you lose a central benefit of standardization. It's nice to see descriptive markup move into the mainstream and be adopted so quickly. I hope that it will let us really move data into forms that will outlast rev 5.3.9.1b of somebody's word processor, and help make bit-rot a non-issue for the future of literature."

Fortunately, XML will be easier to develop than HTML, according to Tim Bray.

"HTML is painfully difficult to evolve," he says, "because it is a mixture of formatting semantics and hypertext semantics and GUI semantics with forms and so on. And trying to evolve all of those capabilities at once without breaking them is very difficult. Now XML, the basic language, has a syntax and there's going to be a style sheet facility and there's going to be various behavior facilities. That doesn't mean that evolving any of this stuff is easy, it just means that you can partition the problems and solve them without having to solve them all at once, which is the problem that HTML faces. So a lot of the advanced capabilities that users of the Web are asking for, I think, are going to be easier to solve in an XML context."

Yet still ahead, after the big technical problems are largely solved, there's another challenge: inspiring people to exploit the new possibilities that come with XML.

"Now that it is reasonable to expect next generation tools to have better control over encoding information," **Dave Hollander** says, "we need to get ready to use these features. My next key initiative is how to get authors, collaborators, and consumers of information to make the best use of the new capabilities."

"Now, we have to encourage the market to create specific horizontal and vertical DTDs, to build common vocabularies," Paoli says. "We need to let content providers generate useful XML data while we, the software and tool builders, build tools which access and uses this data."

There's plenty to do, to be sure. Yet, at this point it appears likely that the early work of the XML ERB has created enough momentum to carry the project to completion.

"What's important, from here on in, is to keep all these activities moving toward the goal we started with in July 1996," Jon Bosak says. "It's more like a snowball gathering speed down a slope now. It doesn't need pushing, it just needs to be kept pointed in the right direction." ■

WORK IN PROGRESS
People & Projects

DAVID SIEGEL
THE WEB IS RUINED AND I RUINED IT

Every so often, dredging through the muck and mire of hopeless self-promotion and autodidacticism saturating the World Wide Web, one encounters an exotic specimen: the Web Head who truly merits it. David Siegel is not merely a self-proclaimed "HTML Terrorist," he has been so anointed by knowledgeable and right-thinking SGML/XML purists everywhere.

This article first appeared in Web Review (www.webreview.com) in the depths of the Tag Wars. It describes how proper separation of structure (HTML), style (CSS), and semantics (XML) make content more compelling and design more effective. Visit David's sites at www.verso.com and www.dsiegel.com. [Ed]

The Roots of HTML Terrorism

Some people say I've ruined the Web, and to them it's true. Web pages can't be seen as easily by search engines and those with low-end machines have a hard time getting much out of my site. On my personal site, I don't even put ALT tags just to send a message to those surfing without images. My life is visual. I love museums. How would you like to visit the Louvre with images turned off?

I ruined the Web by mixing chocolate and peanut butter so they could never become unmixed. I committed the hangable offense of mixing structure with presentation, and in HTML and SGML circles, that's a big no-no.

The reason the HTML purists never carried out their threats is not that they're against violence, it's that they know that if they kill me, someone else will rise to take my place. It seems that structure and presentation have been mixed forever, and the Web is in the fast lane of the road to Hell. Fortunately, nothing on the Web is what it seems, and "forever" lasts only about six months.

Structure versus Layout

First things first: Structure is markup. Markup is structure. To mark up a document is to describe its structure using metadata, also known as tags. Tags were never meant to denote images or frames. Tags are meant to describe contents, not presentation. For example, the <P> tag denotes a paragraph (originally, HTML required a closing p-tag, </P>, but most browsers ignored it, so it fell out of use). A tag would denote something as a recipe, a movie review, a book title, a product description, a grade, a headline, a bowling score, etc. Imagine all the things that go into a newspaper. Properly tagged, you could apply a layout engine, using a set of lay out rules, to layout an entire newspaper automatically. Not surprisingly, this kind of application is exactly where SGML, the grandfather of HTML, came from.

Layout is presentation. Presentation is layout. Apply one set of layout rules and get *The New York Times*. Apply another set and get *The Village Voice*. Notice I am not talking about content! I'm talking about layout. I'm writing this document in Microsoft Word. To tell you that *The New York Times* is a newspaper title, I've used the italic feature, as any good editor would. Now that you're reading it in HTML, someone has put it between <I> and </I> tags, so now you're seeing the title in italics, too. Blasphemy! How dare we use italics, when we mean <newspapertitle>The New York Times </newspapertitle>, don't we? If we had a <newspapertitle> tag, then people with 24x80 terminals in Zimbabwe would see "The New York Times" rather than *The New York Times*, because on a 24x80 terminal, you can't display italics. The browser itself adds the quote marks—*they would not be part of the document.* In this case, the tag indicates meta-information, which the User Agent (also known as a browser) interprets however it can on the target display. Similarly, if this text were being spoken by a speaking browser for the blind (yes, there are some—and no, they're not very good), the <newspapertitle> tag would be a signal to the program to pause and then emphasize the name of the paper. Gripping, isn't it? Are they that extreme, those HTML extremists er, I mean, purists?

Let's take another example. A few sentences earlier, I wrote "they would not be part of the document" in italics. Remember that? Did I mean italics? Or did I really mean *emphasis!* [italics mine] Oh, yeah, that's what I meant, but I'm used to hitting the <I> key, not the <EM> key. Wow. Are they that extreme, those HTML extremists er, I mean, purists? Yes, they are that extreme. They can't believe everyone is using <I> for italics when they really mean <EM>, for emphasis.

The Roots of HTML

Let's look at the sheer beauty of this argument for a second. Separate all your content from its descriptive data (metadata, or markup), and the world suddenly gets interesting. You can see right through newspapers to the stock pages. You can compare movie reviews among 372 newspapers at once. You can search for Marx and find Karl, not Groucho, simply by filtering for the <PROMINENTSOCIALIST CLASS=MANIFESTOWRITER> tag.

In a perfectly tagged world, no one needs a search engine at her own site. In a perfectly tagged world, the big search engines do all the work for us, by searching the Web and storing not only the data, but also the metadata. In a perfectly tagged world, we would standardize our tags, so that everyone would use the same exact tag to denote a <MOVIEREVIEW CLASS=HORROR>, or <RECIPE CLASS=VEGAN>. If one person decided to use a tag called <MOVIEREVIEW> and another used one called <FILMREVIEW>, the search engines would have a hard time keeping up with all the new tags (are you listening, Marc Andreessen?). Hence, the need for standardized markup (there I go again—don't look at my source, okay?).

Go one step further and say what kind of a document you are reading—a play, a newspaper, a Ph.D. thesis, a recipe book, a journal— and you soon need to generalize the language to include the document type, followed by the appropriate markup for that document type. Cookbooks contain recipes, report cards contain grades, plays contain dialogue, scene and action descriptions, and so forth. Standard tags for time sensitivity let visitors choose whether they want to see only the most recent content or see the last ten days' worth of material with every page they visit.

Voilà! I've just performed a magic trick: Now we know what SGML is—Standard Generalized Markup Language. It's a difficult concept, because the generalized part adds a layer of abstraction by first saying what species of document you have, then adds the markup appropriate for that species. Now that you understand it, you see where HTML came from. HTML is a fairly weak, underpowered set of markup tags for marking up hypertext physics papers. When Tim Berners-Lee talks about "inventing" the Web, he means that he came up with a few tags for writing physics papers and linking them together.

The Roots of HTML Terrorism

Just after Tim did his thing, a kid named Marc Andreessen came up with the idea of the <IMG> tag, and the Web was both born and destroyed at that moment. You see, Marc is the founding father of the HTML Terrorist Guild, which now numbers in the thousands. As inventor of the <BLINK> tag, Marc has done as much damage as I have with less effort. All I did was take Marc's <IMG> tag a step further, to use single-pixel GIFs to help lay out a Web page. Seen from the perspectives of the SGML crowd, this is about as far away from the beauty of the original argument as one can get.

But it didn't stop there. I kept wanting to align my backgrounds and foregrounds, forcing readers to see pages my way, not the way they thought they wanted to see them.

Now let's return to the real world of the Web (not an oxymoron at all, in case the thought just crossed your mind). The Web got where it is in six easy steps:

1. The Framers of the Web mark up their papers on their NeXT machines and put them on the first Web servers, delighted to be avoiding FedEx charges to their limited particle-physics budgets. The `<IMG>` tag makes the Web visual, and products like PageMill reinforce the ugly-factor of first-generation sites.

2. I come along and start laying out pages visually, using HTML (admittedly, a markup language, not a page-description language) as it was never intended to be used. I pour narrative text into tables, completely hosing the idea that tables should be used for tabular material. My sites become popular. People start doing what I'm doing. I write a book explaining how to do it, and it becomes the *Amazon.com*[*] number one best-selling book of 1996 in five months. The Web falls apart quickly. The search engines can't tell a picture of Dolly Parton from a picture of Dolly the sheep.

3. HTML changes so rapidly, and site maintenance becomes so difficult, that large sites start using databases to serve up their pages, separating the content from the HTML. Dynamic Web sites that cost $300,000 to build become the norm. Companies like *Organic*[†] grow quickly, taking advantage of the market for database-driven sites. The search engines, which can't see inside databases, break even more.

4. Microsoft comes to the aid of the W3C and puts some muscle behind Cascading Style Sheets (CSS), for the sole reason that they are what Netscape is not doing. Also, as it turns out, the people in Microsoft's browser division saw that it was good to separate style from markup, and they made a good choice. Internet Explorer 3.0 ships with style-sheet capability. Few people write style sheets, but they are a good step forward.

5. NetObjects Fusion, a product based entirely on my principles (you can see my filenames in their code and I didn't get any NetObjects stock—what is it they say about imitation and flattery?). The product takes a baby step toward becoming the first PageMaker of the Web. Databases detect which browser you're using and serve sites adjusted for all the different display bugs. Structurists see Fusion sites being paired with databases and prepare to eat the sleepy applesauce and lay down with purple shrouds over their heads.

6. Style sheets don't solve all layout problems, but they improve typography greatly. Netscape announces a whole bunch of new tags to keep people smoking their

* *http://www.amazon.com*

† *http://www.organic.com*

layout crack. Because Microsoft has aligned with the W3C, Netscape tries to reinvent Director by putting lots of "dynamic HTML" tags into their 4.0 browser. The design community isn't sure what to do.

Keep in mind that the purists are protecting some pretty fetid ground. Most of the content on the Web is garbage, and most of my content turns to garbage after some reasonably short period of time. Trying to find quality on the Web is like trying to find arable land in Antarctica. The Web is a visual medium—not to design is to design. Personally, I'd rather leave the design up to professional designers than programmers, but hey—that's me. It's easy to be proud of your Web site. It's another thing to have people say it was visually appealing and easy to find everything.

Back to Reality

Here in the spring of 1997, I still have to use what works. My clients want to win on the Web, so we employ the method used by more political strategists: Image. We use great-looking sites and compelling experiences to create equity on the Web for our clients. Example: The coming bookstore wars. Amazon.com will have a lot of competition. All of them will have great selection, service, and advice on what to buy. The battle will be fought on design and editorial content, plus extra services that make people feel special. This has nothing to do with "information," but everything to do with attracting and keeping customers. How much information does Nike give out about its products? Not a lot. On the commercial side of the Web, design can make millions of dollars of difference.

Does that mean Amazon.com should use every new gizmo and tag Netscape provides? Does that mean we should suck up to the smarmy <LAYER> tag and leave the standards body behind? I hope not. I support the standards process. Right now, there is an interesting debate in the W3C over something called the OBJECT model. It promises to give us active, dynamic Web sites and still separate content from presentation. For some odd reason, Netscape is actually being quite helpful and conciliatory in this debate, and though we can't figure out why, we certainly see it as a good sign for designers.

I can't say that much about the OBJECT model yet, because there are a bunch of details to work out. Suffice to say it won't involve any new tags, because tags are for markup, not layout. It will involve the use of a special tag, called <DIV>, which we already use today in our work with style sheets. (View the source of *http://www.highfive.com* to see our current use of style sheets.) We expect both fifth-generation browsers to incorporate the still-unapproved OBJECT model within a year.

We are waiting for PNG, the Portable Network Graphics format, to replace GIF.* Let's hope that by the end of the year most images on the Web are PNG, with several levels of transparency and a much richer set of extensions. It's been a political battle, but PNG is

* *http://www.w3.org/TR/REC-prog*

promising and it will come. Add PNG images to your sites—visitors using Netscape Communicator will automatically download the PNG plug-in the first time they encounter one. Let's hope they encounter lots of them. Perhaps professional-quality image standards like Live-Picture and Olivr will take us even further in our quest for low-bandwidth quality.

We are waiting for vector graphics like Flash.* Flash images will be tiny. They will look great. They will be as close as you can get to PostScript without making a PDF.

We are waiting for something in between SGML and HTML. SGML is too general and too complicated for the Web. Instead, we need a junior version, and that's called XML. Just formulated in the fall of 1996, the ideas behind XML are good: to create a generalized markup language independent of presentation that works for most of the document types found on the Web. I'll talk about XML another time, but the early news is that Microsoft is interested and excited about taking HTML in this direction. In a few years, Microsoft Word's underlying data could be marked up in XML, but it's a bit far off to be making predictions like that (I just can't resist trying to tilt the playing field).

We will have to wait before the tools catch up. About two years ago, I said the first halfway decent tools would appear in late 1997. I may get lucky and be on track with that prediction. Then again, we may have to wait a while longer. HTML isn't PostScript. It's hard to build tools that don't suck on top of a set of standards being used in a giant tug-of-war between big companies with millions at stake. Until good tools exist, Web designers will continue to be used as human shields in the browser wars, with our customers being the big losers as they pay us to make two separate versions of everything and serve HTML out of custom databases.

Style Sheets: The Light at the End of the Tunnel

Let's take one thing at a time. If we're going to learn anything, it's that style sheets are the future and tag-based layout is the past. What can style sheets do? They can do a lot of typographic things, like set your margins, indents, drop caps, leading, and other niceties invented in the time of the Romans. No longer should we pour our text into tables, for I have led us through the desert for 40 years (seemed like it, anyway), and we have emerged in the promised land, where style sheets give us the margins we seek. Sure, we still have to use tables to lay out our pages, but in a year or so, we hope to give that up, too. Say goodbye to the single-pixel GIF! Use it only when necessary! Ban the kluges—learn to use style sheets today!

Okay, maybe tomorrow.

Turns out that the Internet Explorer 3.0 version of style sheets is pretty different from the 4.0 version, and the Netscape Communicator version will likely have its differences. We will find the common presentational behavior of both 4.0 browsers and use that. Stay tuned.

* *http://www.macromedia.com/software/flash*

One thing you don't want to do is to commit style-sheet terrorism. Style-sheet terrorism is where you use style-sheet capabilities by brute force, mixing the style primitives right into your content, rather than separating the content from the description of the presentation. Look at *Microsoft's Style Gallery*.* It's shameful. Look at both the code and with Netscape Navigator 3.0. What's going on? To get a drop-shadowed "3," they've used the actual number two times—once dark and once light—positioned on top of each other. Not only that, but the number itself is part of an ordered list—the program should take care of the numbering automatically! The style sheet should describe the behavior of an ordered list in the absence of the list data. I repeat: There should be no use of style sheets to effect typography that is bound to the content. Style sheets must describe content that isn't there, then be applied to content that is. If the style sheet doesn't give the intended result, debug the style sheet, not the data.

To be fair, the gallery was created last summer in a rush. The people hired to make it were just playing around. But they didn't understand the basic concept, and Microsoft let everyone see it as an example of how to use style sheets, mostly because it looks awful in Netscape. If you did it correctly, your pages would just look gray and dull in Netscape, rather than all screwed up, and that would reflect badly on Microsoft, hence the style-sheet terrorism.

The Big-Brother Issue

One of the central questions surrounding the use of style sheets is: Who gets the final say over the look of a document? A small percentage of the readership is colorblind, another group prefers larger type, and others have special viewing requirements. Then there are alternative surfing environments like Web phones, WebTV, and Web dishwashers. Each has its own special browser and its own limitations. Aside from that, issues of available typefaces, available colors, monitor size, and other parameters affect the average surfer every day. Should there only be one way to view a Web page?

My answer is simple: The designer should be able to specify how the page looks under most conditions and give more (but perhaps not total) control to the viewer as a last resort. In other words, designers should be authoritarian, not dictatorial. Fortunately, that is roughly how style sheets work. Style sheets can cascade, and that has two meanings, so let me take them one at a time.

Style sheets can refer by name. A style sheet can include another style sheet simply by naming it, specifying its absolute or relative location on the Web. This lets us build a hierarchy of simple, middle, and more complex style sheets without reinventing the wheel every time we write one. As with Java, the lower-level libraries are just now being built (by no one, actually, but we hope someone starts working on them soon). Then we can write more complicated style sheets based on

* *http://www.microsoft.com/truetype/css/gallery/slide1.htm*

those and place them on public servers. All you'll have to do to use a Dave Siegel style sheet is include its name and location at the top of your file, and its full functionality will apply to your document. Is that going to make using style sheets easy? Yes. You won't have to write anything. You'll just find the style sheets you like and specify them by name.

Style sheets have the capability to degrade gracefully. Today, you can specify which fonts to use for which sections of a site, and if those fonts aren't available, you can specify a second and third choice, and so on. Style sheets go further. If a style sheet is well written, it will contain instructions for what happens when you see a Web page under optimal conditions (big screen, fast modem, lots of colors, etc.), then how it should look under suboptimal conditions (256 colors, 14-inch screen, slow modem), and also how it should look under lousy conditions (WebTV, Microsoft CE, black-and-white screen, etc.). There aren't three levels of cascade, there are as many as the designer can specify.

One of the most vexing things about this approach is that we still don't have standard ways of learning how big or colorful people's systems are, and this is a huge impediment to site designers. The W3C could have long ago specified ways for people to fill out a little profile in their browser, specifying, among other things, how many colors they have, how large their screen is, whether they have sound capability, etc. There are a lot of other Big-Brother issues surrounding profiles, but I'm a strong believer that people will benefit by giving sites a bit of information about themselves (demographics), their lifestyles (psychographics), and their viewing systems (technographics). If the Web is going to be free, it's a small price to pay for getting better service. And anyway, if you don't specify a profile, you don't get the benefit of it. No one would be forced to fill out a profile, but if most people did, it would help sites degrade properly.

Finally, style sheets take the correct stance that the viewer should, in the end, be able to specify her own style sheet for her own viewing. She should be able to set up her browser (User Agent) so it always overrides the designer's style sheets and substitutes her own. There should actually be levels of override. It should be fairly hard to completely throw out a designer's intended style sheet, but if she checks the box marked "Hey, I really really really want to use my own damn style sheet, okay?", then she should be able to get her way.

Turning in My Black Hat

Because both Marc Andreessen and I are HTML terrorists, we are jointly responsible for the mess. Yet here our roads diverge. While Marc and his pals have been slaving away deep in the Netscape laboratory to bring us such visions of beauty as the <SPACER> tag and the <MULTICOL> tag—and now a new set of <LAYER> tags—I am in the process of turning in my black hat.

I am leaning toward structure. The hacks I've espoused, especially the single-pixel GIF, and using frames and tables to do layout, are the duct tape of the Web. They are the designer's finger in the dam, trying to keep the ugly gray sites where they belong—at Yahoo!, not in our portfolios. Several of the things I've mentioned here are part of doing it better.

Some day, the purists and I will see eye-to-eye, while Marc and company keep on tagging, with lame excuses like: "Our customers demand interim, tag-based solutions." Hogwash. When the browser manufacturers let us separate content from presentation, we will gladly comply, for the benefit of surfers everywhere. My personal priorities are that design drives the train, because to hold an audience, you need good content presented well. The best content poorly presented will lose to a better idea hidden by dull presentation (presidential elections aside).

"XML promises to be the Alexandria (I won't say Xanadu) of our digital desert dreams." It will let us build great libraries simply by building our own sites. It will let the average person put together very sophisticated and powerful applications, simply by tagging everything properly so it fits into the larger schema of the Web. Style sheets and the OBJECT model will provide the layout capabilities to make it look good. Then, in that future, we will have databases only to do what databases do best: search for and compare 283 possible ways to get from San Francisco to Denver on July 3 for the lowest fare, find the best combination of 40,000 products for a particular visitor, or to do banking transactions. In this future scenario, Web sites will be big, flat, and tagged full of standard-compliant metadata descriptions. Then the webmaster will tend, or farm, this flat Web site, using automated content-management tools to help keep it all up to date. Meanwhile, the search engines will grow more powerful every day and the average site builder will be able to participate. Radical, yes. You decide who is extreme.

Light at the End of the Tunnel

You're not on the commercial side of the Web, you say? Then why complain? Stick with your human-genome site and put helical horizontal rules all over the place. Wait for the rest of us to catch up. When XML hits, you'll be able to say, "I told you so." Until then, don't expect many visitors. When we have better tools, we will use them. When HTML evolves to the point that we no longer need to do browser detection or dynamic page serving, we will do things simpler, and better. Until then, we're going to go through another round of hacks where we put everything into databases and serve pages from there. It won't help the search engines at all. It will cost millions of dollars. It will all be totally unnecessary. Don't look at me. Look at Netscape. They break the rules; I just do what needs to be done. If I have ruined the Web, I apologize. It was my intention all along. Many people like me have put design and content ahead of structure, and now we can see a light at the end of the tunnel. Netscape has blocked the way, but they may be coming around. Site designers unite. Fight for presentation and structure. If we win, our future will be so bright, we'll have to wear shades. ■

First Combined P3P Meetings

JUNE 26, 1997, *Cambridge, Massachusetts*

The Platform for Privacy Preferences (P3) Project was launched to generate the specification and demonstration of an interoperable way of expressing privacy practices and preferences by Web sites and users respectively. Participants from more than 20 W3C Member organizations discussed Project goals, technology and policy requirements, privacy and profiling issues, results of the FTC hearings, as well as the OPS submission. Two new working groups were formed to address architecture and vocabulary. *http://www.w3.org/P3/*

Tim Berners-Lee Participates at White House Administration's Electronic Commerce Initiative

JULY 1, 1997, *Washington, D.C.*

W3C Director Tim Berners-Lee met with U.S. President Clinton, government officials, and other technology leaders at the White House for the Administration's announcement of a nine-point framework to spur electronic commerce on a global scale. Principles of the framework include the recognition of the uniqueness of the Internet, minimal government restrictions, and the promotion of a predictable and consistent legal environment for electronic commerce. Issues addressed in the framework include online payment, intellectual property protection, security, privacy, content control, and standards development. A prototype from the Platform for Privacy Preferences (P3) Project was demonstrated before the U.S. Federal Trade Commission as a way to allow users to be easily and automatically informed of a site's practices. *http://www.w3.org/Press/Magaziner*

W3C Publishes First Public Working Draft of HTML 4.0

JULY 8, 1997, *Cambridge, Massachusetts*

The HTML 4.0 Working Draft builds on the multimedia and hypertext features which debuted in the HTML 3.2 Recommendation, published in January, 1997. HTML 4.0 adds enhancements such as advanced forms, frame improvements, table enhancements, object support, script and style elements, as well as named entities to make the Web more appealing for both content providers and users. Demonstrating the power of the W3C process, the HTML Working Group includes key industry players such as Adobe Systems, Hewlett Packard, IBM, Microsoft, Netscape Communications, Novell, SoftQuad, Spyglass, and Sun Microsystems; content specialists at HotWired, PathFinder and Verso; and experts in the fields of accessibility and internationalization. *http://www.w3.org/Press/HTML4*

W3C Exhibits Technology at European Ministerial Conference

JULY 8, 1997, *Bonn, Germany*

The European Ministerial Conference on Global Information Networks, hosted by the Federal Republic of Germany and organized in cooperation with the European Commission, convened to outline principles governing the use of global information networks, and to stress the need for international cooperation. Attendees included Ministers from European Union Member States, guest countries and select global organizations. W3C Electronic Commerce Specialist Josef Dietl and Technology & Society Project Manager Daniel Dardailler demonstrated PICS and P3P, two projects featured in the European Initiative in Electronic Commerce. The resultant "Bonn Declaration" is expected to focus on principles such as the free flow of information in the context of secure commerce, user empowerment, and confidence in electronic commerce. *http://www.w3.org/Press/Bonn*

Web Accessibility Initiative (WAI) Working Group Meeting

AUGUST 4-5, 1997, *Cambridge, Massachusetts*

The second meeting of the WAI Working Group addressed technical developments which focus on protocols and data formats aimed at making the Web itself more accessible. Technical issues include HTML, XML, CSS and Aural extensions, HTTP content/feature negotiation, DOM, support for Math, and labeling/rating with PICS. *http://www.w3.org/WAI/*

DOM Working Group Meeting

AUGUST 18-19, 1997, *Vancouver, Canada*

The third working group spun off the former HTML ERB addresses DOM, the Document Object Model, a platform- and language-neutral interface that will allow programs and scripts to dynamically access and update the content, structure, and style of documents. The DOM Working Group, chaired by Lauren Wood of SoftQuad, strives to produce interoperable and scripting-language neutral solutions. *http://www.w3.org/MarkUp/DOM/*

HTML Working Group Meeting

AUGUST 25-26, 1997, *San Jose, California*

The HTML Working Group met at Adobe Systems to continue work on HTML 4.0. The working group, chaired by Dan Connolly, addressed topics which included internationalization, objects, images, applets, presentation, style sheets, frames, forms and scripting, and XML in HTML for Math and RDF. *http://www.w3.org/MarkUp/*

CSS & FP Working Group Meeting

AUGUST 26-27, 1997, *San Jose, California*

Chaired by Chris Lilley, the Cascading Style Sheets and Formatting Properties Working Group met at Adobe Systems to focus on the evolution of CSS, Web Fonts, positioning, tables, ACSS (Aural Cascading Style Sheets), XML, and printing. *http://www.w3.org/Style/*

RDF Working Group Meeting

AUGUST 27–28, 1997, *Redmond, Washington*

Resource Description Framework (RDF) is designed to provide an infrastructure to support metadata across many Web-based activities. RDF is the result of a number of metadata communities bringing together their needs to provide a robust and flexible architecture for supporting metadata on the Internet and WWW. Example applications include sitemaps, content ratings, stream channel definitions, search engine data collection (web crawling), digital library collections, and distributed authoring. The RDF Working Group, chaired by Ralph Swick, convened at Microsoft to discuss issues relevant to the model and syntax working drafts in progress. h*ttp://www.w3.org/Metadata/RDF/*

Jigsaw Receives Award and Announces beta1 Release

AUGUST 26, 1997, *New York City, New York*

SEPTEMBER 1, 1997, *AtSophia-Antipolis, France*

At the Java Internet Business Expo, W3C Director Tim Berners-Lee accepted the finalist award for JavaWorld Editors' Choice "Best Java Application" for Jigsaw, W3C's object-oriented HTTP server written entirely in Java. *http://www.javaworld.com/javaworld/editorschoice97-finalists.html, http://www.w3.org/Jigsaw/*

Technology & Society Interest Group Meetings

SEPTEMBER 2–4, 1997, *Brussels, Belgium*

The three Interest Group meetings were hosted by the European Commission and Riverland Holding, and were attended by more than 40 Members and invited experts. The meeting on Security focused on certificates and certification infrastructure, comparison of X.509, PGP, and SPKI; as well as a discussion of identity certificates. Members of the European Commission and European Parliament presented their views on electronic commerce issues, technical presentations on micropayments and smartcards. In addition, discussions on requirements for Web interoperability took place at the Electronic Commerce meeting. Key public policy issues raised by the Web were addressed by select members of the European Commission and European Parliament. Also discussed at the Public Policy meeting were W3C's role in content regulation through PICS and the next steps in educating policymakers about W3C's emerging technologies. *http://www.w3.org/TandS/IG/*

W3C Workshop on Push Technology

SEPTEMBER 8–9, 1997, *Peabody, Massachusetts*

Over 70 Members and invited experts participated in this workshop chaired by Philipp Hoschka. Participants expressed strong interest for a W3C activity in this area with emphasis in the following: rich descriptions of Web content for the purpose of "push" distribution; HTTP protocol enhancements to facilitate "push" distribution; and multicast protocols for "push" distribution. CDF and DRP, recent submissions to W3C, were presented. Discussion included the relationship of these proposals to ongoing work in W3C and elsewhere. In particular, workshop participants began to evaluate the use of technology in development in W3C's Metadata Activity, i.e., RDF, for description of collections of Web content. *http://www.w3.org/Architecture/9709_Workshop/*

Amaya Source Code Public Release (1.1a beta)

SEPTEMBER 15, 1997, *Grenoble, France*

Amaya is both a browser and an authoring tool conceived to serve as a testbed client for new Web protocols and formats as well as new extensions to existing ones. Amaya was designed as an active client, but also works as an authoring tool that allows for creating new documents, editing existing ones, and publishing these documents on remote Web servers. The 1.1a beta release is the first publically available version for PC/Windows. *http://www.w3.org/Amaya/*

"Network Performance Effects of HTTP/1.1, CSS1, and PNG" presented at ACM SIGCOMM 97

SEPTEMBER 14–18, 1997, *Cannes, France*

HTTP activity lead Henrik Frystyk Nielsen and Jim Gettys, Visiting Engineer from Digital Equipment Corporation presented the acclaimed W3C performance paper on "Network Perfomance Effects of HTTP/1.1, CSS1, and PNG" at the annual SigComm conference's Web and TCP Performance track. *http://www.inria.fr/rodeo/sigcomm97/*

Based on a year of effort by the SGML ERB (which later became the XML WG), XML is an overnight success. The current drafts are already being adopted in commercial products, but the W3C Recommendation process is only beginning. W3C is collecting public comments on the specifications published here as XML proceeds to Proposed Recommendation. The language itself is presented in the "Extensible Markup Language" spec, edited by Tim Bray (Textuality and Netscape), Jean Paoli (Microsoft), and Christopher M. Sperberg-McQueen (University of Illinois at Chicago); the enhanced hypertext link model is entitled "Extensible Link Language," and is edited by Tim Bray and Steve DeRose (Inso Electronic Publishing Solutions). Please stay tuned to http://www.w3.org/XML for the latest news.

While XML is being vetted, other W3C teams have already adopted it to their own ends. The Technology & Society domain is consolidating its metadata efforts on an XML-based format. The User Interface domain is evaluating proposals for XML style sheets. Furthest along is another long-time quest of the Web's framers: interactive, structured, mathematical notation. HP's Dave Raggett, one of the earliest proponents of math markup, has been leading a working group to create an XML format for equations. Patrick Ion of the American Mathematical Society and Robert Miner of NSF Geometry Center at the University of Minnesota summarize the progress to date; see http://www.w3.org/MarkUp/Math/ for the latest updates.

W3C's fundamental strength is its breadth and depth, which allows it to lead the evolution of the Web towards a unified future along several paths. Developers have also been trying to squeeze richer expressiveness into HTML through scripting and other "dynamic" innovations. The Document Object Model WG is chartered to map the potential for client-side automation, hooks for scripting, and plug-ins that will become even more valuable in the migration to a document format with a real information model underneath. Chair Lauren Wood of SoftQuad and Jared Sorenson summarize the group's requirements in our final offering in this section; see http://www.w3.org/MarkUp/DOM/ for the latest updates.

EXTENSIBLE MARKUP LANGUAGE (XML)

Tim Bray, Jean Paoli, C.M. Sperberg-McQueen

Abstract

[W3C Working Draft; WD-xml-970807; Draft 07; August 7, 1997]

Extensible Markup Language (XML) is an extremely simple dialect of SGML which is completely described in this document. The goal is to enable generic SGML to be served, received, and processed on the Web in the way that is now possible with HTML. XML has been designed for ease of implementation and for interoperability with both SGML and HTML.

Status of This Memo

This is a W3C Working Draft for review by W3C members and other interested parties. It is a draft document and may be updated, replaced or obsoleted by other documents at any time. It is inappropriate to use W3C Working Drafts as reference material or to cite them as other than "work in progress." A list of current W3C working drafts can be found at *http://www.w3.org/TR.*

This work is part of the W3C SGML Activity (for current status, see *http://www.w3.org/MarkUp/SGML/Activity*).

1. Introduction

The Extensible Markup Language, abbreviated XML, describes a class of data objects called *XML documents* and partially describes the behavior of computer programs which process them. XML is an application profile or restricted form of SGML, the Standard Generalized Markup Language [4].

XML documents are made up of storage units called entities, which contain either text or binary data. Text is made up of characters, some of which form the character data in the document, and some of which form markup. Markup encodes a description of the document's storage layout and logical structure.

A software module called an *XML processor* is used to read XML documents and provide access to their content and structure. It is assumed that an XML processor is doing its work on behalf of another module, referred to as the *application*. This specification describes the required behavior of an XML processor in terms of how it must read XML data and the information it must provide to the application.

1.1 Origin and Goals

XML was developed by an XML Working Group (originally known as the SGML Editorial Review Board) formed under the auspices of the World Wide Web Consortium (W3C) in 1996 and chaired by Jon Bosak of Sun Microsystems with the very active participation of an XML Special Interest Group (previously known as the SGML Working Group) also organized by the W3C. The membership of the XML Working Group is given in Appendix H. Dan Connolly served as the WG's contact with the W3C.

The design goals for XML are:

1. XML shall be straightforwardly usable over the Internet.
2. XML shall support a wide variety of applications.
3. XML shall be compatible with SGML.
4. It shall be easy to write programs which process XML documents.

5. The number of optional features in XML is to be kept to the absolute minimum, ideally zero.
6. XML documents should be human-legible and reasonably clear.
7. The XML design should be prepared quickly.
8. The design of XML shall be formal and concise.
9. XML documents shall be easy to create.
10. Terseness in XML markup is of minimal importance.

This specification, together with the associated standards, provides all the information necessary to understand XML version 1.0 and construct computer programs to process it.

This version of the XML specification (07 August 1997) is for public review and discussion. It may be distributed freely, as long as all text and legal notices remain intact.

1.2 Relationship to Existing Standards

Standards relevant to users and implementors of XML include:

- *SGML (ISO 8879:1986).* By definition, valid XML documents are conformant SGML documents in the sense described in ISO standard 8879. The current draft of this specification presupposes the successful completion of the current work on a technical corrigendum to ISO 8879 now being prepared by ISO/IEC JTC1/SC18/WG8. If the corrigendum is not adopted in the expected form, some clauses of this specification may change, and some recommendations now labeled for interoperability will become requirements labeled for compatibility.
- *Unicode and ISO/IEC 10646.* This specification depends on the international standard ISO/IEC 10646 (with amendments AM 1 through AM 5) and the *Unicode Standard, Version 2.0,* which define the encodings and meanings of the characters which make up XML text data. All the characters in ISO/IEC 10646 are present, at the same code points, in Unicode.
- *IETF RFC 1738 and RFC 1808.* RFC 1738 and RFC 1808 define the syntax and semantics of Uniform Resource Locators, or URLs.

1.3 Terminology

Some terms used with special meaning in this specification are:

may
: Conforming data and XML processors are permitted to but need not behave as described.

must
: Conforming data and XML processors are required to behave as described; otherwise they are in error.

error
: A violation of the rules of this specification; results are undefined. Conforming software may detect and report an error and may recover from it.

fatal error
: An error which conforming software must detect and report to the application. After encountering a fatal error, an XML processor may continue processing the data to search for further errors and may report such errors to the application. In order to support correction of errors, the processor may make unprocessed text from the document (with intermingled character data and markup) available to the application. Once a fatal error is detected, however, the processor must not continue normal processing (i.e., it must not continue to pass character data and information about the document's logical structure to the application in the normal way).

validity constraint
: A rule which applies to all valid XML documents. Violations of validity constraints are

errors; they must, at user option, be reported by validating XML processors.

well-formedness constraint
: A rule which applies to all well-formed XML documents. Violations of well-formedness constraints are fatal errors.

at user option
: Conforming software may or must (depending on the modal verb in the sentence) behave as described; if it does, it must provide users a means to enable or disable the behavior described.

match
: (Of strings or names:) Case-insensitive match: two strings or names being compared match if they are identical after case-folding. (Of strings and rules in the grammar:) A string matches a grammatical production if it belongs to the language generated by that production. (Of content and content models:) The content of a parent element in a document matches the content model for that element if (a) the content `Mixed` and the content consists of character data and elements whose names match names in the content model, or if (b) the content model matches the rule for `elements`, and the sequence of child elements belongs to the language generated by the regular expression in the content model.

case-folding
: A process applied to a sequence of characters, in which those identified as non-uppercase (in scripts which have case distinctions) are replaced by their uppercase equivalents, as specified in The Unicode Standard, Version 2.0, section 4.1. Note that Unicode recommends folding to lowercase; for compatibility reasons, XML processors must fold to uppercase. Case-folding, as described here, neither requires nor forbids the normalization of Unicode character sequences into canonical form (e.g., as described in The Unicode Standard, section 5.9).

exact(ly) match
: Case-sensitive string match: two strings or names being compared must be identical. Characters with multiple possible representations in ISO/IEC 10646 (e.g., characters with both precomposed and base+diacritic forms) match only if they have the same representation in both strings. At user option, processors may normalize such characters to their canonical form.

for compatibility
: A feature of XML included solely to ensure that XML remains compatible with SGML.

for interoperability
: A non-binding recommendation included to increase the chances that XML documents can be processed by the existing installed base of SGML processors which predate the technical corrigendum to ISO 8879 now in the process of preparation by ISO/IEC JTC1/SC18/WG8.

1.4 Notation

The formal grammar of XML is given using a simple Extended Backus-Naur Form (EBNF) notation. Each rule in the grammar defines one symbol, in the form

```
symbol ::= expression
```

Symbols are written with an initial capital letter if they are defined by a regular expression, or with an initial lowercase letter if a recursive grammar is required for recognition. Literal strings are quoted; unless otherwise noted they are case-insensitive. The distinction between symbols which can and cannot be recognized using simple regular expressions may be used to set the boundary between an implementation's lexical scanner and its parser, but this specification neither constrains the placement of that boundary nor presupposes that all implementations will have one.

Within the expression on the right-hand side of a rule, the meaning of symbols is as shown below.

#xN
: Where *N* is a hexadecimal integer, the expression represents the character in ISO/IEC 10646 whose canonical (UCS-4) bit string, when interpreted as an unsigned binary number, has the value indicated. The number of leading zeroes in the #xN form is insignificant; the number of leading zeroes in the corresponding bit string is governed by the character encoding in use and is not significant for XML.

[a-zA-Z]&, [#xN-#xN]
: Represents any character with a value in the range(s) indicated (inclusive).

[^a-z], [^#xN-#xN]
: Represents any character with a value *outside* the range indicated.

[^abc], [^#xN#xN#xN]
: Represents any character with a value not among the characters given.

"*string*"
: Represents a literal string matching that given inside the double quotes.

string
: Represents a literal string matching that given inside the single quotes.

a b
: *a* followed by *b*.

a | b
: *a* or *b* but not both.

a - b
: The set of strings represented by *a* but not represented by *b*

a?
: *a* or nothing; optional *a*.

a+
: One or more occurrences of *a*.

a*
: Zero or more occurrences of *a*.

%a
: Specifies that *in the external DTD subset* a parameter entity may occur in the text at the position where *a* may occur; if so, its replacement text must match S? *a* S?. If the expression *a* is governed by a suffix operator, then the suffix operator determines both the maximum number of parameter-entity *a* in the replacement text of the parameter entities: %a* means that *a* must occur zero or more times, and that some of its occurrences may be replaced by references to parameter *a*; it is thus a more compact way of writing %(a*)*. Similarly, %a+ means that *a* must occur one or more times, and may be replaced by parameter entities with replacement text matching S? (a S?)+. The recognition of parameter entities in the internal subset is much more highly constrained.

(expression)
: *Expression* is treated as a unit, and may carry the % prefix operator, or a suffix operator: ?, *, or +.

/* ... */
: Comment.

[WFC: ...]
: Well-formedness check; this identifies by name a check for well-formedness associated with a production.

[VC: ...]
: Validity check; this identifies by name a check for validity associated with a production.

1.5 Common Syntactic Constructs

This section defines some symbols used widely in the grammar.

S (white space) consists of one or more space (#x20) characters, carriage returns, line feeds, or tabs. (White Space.)

White Space

```
[1] S ::= (#x20 | #x9 | #xd | #xa)+
```

Legal characters are tab, carriage return, line feed, and the legal graphic characters of Unicode and ISO/IEC 10646. (See Character Range.)

Characters are classified for convenience as letters, digits, or other characters. Letters consist of an alphabetic or syllabic base character possibly followed by one or more combining characters, or of an ideographic character. Certain layout and format-control characters defined by ISO/IEC 10646 [5] should be ignored when recognizing identifiers; these are defined by the classes `Ignorable` and `Extender`. Full definitions of the specific characters in each class are given in Appendix B, "Character Classes."

A `Name` is a token beginning with a letter or underscore character and continuing with letters, digits, hyphens, underscores, or full stops (together known as name characters). Names beginning with the string XML are reserved for standardization in this or future versions of this specification.

NOTE

> The colon character (:) is also allowed within XML names; it is reserved for experimentation with name spaces and schema scoping. Its meaning is expected to be standardized at some future point, at which point those documents using a colon for experimental purposes will need to be updated. (Note that there is no guarantee that any name-space mechanism adopted for XML will in fact use a colon as a name-space delimiter.) In practice, this means that authors should not use colons in XML names except as part of name-space experiments, but that implementors should accept the colon as a name character.

An `Nmtoken` (*name token*) is any mixture of name characters. (See Names and Tokens.)

Literal data is any quoted string not containing the quotation mark used as a delimiter for that string; different forms of literal data may or may not contain angle brackets (< >), entity references, and character references. Literals are used for specifying the replacement text of internal entities (`EntityValue`), the values of attributes (`AttValue`), and external identifiers (`SystemLiteral`); for some purposes, the entire literal can be skipped without scanning for markup within it (`SkipLit`). (See Literals.)

Note that entity references and character references are recognized and processed within `EntityValue` and `AttValue`, but not within `SystemLiteral`.

Character Range

```
[2] Char ::= #x9 | #xA | #xD | [#x20-#xFFFD] | /* any ISO/IEC 10646 UCS-4 code,
             [#x00010000-#x7FFFFFFF]                FFFE and FFFF excluded */
```

Names and Tokens

```
[3] MiscName ::= '.' | '-' | '_' | ':' | CombiningChar | Ignorable | Extender
[4] NameChar ::= Letter | Digit | MiscName
[5]     Name ::= (Letter | '_' | ':') (NameChar)*
[6]    Names ::= Name (S Name)*
[7]  Nmtoken ::= (NameChar)+
[8] Nmtokens ::= Nmtoken (S Nmtoken)*
```

Literals

```
[9]   EntityValue ::= '"' ([^%&"] | PEReference | Reference)* '"' | "'" ([^%&'] |
                      PEReference | Reference)* "'"
[10]     AttValue ::= '"' ([^<&"] | Reference)* '"'
                   |  "'" ([^<&'] | Reference)* "'"
[11]SystemLiteral ::= '"' URLchar* '"' | "'" (URLchar - "'")* "'"
[12]      URLchar ::=  /* See RFC 1738 and 1808  */
[13] PubidLiteral ::= '"' PubidChar* '"' | "'" (PubidChar - "'")* "'"
[14]    PubidChar ::= #x20 | #x9 | #xd | #xa | #x3000
                    | [a-zA-Z0-9] | [-'()+,./:=?]
[15]      SkipLit ::= ('"' [^"]* '"') | ("'" [^']* "'")
```

2. Documents

A textual object is an *XML document* if it is either valid or well-formed, as defined in this specification.

2.1 Logical and Physical Structure

Each XML document has both a logical and a physical structure.

Physically, the document is composed of units called entities. An entity may refer to other entities to cause their inclusion in the document. A document begins in a "root" or document entity.

The logical structure contains declarations, elements, comments, character references, and processing instructions, all of which are indicated in the document by explicit markup.

The two structures must be synchronous: see section 4.1.

2.2 Well-Formed XML Documents

A textual object is said to be a *well-formed* XML document if, first, it matches the production labeled *document*, and if for each entity reference which appears in the document, either the entity has been declared in the document type declaration or the entity name is one of: `amp`, `lt`, `gt`, `apos`, `quot`.

Matching the *document* production implies that:

1. It contains one or more elements.
2. It meets all the well-formedness constraints (WFCs) given in the grammar.
3. There is exactly one element, called the *root*, or document element, for which neither the start-tag nor the end-tag is in the content of any other element. For all other elements, if the start-tag is in the content of another element, the end-tag is in the content of the same element. More simply stated, the elements, delimited by start- and end-tags, nest within each other.

As a consequence of this, for each non-root element *C* in the document, there is one other element *P* in the document such that *C* is in the content of *P*, but is not in the content of any other element that is in the content of *P*. Then *P* is referred to as the *parent* of *C*, and *C* as a *child* of *P*.

2.3 Characters

The data stored in an XML entity is either text or binary. Binary data has an associated notation, identified by name; beyond a requirement to make available the notation's name and the associated system identifier, XML places no constraints on the contents or use of binary entities. So-called binary data might in fact be textual; its identification as binary means that an XML processor need not parse it in the fashion A character is an atomic unit of text; valid characters are specified by ISO/IEC 10646. Users may extend the ISO/IEC 10646 character repertoire by exploiting the private use areas.

The mechanism for encoding character values into bit patterns may vary from entity to entity. All XML processors must accept the UTF-8 and

UCS-2 encodings of 10646; the mechanisms for signaling which of the two are in use, or for bringing other encodings into play, are discussed later, in the discussion of character encodings (section 4.3.3).

Regardless of the specific encoding used, any character in the ISO/IEC 10646 character set may be referred to by the decimal or hexadecimal equivalent of a bit string.

2.4 Character Data and Markup

XML text consists of intermingled *character data* and markup. Markup takes the form of start-tags, end-tags, empty elements, entity references, character references, comments, CDATA sections, document type declarations, and processing instructions.

Character Data

```
[16] PCData ::= [^<&]*
```

All text that is not markup constitutes the character data of the document.

The ampersand character (&) and the left angle bracket (<) may appear in their literal form *only* when used as markup delimiters, or within comments, processing instructions, or CDATA sections. If they are needed elsewhere, they must be escaped using either numeric character references or the strings "`&`" and "`<`". The right angle bracket (>) may be represented using the string "`>`", and must, for compatibility, be so represented when it appears in the string "`]]>`", when that string is not marking the end of a CDATA section.

In the content of elements, character data is any string of characters which does not contain the start-delimiter of any markup. In a CDATA section, character data is any string of characters not including the CDATA-section-close delimiter "`]]>`".

To allow attribute values to contain both single and double quotes, the apostrophe or single-quote character (`'`) may be represented as "`'`", and the double-quote character (`"`) as "`"`".

2.5 Comments

Comments may appear anywhere except in a CDATA section; i.e., within element content, in mixed content, or in a DTD. They must not occur within declarations or tags. They are not part of the document's character data; an XML processor may, but need not, make it possible for an application to retrieve the text of comments. For compatibility, the double hyphen string (`--`) must not occur within comments.

An example of a comment follows:

```
<!-- declarations for <head> & <body> -->
```

2.6 Processing Instructions

Processing instructions (PIs) allow documents to contain instructions for applications.

PIs are not part of the document's character data, but must be passed through to the application. The `Name` is called the *PI target*; it is used to identify the application to which the instruction is directed. XML provides an optional mechanism, NOTATION, for formal declaration of such names. PI targets with names beginning with the string "XML" are reserved for standardization in this or future versions of this specification.

Comments

```
[17] Comment ::= '<!--' (Char* - (Char* '--' Char*)) '-->'
```

Processing Instructions

```
[18] PI ::= '<?' Name S (Char* - (Char* '?>' Char*)) '?>'
```

2.7 CDATA Sections

CDATA sections can occur anywhere character data may occur; they are used to escape blocks of text containing characters which would otherwise be recognized as markup. CDATA sections begin with the string "`<![CDATA[`" and end with the string "`]]>`".

Within a CDATA section, only the **CDEnd** string is recognized, so that left angle brackets (<) and ampersands (&) may occur in their literal form; they need not (and cannot) be escaped using `<` and `&`. CDATA sections cannot nest.

An example of a CDATA section follows:

```
<![CDATA[<greeting>Hello, world!
    </greeting>]]>
```

2.8 White Space Handling

In editing XML documents, it is often convenient to use "white space" (spaces, tabs, and blank lines, denoted by the non-terminal `S` in this specification) to set apart the markup for greater readability. Such white space is typically not intended for inclusion in the delivered version of the document. On the other hand, "significant" white space that must be retained in the delivered version is common, for example in poetry and source code.

An XML processor must always pass all characters in a document that are not markup through to the application. A validating XML processor must distinguish white space in element content from other non-markup characters and signal to the application that white space in element content is not significant.

A special attribute may be inserted in documents to signal an intention that the element to which this attribute applies requires all white space to be treated as significant by applications.

In valid documents, this attribute must be declared as follows, if used:

```
XML-SPACE (DEFAULT|PRESERVE)
    #IMPLIED
```

The value **DEFAULT** signals that applications' default white space processing modes are acceptable for this element; **PRESERVE** indicates the intent that applications preserve all the white space. This declared intent is considered to apply to all elements within the content of this element, unless overriden with another instance of **XML-SPACE** attribute.

The root element of any document is considered to have signaled no intentions as regards application space handling, unless it provides a value for this attribute or the attribute is declared with a default value.

2.9 Prolog and Document Type Declaration

XML documents may, and should, begin with an XML declaration which specifies, among other things, the version of XML being used.

The function of the markup in an XML document is to describe its storage and logical structures, and associate attribute-value pairs with the logical structure. XML provides a mechanism, the document type declaration, to define constraints on that logical structure and to support the use of predefined storage units. An XML document is

CDATA Sections

```
[19]   CDSect ::= CDStart CData CDEnd
[20]  CDStart ::= '<![CDATA['
[21]    CData ::= (Char* - (Char* ']]>' Char*))
[22]    CDEnd ::= ']]>'
```

XML Document

```
[23]    document ::= prolog element Misc*
[24]      prolog ::= XMLDecl? Misc* (doctypedecl Misc*)?
[25]     XMLDecl ::= '<?XML' VersionInfo EncodingDecl? RMDecl? S? '?>'
[26] VersionInfo ::= S 'version' Eq ('"1.0"' | "'1.0'")
[27]        Misc ::= Comment | PI | S
```

said to be *valid* if there is an associated document type declaration and if the document complies with the constraints expressed in it.

The document type declaration must appear before the first start-tag in the document.

The identification of the XML version as "1.0" does not indicate a commitment to produce any future versions of XML, nor if any are produced, to use any particular numbering scheme. Since future versions are not ruled out, this construct is provided as a means to allow the possibility of automatic version recognition, should it become necessary.

For example, the following is a complete XML document, well-formed but not valid:

```
<?XML version="1.0"?>
<greeting>Hello, world!</greeting>
```

and so is this:

```
<greeting>Hello, world!</greeting>
```

The XML document type declaration may include a pointer to an external entity containing a subset of the necessary markup declarations, and may also directly include another, internal, subset.

These two subsets make up the *document type definition*, abbreviated *DTD*. The DTD, in effect, provides a grammar which defines a class of documents. Properly speaking, the DTD consists of both subsets taken together, but it is a common practice for the bulk of the markup declarations to appear in the external subset, and for this subset, usually contained in a file, to be referred to as "the DTD" for a class of documents.

Validity Constraint: Root Element Type
The `Name` in the document-type declaration must match the element type of the root element.

Validity Constraint: Non-null DTD
The internal and external subsets of the DTD must not both be empty.

Well-Formedness Constraint: Integral Declarations
A parameter-entity reference recognized in this context must have replacement text consisting of zero or more complete declarations; i.e., matching the production for the non-terminal `markupdecl`.

The *external subset* must obey substantially the same grammatical constraints as the internal subset; i.e., it must match the production for the non-terminal symbol `markupdecl`. In the external subset, however, parameter-entity references can be used to replace constructs prefixed by `%` in a

Document Type Definition

```
[28]   doctypedecl ::= '<!DOCTYPE' S Name (S            [ VC: Root Element
                       ExternalID)? S? ('['               Type ]
                       %markupdecl* ']' S?)? '>'
                                                        [ VC: Non-null DTD]
[29]    markupdecl ::= ( %elementdecl |
                       %AttlistDecl | %EntityDecl |
                       %NotationDecl  | %PI | %S |
                       %Comment | InternalPERef )*
[30] InternalPERef ::= PEReference                      [ WFC: Integral
                                                          Declarations ]
```

External Subset

```
[31] extSubset ::= ( %markupdecl | %conditionalSect )*
```

production of the grammar, and conditional sections may occur. In the internal subset, by contrast, conditional sections may not occur and the only parameter-entity references allowed are those which match `InternalPERef` within the rule for `markupdecl`.

For example:

```
<?XML version="1.0"?>
<!DOCTYPE greeting SYSTEM "hello.
   dtd">
<greeting>Hello, world!</greeting>
```

The system identifier `hello.dtd` indicates the location of a DTD for the document.

The declarations can also be given locally, as in this example:

```
<?XML version="1.0" encoding=
   "UTF-8" ?>
<!DOCTYPE greeting [
  <!ELEMENT greeting (#PCDATA)>
]>
<greeting>Hello, world!</greeting>
```

If both the external and internal subsets are used, an XML processor must read the internal subset first, then the external subset. This has the effect that entity and attribute declarations in the internal subset take precedence over those in the external subset.

2.10 Required Markup Declaration

In some cases, an XML processor can read an XML document and accomplish useful tasks without having first processed the entire DTD. However, certain declarations can substantially affect the actions of an XML processor. It is desirable, therefore, to be able to specify whether a document contains any such declarations. A document author can communicate whether or not DTD processing is necessary using a *required markup declaration* (abbreviated RMD), which appears as a component of the XML declaration.

In an RMD, the value `NONE` indicates that an XML processor can parse the containing document correctly without first reading any part of the DTD. The value `INTERNAL` indicates that the XML processor must read and process the internal subset of the DTD, if provided, to parse the containing document correctly. The value `ALL` indicates that the XML processor must read and process the declarations in both the subsets of the DTD, if provided, to parse the containing document correctly.

The RMD must indicate that the entire DTD is required if the external subset contains any declarations of:

- Attributes with default values, if elements to which these attributes apply appear in the document without specifying values for these attributes, or
- Entities (other than `amp`, `lt`, `gt`, `apos`, `quot`), if references to those entities appear in the document, or
- Element types with element content, if white space occurs directly within any instance of those types.

If such declarations occur in the internal but not the external subset, the RMD must take the value `INTERNAL`. It is an error to specify `INTERNAL` if the external subset is required, or to specify `NONE` if the internal or external subset is required.

Required Markup Declaration

```
[32] RMDecl ::=  S 'RMD' Eq "'" ('NONE' | 'INTERNAL' | 'ALL') "'"
               | S 'RMD' Eq '"' ('NONE' | 'INTERNAL' | 'ALL') '"'
```

Start-tag

```
[33]       STag ::= '<' Name (S Attribute)* S? '>'   [ WFC: Unique Att Spec ]
[34] Attribute ::= Name Eq AttValue                  [ VC: Attribute Value Type ]
                                                     [ WFC: No External Entity
                                                       References ]
[35]         Eq ::= S? '=' S?
```

If no RMD is provided, an XML processor must behave as though an RMD had been provided with the value ALL.

An example XML declaration with an RMD follows:

```
<?XML version="1.0" RMD='INTERNAL'?>
```

3. Logical Structures

Each XML document contains one or more *elements*, the boundaries of which are either delimited by start-tags and end-tags, or, for empty elements by an empty-element tag. Each element has type, idntified by name (sometimes called its *generic identifier* or *GI*), and may have a set of attributes. Each attribute has a name and a value.

This specification does not constrain the semantics, use, or (beyond syntax) names of the elements and attributes, except that names beginning with the string XML are reserved for standardization in this on future versions of this specification.

3.1 Start-Tags, End-Tags, and Empty-Element Tags

The beginning of every non-empty XML element is marked by a *start-tag*.

The Name in the start- and end-tags gives the element's *type*. The Name-AttValue pairs are referred to as the *attribute specifications* of the element, with the Name referred to as the *attribute name* and the content of the AttValue (the characters between the ' or " delimiters) as the *attribute value*.

Validity Constraint: Unique Att Spec
No attribute may appear more than once in the same start-tag or empty-element tag.

Validity Constraint: Attribute Value Type
The attribute must have been declared; the value must be of the type declared for it. (For attribute types, see the discussion of attribute declarations.)

Well-Formedness Constraint: No External Entity References
Attribute values cannot contain entity references to external entities.

An example of a start-tag follows:

```
<termdef id="dt-dog" term="dog">
```

The end of every element may (for elements which are not empty, must) be marked by an *end-tag* containing a name that echoes the element's type as given in the start-tag.

End-tag

```
[36] ETag ::= '</' Name S? '>'
```

An example of an end-tag follows:

```
</termdef>
```

The text between the start-tag and end-tag is called the element's *content*.

Content of Elements

```
[37] content ::= (element | PCData | Reference |        [ VC: Content ]
                 CDSect | PI | Comment)*
[38] element ::= EmptyElement
                 | STag content ETag                    [ WFC: GI Match ]
```

Tags for Empty Elements

```
[39] EmptyElement ::= '<' Name (S Attribute)* S? '/>'      [ WFC: Unique Att Spec ]
```

Validity Constraint: Content

Each element type used must be declared. The content of an element instance must match the content model declared for that element type.

Well-Formedness Constraint: GI Match

The `Name` in an element's end-tag must match that in the start-tag.

If an element is *empty*, it may be represented either by a start-tag immediately followed by an end-tag, or by an *empty-element tag*. An Empty-element tag takes a special form.

Empty-element tags may be used for any element which has no content, whether or not they are declared using the keyword EMPTY.

Examples of empty elements follow:

```
<IMG align="left"
 src="http://www.w3.org/Icons/
      WWW/w3c_home" />
<br></br>
<br/>
```

3.2 Element Declarations

The element structure of an XML document may, for validation purposes, be constrained using element and attribute declarations.

An *element declaration* constrains the element's type and its content.

Element declarations often constrain which element types can appear as children of the element. At user option, an XML processor may issue a warning when a reference is made to an element type for which no declaration is provided, but this is not an error.

An *element declaration* takes the form shown below, where the `Name` gives the type of the element.

Validity Constraint: Unique Element Declaration

No element type may be declared more than once.

An element can be declared using a *content model*, in which case its content can be categorized as element content or mixed content, as explained below.

An element declared using the keyword EMPTY must be empty and may be tagged using an empty-element tag when it appears in the document.

If an element type is declared using the keyword ANY, then there are no validity constraints on its content: it may contain child elements of any type and number, interspersed with character data.

Examples of element declarations follow:

```
<!ELEMENT br EMPTY>
<!ELEMENT %name.para; %content.
   para; >
<!ELEMENT container ANY>
```

3.2.1 Element content

An element type may be declared to have element content, which means that elements of that type may only contain other elements (no character data). In this case, the constraint includes a content model, a simple grammar governing the allowed types of the child elements and the order in which they appear. The grammar is built on content particles (CPs), which consist of names, choice lists of content particles, or sequence lists of content particles.

Element Declaration

```
[40] elementdecl ::= '<!ELEMENT' S %Name S (%S      [ VC:  Unique Element
                     S)? %contentspec S? '>'          Declaration   ]
[41] contentspec ::= 'EMPTY' | 'ANY' | Mixed | elements
```

In *Element-content models*, each **Name** gives the type of an element which may appear as a child. Any content particle in a choice list may appear in the element content at the appropriate location; content particles occurring in a sequence list must each appear in the element content in the order given. The optional character following a name or list governs whether the element or the content particles in the list may occur one or more (+), zero or more (*), or zero or one times (?). The syntax and meaning are identical to those used in the productions in this specification.

The content of an element matches a content model if and only if it is possible to trace out a path through the content model, obeying the sequence, choice, and repetition operators and matching each element in the content against an element name in the content model. For compatibility reasons, it is an error if an element in the document can match more than one occurrence of an element name in the content model. More formally: a finite state automaton may be constructed from the content model using the standard algorithms; e.g., algorithm 3.5 in section 3.9 of [1]. In many such algorithms, a follow set is constructed for each position in the regular expression (i.e., each leaf node in the syntax tree for the regular expression); if any position has a follow set in which more than one following position is labeled with the same element type name, then the content model is in error and may be reported as an error. For more information, see Appendix D, "Deterministic Content Models."

Examples of element-content models follow:

```
<!ELEMENT spec (front, body, back?)>
<!ELEMENT div1 (head, (p | list |
   note)*, div2*)>
<!ELEMENT head (%head.content; |
   %head.misc;)*>
```

3.2.2 Mixed content

An element type may be declared to contain mixed content, that is, text comprising character data optionally interspersed with child elements. In this case, the types of the child elements are constrained, but not their order nor their number of occurrences, where the **Names** give the types of elements that may appear as children. The same name must not appear more than once in a single *mixed-content declaration.*

Examples of mixed content declarations follow:

```
<!ELEMENT p (#PCDATA|a|ul|b|i|em)*>
<!ELEMENT p (#PCDATA | %font;
    | %phrase; | %special;
    | %form;)* >
<!ELEMENT b (#PCDATA)>
```

3.3 Attribute-List Declarations

Attributes are used to associate name-value pairs with elements. Attributes may appear only within start-tags; thus, the productions used to recognize them appear in the discussion of start-tags. Attribute-list declarations may be used:

- To define the set of attributes pertaining to a given element type
- To establish a set of type constraints on these attributes
- To provide default values for attributes

Element-Content Models

```
[42] elements ::= (choice | seq) ('?' | '*' | '+')?
[43]       cp ::= (Name | choice | seq) ('?' | '*' | '+')?
[44]      cps ::= S? %cp S?
[45]   choice ::= '(' S? %ctokplus (S? '|' S? %ctoks)* S? ')'
[46] ctokplus ::= cps ('|' cps)+
[47]    ctoks ::= cps ('|' cps)*
[48]      seq ::= '(' S? %stoks (S? ',' S? %stoks)* S? ')'
[49]    stoks ::= cps (',' cps)*
```

Mixed-Content Declaration

```
[50] Mixed ::= '(' S? %( %'#PCDATA' (S? '|' S? %Mtoks)* ) S? ')*'
             | '(' S? %('#PCDATA') S? ')'
[51] Mtoks ::= %Name (S? '|' S?  %Name)*
```

Attribute-list declarations specify the name, data type, and default value (if any) of each attribute associated with a given element type.

The **Name** in the **AttlistDecl** rule is the type of an element. At user option, an XML processor may issue a warning if attributes **Name** in the **AttDef** rule is the name of the attribute.

When more than one **AttlistDecl** is provided for a given element type, the contents of all those provided are merged. When more than one definition is provided for the same attribute of a given element type, the first declaration is binding and later declarations are ignored. For interoperability, writers of DTDs may choose to provide at most one attribute-list declaration for a given element type, and at most one attribute definition for a given attribute name. For interoperability, an XML processor may at user option issue a warning when more than one attribute-list declaration is provided for a given element type, or more than one attribute definition for a given attribute name, but this is not an error.

3.3.1 Attribute types

XML *attribute types* are of three kinds: a string type, a set of tokenized types, and enumerated types. The string type may take any literal string as a value; the tokenized types have varying lexical and semantic constraints, as noted:

Validity Constraint: ID
: Values of this type must be valid **Name** symbols. A name must not appear more than once in an XML document as a value of this type; i.e., ID values must uniquely identify the elements which bear them.

Validity Constraint: Idref
: Values of this type must match the **Name** (for IDREFS, the **Names**) production; each **Name** must match the value of an ID attribute on some element in the XML document; i.e., IDREF values must match some ID.

Validity Constraint: Entity Name
: Values of this type must match the production for **Name** (for ENTITIES, **Names**); each **Name** must exactly match the name of an external binary general entity declared in the DTD.

Validity Constraint: Name token
: Values of this type must consist of a string matching the **Nmtoken** nonterminal (for NMTOKENS, the **Nmtokens** nonterminal) of the grammar defined in this specification.

The XML processor must normalize attribute values before passing them to the application, as described in section 3.3.3, "Attribute-Value Normalization."

Enumerated attributes can take one of a list of values provided in the declaration; there are two types.

Validity Constraint: Notation Attributes
: The names in the declaration of NOTATION attributes must be names of declared notations (see the discussion of notations in section 4.6). Values of this type must match one of the notation names included in the declaration.

Attribute List Declaration

```
[52] AttlistDecl ::= '<!ATTLIST' S %Name S? %AttDef+ S? '>'
[53]      AttDef ::= S %Name S %AttType S %Default
```

Attribute Types

```
[54]        AttType ::= StringType | TokenizedType | EnumeratedType
[55]     StringType ::= 'CDATA'
[56] TokenizedType ::= 'ID'                        [ VC: ID  ]
                     | 'IDREF'                     [ VC: Idref  ]
                     | 'IDREFS'                    [ VC: Idref  ]
                     | 'ENTITY'                    [ VC: Entity Name  ]
                     | 'ENTITIES'                  [ VC: Entity Name  ]
                     | 'NMTOKEN'                   [ VC: Name Token  ]
                     | 'NMTOKENS'                  [ VC: Name Token  ]
```

Validity Constraint: Enumeration

Values of this type must match one of the **Nmtoken** tokens in the declaration. For interoperability, the same **Nmtoken** should not occur more than once in the enumerated attribute types of a single element type.

3.3.2 Attribute defaults

An attribute declaration provides information on whether the attribute's presence is required, and if not, how an XML processor should react if a declared attribute is absent in a document (see *Attribute Defaults*).

#REQUIRED means that the document is invalid should the processor encounter a start-tag for the element type in question which specifies no value for this attribute. **#IMPLIED** means that if the attribute is omitted from an element of this type, the XML processor must inform the application that no value was specified; no constraint is placed on the behavior of the application.

If the attribute is neither **#REQUIRED** nor **#IMPLIED**, then the **AttValue** value contains the declared *default* value. If the **#FIXED** is present, the document is invalid if the attribute is present with a different value from the default. If a default value is declared, when an XML processor encounters an omitted attribute, it is to behave as though the attribute were present with its value being the declared default value.

Validity Constraint: Attribute Default Legal

The declared default value must meet the constraints of the declared attribute type.

The following contains examples of attribute-list declarations.

```
<!ATTLIST termdef
          id       ID       #REQUIRED
          name     CDATA    #IMPLIED>
<!ATTLIST list
          type (bullets|ordered|
               glossary) "ordered">
<!ATTLIST form
          method  CDATA    #FIXED
                              "POST">
```

Enumerated Attribute Types

```
[57] EnumeratedType ::= NotationType | Enumeration
[58]   NotationType ::= %'NOTATION' S '(' S?        [ VC: Notation Attributes  ]
                        %Ntoks (S? '|' S?
                        %Ntoks)* S? ')'
[59]          Ntoks ::= %Name (S? '|' S?  %Name)*
[60]    Enumeration ::= '(' S? %Etoks (S? '|' S?    [ VC: Enumeration ]
                        %Etoks)* S? ')'
[61]          Etoks ::= %Nmtoken (S? '|' S?  %Nmtoken)*
```

Attribute Defaults

```
[62] Default ::= '#REQUIRED' | '#IMPLIED'         [ VC: Attribute Default Legal  ]
               | ((%'#FIXED' S)? %AttValue)
```

3.3.3 Attribute-value normalization

Before the value of an attribute is passed to the application, the XML processor must normalize it as follows:

1. Line-end characters (or, on some systems, record boundaries) must be replaced by single space (`#x20`) characters.
2. Character references and references to internal text entities must be expanded. References to external entities are an error.
3. If the attribute is not of type CDATA, all strings of white space must be normalized to single space characters (`#x20`), and leading and trailing white space must be removed.
4. Values of type ID, IDREF, IDREFS, NMTOKEN, NMTOKENS, or of enumerated or notation types, must be folded to uppercase.

If no DTD is present, attributes should be treated as CDATA.

3.4 Conditional Sections

Conditional sections are portions of the document type declaration external subset which are included in, or excluded from, the logical structure of the DTD based on the keyword which governs them.

Like the internal and external DTD subsets, a conditional section may contain one or more complete declarations, comments, processing instructions, or nested conditional sections, intermingled with white space.

If the keyword of the conditional section is INCLUDE, then the conditional section is read and processed in the normal way. If the keyword is IGNORE, then the declarations within the conditional section are ignored; the processor must read the conditional section to detect nested conditional sections and ensure that the end of the outermost (ignored) conditional section is properly detected. If a conditional section with a keyword of INCLUDE occurs within a larger conditional section with a keyword of IGNORE, both the outer and the inner conditional sections are ignored.

If the keyword of the conditional section is a parameter entity reference, the parameter entity is replaced before the processor decides whether to include or ignore the conditional section.

An example follows:

```
<!ENTITY % draft 'INCLUDE' >
<!ENTITY % final 'IGNORE' >

<![%draft;[
<!ELEMENT book (comments*, title,
   body, supplements?)>
]]>
<![%final;[
<!ELEMENT book (title, body,
   supplements?)>
]]>
```

4. Physical Structures

An XML document may consist of one or many virtual storage units. These are called *entities*; they are identified by name and have *content*. An entity may be stored in, but need not comprise the whole of, a single physical storage object such as a file or database field. Each XML document has one entity called the document entity, which serves as the starting point for the XML

Conditional Sections

```
[63]     conditionalSect ::= includeSect | ignoreSect
[64]         includeSect ::= '<![' %'INCLUDE' '[' (%markupdecl*)* ']]>'
[65]          ignoreSect ::= '<![' %'IGNORE' '[' ignoreSectContents* ']]>'
[66] ignoreSectContents ::= ((SkipLit | Comment | PI) - (Char* ']]>' Char*))
                          | ('<![' ignoreSectContents* ']]>')
                          | (Char - (']' | [<'"]))
                          | ('<!' (Char - ('-' | '[')))
```

processor (and may contain the whole document).

Entities may be either binary or text. A text entity contains text data which is considered as an integral part of the document. A binary entity contains binary data with an associated notation. Only text entities may be referred to using entity references; only the names of binary entities may be given as the value of ENTITY attributes.

4.1 Logical and Physical Structures

The logical and physical structures (elements and entities) in an XML document must be synchronous. Tags and elements must each begin and end in the same entity, but may refer to other entities internally; comments, processing instructions, character references, and entity references must each be contained entirely within a single entity. Entities must each contain an integral number of elements, comments, processing instructions, and references, possibly together with character data not contained within any element in the entity, or else they must contain non-textual data, which by definition contains no elements.

4.2 Character and Entity References

A *character reference* refers to a specific character in the ISO/IEC 10646 character set; e.g., one not directly accessible from available input devices.

An *entity reference* refers to the content of a named entity. General entities are text entities for use within the document itself; references to them use ampersand (`&`) and semicolon (`;`) as delimiters. In this specification, general entities are sometimes referred to with the unqualified term entity when this leads to no ambiguity. Parameter entities are text entities for use within the DTD, or to control processing of conditional sections; references to them use percent-sign (`%`) and semicolon (`;`) as delimiters.

Well-Formedness Constraint: Entity Declared

The `Name` given in the entity reference must exactly match the name given in the declaration of the entity, except that well-formed documents need not declare any of the following entities: `amp`, `lt`, `gt`, `apos`, `quot`. In valid documents, these entities must be declared, in the form specified in the section on predefined entities. In the case of parameter entities, the declaration must precede the reference.

Well-Formedness Constraint: Text Entity

An entity reference must not contain the name of a binary entity. Binary entities may be referred to only in attribute values declared to be of type ENTITY or ENTITIES.

Character Reference

```
[67] CharRef ::= '&#' [0-9]+ ';'
               | '&#x' [0-9a-fA-F]+ ';'
```

Entity Reference

```
[68]    Reference ::= EntityRef | CharRef
[69]    EntityRef ::= '&' Name ';'          [ WFC: Entity Declared ]
                                            [ WFC: Text Entity  ]
                                            [ WFC: No Recursion ]
[70] PEReference ::= '%' Name ';'           [ WFC: Entity Declared ]
                                            [ WFC: Text Entity  ]
                                            [ WFC: No Recursion ]
                                            [ WFC: In DTD ]
```

Well-Formedness Constraint: No Recursion

A text or parameter entity must not contain a recursive reference to itself, either directly or indirectly.

Well-Formedness Constraint: In DTD

In the external DTD subset, a parameter-entity reference is recognized only at the locations where the `PEReference` or the special operator `%` appears in a production of the grammar. In the internal subset, parameter-entity references are recognized only when they match the `InternalPERef` non-terminal in the production for `markup-decl`.

Examples of character and entity references follow:

```
Type <key>less-than</key> (&#x3C;) to
    save options.
This document was prepared on
    &docdate; and is classified
    &security-level;.
```

An example of a parameter-entity reference follows:

```
<!ENTITY % ISOLat2
    SYSTEM "http://www.xml.com/iso/
             isolat2-xml.entities" >
%ISOLat2;
```

4.3 Entity Declarations

Entities are declared as shown below.

The `Name` is that by which the entity is invoked by exact match in an entity reference. If the same entity is declared more than once, the first declaration encountered is binding; at user option, an XML processor may issue a warning if entities are declared multiple times.

4.3.1 Internal entities

If the entity definition is an `EntityValue`, the defined entity is called an *internal* entity. There is no separate physical storage object, and the replacement text of the entity is given in the declaration. Within the `EntityValue`, parameter-entity references and character references are recognized and expanded immediately. General-entity references within the replacement text are not recognized at the time the entity declaration is parsed, though they may be recognized when the entity itself is referred to.

An internal entity is a text entity.

Here is an example of an internal entity declaration:

```
<!ENTITY Pub-Status "This is a pre-
    release of the specification.">
```

4.3.2 External entities

If the entity is not internal, it is an external entity, declared in *External Entity Declaration.*

If the `NDataDecl` is present, this is a binary data entity, otherwise a text entity.

Validity Constraint: Notation Declared

The `Name` must match the declared name of a notation.

The `SystemLiteral` that follows the keyword SYSTEM is called the entity's *system identifier.* It is a URL, which may be used to retrieve the entity. Unless otherwise provided by information outside the scope of this specification (e.g., a special XML element defined by a particular DTD, or a processing instruction defined by a particular application specification), relative URLs are relative to the location of the entity or file within which the entity declaration occurs. Relative URLs in entity declarations within the internal DTD subset are thus relative to the location of the document; those in entity declarations in the external subset are relative to the location of the files containing the external subset.

In addition to a system literal, an external identifier may include a public identifier. An XML processor may use the public identifier to try to generate an alternative URL. If the processor is unable to do so, it must use the URL specified in the system literal.

Examples of external entity declarations follow:

```
<!ENTITY open-hatch
    SYSTEM "http://www.textuality.
        com/boilerplate/OpenHatch.
        xml">
```

Entity Declaration

```
[71] EntityDecl ::= '<!ENTITY' S %Name S              /* General entities */
                    %EntityDef S? '>'
                    | '<!ENTITY' S '%' S %Name S       /* Parameter
                    %EntityDef S? '>'                     entities */
[72]  EntityDef ::= EntityValue | ExternalDef
```

External Entity Declaration

```
[73] ExternalDef ::= ExternalID %NDataDecl?
[74]  ExternalID ::= 'SYSTEM' S SystemLiteral
                     | 'PUBLIC' S PubidLiteral S
                     SystemLiteral
[75]   NDataDecl ::= S %'NDATA' S %Name            [ VC: Notation Declared  ]
```

```
<!ENTITY open-hatch
    PUBLIC "-//Textuality//
          TEXT Standard open-hatch
          boilerplate//"http://www.
          textuality.com/boilerplate/
           OpenHatch.xml">
<!ENTITY hatch-pic
    SYSTEM "../grafix/OpenHatch.gif"
         NDATA gif >
```

4.3.3 Character encoding in entities

Each external text entity in an XML document may use a different encoding for its characters. All XML processors must be able to read entities in either UTF-8 or UCS-2. It is recognized that for some purposes, the use of additional ISO/IEC 10646 [5] planes other than the Basic Multilingual Plane may be required. A facility for handling characters in these planes is therefore a desirable characteristic in XML processors and applications.

Entities encoded in UCS-2 must begin with the Byte Order Mark described by ISO/IEC 10646 Annex E and Unicode Appendix B [8] (the ZERO WIDTH NO-BREAK SPACE character, **#xFEFF**). This is an encoding signature, not part of either the markup or character data of the XML document. XML processors must be able to use this character to differentiate between UTF-8 and UCS-2 encoded documents.

Although an XML processor is only required to read entities in the UTF-8 and UCS-2, it is recognized that many other encodings are in daily use around the world, and it may be advantageous for XML processors to read entities that use these encodings. For this purpose, XML provides an encoding declaration processing instruction, which, if it occurs, must appear at the beginning of a system entity, before any other character data or markup. In the document entity, the encoding declaration is part of the XML declaration; in other entities, it is part of an encoding processing instruction.

Well-Formedness Constraint: Start of System Entity
An XML encoding declaration may occur at the beginning of a system entity; it must not occur within the body of any entity.

The values `UTF-8`, `UTF-16`, `ISO-10646-UCS-2`, and `ISO-10646-UCS-4` should be used for the various encodings and transformations of Unicode/ ISO/IEC 10646, the values `ISO-8859-1`, `ISO-8859-2`, . . . `ISO-8859-9` should be used for the parts of ISO 8859, and the values `ISO-2022-JP`, `Shift_JIS`, and `EUC-JP` should be used for the various encoded forms of JIS X-0208. XML processors may recognize other encodings; it is recommended that character encodings registered (as charsets) with the Internet Assigned Numbers Authority (IANA), other than those just listed, should be referred to using their registered names.

It is an error for an entity including an encoding declaration to be presented to the XML processor in an encoding other than that named in the declaration.

An entity which begins with neither a Byte Order Mark nor an encoding declaration must be in the UTF-8 encoding.

While XML provides mechanisms for distinguishing encodings, it is recognized that in a heterogeneous networked environment, it may be difficult to signal the encoding of an entity reliably. Errors in this area fall into two categories:

1. Failing to read an entity because of inability to recognize its actual encoding, and
2. Reading an entity incorrectly because of an incorrect guess of its proper encoding.

The first class of error is extremely damaging, and given a correct encoding declaration, the second class is extremely unlikely. For these reasons, XML processors should make an effort to use all available information, internal and external, to aid in detecting an entity's correct encoding. Such information may include, but is not limited to:

- Using information from an HTTP header
- Using a MIME header obtained other than through HTTP
- Metadata provided by the native OS file system or by document management software
- Analysing the bit patterns at the front of an entity to determine if the application of any known encoding yields a valid encoding declaration. See Appendix E, "Autodetection of Character Encodings" for a fuller description.

If an XML processor encounters an entity with an encoding that it is unable to process, it may inform the application of this fact and may allow the application to request either that the entity should be treated as an binary entity, or that processing should cease.

Examples of *encoding declarations* follow:

```
<?XML ENCODING='UTF-8'?>
<?XML ENCODING='EUC-JP'?>
```

4.3.4 Document entity

The *document entity* serves as the root of the entity tree and a starting-point for an XML processor. This specification does not specify how the document entity is to be located by an XML processor; unlike other entities, the document entity might well appear on an input stream of the processor without any identification at all.

4.4 XML Processor Treatment of Entities

XML allows character and general-entity references in two places: the content of elements (*content*) and attribute values (`AttValue`). When an XML processor encounters such a reference, or the name of an external binary entity as the value of an ENTITY or ENTITIES attribute, then:

1. In all cases, the XML processor may inform the application of the reference's occurrence and its identifier (for an entity reference, the

Encoding Declaration

```
[76] EncodingDecl ::=  S 'encoding' Eq               [ WFC: Start of System
                       QEncoding                        Entity ]
[77]   EncodingPI ::= '<?XML' S 'encoding' Eq
                       QEncoding S? '?>'
[78]    QEncoding ::= '"' Encoding '"' | "'"
                      Encoding "'"
[79]     Encoding ::= LatinName
[80]    LatinName ::= [A-Za-z] ([A-Za-z0-9._]         /* Name containing only
                      | '-')*                           Latin characters */
```

character number in decimal, hexadecimal, or binary form).

2. For both character and entity references, the processor must remove the reference itself from the text data before passing the data to the application.

3. For character references, the processor must pass the character indicated to the application in place of the reference.

4. For an external entity, the processor must inform the application of the entity's system identifier if any.

5. If the external entity is binary, the processor must inform the application of the associated notation name, and the notation's associated system and public (if any) identifiers.

6. For an internal (text) entity, the processor must *include* the entity; that is, retrieve its replacement text and process it as a part of the document (i.e., as *content* or `AttValue`, whichever was being processed when the reference was recognized), passing the result to the application in place of the reference. The replacement text may contain both text and markup, which must be recognized in the usual way, except that the replacement text of entities used to escape markup delimiters (the entities `amp`, `lt`, `gt`, `apos`, `quot`) is always treated as data. (The string `AT&T` expands to `AT&T`; the remaining ampersand is not recognized as an entity-reference delimiter.) Since the entity may contain other entity references, an XML processor may have to repeat the inclusion process recursively.

7. If the entity is an external text entity, then in order to validate the XML document, the processor must include the content of the entity.

8. If the entity is an external text entity, and the processor is not attempting to validate the XML document, the processor may, but need not, include the entity's content. This rule is based on the recognition that the automatic inclusion provided by the SGML and XML text entity mechanism, primarily designed to support modularity in authoring, is not necessarily appropriate for other applications, in particular document browsing. Browsers, for example, when encountering an external text entity reference, might choose to provide a visual indication of the entity's presence and retrieve it for display only on demand.

Entity and character references can both be used to escape the left angle bracket, ampersand, and other delimiters. A set of general entities (`amp`, `lt`, `gt`, `apos`, `quot`) is specified for this purpose. Numeric character references may also be used; they are expanded immediately when recognized, and must be treated as character data, so the numeric character references `<` and `&` may be used to escape < and & when they occur in character data.

XML allows parameter-entity references in a variety of places within the DTD. Parameter-entity references are always expanded immediately upon being recognized, and the DTD must match the relevant rules of the grammar after all parameter-entity references have been expanded. In addition, parameter entities referred to in specific contexts are required to satisfy certain constraints in their replacement text; for example, a parameter entity referred to within the internal DTD subset must match the rule for `markupdecl`.

Implementors of XML processors need to know the rules for expansion of references in more detail. These rules only come into play when the replacement text for an internal entity itself contains other references.

1. In the replacement text of an internal entity, parameter-entity references and character references in the replacement text are recognized and resolved when the entity declaration is parsed, before the replacement text is stored in the processor's symbol table. General-entity references in the replacement text

are not resolved when the entity declaration is parsed.

2. In the document, when a general-entity reference is resolved, its replacement text is parsed. Character references encountered in the replacement text are resolved immediately; general-entity references encountered in the replacement text may be resolved or left unresolved, as described above. Character and general-entity references must be contained entirely within the entity's replacement text.

Simple character references do not suffice to escape delimiters within the replacement text of an internal entity: they will be expanded when the entity declaration is parsed, before the replacement text is stored in the symbol table. When the entity itself is referred to, the replacement text will be parsed again, and the delimiters (no longer character references) will be recognized as delimiters. To escape the characters `amp`, `lt`, `gt`, `apos`, `quot` in an entity replacement text, use a general-entity reference or a doubly-escaped character reference. See Appendix C, "Expansion of Entity and Character References" for detailed examples.

4.5 Predefined Entities

As mentioned in the discussion of character data and markup, the characters used as markup delimiters by XML may all be escaped using entity references (for the enties `amp`, `lt`, `gt`, `apos`, `quot`).

All XML processors must recognize these entities whether they are declared or not. Valid XML documents must declare these entities, like any others, before using them.

If the entities in question are declared, they must be declared as internal entities whose replacement text is the single character being escaped, as shown below.

```
<!ENTITY lt      "&#60;">
<!ENTITY gt      "&#62;">
<!ENTITY amp     "&#38;">
<!ENTITY apos    "'">
<!ENTITY quot    '"'>
```

4.6 Notation Declarations

Notations identify by name the format of external binary entities, or the application to which processing instructions are addressed.

Notation declarations provide a name for the notation, for use in entity and attribute-list declarations and in attribute-value specifications, and an external identifier for the notation which may allow an XML processor or its client application to locate a helper application capable of processing data in the given notation.

XML processors must provide applications with the name and external identifier of any notation declared and referred to in an attribute value, attribute definition, or entity declaration. They may additionally resolve the external identifier into the system identifier, file name, or other information needed to allow the application to call a processor for data in the notation described. (It is not an error, however, for XML documents to declare and refer to notations for which notation-specific applications are not available on the system where the XML processor or application is running.)

5. Conformance

Conforming XML processors fall into two classes: validating and non-validating.

Validating and non-validating systems alike must report violations of the well-formedness constraints given in this specification.

Validating processors must report locations in which the document does not comply with the

Notation Declarations

```
[81] NotationDecl ::= '<!NOTATION' S %Name S %ExternalID S? '>'
```

constraints expressed by the declarations in the DTD. They must also report all failures to fulfill the validity constraints given in this specification.

Appendix A: XML and SGML

XML is designed to be a subset of SGML, in that every valid XML document should also be a conformant SGML document, using the same DTD, and that the parse trees produced by an SGML parser and an XML processor should be the same. To achieve this, XML was defined by removing features and options from the specification of SGML.

The following list describes syntactic characteristics which XML does not allow but which are legal in SGML. The list may not be complete.

1. No tag omission.
2. Special tag-form for empty elements.
3. Comment declarations must have the delimiters `<!-- comment text -->` and can't have spaces within the markup of `<!--` or `-->`.
4. No comments (`-- . . . --`) inside markup declarations.
5. Comment declarations can't jump in and out of comments with `-- --`.
6. No name groups for declaring multiple elements or making a single ATTLIST declaration apply to multiple elements.
7. No RANK feature.
8. No CDATA or RCDATA declared content in element declarations. (Use CDATA sections instead.)
9. No exclusions or inclusions on content models.
10. No minimization parameters on element declarations.
11. Mixed content models must be optional-repeatable OR-groups, with #PCDATA first.
12. No AND (&) content model groups.
13. No NAME[S], NUMBER[S], or NUTOKEN[S] declared values for attributes. (Use NMTOKEN[S] or CDATA with application-specific validation instead.)
14. No #CURRENT or #CONREF declared values for attributes.
15. Attribute default values must be quoted.
16. Marked sections can't have spaces within the markup of `<![`*keyword*`[` or `]]>`.
17. No RCDATA, TEMP, IGNORE, or INCLUDE marked sections in document instances.
18. Marked sections in document instances must use the CDATA keyword literally, not a parameter entity.
19. No CDATA, RCDATA, or TEMP marked sections in the DTD.
20. Some restrictions on the content of ignored marked-sections: comments, literals, and processing instructions in ignored sections may not contain the delimiter string `]]>`; this helps ensure that the end-point of the conditional section does not change when the section is changed from IGNORE to INCLUDE.
21. No SDATA, CDATA, or bracketed internal entities.
22. No SUBDOC, CDATA, or SDATA external entities.
23. External entities must have a system identifier.
24. Parameter-entity references in the internal DTD subset may occur only between declarations.
25. Parameter-entity references in the external DTD subset are restricted to certain positions in the grammar, and must replace whole non-terminals of the grammar; this ensures that all valid XML documents are valid SGML, and makes the restrictions on param-

eter-entity replacement easier to understand and implement.

26. No data attributes on NOTATIONs or attribute value specifications on ENTITY declarations.
27. No SHORTREF declarations.
28. No USEMAP declarations.
29. No LINKTYPE declarations.
30. No LINK declarations.
31. No USELINK declarations.
32. No IDLINK declarations.
33. No SGML declarations.

In most current SGML systems, XML documents should be able to use the SGML declaration in Example 1. Some systems (those which take the document character set to be a description of the input stream) may require different declarations, depending on the character set and the capacities and quantities required.

Example 1 SGML Declaration for XML

```
<!SGML -- SGML Declaration for XML --
    "ISO 8879:1986 (ENR)"

    CHARSET
        BASESET
            "ISO Registration Number 176//CHARSET
            ISO/IEC 10646-1:1993 UCS-2 with implementation
            level 3//ESC 2/5 2/15 4/5"
        DESCSET
            0       9 UNUSED
            9       2 9
            11      2 UNUSED
            13      1 13
            14     18 UNUSED
            32     95 32
            127     1 UNUSED
            128    32 UNUSED
            160 65376 160

    CAPACITY SGMLREF
        -- Capacities are not restricted in XML --
        TOTALCAP 99999999
        ENTCAP   99999999
        ENTCHCAP 99999999
        ELEMCAP  99999999
        GRPCAP   99999999
        EXGRPCAP 99999999
        EXNMCAP  99999999
        ATTCAP   99999999
        ATTCHCAP 99999999
        AVGRPCAP 99999999
        NOTCAP   99999999
        NOTCHCAP 99999999
        IDCAP    99999999
        IDREFCAP 99999999
        MAPCAP   99999999
        LKSETCAP 99999999
        LKNMCAP  99999999
```

Example 1 SGML Declaration for XML *(continued)*

```
SCOPE DOCUMENT

SYNTAX
    SHUNCHAR NONE
    BASESET "ISO Registration Number 176//CHARSET
            ISO/IEC 10646-1:1993 UCS-2 with implementation
            level 3//ESC 2/5 2/15 4/5"
    DESCSET
        0 65536 0
    FUNCTION
        RE    13
        RS    10
        SPACE 32
        TAB   SEPCHAR 9
        ITAB  SEPCHAR 12288 -- ideographic space --

    NAMING
        LCNMSTRT
            224-246 248-255 257 259 261 263 265 267 269 271 273
            275 277 279 281 283 285 287 289 291 293 295 297 299
            301 303 305 307 309 311 314 316 318 320 322 324 326
            328 331 333 335 337 339 341 343 345 347 349 351 353
            355 357 359 361 363 365 367 369 371 373 375 378 380
            382 383 387 389 392 396 402 409 417 419 421 424 429
            432 436 438 441 445 453 454 456 457 459 460 462 464
            466 468 470 472 474 476 479 481 483 485 487 489 491
            493 495 498 499 501 507 509 511 513 515 517 519 521
            523 525 527 529 531 533 535 595 596 598-601 603 608
            611 616 617 623 626 643 648 650 651 658 940-943
            945-961 963-974 976 977 981 982 995 997 999 1001
            1003 1005 1007-1009 1072-1103 1105-1116 1118 1119
            1121 1123 1125 1127 1129 1131 1133 1135 1137 1139
            1141 1143 1145 1147 1149 1151 1153 1169 1171 1173
            1175 1177 1179 1181 1183 1185 1187 1189 1191 1193
            1195 1197 1199 1201 1203 1205 1207 1209 1211 1213
            1215 1218 1220 1224 1228 1233 1235 1237 1239 1241
            1243 1245 1247 1249 1251 1253 1255 1257 1259 1263
            1265 1267 1269 1273 1377-1414 7681 7683 7685 7687
            7689 7691 7693 7695 7697 7699 7701 7703 7705 7707
            7709 7711 7713 7715 7717 7719 7721 7723 7725 7727
            7729 7731 7733 7735 7737 7739 7741 7743 7745 7747
            7749 7751 7753 7755 7757 7759 7761 7763 7765 7767
            7769 7771 7773 7775 7777 7779 7781 7783 7785 7787
            7789 7791 7793 7795 7797 7799 7801 7803 7805 7807
            7809 7811 7813 7815 7817 7819 7821 7823 7825 7827
            7829 7841 7843 7845 7847 7849 7851 7853 7855 7857
            7859 7861 7863 7865 7867 7869 7871 7873 7875 7877
            7879 7881 7883 7885 7887 7889 7891 7893 7895 7897
            7899 7901 7903 7905 7907 7909 7911 7913 7915 7917
            7919 7921 7923 7925 7927 7929 7936-7943 7952-7957
            7968-7975 7984-7991 8000-8005 8017 8019 8021 8023
            8032-8039 8048-8061 8064-8071 8080-8087 8096-8103
            8112 8113 8115 8131 8144 8145 8160 8161 8165 8179
            8560-8575 65345-65370
```

Example 1 SGML Declaration for XML *(continued)*

```
UCNMSTRT
    -- 305 and 383 should be 73 and 83 respectively,
    but SGML does not allow a letter to be assigned
    to UCNMSTRT --
    192-214 216-222 376 256 258 260 262 264 266 268 270
    272 274 276 278 280 282 284 286 288 290 292 294 296
    298 300 302 305 306 308 310 313 315 317 319 321 323
    325 327 330 332 334 336 338 340 342 344 346 348 350
    352 354 356 358 360 362 364 366 368 370 372 374 377
    379 381 383 386 388 391 395 401 408 416 418 420 423
    428 431 435 437 440 444 452 452 455 455 458 458 461
    463 465 467 469 471 473 475 478 480 482 484 486 488
    490 492 494 497 497 500 506 508 510 512 514 516 518
    520 522 524 526 528 530 532 534 385 390 393 394 398
    399 400 403 404 407 406 412 413 425 430 433 434 439
    902 904-906 913-929 931-939 908 910 911 914 920 934
    928 994 996 998 1000 1002 1004 1006 922 929
    1040-1071 1025-1036 1038 1039 1120 1122 1124 1126
    1128 1130 1132 1134 1136 1138 1140 1142 1144 1146
    1148 1150 1152 1168 1170 1172 1174 1176 1178 1180
    1182 1184 1186 1188 1190 1192 1194 1196 1198 1200
    1202 1204 1206 1208 1210 1212 1214 1217 1219 1223
    1227 1232 1234 1236 1238 1240 1242 1244 1246 1248
    1250 1252 1254 1256 1258 1262 1264 1266 1268 1272
    1329-1366 7680 7682 7684 7686 7688 7690 7692 7694
    7696 7698 7700 7702 7704 7706 7708 7710 7712 7714
    7716 7718 7720 7722 7724 7726 7728 7730 7732 7734
    7736 7738 7740 7742 7744 7746 7748 7750 7752 7754
    7756 7758 7760 7762 7764 7766 7768 7770 7772 7774
    7776 7778 7780 7782 7784 7786 7788 7790 7792 7794
    7796 7798 7800 7802 7804 7806 7808 7810 7812 7814
    7816 7818 7820 7822 7824 7826 7828 7840 7842 7844
    7846 7848 7850 7852 7854 7856 7858 7860 7862 7864
    7866 7868 7870 7872 7874 7876 7878 7880 7882 7884
    7886 7888 7890 7892 7894 7896 7898 7900 7902 7904
    7906 7908 7910 7912 7914 7916 7918 7920 7922 7924
    7926 7928 7944-7951 7960-7965 7976-7983 7992-7999
    8008-8013 8025 8027 8029 8031 8040-8047 8122 8123
    8136-8139 8154 8155 8184 8185 8170 8171 8186 8187
    8072-8079 8088-8095 8104-8111 8120 8121 8124 8140
    8152 8153 8168 8169 8172 8188 8544-8559 65313-65338

NAMESTRT
    58 95
    170 181 186 223 304 312 329 384 397 405 410 411 414
    415 422 426 427 442 443 446-451 477 496 592-594 597
    602 604-607 609 610 612-615 618-622 624 625 627-642
    644-647 649 652-657 659-680 688-696 699-705 736-740
    768-837 864 865 890 912 944 962 978-980 986 988 990
    992 1010 1011 1155-1158 1216 1369 1415 1425-1441
    1443-1465 1467-1469 1471 1473 1474 1476 1488-1514
    1520-1522 1569-1594 1601-1618 1648-1719 1722-1726
    1728-1742 1744-1747 1749-1768 1770-1773 2305-2307
    2309-2361 2364-2381 2385-2388 2392-2403 2433-2435
```

Example 1 SGML Declaration for XML *(continued)*

```
    2437-2444 2447 2448 2451-2472 2474-2480 2482
    2486-2489 2492 2494-2500 2503 2504 2507-2509 2519
    2524 2525 2527-2531 2544 2545 2562 2565-2570 2575
    2576 2579-2600 2602-2608 2610 2611 2613 2614 2616
    2617 2620 2622-2626 2631 2632 2635-2637 2649-2652
    2654 2672-2676 2689-2691 2693-2699 2701 2703-2705
    2707-2728 2730-2736 2738 2739 2741-2745 2748-2757
    2759-2761 2763-2765 2784 2817-2819 2821-2828 2831
    2832 2835-2856 2858-2864 2866 2867 2870-2873
    2876-2883 2887 2888 2891-2893 2902 2903 2908 2909
    2911-2913 2946 2947 2949-2954 2958-2960 2962-2965
    2969 2970 2972 2974 2975 2979 2980 2984-2986
    2990-2997 2999-3001 3006-3010 3014-3016 3018-3021
    3031 3073-3075 3077-3084 3086-3088 3090-3112
    3114-3123 3125-3129 3134-3140 3142-3144 3146-3149
    3157 3158 3168 3169 3202 3203 3205-3212 3214-3216
    3218-3240 3242-3251 3253-3257 3262-3268 3270-3272
    3274-3277 3285 3286 3294 3296 3297 3330 3331
    3333-3340 3342-3344 3346-3368 3370-3385 3390-3395
    3398-3400 3402-3405 3415 3424 3425 3585-3630
    3632-3642 3648-3653 3655-3662 3713 3714 3716 3719
    3720 3722 3725 3732-3735 3737-3743 3745-3747 3749
    3751 3754 3755 3757 3758 3760-3769 3771-3773
    3776-3780 3784-3789 3804 3805 3864 3865 3893 3895
    3897 3902-3911 3913-3945 3953-3972 3974-3979
    3984-3989 3991 3993-4013 4017-4023 4025 4256-4293
    4304-4342 4352-4441 4447-4514 4520-4601 7830-7835
    8016 8018 8020 8022 8114 8116 8118 8119 8126 8130
    8132 8134 8135 8146 8147 8150 8151 8162-8164 8166
    8167 8178 8180 8182 8183 8319 8400-8412 8417 8450
    8455 8458-8467 8469 8472-8477 8484 8486 8488
    8490-8497 8499-8504 8576-8578 12295 12321-12335
    12353-12436 12441 12442 12449-12538 12549-12588
    12593-12686 19968-40869 44032-55203 63744-64045
    64256-64262 64275-64279 64286-64296 64298-64310
    64312-64316 64318 64320 64321 64323 64324
    64326-64433 64467-64829 64848-64911 64914-64967
    65008-65019 65056-65059 65136-65138 65140
    65142-65276 65382-65391 65393-65437 65440-65470
    65474-65479 65482-65487 65490-65495 65498-65500

LCNMCHAR "-."
UCNMCHAR "-."

NAMECHAR
    183 720 721 1600 1632-1641 1776-1785 2406-2415
    2534-2543 2662-2671 2790-2799 2918-2927 3047-3055
    3174-3183 3302-3311 3430-3439 3654 3664-3673 3782
    3792-3801 3872-3881 8204-8207 8234-8238 8298-8303
    12293 12337-12341 12443-12446 12540-12542 65279
    65296-65305 65392 65438 65439
NAMECASE
    GENERAL YES
    ENTITY  NO
```

Example 1 SGML Declaration for XML *(continued)*

```
        DELIM
            GENERAL SGMLREF
            NET "/>"
            PIC "?>"
            SHORTREF NONE
        NAMES
            SGMLREF

        QUANTITY SGMLREF
            -- Quantities are not restricted in XML --
            ATTCNT      99999999
            ATTSPLEN    99999999
            -- BSEQLEN  not used --
            -- DTAGLEN  not used --
            -- DTEMPLEN not used --
            ENTLVL      99999999
            GRPCNT      99999999
            GRPGTCNT    99999999
            GRPLVL      99999999
            LITLEN      99999999
            NAMELEN     99999999
            -- no need to change NORMSEP --
            PILEN       99999999
            TAGLEN      99999999
            TAGLVL      99999999

    FEATURES
        MINIMIZE
            DATATAG NO
            OMITTAG NO
            RANK NO
            SHORTTAG YES -- SHORTTAG is needed for NET --
        LINK
            SIMPLE NO
            IMPLICIT NO
            EXPLICIT NO
        OTHER
            CONCUR NO
            SUBDOC NO
            FORMAL NO
    APPINFO NONE
>
```

Appendix B: Character Classes

Following the characteristics defined in the Unicode standard, characters are classed as base characters (among others, these contain the alphabetic characters of the Latin alphabet, without diacritics), ideographic characters, combining characters (among others, this class contains most diacritics); these classes combine to form the class of letters. Digits, extenders, and characters which should be ignored for purposes of recognizing identifiers are also distinguished.

Example 2 Characters

```
[82]    BaseChar ::=[#x41-#x5A] | [#x61-#x7A]        /* Latin 1 upper
                                                       and lowercase */
                  | #xAA | #xB5 | #xBA               /* Latin 1
                  | [#xC0-#xD6] | [#xD8-#xF6]           supplementary */
                  | [#xF8-#xFF]
                  | [#x0100-#x017F]                  /* Extended
                  | [#x0180-#x01F5]                     Latin-A and B */
                  | [#x01FA-#x0217]
                  | [#x0250-#x02A8]                  /* IPA Extensions */

                  | [#x02B0-#x02B8]                  /* Spacing
                  | [#x02BB-#x02C1]                     Modifiers */
                  | [#x02E0-#x02E4]
                  | #x037A | #x0386                  /* Greek and
                  | [#x0388-#x038A] | #x038C            Coptic */
                  | [#x038E-#x03A1]
                  | [#x03A3-#x03CE]
                  | [#x03D0-#x03D6] | #x03DA
                  | #x03DC | #x03DE | #x03E0
                  | [#x03E2-#x03F3]
                  | [#x0401-#x040C]                  /* Cyrillic */
                  | [#x040E-#x044F]
                  | [#x0451-#x045C]
                  | [#x045E-#x0481]
                  | [#x0490-#x04C4]
                  | [#x04C7-#x04C8]
                  | [#x04CB-#x04CC]
                  | [#x04D0-#x04EB]
                  | [#x04EE-#x04F5]
                  | [#x04F8-#x04F9]
                  | [#x0531-#x0556] | #x0559         /* Armenian */
                  | [#x0561-#x0587]
                  | [#x05D0-#x05EA]                  /* Hebrew */
                  | [#x05F0-#x05F2]
                  | [#x0621-#x063A]                  /* Arabic */
                  | [#x0641-#x064A]
                  | [#x0671-#x06B7]
                  | [#x06BA-#x06BE]
                  | [#x06C0-#x06CE]
                  | [#x06D0-#x06D3] | #x06D5
                  | [#x06E5-#x06E6]
                  | [#x0905-#x0939] | #x093D         /* Devanagari */
                  | [#x0958-#x0961]
                  | [#x0985-#x098C]                  /* Bengali */
                  | [#x098F-#x0990]
                  | [#x0993-#x09A8]
                  | [#x09AA-#x09B0] | #x09B2
                  | [#x09B6-#x09B9]
                  | [#x09DC-#x09DD]
                  | [#x09DF-#x09E1]
                  | [#x09F0-#x09F1]
                  | [#x0A05-#x0A0A]                  /* Gurmukhi */
                  | [#x0A0F-#x0A10]
                  | [#x0A13-#x0A28]
```

Example 2 Characters *(continued)*

```
| [#x0A2A-#x0A30]
| [#x0A32-#x0A33]
| [#x0A35-#x0A36]
| [#x0A38-#x0A39]
| [#x0A59-#x0A5C] | #x0A5E
| [#x0A72-#x0A74]
| [#x0A85-#x0A8B] | #x0A8D
| [#x0A8F-#x0A91]                    /* Gujarati */
| [#x0A93-#x0AA8]
| [#x0AAA-#x0AB0]
| [#x0AB2-#x0AB3]
| [#x0AB5-#x0AB9] | #x0ABD
| #x0AE0
| [#x0B05-#x0B0C]                    /* Oriya */
| [#x0B0F-#x0B10]
| [#x0B13-#x0B28]
| [#x0B2A-#x0B30]
| [#x0B32-#x0B33]
| [#x0B36-#x0B39] | #x0B3D
| [#x0B5C-#x0B5D]
| [#x0B5F-#x0B61]
| [#x0B85-#x0B8A]                    /* Tamil */
| [#x0B8E-#x0B90]
| [#x0B92-#x0B95]
| [#x0B99-#x0B9A] | #x0B9C
| [#x0B9E-#x0B9F]
| [#x0BA3-#x0BA4]
| [#x0BA8-#x0BAA]
| [#x0BAE-#x0BB5]
| [#x0BB7-#x0BB9]
| [#x0C05-#x0C0C]                    /* Telugu */
| [#x0C0E-#x0C10]
| [#x0C12-#x0C28]
| [#x0C2A-#x0C33]
| [#x0C35-#x0C39]
| [#x0C60-#x0C61]
| [#x0C85-#x0C8C]                    /* Kannada */
| [#x0C8E-#x0C90]
| [#x0C92-#x0CA8]
| [#x0CAA-#x0CB3]
| [#x0CB5-#x0CB9] | #x0CDE
| [#x0CE0-#x0CE1]
| [#x0D05-#x0D0C]                    /* Malayalam */
| [#x0D0E-#x0D10]
| [#x0D12-#x0D28]
| [#x0D2A-#x0D39]
| [#x0D60-#x0D61]
| [#x0E01-#x0E2E] | #x0E30         /* Thai */
| [#x0E32-#x0E33]
| [#x0E40-#x0E45]
| [#x0E81-#x0E82] | #x0E84         /* Lao */
| [#x0E87-#x0E88] | #x0E8A
| #x0E8D | [#x0E94-#x0E97]
| [#x0E99-#x0E9F]
| [#x0EA1-#x0EA3] | #x0EA5
```

Example 2 Characters *(continued)*

```
| #x0EA7 | [#x0EAA-#x0EAB]
| [#x0EAD-#x0EAE] | #x0EB0
| [#x0EB2-#x0EB3] | #x0EBD
| [#x0EC0-#x0EC4]
| [#x0EDC-#x0EDD]
| [#x0F40-#x0F47]                /* Tibetan */
| [#x0F49-#x0F69]
| [#x10A0-#x10C5]                /* Georgian */
| [#x10D0-#x10F6]
| [#x1100-#x1159]                /* Hangul Jamo */
| [#x115F-#x11A2]
| [#x11A8-#x11F9]
| [#x1E00-#x1E9B]                /* Add'l Extended
| [#x1EA0-#x1EF9]                   Latin */
| [#x1F00-#x1F15]                /* Greek
| [#x1F18-#x1F1D]                   Extensions */
| [#x1F20-#x1F45]
| [#x1F48-#x1F4D]
| [#x1F50-#x1F57] | #x1F59
| #x1F5B | #x1F5D
| [#x1F5F-#x1F7D]
| [#x1F80-#x1FB4]
| [#x1FB6-#x1FBC] | #x1FBE
| [#x1FC2-#x1FC4]
| [#x1FC6-#x1FCC]
| [#x1FD0-#x1FD3]
| [#x1FD6-#x1FDB]
| [#x1FE0-#x1FEC]
| [#x1FF2-#x1FF4]
| [#x1FF6-#x1FFC]
| #x207F                         /* Super-,
                                    subscripts */
| #x2102 | #x2107               /* Letterlike
| [#x210A-#x2113] | #x2115         Symbols */
| [#x2118-#x211D] | #x2124
| #x2126 | #x2128
| [#x212A-#x2131]
| [#x2133-#x2138]
| [#x2160-#x2182]                /* Number forms */
| [#x3041-#x3094]                /* Hiragana */
| [#x30A1-#x30FA]                /* Katakana */
| [#x3105-#x312C]                /* Bopomofo */
| [#x3131-#x318E]                /* Hangul Jamo */
| [#xAC00-#xD7A3]                /* Hangul
                                    syllables */
| [#xFB00-#xFB06]                /* Alphabetic
| [#xFB13-#xFB17]                   presentation
| [#xFB1F-#xFB28]                   forms */
| [#xFB2A-#xFB36]
| [#xFB38-#xFB3C] | #xFB3E
| [#xFB40-#xFB41]
| [#xFB43-#xFB44]
| [#xFB46-#xFB4F]
| [#xFB50-#xFBB1]                /* Arabic
```

Example 2 Characters *(continued)*

```
                        | [#xFBD3-#xFD3D]                presentation
                        | [#xFD50-#xFD8F]                forms */
                        | [#xFD92-#xFDC7]
                        | [#xFDF0-#xFDFB]
                        | [#xFE70-#xFE72] | #xFE74
                        | [#xFE76-#xFEFC]
                        | [#xFF21-#xFF3A]             /* Half- and
                        | [#xFF41-#xFF5A]                fullwidth
                        | [#xFF66-#xFF6F]                forms */
                        | [#xFE71-#xFF9D]
                        | [#xFFA0-#xFFBE]
                        | [#xFFC2-#xFFC7]
                        | [#xFFCA-#xFFCF]
                        | [#xFFD2-#xFFD7]
                        | [#xFFDA-#xFFDC]
[83]   Ideographic ::=[#x4E00-#x9FA5]
                        | [#xF900-#xFA2D] | #x3007
                        | [#x3021-#x3029]
[84] CombiningChar ::=[#x0300-#x0345]
                        | [#x0360-#x0361]
                        | [#x0483-#x0486]
                        | [#x0591-#x05A1]
                        | [#x05A3-#x05B9]
                        | [#x05BB-#x05BD] | #x05BF
                        | [#x05C1-#x05C2] | #x05C4
                        | [#x064B-#x0652] | #x0670
                        | [#x06D6-#x06DC]
                        | [#x06DD-#x06DF]
                        | [#x06E0-#x06E4]
                        | [#x06E7-#x06E8]
                        | [#x06EA-#x06ED]
                        | [#x0901-#x0903] | #x093C
                        | [#x093E-#x094C] | #x094D
                        | [#x0951-#x0954]
                        | [#x0962-#x0963]
                        | [#x0981-#x0983] | #x09BC
                        | #x09BE | #x09BF
                        | [#x09C0-#x09C4]
                        | [#x09C7-#x09C8]
                        | [#x09CB-#x09CD] | #x09D7
                        | [#x09E2-#x09E3] | #x0A02
                        | #x0A3C | #x0A3E | #x0A3F
                        | [#x0A40-#x0A42]
                        | [#x0A47-#x0A48]
                        | [#x0A4B-#x0A4D]
                        | [#x0A70-#x0A71]
                        | [#x0A81-#x0A83] | #x0ABC
                        | [#x0ABE-#x0AC5]
                        | [#x0AC7-#x0AC9]
                        | [#x0ACB-#x0ACD]
                        | [#x0B01-#x0B03] | #x0B3C
                        | [#x0B3E-#x0B43]
                        | [#x0B47-#x0B48]
                        | [#x0B4B-#x0B4D]
                        | [#x0B56-#x0B57]
```

```
                    | [#x0B82-#x0B83]
                    | [#x0BBE-#x0BC2]
                    | [#x0BC6-#x0BC8]
                    | [#x0BCA-#x0BCD] | #x0BD7
                    | [#x0C01-#x0C03]
                    | [#x0C3E-#x0C44]
                    | [#x0C46-#x0C48]
                    | [#x0C4A-#x0C4D]
                    | [#x0C55-#x0C56]
                    | [#x0C82-#x0C83]
                    | [#x0CBE-#x0CC4]
                    | [#x0CC6-#x0CC8]
                    | [#x0CCA-#x0CCD]
                    | [#x0CD5-#x0CD6]
                    | [#x0D02-#x0D03]
                    | [#x0D3E-#x0D43]
                    | [#x0D46-#x0D48]
                    | [#x0D4A-#x0D4D] | #x0D57
                    | #x0E31 | [#x0E34-#x0E3A]
                    | [#x0E47-#x0E4E] | #x0EB1
                    | [#x0EB4-#x0EB9]
                    | [#x0EBB-#x0EBC]
                    | [#x0EC8-#x0ECD]
                    | [#x0F18-#x0F19] | #x0F35
                    | #x0F37 | #x0F39 | #x0F3E
                    | #x0F3F | [#x0F71-#x0F84]
                    | [#x0F86-#x0F8B]
                    | [#x0F90-#x0F95] | #x0F97
                    | [#x0F99-#x0FAD]
                    | [#x0FB1-#x0FB7] | #x0FB9
                    | [#x20D0-#x20DC] | #x20E1
                    | [#x302A-#x302F] | #x3099
                    | #x309A | #xFB1E
                    | [#xFE20-#xFE23]
[85]    Letter ::=BaseChar | Ideographic
[86]     Digit ::=[#x30-#x39]                   /* ISO 646 digits */
                    | [#x0660-#x0669]           /* Arabic-Indic
                                                   digits */
                    | [#x06F0-#x06F9]           /* Eastern
                                                   Arabic-Indic
                                                   digits */
                    | [#x0966-#x096F]           /* Devanagari
                                                   digits */
                    | [#x09E6-#x09EF]           /* Bengali digits
                                                   */
                    | [#x0A66-#x0A6F]           /* Gurmukhi
                                                   digits */
                    | [#x0AE6-#x0AEF]           /* Gujarati
                                                   digits */
                    | [#x0B66-#x0B6F]           /* Oriya digits */

                    | [#x0BE7-#x0BEF]           /* Tamil digits
                                                   (no zero) */
                    | [#x0C66-#x0C6F]           /* Telugu digits */
```

Example 2 Characters *(continued)*

```
                    | [#x0CE6-#x0CEF]          /* Kannada digits */

                    | [#x0D66-#x0D6F]          /* Malayalam
                                                  digits */
                    | [#x0E50-#x0E59]          /* Thai digits */
                    | [#x0ED0-#x0ED9]          /* Lao digits */
                    | [#x0F20-#x0F29]          /* Tibetan digits */

                    | [#xFF10-#xFF19]          /* Fullwidth
                                                  digits */
[87]    Ignorable ::=[#x200C-#x200F]           /* zw layout */
                    | [#x202A-#x202E]          /* bidi
                                                  formatting */
                    | [#x206A-#x206F]          /* alt formatting */

                    | #xFEFF                   /* zw nonbreak
                                                  space */
[88]     Extender ::=#xB7 | #x02D0 | #x02D1 | #x0387
                    | #x0640 | #x0E46 | #x0EC6
                    | #x3005 | [#x3031-#x3035]
                    | [#x309B-#x309E]
                    | [#x30FC-#x30FE] | #xFF70
                    | #xFF9E | #xFF9F
```

Appendix C: Expansion of Entity and Character References

This appendix contains some examples illustrating the sequence of entity- and character-reference recognition and expansion.

If the DTD contains the declaration

```
<!ENTITY example "<p>An ampersand
    (&#38;#38;) may be escaped
    numerically (&#38;#38;#38;) or
    with a general entity (&amp;amp;).
</p>">
```

then the XML processor will recognize the character references when it parses the entity declaration, and resolve them before storing the following string as the value of the entity *example*:

```
<p>An ampersand (&#38;) may be
    escaped numerically (&#38;#38;)
    or with a general entity
    (&amp;amp;).</p>
```

A reference in the document to **&example;** will cause the text to be reparsed, at which time the start- and end-tags of the p element will be recognized and the three references will be recognized and expanded, resulting in a p element with the following content (all data, no delimiters or markup):

```
An ampersand (&) may be escaped
    numerically (&#38;) or with a
    general entity (&amp;).
```

A more complex example will illustrate the rules and their effects fully. In the following example, the line numbers are solely for reference.

```
1 <?XML version='1.0'?>
2 <!DOCTYPE test [
3 <!ELEMENT test (#PCDATA) >
4 <!ENTITY % xx '&#37;zz;'>
5 <!ENTITY % zz '&#60;!ENTITY
    tricky "error-prone" >'>
6 %xx;
7 ]>
8 <test>This sample shows a
    &tricky; method.</test>
```

This produces the following:

1. In line 4, the reference to character 37 is expanded immediately, and the parameter entity **xx** is stored in the symbol table with

the value %zz;. Since the replacement text is not rescanned, the reference to parameter entity zz is not recognized. (And it would be an error if it were, since zz is not yet declared.)

2. In line 5, the character reference < is expanded immediately and the parameter entity zz is stored with the replacement text <!ENTITY tricky "error-prone" >, which is a well-formed entity declaration.
3. In line 6, the reference to xx is recognized, and the replacement text of xx (namely %zz;) is parsed. The reference to zz is recognized in its turn, and its replacement text (<!ENTITY tricky "error-prone" >) is parsed. The general entity tricky has now been declared, with the replacement text error-prone.
4. In line 8, the reference to the general entity tricky is recognized, and it is expanded, so the full content of the test element is the self-describing (and ungrammatical) string. This sample shows a error-prone method.

Appendix D: Deterministic Content Models

For compatibility, it is required that content models in element declarations be deterministic. SGML requires deterministic content models (it calls them "unambiguous"); XML processors built using SGML systems may flag non-deterministic content models as errors.

For example, the content model

```
((b, c) | (b, d))
```

is non-deterministic, because given an initial b the parser cannot know which b in the model is being matched without looking ahead to see which element follows the b. In this case, the two references to b can be collapsed into a single reference, making the model read

```
(b, (c | d))
```

An initial b now clearly matches only a single name in the content model. The parser doesn't need to look ahead to see what follows; either c or d would be accepted.

Algorithms exist which allow many but not all non-deterministic content models to be reduced automatically to equivalent deterministic models; see [3].

Appendix E: Autodetection of Character Encodings

The XML encoding declaration functions as an internal label on each entity, indicating which character encoding is in use. Before an XML processor can read the internal label, however, it apparently has to know what character encoding is in use—which is what the internal label is trying to indicate. In the general case, this is a hopeless situation. It is not entirely hopeless in XML, however, because XML limits the general case in two ways: each implementation is assumed to support only a finite set of character encodings, and the XML encoding declaration is restricted in position and content in order to make it feasible to autodetect the character encoding in use in each entity in normal cases.

Because each XML entity not in UTF-8 or UCS-2 format *must* begin with an XML encoding declaration, in which the first characters must be <?XML, any conforming processor can detect, after two to four octets of input, which of the following cases apply (in reading this list, it may help to know that in UCS-4, < is #x0000003C and ? is #x0000003F, and the Byte Order Mark required of UCS-2 data streams is #xFEFF):

00 00 00 3C
: UCS-4, big-endian machine (1234 order)

3C 00 00 00
: UCS-4, little-endian machine (4321 order)

00 00 3C 00
: UCS-4, unusual octet order (2143)

00 3C 00 00
: UCS-4, unusual octet order (3412)

`FE FF`
: UCS-2, big-endian

`FF FE`
: UCS-2, little-endian

`00 3C 00 3F`
: UCS-2, big-endian, no Byte Order Mark (and thus, strictly speaking, in error)

`3C 00 3F 00`
: UCS-2, little-endian, no Byte Order Mark (and thus, strictly speaking, in error)

`3C 3F 58 4D`
: UTF-8, ISO 646, ASCII, some part of ISO 8859, Shift-JIS, EUC, or any other 7-bit, 8-bit, or mixed-width encoding which ensures that the characters of ASCII have their normal positions, width, and values; the actual encoding declaration must be read to detect which of these applies, but since all of these encodings use the same bit patterns for the ASCII characters, the encoding declaration itself may be read reliably

`4C 6F E7 D4`
: EBCDIC (in some flavor; the full encoding declaration must be read to tell which code page is in use)

Other
: UTF-8 without an encoding declaration, or else the data are corrupt, fragmentary, or enclosed in a wrapper of some kind

This level of autodetection is enough to read the XML encoding declaration and parse the character-encoding identifier, which is still necessary to distinguish the individual members of each family of encodings (e.g., to tell UTF-8 from 8859, and the parts of 8859 from each other, or to distinguish the specific EBCDIC code page in use, and so on).

Because the contents of the encoding declaration are restricted to ASCII characters, a processor can reliably read the entire encoding declaration as soon as it has detected which family of encodings is in use. Since in practice, all widely used character encodings fall into one of the categories above, the XML encoding declaration allows reasonably reliable in-line labeling of character encodings, even when external sources of information at the operating-system or transport-protocol level are unreliable.

Once the processor has detected the character encoding in use, it can act appropriately, whether by invoking a separate input routine for each case, or by calling the proper conversion function on each character of input.

Like any self-labeling system, the XML encoding declaration will not work if any software changes the entity's character set or encoding without updating the encoding declaration. Implementors of character-encoding routines should be careful to ensure the accuracy of the internal and external information used to label the entity.

Appendix F: A Trivial Grammar for XML Documents

The grammar given in the body of this specification is relatively simple, but for some purposes it is convenient to have an even simpler one. A very simple, though non-conforming, XML processor could parse a well-formed XML document using the simplified grammar in Example 3, recognizing all element boundaries correctly, though not expanding entity references and not detecting all errors.

Most processors will require the more complex grammar given in the body of this specification.

Example 3 Trivial Text Grammar

```
[89] simpleDoc ::= (SimpleData | Markup)*
[90] SimpleData ::= [^<&]*                        /* cf. PCData */
[91] SimpleLit ::= ('"' [^"]* '"')
                   |("'" [^']* "'")               /* cf. SkipLit */
[92]    Markup ::= '<' Name (S Name S? '=' S?     /* start-tags */
```

Example 3 Trivial Text Grammar *(continued)*

```
                     SimpleLit)* S? '>'
                     | '<' Name (S Name S? '='      /* empty elements */
                     S? SimpleLit)* S? '/>'
                     | '</' Name S? '>'             /* end-tags  */
                     | '&' Name ';'                 /* entity references  */
                     | '&#' [0-9]+ ';'              /* decimal character references */
                     | '&#x' [0-9a-fA-F]+ ';'       /* hexadecimal
                                                       character references*/
                     | '<!--' (Char* - (Char*       /* comments  */
                     '--' Char*)) '-->'
                     | '<?' (Char* - (Char*         /* processing
                     '?>' Char*)) "?>"                instructions  */
                     | '<![CDATA[' (Char* -         /* CDATA sections */
                     (Char* ']]>' Char*)) ']]>'
                     | '<!DOCTYPE' (Char - ('['     /* doc type declaration /*
                     | ']'))+ ('[' simpleDTD*
                     ']')? '>'
[93] simpleDTD ::= '<!--' (Char* - (Char*           /* comment  */
                     '--' Char*)) '-->'
                     | '<?' (Char* - (Char*         /* processing
                     '?>' Char*))  ?>                  instruction  */
                     SimpleLit
                     (Char - (']' | '<' | '"' |
                     "'"))+
                     '<!' (Char - ('-'))+           /* declarations other
                                                       than comment */
```

Appendix G: W3C XML Working Group

This specification was prepared and approved for publication by the W3C XML Working Group (WG). WG approval of this specification does not necessarily imply that all WG members voted for its approval. At the

Jon Bosak, Sun *(Chair)*; James Clark *(Technical Lead)*; Tim Bray, Textuality and Netscape *(XML Co-editor)*; Jean Paoli, Microsoft *(XML Co-editor)*; C. M. Sperberg-McQueen, U. of Ill. *(XML Co-editor)*; Steve DeRose, INSO; Dave Hollander, HP; Eliot Kimber, Highland; Tom Magliery, NCSA; Eve Maler, ArborText; Murray Maloney, Grif; Peter Sharpe, SoftQuad. ■

References

1. Aho, Alfred V., Ravi Sethi, and Jeffrey D. Ullman. *Compilers: Principles, Techniques, and Tools.* Reading: Addison-Wesley, 1986, rpt. corr. 1988.
2. Brüggemann-Klein, Anne. *Regular Expressions into Finite Automata.* Universität Freiburg, Institut für Informatik, Bericht 33, Juli 1991.
3. Brüggemann-Klein, Anne, and Derick Wood. *Deterministic Regular Languages.* Universität Freiburg, Institut für Informatik, Bericht 38, Oktober 1991.
4. ISO (International Organization for Standardization). *ISO/IEC 8879-1986 (E). Information processing—Text and Office Systems—Standard Generalized Markup.* First edition—1986-10-15. [Geneva]: International Organization for Standardization, 1986.
5. ISO (International Organization for Standardization). *ISO/IEC 10646-1993 (E). Information technology—Universal Multiple-Octet Coded Character Set (UCS)* [Geneva]: International Organization for Standardization, 1993 (plus amendments AM 1 through AM 5).
6. ISO (International Organization for Standardization). *ISO/IEC 10744-1992 (E). Information technology—Hypermedia/Time-based Structuring Language (HyTime).* [Geneva]: International Organization for Standardization, 1992. *Extended Facili-*

ties Annexe. [Geneva]: International Organization for Standardization, 1996.

7. IETF (Internet Engineering Task Force). *RFC 1738: Uniform Resource Locators*. 1991.
8. The Unicode Consortium. *The Unicode Standard, Version 2.0*. Reading, Mass.: Addison-Wesley Developers Press, 1996.

About the Authors

Tim Bray
321–3495 Cambie Street
Vancouver, B.C., Canada V5Z 4R3
tbray@textuality.com

Tim Bray is a Canadian. He entered the software profession in 1981; after on-the-job training from Digital and GTE, he became manager of the New Oxford English Dictionary Project at the University of Waterloo in 1986. He co-founded Open Text Corporation in 1989, and started an independent consulting practice under the name Textuality in 1996. He is a Seybold Fellow, editor of the *Gilbane Report*, and co-editor of the World Wide Web Consortium's "Extensible Markup Language Specification."

Jean Paoli
1 Microsoft Way
Redmond, WA 98052-6399
jeanpa@microsoft.com

Jean Paoli is a Product Manager in the Internet Explorer 4.0 team where he manages the XML and databinding effort. Prior to joining Microsoft in May 1996, he was the technical director of GRIF S.A., a leader in the creation of SGML authoring tools. Jean has a strong background in SGML and designed for important corporations a lot of systems where SGML, in its approach of structuring and storing information, ensured the long life and easy exchangeability of the data. Jean is a co-editor of the XML standard and co-created with Jon Bosak (and others) the W3C XML working group in July 1996.

C.M Sperberg-McQueen
University of Illinois at Chicago
Computer Center (M/C 135)
1940 W. Taylor
Rm. 124
Chicago IL 60612-7352
emsmcq@uic.edu

C.M. Sperberg-McQueen is a senior research programmer at the University of Illinois at Chicago. He has a Ph.D. in comparative literature but strayed into computing as a student and never strayed back out. With Lou Burnard (Oxford) he edited the Text Encoding Initiative's *Guidelines for Electronic Text Encoding and Interchange* (1994), and with Tim Bray (Textuality), and Jean Paoli (Microsoft) he serves as editor of the XML language specification.

Extensible Markup Language (XML) Part 2: Linking

Tim Bray, Steve DeRose

Abstract

[W3C Working Draft; WD-xml-link-970731; July 31, 1997]

This document specifies a simple set of constructs that may be inserted into XML documents to describe links between objects and to support addressing into the internal structures of XML documents. It is a goal to use the power of XML to create a structure that can describe the simple unidirectional hyperlinks of today's HTML as well as more sophisticated multi-ended, typed, self-describing links.

Status of This Memo

This is a W3C Working Draft for review by W3C members and other interested parties. It is a draft document and may be updated, replaced or obsoleted by other documents at any time. It is inappropriate to use W3C Working Drafts as reference material or to cite them as other than "work in progress." A list of current W3C working drafts can be found at *http://www.we.org/TR.*

Note that some of the work that is still be done in this particular draft is described in Appendix A. This work is part of the W3C SGML Activity (for current status, see *http://www.w3.org/MarkUp/SGML/Activity*).

1. Introduction

This document specifies a set of constructs which may be inserted in XML documents to describe links. A *link*, as the term is used here, is a relationship which is asserted to exist between two or more data objects or portions of data objects. This specification is concerned with the syntax used to assert link existence and describe link characteristics. Implicit (unasserted) relationships, for example that of one word to the next, or that of a word in a text to its entry in an on-line dictionary, are outside its scope. Explicitly asserted links do not constitute the only useful kind of link, but this specification is intended neither to provide machinery for every possible kind of link nor to preclude the use of such machinery.

The existence of links is asserted by the presence of elements contained in XML documents. They may or may not reside at the locations of, or in the same documents with, the objects which they serve to connect.

1.1 Origin and Goals

This specification aims to provide an effective, compact structure for representing links that can be in documents or external to them, and that can have multiple typed locators, indirection, and precise specification of resource locations in XML and SGML data. It also aims to represent the abstract structure and significance of links, leaving formatting issues to stylesheets or other mechanisms as far as is practical.

1.2 Relationship to Existing Standards

Three standards have been especially influential:

HTML

Defines several SGML element types that represent links as well as popularizing a location specifier type, the URL, mainly focused on pointing to entire data objects, though with some provision for linking to elements with IDs, regions in graphics, and so on.

HyTime

Defines location specifier types applicable to all kinds of data, as well as in-line and out-of-line link structures, and some semantic features, including traversal control and placement of objects into a display or other space.

Text Encoding Initiative Guidelines (TEI P3)

Provides a formal syntax for location specifiers for structured data, graphics, and other data, and structures for creating links and link collections out of them.

Many other linking systems have also informed this design, including Dexter, MicroCosm, and InterMedia.

1.3 Terminology

The following basic terms apply in this document:

resource

In the abstract sense, an addressable unit of information or service which is participating in a link. Examples include files, images, documents, programs, and query results. Concretely, anything which happens to be reachable by the use of a locator in some linking element. Note that this term and its definition are taken from the basic specifications governing the World Wide Web.

linking element

An element which asserts the existence and describes the characteristics of a link.

locator

A character string appearing in a linking element, which may be used to locate a resource.

title

A caption associated with a resource, suitable for showing users as a means of explaining the significance of the part played in the link by that resource.

traversal

The action of using a link; that is, of accessing a resource. Traversal may be initiated by a user action (for example, clicking on the displayed content of a linking element) or occur under program control.

multi-directional link

A link that can be traversed starting at more than one of its resources. Note that being able to "go back" after following a one-directional link does not make the link multi-directional.

in-line link

Abstractly, a link which serves as one of its own resources. Concretely, in the language of this specification, a link where the content of the linking element serves as a resource. HTML `A`, HyTime `clink`, and TEI `XREF` are all examples of in-line links.

out-of-line link

A link which does not serve as one of its own resources. Such links only make sense given a notion like link groups, which instruct applications where to look for links. Nevertheless, out-of-line links are required to support multi-directional traversal and for creating links with resources which can be traversed starting from read-only data objects.

1.4 Notation

The formal grammar for locators is given using a simple Extended Backus-Naur Form (EBNF) location, as described in Part 1.

1.5 Types of Link Types

There is an extensive literature on link typology. Some well-known axes are:

link relationships

Links express various kinds of relationships between the data objects or portions they connect, in terms of conceptual significance to the author and user. Some links may be criticisms, others add support or background, while others have a very different meaning such as providing access to demographic information about a data object (its author's name, version number, etc.), or to navigational tools such as index, glossary, and summary.

link topology
: In-line and out-of-line links differ in their structure, as do links involving varying numbers of resources.

locator language
: There are many languages available for use in locating resources; examples are URLs, SQL queries, and and file names.

formatting
: Links may be presented in a variety of ways. The discussion of this area is complicated by the fact that link formatting and link behavior are inextricably connected. This specification does not discuss, or provide mechanisms for, the provision or use of link formatting information.

link behavior
: Links may have a wide variety of effects when traversed, such as opening, closing, or scrolling windows or panes; displaying the data from various resources in various ways; testing, authenticating, or logging user and context information; or executing various programs. Ideally, link behavior should be determined by a semantic specification based on link types, resource roles, user circumstances, and other factors; just as element formatting is determined by a stylesheet based on element type, context, and other factors.

2. Link Recognition

2.1 Linking Element Recognition

The existence of a link is asserted by a linking element. Linking elements must be recognized reliably by software in order to provide appropriate display and behavior. XML linking elements are recognized based on the use of a designated attribute named `XML-LINK`. Possible values are `SIMPLE`, `EXTENDED`, `LOCATOR`, `GROUP`, and `DOCUMENT`, signalling in each case that the element in whose start-tag the attribute appears is to be treated as an element of the indicated type, as described in this specification.

An example of such a link follows:

```
<A XML-LINK="SIMPLE" HREF="http://
   www.w3.org/"The W3C</A>
```

2.2 Attribute Remapping

This specification describes many attributes that can be attached to linking elements to describe various aspects of links. Each is given a name in this specification. It may be desired to use existing elements in XML documents as linking elements, but such elements might already have attributes whose names conflict with those described in this document. To avoid collisions, user-chosen attributes can be declared as equivalent to those described in this specification using the `XML-ATTRIBUTES` attribute.

This attribute must contain an even number of white-space-separated names, which are treated as pairs. In each pair, the first name must be one of those described in this specification: (`ROLE`, `HREF`, `TITLE`, `SHOW`, `INLINE`, `CONTENT-ROLE`, `CONTENT-TITLE`, `ACTUATE`, `BEHAVIOR`, `STEPS`). The second name, when recognized in the document, will be treated as though it were playing the role assigned to the first. For example, consider a DTD with the declaration shown in Example 1.

If it were desired to use this as a simple link, it would be necessary to remap a couple of attributes, which could be accomplished in the internal subset shown in Example 2.

Then in the document, Example 3 would be recognized as a simple link.

Example 1

```
<!ELEMENT TEXT-BOOK ANY>
<!ATTLIST TEXT-BOOK TITLE CDATA                   #IMPLIED
                    ROLE  (PRIMARY|SUPPORTING) #IMPLIED>
```

Example 2

```
<!ATTLIST TEXT-BOOK XML-LINK       CDATA #FIXED "SIMPLE"
                    XML-ATTRIBUTES CDATA #FIXED
                                         "TITLE XL-TITLE ROLE XL-ROLE">
```

Example 3

```
<TEXT-BOOK TITLE="Compilers: Principles, Techniques, and Tools"
           ROLE="PRIMARY" XL-TITLE="Primary Textbook for the Course"
           XL-ROLE="ONLINE-PURCHASE"
           HREF="/cgi/auth-search?q="+Aho+Sethi+Ullman"/>
```

2.3 Operational Issues Concerning Link Recognition

There are two distinct mechanisms that may be used to associate the **XML-LINK** and **XML-ATTRIBUTES** attributes with a linking element. The simplest is to provide it explicitly. However, this practice is verbose, and would be not only cumbersome but wasteful of network bandwidth in the case where there are large numbers of linking elements. Fortunately, XML's facilities for declaring default attribute values can be used to address this problem. For example, the following would accomplish the declaration of the **A** element as an XML **SIMPLE** link:

```
<!ATTLIST A XML-LINK CDATA #FIXED
    "SIMPLE">
```

Such a declaration may be placed in either the external or the internal subset of the Document Type Declaration. Placing it in both subsets would be the obvious thing to do for convenient network operation. So doing, at the time of creation of this specification, would cause the document to fail to be valid. Note that the successful completion of the current work on a technical corrigendum to ISO 8879 that is in the process of international ballot would resolve this problem and allow this practice in valid documents. However, for interoperability, the declaration should not be placed in both subsets.

3. Linking Elements

This specification defines two types of linking elements. First, a simple link, which is usually in-line and always one-directional, very like the HTML **A** element. Second, a much more general extended link which may be either in-line or out-of-line and may be used for multi-directional links, links into read-only data, and so on.

3.1 Information Associated with Links

This specification describes a variety of information that may be (and in some cases is required to be) associated with linking elements:

Role

Every link may have a role, a string used to identify to the application program the meaning of the link. Furthermore, each resource participating in a link may be given its own role. The **ROLE** attribute is used to provide both link and resource roles.

Resource

Every locator must identify a resource in some fashion. This is done using the **HREF** attribute, as described in section 5, "Addressing."

Title

Every locator may be associated with a title in the TITLE attribute. This specification does not require that applications make any particular use of the title.

Behavior

The SHOW and ACTUATE attributes may be used by an author to communicate general policies concerning the traversal behavior of the link; this specification defines a small set of policies for this purpose. The BEHAVIOR attribute may be used to communicate detailed instructions for traversal behavior; this specification does not constrain the contents, format, or meaning of this attribute.

In/Out-of-Line

The INLINE attribute may be used to communicate whether the linking element is inline or not.

3.2 Content of Linking Elements

This specification places no constraints on the contents of linking elements; for this reason, in the sample declarations given below, they are given declared content of ANY.

Any element may be recognized as a linking element based on use of the XML-LINK attribute; in a valid document, each such element must conform to the constraints expressed in its governing DTD.

3.3 Simple Links

Simple links are very much like HTML A or TEI XREF elements, but with more general reference capabilities. A simple link may contain only one locator; thus there is no necessity for a separate child element, and the locator attributes are attached directly to the linking elements.

Example 4 is a sample declaration for an XML simple link; note that the element type need not be SIMPLE, since the linking element will be recognized based on the value of the XML-LINK attribute.

3.4 Extended Links

An extended link can involve any number of resources, and need not be co-located with any of them. An application may be expected to provide traversal among all of them (subject to semantic constraints outside the scope of this paper). The key issue with extended links is how to manage and find them, since they do not necessarily co-occur with any of their resources, and often are located in completely separate documents. This process is discussed in Section 7, "Extended Link Groups."

A extended link's locators are contained in child elements of the linking element, each with its own set of attributes. Once again, in the sample declaration in Example 5, the element types need not be EXTENDED and LOCATOR; recognition depends on the XML-LINK attribute.

Example 4

```
<!ELEMENT SIMPLE ANY>
<!ATTLIST SIMPLE
          XML-LINK      CDATA                  #FIXED "SIMPLE"
          ROLE          CDATA                  #IMPLIED
          HREF          CDATA                  #REQUIRED
          TITLE         CDATA                  #IMPLIED
          INLINE        (TRUE|FALSE)           "TRUE"
          CONTENT-ROLE  CDATA                  #IMPLIED
          CONTENT-TITLE CDATA                  #IMPLIED
          SHOW          (EMBED|REPLACE|NEW)    "REPLACE"
          ACTUATE       (AUTO|USER)            "USER"
          BEHAVIOR      CDATA                  #IMPLIED
>
```

The declared content of ANY for the linking element is perhaps misleading; the idea is that locator elements should appear as children of the linking elements, along with any other content that is appropriate.

Note that many of the attributes may be provided for both the parent linking element and the child locator element. If any such attribute is provided in the linking element but not in a locator element, the value provided in the linking element is to be used in processing the locator element. In other words, the attributes provided in the linking element may serve as defaults for the (possibly many) locator elements.

3.5 In-Line and Out-of-Line Links

The INLINE attribute can take the values TRUE and FALSE. The value TRUE, which is the default, means that all of the content of the linking element is to be considered a resource of the link, except for any child locator elements (which are considered part of the linking element machinery).

When the link is in-line, the CONTENT-ROLE and CONTENT-TITLE attributes may be used to provide the title and role information for this "content" resource. If INLINE is FALSE, it is not an error to provide the CONTENT-TITLE or CONTENT-ROLE attributes, but they have no effect.

4. Link Behavior

This specification provides a mechanism for the authors of linking elements to signal their intentions as to the timing and effects of traversal. Such intentions can be expressed along two axes, labeled SHOW and ACTUATE. These are used to express *policies* rather than *mechanisms*; programs which are processing links in XML documents are free to devise their own mechanisms, best suited to the user environment and processing mode, to implement the requested policies.

In many cases, there will be a requirement for much finer control over the details of traversal behavior; existing hypertext software typically provides such control. Such fine control of link traversal is outside the scope of this specification; however, the BEHAVIOR attribute is provided as

Example 5

```
<!ELEMENT EXTENDED ANY>
<!ELEMENT LOCATOR  ANY>
<!ATTLIST EXTENDED
          XML-LINK      CDATA                    #FIXED "EXTENDED"
          ROLE          CDATA                    #IMPLIED
          TITLE         CDATA                    #IMPLIED
          INLINE        (TRUE|FALSE)             "TRUE"
          CONTENT-ROLE  CDATA                    #IMPLIED
          CONTENT-TITLE CDATA                    #IMPLIED
          SHOW          (EMBED|REPLACE|NEW)      "REPLACE"
          ACTUATE       (AUTO|USER)              "USER"
          BEHAVIOR      CDATA                    #IMPLIED
<!ATTLIST LOCATOR
          XML-LINK CDATA                    #FIXED "LOCATOR"
          ROLE     CDATA                    #IMPLIED
          HREF     CDATA                    #REQUIRED
          TITLE    CDATA                    #IMPLIED
          SHOW     (EMBED|REPLACE|NEW)      "REPLACE"
          ACTUATE  (AUTO|USER)              "USER"
          BEHAVIOR CDATA                    #IMPLIED
>
```

a standard place for authors to provide, and in which programs should look for, such detailed behavioral instructions.

4.1 The SHOW Axis

The `SHOW` attribute is used to express a policy as to the context in which a resource that is traversed to should be displayed or processed. It may take one of three values:

`EMBED`
: Directs that upon traversal of the link, the designated resource should be embedded, for the purposes of display or processing, in the body of the resource, and at the location, where the traversal started.

`REPLACE`
: Directs that upon traversal of the link, the designated resource should, for the purposes of display or processing, replace the resource where the traversal started.

`NEW`
: Directs that upon traversal of the link, the designated resource should be displayed or processed in a new context, not affecting that of the resource where the traversal started.

4.2 The ACTUATE Axis

The `ACTUATE` attribute is used to express a policy as to when traversal of a link should occur. It may take one of two values:

`AUTO`
: Directs that the link should be traversed when encountered, and that the display or processing of the resource where the traversal started is not considered complete until this is done.

`USER`
: Directs that the link should not be traversed until there is an explicit external request for this to happen.

5. Addressing

The locator value for a resource is provided in the `HREF` attribute. `HREF` may have at one point stood for "Hypertext reference"; the name is adopted for compatibility with existing practice.

5.1 Locator Syntax in General

A *locator* always contains a URL, as described in IETF RFCs 1738 [2] and 1808 [3]. As these RFCs state, the URL may include a trailing *query* (marked by a `?`), and be followed by a `#` and a *fragment identifier*, with the query interpreted by the host providing the indicated resource, and the interpretation of the fragment identifier dependent on the data type of the indicated resource. Thus, when a locator in an XML linking element identifies a resource that is not an XML document (for example, an HTML or PDF document), this specification does not constrain the syntax or semantics of the query nor of the fragment identifier.

5.2 Locator Syntax for XML Resources

When a locator identifies a resource that is an XML document, the locator value may contain either or both a URL and a fragment identifier, which in this case is a TEI-derived "Extended Pointer" (hereinafter XPointer). Special syntax may be used to request the use of particular processing models in accessing the locator's

Locator

```
[1]    Locator   ::=  URL
                      | Connector (XPointer | Name)
                      | URL Connector (XPointer | Name)
[2] Connector    ::=  '#' | '|'
[3]         URL  ::=  URLchar*
```

resource. This is designed to reflect the realities of network operation, where it may or may not be desirable to exercise fine control over the distribution of work between local and remote processors.

In this discussion, the term *designated resource* refers to the resource participating in the link which the locator serves to locate. The following rules apply:

- The URL, if provided, locates a resource called the *containing resource.*
- If the URL is not provided, the containing resource is considered to be the document in which the linking element is contained.
- If the XPointer is provided, the designated resource is a "sub-resource" of the containing resource; otherwise the designated resource is the containing resource.
- If the `Connector` is followed by a `Name`, the `Name` is shorthand for the XPointer "`ID(Name)`"; i.e., the sub-resource is the element in the containing resource that has an XML ID attribute whose value matches the `Name`. This shorthand is to encourage use of the robust `ID` addressing mode.
- If the connector is "`#`", this signals an intent that the containing resource is to be fetched as a whole from the host that provides it, and that the XPointer processing to extract the sub-resource is to be performed on the client, that is to say on the same system where the linking element is recognized and processed.
- If the connector is "`|`", no intent is signaled as to what processing model is to be used to go about accessing the designated resources.

In the case where the URL contains a *query* (to be interpreted by the server) information providers and authors of server software are urged to use queries as shown in *Query Syntax.*

6. Extended Pointers

XML uses a locator syntax derived from that for TEI extended pointers; the XML version of a TEI extended pointer is referred to as an XPointer. XPointers operate in a straightforward way on the element tree which is defined by the elements of an XML document.

The basic form of an XPointer is a series of location terms, each of which specifies a location, either absolute or (more frequently) relative to the prior one. Each term has a keyword such as `ID`, `CHILD`, `ANCESTOR`, and so on, and can be qualified by parameters such as an instance number, element type, or attribute.. For example, the locator string

```
CHILD(2,CHAP)(4,SEC)(3)
```

refers to the third child of the fourth SEC within the second CHAP within the referenced document.

The syntax for TEI Extended Pointers has been adjusted in order to allow them to be packaged naturally with URLs without requiring URL-escaping of space characters:

- Parameters in locator terms must be separated by commas to facilitate including XPointers within URLs, where spaces would otherwise need to be escaped.
- A locator may contain two XPointers separated by the string "`..`". These define the beginning and end of a span which constitutes the resource. This merely combines the capability of the TEI `FROM` and `TO` attributes into the locator syntax.

Query Syntax

```
[4] Query  ::=  'XML-XPTR=' (XPointer | Name)
```

6.1 XPointer Structure

At the heart of the *XPointer* is the location term. Location terms are designed to work in sequences and are explained fully below.

A locator can contain either one or two XPointers; if there are two, they are separated by the string "`..`". For a locator with one XPointer, the designated resource is the element or location selected by the sequence of location terms it contains. With two XPointers, the designated resource is all of the text from the location, or start of the element, selected by the first, through to the location, or the end of the element, selected by the second.

Note that the implementation of traversal to a resource is not constrained by this specification. In particular, handling a resource designated by a span is probably highly application-dependent. In a display-oriented application, such traversal might simply be implemented by highlighting the designated characters. In particular, it should be noted that a span cannot safely be treated as a set of elements; most spans will include partial elements.

A location term is an atomic unit of addressing information; XPointers consist of combinations of location terms. Location terms are grouped into *absolute terms, relative terms, and string-match terms.* Absolute terms select one or more elements or locations in an XML document; if an XPointer contains only an absolute term, that term identifies its designated resource. If the absolute term is followed by any relative or string-match terms, the elements or locations that it designates are termed a *location source* and serve as a starting point for the operations of the location terms in Absolute, Relative, and String-match.

6.2 Absolute Location Terms

The keywords described in this section do not depend on the existence of a location source. They can be used to establish a location source or as standalone self-contained XPointers.

If an XPointer omits any leading *absolute location* terms (i.e., consists only of relative and string-match terms) it is assumed to have a leading `ROOT()` absolute location term.

The empty parentheses after `ROOT`, `HERE`, and `DITTO` are for consistency with other keywords and to avoid ambiguous interpretation of an extended pointer containing just the string "ROOT" or "HERE".

6.2.1 The ROOT keyword

If an XPointer is preceded by `ROOT()`, the location source is the root element of the containing resource. This is the default behavior. `ROOT` keyword has no effect on the interpretation of the locator; it exists in the interests of design clarity.

6.2.2 The HERE keyword

If the first or second XPointer is preceded by `HERE()`, the location source for the first location term of that series is the linking element containing the locator rather than the default root element. This allows extended pointers to select items such as "the paragraph immediately preceding the one within which this pointer occurs." It is an error to use `HERE` in a locator where a URL is also provided and identifies a resource different from the document which contains the linking elements.

XPointer

```
[5] XPointer   ::=  First ('..' Second)?
```

Absolute, Relative, and String-match

```
[6]  First   ::=  AbsTerm? RelTerm* StringTerm?
[7] Second   ::=  AbsTermOrDitto? RelTerm* StringTerm?
```

Absolute Location Terms

```
[8]         AbsTerm  ::=  'ROOT()' | 'HERE()' | IdLoc | HTMLAddr
[9] AbsTermOrDitto   ::=  'DITTO()' | AbsTerm
[10]          IdLoc  ::=  'ID(' Name ')'
[11]       HTMLAddr  ::=  'HTML(' SkipLit ')'
```

6.2.3 The DITTO keyword

If the second XPointer is preceded by `DITTO()`, the location source for its first location term is the location source specified by the entire first XPointer in order to facilitate relative specification of a span.

6.2.4 The ID keyword

If the first or second XPointer is preceded by `ID(Name)`, the location source for the first location term is the element in the containing resource which has an attribute of type ID with a value matching the given `Name`.

For example, the location specification

```
ID(a27)
```

chooses the necessarily unique element of the containing resource which has an attribute declared to be of type `ID` whose value is `a27`.

6.2.5 The HTML keyword

The location term `HTML(NAMEVALUE)` selects the first element whose type is `A` and which has a `NAME` attribute whose value is the same as the supplied `NAMEVALUE`; this is exactly the function performed by the "#"-fragment in the context of an HTML document.

6.3 Relative Location Terms

The keywords described in this section and shown in *Relative Location Terms* depend on the existence of a location source. They provide facilities for navigating forward, backward, up, and down through the element tree.

The keyword selects zero or more elements relative to the location source, which are referred to as candidate locations. Each keyword summarized here is described in detail in following sections.

`CHILD`
: Selects child elements of the location source.

`DESCENDANT`
: Selects elements appearing within the content of the location source.

`ANCESTOR`
: Selects elements in whose content the location source is found.

`PRECEDING`
: Selects elements which appear before the location source.

`PSIBLING`
: Selects preceding sibling elements of the location source.

`FOLLOWING`
: Selects elements which appear after the location source.

`FSIBLING`
: Selects following sibling elements of the location source.

Relative Location Terms

```
[12] RelTerm  ::=  Keyword Arguments+
[13] Keyword  ::=  'CHILD' | 'DESCENDANT' | 'ANCESTOR' | 'PRECEDING' | 'PSIBLING'
```

Relative Location Term Arguments

```
[14] Arguments  ::=  '(' Instance ',' ElType (',' Attr ',' Val)* ')'
```

6.3.1 Relative location term arguments

All relative location terms operate using *arguments*; each keyword takes the same set of arguments. Multiple sets of arguments can be attached to a single keyword as a shorthand for repeated occurrences of that keyword.

Multiple argument lists are a shorthand in which the keyword is considered to have been repeated between each of the steps. That is to say, the following two XPointers are equivalent:

```
CHILD(2,SECTION)(1,SUBSECTION)
CHILD(2,SECTION)CHILD(1,SUBSECTION)
```

6.3.2 Selection by Instance number

Candidates can be selected by occurrence number.

When the value of *Instance* is the number *N*, it selects the *N*th of the candidate locations. If the special value `ALL` is given, then *all* the candidate locations are selected. Negative numbers count from the last candidate location to the first; numbers out of range constitute an error.

6.3.3 Selection by element type

Candidates can be selected by *element type* as well as number.

The `ElType` gives an XML element type; only elements of that type will be selected from among the candidate locations. For example, the location term

```
CHILD(3,DIV1)(4,DIV2)(29,P)
```

selects the 29th paragraph of the fourth sub-division of the third major division of the location source.

The XPointer

```
DESCENDANT(-1,EXAMPLE)>
```

selects the last example in the document.

Selection by type is strongly recommended because it makes links more perspicuous and more robust. It is perspicuous because humans typically refer to things by type: as "the second section," "the third paragraph," etc. It is robust because it increases the chance of detecting breakage if (due to document editing) the target originally pointed at no longer exists.

The type may be specified by `Name` or by using one of the values "`.`", "`*CDATA`", or "`*`". If the type is specified as "`.`", candidate elements of any type are matched. If the type is specified as "`*CDATA`", the location term selects only untagged sub-portions of an element with mixed content (these are generally referred to as pseudo-elements). Finally, `*` selects among child elements and pseudo-elements.

Consider the following example:

```
<SPEECH ID="a27"><SPEAKER>Polonius
    </SPEAKER>
<DIRECTION>crossing downstage
    </DIRECTION>Fare you well,
    my lord. <DIRECTION>To Ros.
    </DIRECTION>
You go to seek Lord Hamlet? There he is.
    </SPEECH>
```

Instance

```
[15] InstanceOrAll  ::=  'ALL' | Instance
[16]      Instance  ::=  ('+' | '-')? Digit+
```

Element Type

```
[17] ElType   ::=  '*CDATA'  /* selects text pseudo-elements */
                 | '*'       /* elements and pseudo-elements */
                 | '.'       /* elements only */
                 | Name      /* elements of this type */
```

ID(a27),CHILD(2,DIRECTION)
: Selects the second "DIRECTION" element, "To Ros."

ID(a27),CHILD(2,.)
: Selects the second child element, which is the first direction "crossing downstage".

ID(a27),CHILD(2,*CDATA)
: Selects the second pseudo-element (the line-break between the "SPEAKER" and "DIRECTION" elements is the first), "Fare you well, my lord."

ID(a27),CHILD(2,*)
: Selects the second element or pseudo-element among the children, the line-break between the "SPEAKER" and "DIRECTION" elements.

6.3.4 Selection by attribute

Candidates can be selected based on *attribute* name and value.

The Attr and Val are used to provide attribute names and values to use in selecting among candidates.

If specified within quotation marks, the attribute-value parameter is case-sensitive; otherwise not.

As with generic identifiers, attribute names may be specified as * in location terms in the (unlikely) event that an attribute value constitutes a constraint regardless of what attribute name it is a value for.

For example, the location term

```
CHILD(1,*,TARGET,*)
```

selects the first child of the location source for which the attribute TARGET has a value.

The location specification

```
CHILD(1,*,N,2)(1,*,N,1)
```

chooses an element using the N attribute. Beginning at the location source, the first child (whatever element type it is) with an N attribute having the value 2 is chosen; then that element's first child element having the value 1 for the same attribute is chosen.

The location specification

```
CHILD(1,FS,RESP,*IMPLIED)
```

selects the first child of the location source which is an FS element for which the RESP attribute has been left unspecified.

Note that the HTML keyword is a synonym for a very specific instance of attribute-based addressing such that the following two XPointers are equivalent:

```
HTML(Sec3.2)
ROOT()DESCENDANT(1,*,A,"Sec3.2")
```

6.3.5 The DESCENDANT keyword

The location specification

```
ID(a23)DESCENDANT(2,TERM,LANG,DE)
```

selects the second TERM element with a LANG attribute whose value is DE occurring within the element with an ID attribute whose value is A23. The search for matching elements occurs in the same order as the XML data stream (depth-first, left-to-right).

If an instance number is negative, the search is depth-first right-to-left, in which the right-most,

Attribute

```
[18] Attr  ::=  '*'          /* any attribute name */
              | Name
[19] Val   ::=  '*IMPLIED'   /* no value specified, no default */
              | '*'          /* any value */
              | Name         /* case and space normalized */
              | SkipLit      /* exact match */
```

deepest matching element is numbered -1, etc. The location specification

```
ROOT()DESCENDANT(-1,NOTE)
```

thus chooses the last `NOTE` element in the document, that is, the one with the rightmost start-tag.

6.3.6 The ANCESTOR keyword

The `ANCESTOR` location term selects an element from among the direct ancestors of the location source. The parameters are for `CHILD`. However, the `ANCESTOR` keyword selects elements from the list of containing elements or "ancestors" of the location source, counting upwards from the parent of the location source (which is ancestor number 1) to the root of the document instance (which is ancestor number -1).

For example, the location term

```
ANCESTOR(1,*,N,1)(1,DIV)
```

first chooses the smallest element properly containing the location source and having attribute `N` with value `1` and then the smallest `DIV` element properly containing it.

Note that the `ANCESTOR` keyword's second (element type) argument cannot be `*` or `*CDATA`.

6.3.7 The PRECEDING keyword

The `PRECEDING` keyword selects an element or pseudo-element from among those which precede the location source. The set of elements and pseudo-elements which may be selected is the set of all those in the entire document which occur or begin before the location source. (For purposes of the keywords `PRECEDING` and `FOLLOWING`, elements are interpreted as occurring where they start.) The result of the `PRECEDING` keyword is not guaranteed to be a subset of its location source.

The instance number in the location value of a `preceding` term designates the nth element or pseudo-element preceding the location source, counting from most recent to less recent. The XPointer

```
ID(a23)PRECEDING(5,.)
```

thus designates the fifth element or pseudo-element before the element with an `ID` of `a23`. Negative instance numbers also designate preceding elements or pseudo-elements counting from the eldest to the youngest. The value `ALL` may be used to select the entire portion of the document preceding the beginning of the location source.

6.3.8 The PSIBLING keyword

The `PSIBLING` keyword selects an element or pseudo-element from among those which precede the location source within the same parent element. We speak of the elements and pseudo-elements contained by the same parent element as siblings; those which precede the location in the document are its elder siblings; those which follow it are its younger siblings.

The instance number in the location value of a `PSIBLING` term designates the nth elder sibling of the location source, counting from most recent to less recent. The location source must have at least as many elder siblings as the absolute value of the instance number; otherwise, the `PSIBLING` term fails.

```
ID(a23)PSIBLING(1,.)
```

thus designates the element immediately preceding the element with an `ID` of `a23`. Negative instance numbers also designate elder siblings, but counting from the eldest left sibling to the youngest. If the location source has at least one elder sibling, then the location term

```
PSIBLING(-1,.)
```

designates the very eldest sibling and is synonymous with

```
ANCESTOR(1,.)CHILD(1,.)
```

The value `ALL` may be used to select the entire range of elder siblings of an element:

```
ID(a23)PSIBLING(ALL,.)
```

thus designates the set of elements preceding the element with an `ID` of `a23` and contained by the same parent.

6.3.9 The FOLLOWING keyword

The keyword `FOLLOWING` behaves like `PRECEDING` but selects from the portion of the document following the location source, not preceding it.

6.3.10 The FSIBLING keyword

The keyword `FSIBLING` behaves like `PSIBLING` but selects from the younger siblings of the location source, not the elder siblings. The XPointer

```
ID(a23)FSIBLING(1,.)
```

thus designates the element immediately following the element which has an `ID` of `A23`. Negative instance numbers designate younger siblings counting from the youngest sibling toward the location source. If the location source has at least one younger sibling, then the location term

```
FSIBLING(-1,.)
```

designates its youngest sibling.

6.4 String-Match Location Terms

A *string-match* sub-element address may optionally appear as the last in the series of location terms in an XPointer.

In this case the designated resource is a location which is found by searching the textual content of the current location source for occurrences of the `SkipLit` string given in the second argument. The `Index` is a number which selects among these occurrences, and the `Offset` is a number which gives a character offset from the start of the match to the designated location. Thus, the XPointer

```
ROOT()STRING(3,"Thomas Pynchon",7)
```

selects the letter `P` (seven from the start of the string) in the third occurrence of the string "`Thomas Pynchon`".

```
ID(a27)STRING(5,'!',1)
```

selects the character immediately following the fifth exclamation mark.

For purposes of string matching, the "text of the element" means all the character data in the element(s) in the current location source and descendant elements, all markup characters being ignored in the pattern matching. Thus in the example above, the string "`Thomas Pynchon`" would match and designate a reference in

```
<authname><first>Thomas</first>
    <family>Pynchon</family>
    </authname>
```

The pattern matching is exact and character-for-character. No case, space, or combining-character normalization of any kind is to be performed. Thus, there would be no match to "Thomas Pynchon" in the following:

```
<example>thomas pynchon,
<auth><first>Thomas</first>
    <family>Pynchon</family></auth>,
Thomas
Pynchon</example>
```

7. Extended Link Groups

Hyperlinked documents are often best processed in groups rather than one at a time. If it is desired to highlight resources to advertise that traversal can be initiated, and if at the same time use is being made of out-of-line links, it may be an absolute requirement to read other documents to find these links and discover where the resources are.

In these cases, the Extended Link Group element may be used to store a list of links to other documents that together constitute an interlinked document group. Each such document is identified using the `HREF` attribute of an Extended Link Document element, which is a child element of

String-Match Term

```
[20] StringTerm  ::=  'STRING(' Instance ',' SkipLit ',' Offset ')'
[21]     Offset  ::=  Digit+
```

Example 6

```
<!ELEMENT GROUP (DOCUMENT*)>
<!ATTLIST GROUP
          XML-LINK CDATA #FIXED "GROUP"
          STEPS    CDATA #IMPLIED
>
<!ELEMENT DOCUMENT EMPTY>
<!ATTLIST DOCUMENT
          XML-LINK CDATA #FIXED "DOCUMENT"
          HREF     CDATA #REQUIRED
>
```

the GROUP. The value of the HREF attribute is a locator, with the same interpretation as described above.

These elements, just as with EXTENDED, SIMPLE, or LOCATOR elements, are recognized by the use of the XML-LINK attribute with the value GROUP or DOCUMENT.

Example 6 contains sample declarations for the GROUP and DOCUMENT elements.

The STEPS attribute may be used by an author to help deal with the situation where an Extended Link Group directs a processor to another document, which proves to contain an Extended Link Group of its own. Clearly, there is a potential here for infinite regress, and yet there are situations where processing several levels of Extended Link Groups is useful. The STEPS attribute should have a numeric value that serves as a hint from the author to any link processor as to how many steps of Extended Link Group processing should be undertaken. It does not have any normative effect.

For example, should a group of documents be organized with a single "hub" document containing all the out-of-line links, it might well make sense for each non-hub document to have an Extended Link Group containing only one reference to the hub document. In this case, the best value for STEPS would be 2.

Appendix A: Unfinished Work

A.1 Structured Titles

The simple title mechanism described in this draft is insufficiently flexible to cope with internationalization or the use of multimedia in link titles. A future version will provide a mechanism for the use of structured link titles.

A.2 Case Sensitivity in Attribute Values

It is possible to specify a link's resource based on the value of an attribute. It is is difficult to decide what the correct behavior is as regards case-sensitivity in matching. Ideally, the declared type of the attribute value should be taken into account, but that presupposes fetching and reading the document's DTD, which may not be appropriate in many XML applications. The current system, while easy to explain, may not prove suitable in the long run.

Appendix B: XPointers and Other SGML Standards

Formally, the operations of the XPointer mechanism may be specified as operating on groves as defined in the HyTime standard. Every construct in such locators has a corresponding expression in SDQL, and most also have direct equivalents in the HyTime location module. ■

References

1. ISO (International Organization for Standardization). *ISO/IEC 10744-1992 (E). Information technology—Hypermedia/Time-based Structuring Language (HyTime).* [Geneva]: International Organization for Standardization, 1992. *Extended Facilities Annex.* [Geneva]: International Organization for Standardization, 1996. (See *http://www.ornl.gov/sgml/wg8/hytime/html/is10744r.html*).
2. IETF (Internet Engineering Task Force). *RFC 1738: Uniform Resource Locators.* 1991. (See *http://www.w3.org/Addressing/rfc1738.txt*).
3. IETF (Internet Engineering Task Force). *RFC 1808: Relative Uniform Resource Locators.* 1995. (See *http://www.w3.org/Addressing/rfc1808.txt*).
4. Sperberg-McQueen, C.M., and Lou Burnard, editors. *Guidelines for Electronic Text Encoding and Interchange.* Association for Computers and the Humanities (ACH), Association for Computational Linguistics (ACL), and Association for Literary and Linguistic Computing (ALLC). Chicago, Oxford: Text Encoding Initiative, 1994.

About the Authors

Tim Bray
321–3495 Cambie Street
Vancouver, B.C., Canada V5Z 4R3
tbray@textuality.com

Tim Bray is a Canadian. He entered the software profession in 1981; after on-the-job training from Digital and GTE, he became manager of the New Oxford English Dictionary Project at the University of Waterloo in 1986. He co-founded Open Text Corporation in 1989, and started an independent consulting practice under the name Textuality in 1996. He is a Seybold Fellow, editor of the *Gilbane Report*, and co-editor of the World Wide Web Consortium's "Extensible Markup Language Specification."

Steve J. DeRose
Chief Scientist
Inso Electronic Publishing Systems
1 Richmond Square
Providence, RI 02771
sderose@eps.inso.com

Steve DeRose work with hypermedia systems began with FRESS (at Brown University) in 1979. In 1989 he co-founded Electronic Book Technologies and designed DynaText, the first SGML online delivery engine, and other products. He is now Chief Scientist for Inso, EBT's parent company. He is active in standards with ISO, the TEI, SGML Open, and W3C, and is co-editor of XLL. He is a frequent speaker in industry and academe, and has written many papers and two books: *Making Hypermedia Work* (with David Durand), and *The SGML FAQ Book*.

HTML-MATH

MATHEMATICAL MARKUP LANGUAGE WORKING DRAFT

Robert R. Miner, Patrick D.F. Ion

Abstract

The HTML-Math Working Group recently released another revision of its Working Draft of MathML. The full text of this Working Draft is available at http://www.w3.org/TR/WD-math. This note should serve to point the way to the proposal outlined in the full Working Draft, and will describe a little of the history, current state, and future of the HTML-Math work.

Communicating mathematical and other technical notation is a challenging and important task. The intricate expression structure of mathematical notation reflects the internal logic of mathematics in a subtle way. Mathematical notation not only involves the use of a large extended symbol set, it relies on a rich collection of 2-dimensional layout schema, such as fractions, exponents, radicals, and matrices.

At present, HTML has limited utility for the transmission of scientific and technical material over the Web. At the same time, the demand is high for an effective means of electronic scientific communication. Increasingly researchers, scientists, engineers, educators, students, and technicians find themselves working at a distance and relying on electronic communication.

The HTML-Math Working Group [1] of the World Wide Web Consortium (W3C) has been working on the problem of getting mathematics onto the Web in a way that gives it a presence as a native form of text in that environment. The Working Group brings together a disparate group of interests and concerns united by their belief that mathematical discourse should be natural in the context of the Web, but differing in what they feel the content of mathematical discourse is.

The Working Group, after considerable discussion resulting from the need for members to get to know each others' points of view, decided upon a layered approach. First, a fundamental language, at least capable of expressing the complexities of the visual conventions of everyday mathematics, is to be developed, along with prototype implementations of renderers. The first renderers are, of course, for visual presentation, but the language design is intended to facilitate support of audio output.

Then, in a second phase, facilities for the extension of this basic language, such as macros, will be added, and a variety of input types explored. Unlike conventional printed rendering of mathematical notation, a uniform style has not been developed for inputting mathematical expressions into computers. There are already several established ways of input ranging from proprietary pick and place methods, through publicly accepted codings (such as those of TeX and eqn), to the sometimes arcane proprietary encodings of production typesetting and computer algebra systems.

The fundamental language, which came to be known as Mathematical Markup Language (MathML), will be put forward to the W3C as the Working Group's proposed recommendation in October 1997, after the group's next face-to-face meeting. By that time there will be at least two prototype renderers available.

During the rest of the presently chartered life of the Working Group, which runs until August, 1998, recommendations will be made on macros; on input methods; on further extensions to basic MathML; and on other implementations.

MathML Background

Efforts to define a specification for mathematics in HTML have been underway in the World Wide Web Consortium (W3C) for several years. Dave Raggett of the W3C made a proposal for Math extensions to HTML in 1994. That proposal was not ultimately incorporated into the HTML 3.2 revision, although it was mentioned in several published books on HTML. However, a panel discussion at the WWW4 Conference in Darmstadt, April 1995, demonstrated that there was clear interest in pursuing specifications for mathematics on the Web. A group was formed to discuss the problem further.

In the intervening two years, the W3C and the Math Working Group have both evolved substantially. The small informal math group has grown, and has been formally reconstituted as the W3C HTML-Math Working Group. The current Working Group is composed of experts from commercial publishers and software vendors, as well as from not-for-profit publishers and research organizations in both Europe and North America.

Now that the first phase of its work has almost ended, the Working Group is in the process of reaching out to a wider circle of experts by forming an Advisory Interest Group to encourage better feedback from the community of math users and to promote awareness of the progress it has achieved.

Early on in the Working Group's discussions, a few fundamental observations were noted:

- The potential audience for a mathematics specification for the Web is large, encompassing students and teachers at nearly all educational levels, professional researchers from many different scientific disciplines, software vendors, scientific publishers, etc.
- Current technologies for rendering mathematics on the Web (e.g., as in-line graphics or using complex HTML font and positioning commands) contain drawbacks serious enough to prevent their widespread use.

As the Working Group began its progress toward a more robust method of rendering mathematics in the Web environment, it also became evident that the motivation within the Group for defining a mathematics specification for the Web came primarily from two distinct sources:

- *From publishers,* who have an immediate need for displaying mathematical content on the Web. Publishers have legacy data marked up using TeX and SGML, and they presently have very limited options for displaying such documents on the Web. Publishing production using existing SGML compliant methods is too complicated when high quality typography is a goal.
- *From software vendors,* who wish to link their products for manipulating mathematical expressions to the mathematics in Web pages. This might be accomplished by cutting and pasting a mathematical expression from a Web page into the mathematical software, or by other more direct means.

The HTML-Math group, therefore, began its work by taking on the definition of a markup language that would be rich enough to capture all that the various interested parties needed for their intended processing. An attempt has been made to include concerns from the ICADD community, but this has not dominated the development. It is clear that just defining a relatively low-level markup language for mathematics does not make the appearance of mathematical formalism on the Web automatic. The authoring aspect of things has to be addressed too, and implementations using the language provided.

In just over a year since the HTML-Math WG's formal constitution, it will come up with a recommendation to be proposed to the W3C for MathML. MathML was written as compliant with the emergent XML standard; in its second year, the WG will extend that language by macro mechanisms, and will address the ease of use of alternative input syntaxes for different groups of users. These subjects are being discussed on the side thus far, since the main effort has been devoted to the development of the MathML proposal.

The MathML specification responds directly to the needs of both publishers, to ensure an effective language for a production environment, and those of the software industry, for a public portable standard. The HTML-Math WG has amongst its members people who can implement prototype engines that use MathML. There are already two early rendering prototypes:

- WebEQ, a Java development, from the Geometry Center at the University of Minnesota
- An inclusion in the Techexplorer product from the Interactive Document labs of IBM

In addition, there is a project planned by a consortium including scientific societies to produce a LaTeX to MathML conversion utility. Design Science, makers of the popular MathType tool and of the equation editor for Microsoft Word, have also announced that they will support MathML as an output option from MathType. Moreover, it is hoped—indeed expected—that both Mathematica and Maple, who are well represented on the HTML-Math WG, will soon be supporting MathML. Early examples of parsing have been demonstrated as aids to the WG discussions.

MathML has been prepared with a true SGML DTD, but this is not enough to capture fully the specifications required. The full language description, including examples of encouraged and deprecated usage, is much longer. MathML provides both Presentation elements to specify how mathematics should be rendered within a Web page, and Content elements that can be used to capture the meaning of the mathematics being encoded. The tag sets for these elements are further explained below.

The MathML Specification

MathML is an XML application that adheres to the current XML specification, which itself is a Working Draft under the W3C. XML, which stands for eXtensible Markup Language, is a proposed extension to HTML for delivering content on the Web. XML is designed to interoperate with current HTML specifications. See [2] for the full XML Working Draft.

The MathML Presentation Tags correspond to the constructors of traditional math notation, while also providing mechanisms to finetune the visual rendering of mathematics in a Web environment. MathML Presentation elements are at least as powerful as the markup of TeX in their ability to control the visual representation of math. MathML Presentation Tags can therefore be used to render sophisticated research-level mathematical notation on the Web.

The MathML Content Tags are intended to support the encoding of the underlying mathematical content of an expression. Mathematics encoded with Content Tags could, for example, be cut from a Web document and pasted into mathematical software (such as computer algebra systems) where the mathematics could be further manipulated. MathML Content Tags should be adequate for coding most formulas used in education through the U.S. high school level, and probably beyond that, through the first two years of U.S. college.

MathML Presentation and Content Tags may be mixed within the encoding of a single mathematical expression. By proper use of Presentation Tags alone, the mathematical structure of an expression can, in principle, be represented well enough to permit its manipulation by computer algebra systems which make appropriate assumptions about the meanings of individual symbols. When a potential for ambiguity exists, Content Tags may be employed to specify more precisely the intended mathematical meaning. An author may in fact choose to write at any level along a spectrum of specification, from purely using Presentation Tags to purely using Content Tags, according to how precisely the mathematical content of an expression needs to be specified.

Whether using Presentation Tags or Content Tags, MathML is designed to be mixed in with ordinary HTML commands, just, for example, as markup for frames mixes with HTML. However, MathML markup is necessarily verbose and is not optimized for hand entry. While some simple examples may be entered by hand, it is likely that most MathML markup will be generated by translators or filters that convert from other mathematical markup languages (e.g., TeX, some SGML specifications, etc.) into MathML, or by authoring tools that output MathML directly. Translators from SGML or TeX will probably choose to convert these formats into MathML Presentation Tags, while WYSIWYG authoring tools may choose to output either MathML Content Tags or MathML Presentation Tags.

The HTML-Math Working Group fully recognizes the need for simplified mathematical input syntaxes that are better suited for human entry, in addition to the more machine-friendly MathML notation. The Working Group's first task in its second year is to come up with support for other suitable input forms.

Embedding MathML in HTML Pages

Within an HTML document, MathML notation appears between the tags `<MATH>...</MATH>` (for in-line math) and `<MATHDISP>...</MATHDISP>` (for display math). In SGML parlance, the pair of tags `<MATH>` and `</MATH>` mark the extent of a MATH element whose content is the material between the tags. In a short note such as this all one can do is illustrate some of the basic principles involved in as complex a specification as that for MathML, which is over 100 standard printed pages long (not counting extensive appendices listing such things as default values and several hundred special entities). Example 1 illustrates MathML encoding using both Presentation Tags and Content Tags for the expression $\chi^2 + 4\chi + 4 = 0$.

Example 1 Presentation Tags

```
<MATH>
<MROW>
  <MROW>
    <MSUP>

<MI>x</MI>
      <MN>2</MN>
    </MSUP>

<MO>+</MO>
    <MROW>
      <MN>4</MN>

<MO>&InvisibleTimes;</MO>
      <MI>x</MI>

</MROW>
    <MO>+</MO>
    <MN>4</MN>

</MROW>
  <MO>=</MO>

<MN>0</MN>
</MROW>
</MATH>
```

On the outside we have the $...$ that identify math markup to a browser, and immediately within that an <MROW>...</MROW> pair, delimiting a horizontal row construction containing a list of subexpressions. Here the first subexpression, the left-hand side of the quadratic equation, is itself an MROW element containing a superscript construction between <MSUP>... </MSUP> tags. There are two arguments that make up the content of an MSUP element, the base expression and its superscript. Here they are an identifier, explicitly tagged as such in <MI>x</MI> and an explicitly tagged number, <MN>2</MN>, which is to be a superscript.

After the superscript fragment comes a symbol explicitly tagged as a math operator <MO>+</MO>, and then another subexpression in an MROW element. The numerical coefficient <MN>4</MN> and the variable identifier <MI>x</MI> are separated by an operator, <MO>⁢</MO>, whose content is a special entity, ⁢, which will not be printed but is useful as a clue to audio rendering and for fine typesetting. The left-hand side is closed with another operator, <MO>+</MO>, and a final number, <MN>4 </MN>.

The outer MROW finishes with the equality operator <MO>=</MO> and a number <MN>0</MN>.

This description makes obvious how much we save with ordinary math notation over the description of equations in prose. It should also bring out how much of notation's interpretation we draw from the mental contexts we have acquired from long years of schooling. In fact the notation even for equations as simple as this one was not always the modern one. The pedantic completeness of the tagging serves the machinery we want to work with, which requires complete clarity of description in order to do a high-quality job of rendering.

There is a vocabulary of about 30 Presentation Tags covering all the layout types that are presently common in math. The elements have many special attributes permitting fine control of rendering. For simplicity, none of these attributes was mentioned above.

In Example 2, we consider the markup of the same simple equation using Content tagging. The intent of MathML Content markup is to encode mathematical expressions in such a way that they retain a clear, unambiguous meaning that can be dependably evaluated. It will be noted that this markup emphasizes the tree structure of mathematical notation. There about 50 different Content tags.

Example 2 Content Tags

```
<MATH>
<EXPR>
  <EXPR>
    <EXPR>

<MCI>x</MCI>
      <POWER/>

<MCN>2</MCN>
    </EXPR>
    <PLUS/>

<EXPR>
      <MCN>4</MCN>
      <TIMES/>

<MCI>x</MCI>
```

Example 2 Content Tags *(continued)*

```
    </EXPR>
    <PLUS/>

<MCN>4</MCN>
  </EXPR>
  <E/>

<MCN>0</MCN>
</EXPR>
</MATH>
```

Within the outer tags of the MATH element we find the <EXPR>...</EXPR> pair, which serve to group the contents as a mathematical unit. The MROW element, by contrast, connotes no assumption about the mathematical significance of its contents; it just specifies a horizontal row type of layout. Subexpressions are similarly marked with <EXPR>...</EXPR> pairs. The first subunit here is the square term, specified here by an expression containing the identifier <MCI>x</MCI> and the numerical exponent <MCN>2</MCN>, separated by the tag <POWER/>, indicating the algebraic type of the expression.

NOTE

> The POWER element is (in a technical sense) empty since it has no corresponding end tag (it already has an ending / in its name) and contains no data. It is, however, a marker full of significance.

Another change is to the tags <MCI> and <MCN> for identifiers and numbers, respectively. The attributes which may be added to these will be able to carry more semantic information over to other math processing platforms than the information about presentation that goes with the presentational <MI> and <MN> tags.

The rest of the equation is marked up similarly using the analogous non-container elements with the tags <PLUS/> <TIMES/>, and <E/> within EXPR containers.

NOTE

> There is a difference between the printable character entities and their corresponding Content tags. For each of the Content tags there has also to be specified a standard presentation form which will normally be used for display. Though there are facilities for overriding these defaults, this discussion is not within the scope of this article.

The additional top-level HTML tags <F>...</F> and <FD>...</FD> are being reserved for alternate mathematical input notation (i.e., notations other than MathML). <F>...</F> and <FD>...</FD> are mnemonics for "formula" and "formula display," in analogy to the <MATH> and <MATHDISP> tags. Until Web browsers provide a native implementation of MathML, rendering plug-ins will have to be invoked to do the rendering job. The dialect of math input chosen will be conveyed through a MIME-type attribute. For example, a plug-in capable of interpreting some restricted form of TeX, arbitrarily called pTeX here, might be invoked as follows:

```
<FD
TYPE="application/x-
    ptex">2x^2+3y=z</FD>
```

The rendering plug-in would convert the TeX-style syntax to an internal representation of MathML, which would be passed to a MathML rendering engine. MathML compliance requires that the program can be queried for a corresponding MathML markup.

The examples mentioned above are to be used in this fashion. Both IBM's techexplorer [3] (a plug-in) and WebEQ [4] (a Java applet) from the Geometry Center at the University of Minnesota are beginning to support MathML. Both are freely available.

MathML Timetable

The HTML-Math Working Group issued the initial MathML Working Draft on May 15, 1997 on schedule, according to its publicly announced timetable. Revisions have been taking place through the summer and fall of 1997. The Working Group has the goal of promoting the Working Draft to a W3C Proposed Recommendation in October 1997.

After the MathML specification is put forward for ratification by the W3C, the HTML-Math Working Group will turn its attention to several other matters, such as simplified input syntaxes suitable for hand editing elementary mathematical notation to be put inside the <F> and <FD> tags, and macro mechanisms for MathML itself. A second Working Draft covering these and other considerations extending MathML to a workable solution for HTML-Math, is planned for May 1998. Implementation prototypes will continue to appear along with the development of the specifications. ■

References

1. *http://www.w3.org/Math/*
2. *www.w3.org/TR/WD-xml.html*
3. *http://www.ics.raleigh.ibm.com/ics/techexp.htm*
4. *http://www.geom.umn.edu/software/WebEQ*

About the Authors

Robert R. Miner
The Geometry Center
400 Lind Hall 207 Church Street S.E.
Minneapolis, MN 55455
rminer@geom.umn.edu

Robert Miner, W3C HTML-Math Working Group co-chair, has been a technical researcher since 1995 at the Geometry Center at the University of Minnesota, a National Science Foundation Science and Technology Center. Prior to that, Miner was a memeber of the mathematics faculty at the University of Oklahoma (1991–95) after receiving his Ph.D. from the University of Maryland. His current research interests focus on the uses of electronic media in scientific research and teaching. His primary mathematical interest is differential geometry.

Patrick D.F. Ion
Mathematical Reviews
P. O. Box 8604
416 Fourth Street
Ann Arbor, MI 48107-8604
ion@math.ams.org

Patrick Ion, W3C HTML-Math Working Group co-chair, has been a mathematician Associate Editor at Mathematical Reviews for the American Mathematical Society since 1980. Previous positions in Heidelberg (1974–80), Kyoto (1972–74), Groningen, and London, England followed a Ph.D. from Imperial College, London. His present interests include the communication of mathematics, the preservation and use of its permanent record, quantum probability and quantum groups, special functions and non-commutative geometry.

Document Object Model Requirements

Lauren Wood, Jared Sorensen

[W3C Working Draft; September 2, 1997]

Status of This Document

This draft is work under review by the W3C DOM Working Group, for use in an upcoming version of the Document Object Model specification. Please remember this is subject to change at any time, and may be updated, replaced or obsoleted by other documents at any time. It is inappropriate to use W3C Working Drafts as reference material or to cite them as other than "work in progress."

A list of current W3C Working Drafts can be found at *http://www.w3.org/TR*.

Public discussion of the Document Object Model, including discussion of this draft, takes place on *www-dom@w3.org*. To subscribe send a message to *www-dom-request@w3.org* with the word "subscribe" in the subject line.

This document defines the high-level requirements for the Document Object Model (DOM). References to XML and HTML documents generally denote the physical files that contain structural markup. Some requirements are not implemented in DOM Level 1. Those requirements are identified in this document with the notation [*After Level 1*].

General Requirements

Listed below are the general requirements of the Document Object Model.

1. The Object Model is language neutral and platform independent.
2. There will be a core DOM that is applicable to HTML, CSS, and XML documents.
3. The Object Model can be used to construct and deconstruct the document.
4. The Object Model will not preclude use by either agents external to the document content, or scripts embedded within the document.
5. Consistent naming conventions must be used through all levels of the Object Model.
6. A visual UI component will not be required for a conforming implementation of the Object Model.
7. The specific HTML, CSS, or XML document object models will be driven by the underlying constructs of those languages.
8. It must be possible to read in a document and write out a structurally identical document to disk (both documents can be represented by the same raw structural model).
9. The Object Model will not expose the user to problems with security, validity, or privacy.
10. The Object Model will not preclude other mechanisms for manipulating documents.

Structure Navigation

This refers to the navigation around a document, such as finding the parent of a given element, or what children elements a given parent element contains.

General Requirements

1. All document content, including elements and attributes, will be programmatically accessible and manipulable.

2. Navigation from any element to any other element will be possible, except where such navigation would compromise security.

3. There will be a way to uniquely and reproducibly enumerate the structure of static documents.

4. There will be a way to query for elements and attributes, subject to security and privacy considerations.

5. Basic low-level functions (get first, get next, etc.) will be provided, along with convenience functions that build upon them, but have a consistent access method.

HTML Requirements

These are specific to HTML documents.

1. All elements known to the user agent are exposed.

2. Unknown tags and attributes are exposed.

3. Implied elements are exposed even if not explicitly defined in the document (e.g., HTML, HEAD, BODY).

4. There will be guidelines for the inclusion of new elements and attributes in the object model.

Document Manipulation

1. There will be a way to add, remove, and change elements and/or tags (if permitted by the Document Type Definition and not precluded by security or validity considerations) in the document structure.

2. There will be a way to add, remove, and change attributes (if permitted by the Document Type Definition and not precluded by security or validity considerations) in the document structure.

3. Operations must restore consistency before they return.

4. A valid static document acted upon by the DOM will deliver a consistent reproducible document structure.

Content Manipulation

1. There will be a way to determine the containing element from any text part of the document (subject to security considerations).

2. There will be a way to manipulate (add, change, delete) content.

3. There will be a way to navigate content.

Event Model [After Level 1]

The event model must be rich enough to create completely interactive documents. This requires the ability to respond to any user action that may occur on the document. Therefore, many of these requirements only apply if a UI component is involved.

1. All elements will be capable of generating events.

2. There will be interaction events, update events, and change events.

3. The event model will allow responses to user interactions.

4. The event delivery mechanism will allow for overriding of default behavior.

5. Events will bubble through the structural hierarchy of the document.

6. Events are synchronous.

7. Events will be defined in a platform independent and language neutral way.

8. There will be an interface for binding to events.

Stylesheet Object Model [After Level 1]

Cascading Style Sheets (CSS) is one model for manipulating the style of the document. The Stylesheet Object Model exposes the ability to create, modify, and associate CSS style sheets with the document. The stylesheet model will be extensible to other stylesheet formats in the future.

1. All style sheets will be represented in the object model.
2. There will be a CSS stylesheet model. The CSS object model will be defined as part of a stylesheet embedding model, where the core part of the model may be applicable to other style languages.
3. Selectors, rules, and properties of individual style sheets can be added, removed and changed.
4. All elements of a CSS style can be added, removed, and changed in the object model. This includes but is not limited to:
   - Linked style sheets
   - Imported style sheets
   - Alternative style sheets
   - CSS pseudo-classes and CSS pseudo-elements
   - Contextual selectors
   - Inline styles
5. All properties as defined in the CSS specification, including but not limited to font properties, colors, backgrounds, and box properties.

DTD Manipulation

1. [*After Level 1*] There will be a way to determine the presence of a DTD.
2. There will be a way to query declarations in the underlying DTD (if available).
3. [*After Level 1*] There will be a way to add, remove, and change declarations in the underlying DTD (if available).
4. [*After Level 1*] There will be a way to test conformance of all or part of the given document against a DTD (if available). (See Document Manipulation, item 3).

Error Reporting

1. The DOM will provide a document-wide error logging and reporting mechanism.
2. Error reporting will be primarily via exceptions.
3. The DOM error state can be queried.

Security, Validity, and Privacy

Security, validity, and privacy considerations are interrelated and entwined. DOM Level 1 will provide simple "sandbox" security; subsequent levels are expected to incorporate more sophisticated mechanisms.

1. Each object must be responsible for maintaining its own internal consistency.
2. It must be safe to have multiple threads operating on the same object.
3. Object locking must be incorporated to ensure consistent results.
4. It must be possible to prevent scripts on one page from accessing another page.
5. Firewall boundaries must be respected.
6. It must be possible to restrict access and navigation to specific elements.
7. [*After Level 1*] An external security API will be provided.

Document Meta Information

These are requirements for what must be exposed about the document:

1. There will be information about the document and its embedded objects such as source location, date created, and associated cookies.

UA Information

These are requirements for information about the user agent environment, if applicable:

1. There will be a way of obtaining relevant information about the display environment, including the UA brand information and version number, and, where appropriate, the HTTP header.

2. [*After Level 1*] A way of determining support for a MIME type will be available. ■

About the Authors

Lauren Wood
Technical Product Manager
SoftQuad, Inc.
108-10070 King George Hwy
Surrey B.C. Canada V3T 2W4
lauren@sqwest.bc.ca

Lauren Wood is Technical Product Manager at SoftQuad, Inc., one of the leading vendors of Internet, Intranet, and SGML document solutions. She plays a major role in the design of SoftQuad's authoring tools, as well as taking part in various technical committees, such as the W3C HTML Working Group, the CSS and Formatting Properties Working Group, and the XML Working Group. She chairs the W3C Document Object Model Working Group. Lauren holds a Ph.D. in theoretical nuclear physics from the University of Melbourne, Australia.

Jared N. Sorensen
Manager, Documentation Products Group
Novell, Inc.
1555 N. Technology Way
M/S ORM-Q354
Orem, UT 84097
jnsorensen@novell.com

Jared N. Sorensen manages documentation engineering efforts at Novell, Inc. He is also the webmaster of the Novell Product Documentation Web site, one of the largest on the World Wide Web. Mr. Sorensen is Novell's representative on three working groups of the W3C: DOM, CSS, and HTML. An accomplished programmer, linguist, and technical writer, he has worked in management capacities for several software development companies and has been a popular speaker at publishing conferences around the world.

Guest Editor Dan Connolly has drawn on the XML development community to compile this movable feast of papers exploring the XML specifications, the philosophy behind it, its applications, implementations, and future directions. Norman Walsh of ArborText reprises his W3J role as an able guide to the technical details presented in Section 2 with "A Guide to XML." Users do not live by documents alone, though; it is essential to present XML-formatted data in mulitple media. Michael Leventhal from Grif surveys the latest adaptations to use "XML and CSS" together.

Understanding the mechanical details of XML is only the first step in the journey of wisdom. Two invited papers consider the philosophy behind the development of XML and come to opposing views. On one side, Dan Connolly of W3C, Rohit Khare of UC Irvine, and Adam Rifkin from Caltech extol "The Evolution of Web Documents: The Ascent of XML." Hypertext's founding father Ted Nelson artfully lays out the opposing view in "Embedded Markup Considered Harmful," subtly echoing Edsger Dijkstra's famous 1968 missive on goto abuse. Ted is currently teaching at Keio University's Shonan Fujisawa campus, which is also the North Pacific home of W3C.

XML's essential goal is to make it easier to capture the data structures and definitions used in specific applications. As XML makes it cheaper to extend new tags and document their use on the Web, its DTDs begin to represent community ontologies. Two papers consider the challenges of pinning down local usage and jargon in "Chemical Markup Language: A Simple Introduction to Structured Documents," by Peter Murray-Rust from Nottingham University, and "Codifying Medical Records in XML: Philosophy and Engineering," by Thomas L. Lincoln of RAND and the University of Illinois at Chicago.

XML's power will be proportional to its adoption across the World Wide Web. XML's designers thus placed a premium on simplifying implementations, as demonstrated by the four separate systems dissected in this section: "XML: Can the Desparate Perl Hacker Do It?" by Michael Leventhal; "XML Processing with Lark" by Tim Bray; "Building Microsoft's XML Parsers in Internet Explorer 4," by Jean Paoli from Microsoft, and Peter Murray-Rust's "JUMBO—An Object-Based XML Browser."

Looking further ahead, XML could become a compelling container for data of all kinds, making it easier to automate the Web with mobile code and transaction processing. Khare and Rifkin encourage "Capturing the State of Distributed Systems with XML"; Jon Bosak of Sun Microsystems reflects on "XML, Java, and the Future of the Web"; and Charles Axel Allen present's webMethods' plans for "Automating the Web with WIDL."

A Guide to XML

Norman Walsh

Abstract

This article provides a technical introduction to XML with an eye towards guiding the reader to appropriate sections of the XML specification when greater technical detail is desired. This introduction is geared towards a reader with some HTML or SGML experience, although that experience is not absolutely necessary. The XML Link and XML Style specifications are also briefly outlined.

Introduction

Because other articles in this issue of the *Web Journal* describe the motivations for XML and some of its goals, this article is intended to serve as a slightly more technical introduction to XML and as an overview of the specification. Throughout this document you will find references of the form [Section 1]; these are references to the XML language specification included in this issue. If you are interested in more technical detail about a particular topic, please consult the specification.

Understanding the Specs

For the most part, reading and understanding the XML specifications does not require extensive knowledge of SGML or any of the related technologies.

One topic that may be new is the use of EBNF to describe the syntax of XML. Please consult the discussion of EBNF in Appendix A for a detailed description of how this grammar works.

What Do XML Documents Look Like?

If you are conversant with SGML or HTML, XML documents will look familiar. Here is a simple XML document:

```
<?XML version="1.0"?>
<oldjoke>
<burns>Say <quote>goodnight
    </quote>, Gracie.</burns>
<allen><quote>Goodnight, Gracie.
    </quote></allen>
<applause/>
</oldjoke>
```

A few things may stand out to you:

- The document begins with a processing instruction: `<?XML ...?>`. This is the XML markup declaration [Section 2.9]. While it is not required, its presence explicitly identifies the document as an XML document and indicates the version of XML to which it was authored.
- There's no document type declaration. Unlike SGML, XML does not require a document type declaration. However, a document type declaration can be supplied, and some documents will require one.
- Empty elements (`<applause/>` in the example above) have a modified syntax. While most elements in a document are wrappers around some content, empty elements are simply markers where something occurs (a horizontal rule for HTML's `hr` tag, for example, or an `xref` cross reference in DocBook). The trailing slash in the modified syntax, `<name/>`, indicates to a program processing the XML document that the element is empty and no matching end-tag should be sought. Since XML documents do not require a document type declaration, without this clue it could be impossible for an XML parser to determine which tags were

intentionally empty and which had been left empty by mistake.

In a very recent modification to the specification, another alternate syntax has been introduced for empty elements which allows the end-tag to be present, *if* it immediately follows the start-tag. Under this syntax, `<applause></applause>` would be acceptable as well.

XML documents are composed of markup and content. There are six kinds of markup that can occur in an XML document: elements, entity references, comments, processing instructions, marked sections, and document type declarations. The following sections introduce each of these markup concepts.

Elements

Elements are the most common form of markup. Delimited by angle brackets (< >), most elements identify the nature of the content they surround. Some elements may be empty, as seen above, in which case they have no content. If an element is not empty, it begins with a start-tag, `<element>`, and ends with an end-tag, `</element>`.

Attributes

Attributes are name-value pairs that occur inside tags after the element name. For example, `<div class="preface">` is the `div` element with the attribute `class` having the value `preface`. In XML, all attribute values must be quoted.

Entity References

In order to introduce markup into a document, some characters have been reserved to identify the start of markup. The left angle bracket (<), for instance, identifies the beginning of an element start- or end-tag. In order to insert these characters into your document as content, there must be an alternative way to represent them. In XML, entities are used to represent these special characters. Entities are also used to refer to often repeated or varying text and to include the content of external files.

Every entity must have a unique name. Defining your own entity names is discussed in the section "Entity Declarations" below. In order to use an entity, you simply reference it by name. Entity references begin with the ampersand character (&) and end with a semicolon (`;`).

For example, the `amp` entity inserts a literal ampersand into a document. So the string "O'Reilly & Associates, Inc." can be represented in an XML document as `O'Reilly & Associates, Inc.`

A special form of entity reference, called a character reference [Section 4.2], can be used to insert arbitrary Unicode characters into your document. This is a mechanism for inserting characters that cannot be directly typed.

Character references take one of two forms:

- Decimal references (`℞`)
- Hexadecimal references (`℞`)

Both of these refer to character number U+211E from Unicode (which is the standard Rx prescription symbol).

Comments

Comments begin with `<!--` and end with `-->`. Comments can contain any data except the literal string "`--`". You can place comments between markup anywhere in your document.

Comments are not part of the textual content of an XML document; an XML processor is not required to pass them along to an application.

Processing Instructions

Processing instructions (PIs) are an escape hatch to provide information to an application. Like comments, they are not textually part of the XML document, but the XML processor is required to pass them to an application.

Processing instructions have the form: `<?name pidata?>`. The name, called the *PI target*, identifies the PI to the application. Applications should process only the targets they recognize and ignore all other PIs. Any data that follows the PI target is optional; the data is for the application that recognizes the target. The names used in PIs may be declared as notations in order to formally identify them.

PI names beginning with `XML` are reserved for XML standardization.

CDATA Sections

In a document, a CDATA section instructs the parser to ignore most markup characters.

Consider a source code listing in an XML document. It might contain characters that the XML parser would ordinarily recognize as markup (< and &, for example). In order to prevent this, a CDATA section can be used.

```
<![CDATA[
*p = &q;
b = (i <= 3);
]]>
```

Between the start of the section `<![CDATA[` and the end of the section, `]]>`, all character data is passed directly to the application. The only string that cannot occur in a CDATA section is `]]>`.

NOTE

Comments are not recognized in a CDATA section. If present, the literal text `<!--comment-->` will be passed directly to the application.

Document Type Declarations

A large percentage of the XML specification deals with various sorts of declarations that are allowed in XML. If you have experience with SGML, you will recognize these declarations from SGML DTDs (Document Type Definitions). If you have never seen them before, their significance may not be immediately obvious.

One of the greatest strengths of XML is that it allows you to create your own tag names. But for any given application, it is probably not meaningful for tags to occur in a completely arbitrary order. Consider the old joke example introduced earlier. Would this be meaningful?

```
<quote><oldjoke>Goodnight,
    <applause/>Gracie</oldjoke>
    </quote>
<burns><gracie>Say
    <quote>goodnight</quote>,
    </gracie>Gracie.</burns>
```

It's so far outside the bounds of what we normally expect that it's nonsensical. It just doesn't mean anything.

However, from a strictly syntactic point of view, there's nothing wrong with that XML document. So, if the document is to have meaning, and certainly if you're writing a stylesheet to present it, there must be some constraint on the sequence and nesting of tags. Declarations are where these constraints can be expressed.

More generally, declarations allow a document to communicate meta-information to the parser about its content. Meta-information includes the allowed sequence and nesting of tags, attribute values and their types and defaults, the names of external files that may be referenced and whether or not they contain XML, the formats of some external (non-XML) data that may be included, and entities that may be encountered.

There are four kinds of declarations in XML: element declarations, attribute list declarations, entity declarations, and notation declarations.

Element declarations

Element declarations [Section 3.2] identify the names of elements and the nature of their content. A typical element declaration looks like this:

```
<!ELEMENT oldjoke (burns+, allen,
    applause?)>
```

This declaration identifies the element named `oldjoke`. Its "content model" follows the element name. The content model defines what an element may contain. In this case, an oldjoke must contain burns and allen and may contain applause. The commas (,) between element names indicate that they must occur in succession. The plus (+) after burns indicates that it may be repeated more than once but must occur at least once. The question mark (?) after applause indicates that it is optional. A name with no punctuation, such as allen, must occur exactly once.

Declarations for burns, allen, applause, and all other elements used in any content model must also be present for an XML processor to check the validity of a document.

In addition to element names, the special symbol #PCDATA is reserved to indicate character data. The moniker PCDATA stands for "parseable character data."

Elements with both element content [Section 3.2.1] and PCDATA content are said to have "mixed content" [Section 3.2.2].

For example, the definition for burns might be

```
<!ELEMENT burns (#PCDATA | quote)*>
```

The vertical bar (|) indicates an "or" relationship and the asterisk (*) indicates that the content is optional (may occur zero or more times); therefore, by this definition, burns may contain zero or more characters and quote tags. All content models that include PCDATA must have this form: PCDATA must come first, all of the elements must be separated by vertical bars, and the entire group must be optional.

Two other content models are possible:

- EMPTY indicates that the element has no content (and consequently no end-tag)
- ANY indicates that any content is allowed

The ANY content model is sometimes useful during document conversion, but should be avoided at almost any cost in a production environment because it disables all content checking in that element.

Here is a complete set of element declarations for the example used at the beginning of this article:

```
<!ELEMENT oldjoke  (burns+, allen,
   applause?)>
<!ELEMENT burns    (#PCDATA |
   quote)*>
<!ELEMENT allen    (#PCDATA |
   quote)*>
<!ELEMENT quote    (#PCDATA)*>
<!ELEMENT applause empty>
```

Attribute declarations

Attribute declarations [Section 3.3] identify which elements may have attributes, what attributes they may have, what values the attributes may hold, and what default value each attribute has. A typical attribute declaration looks like this:

```
<!ATTLIST oldjoke
    name   ID            #required
    label  CDATA         #implied
    status ( funny | notfunny )
      'funny'>
```

In this example, the oldjoke element has three attributes:

- name, which is an ID and is required
- label, which is a string (character data) and is not required
- status, which must be either funny or notfunny and defaults to funny if not specified.

Each attribute in a declaration has three parts: a name, a type, and a default value. You are free to select any name you wish, subject to some slight restrictions [Section 1.5, production 5], but names cannot be repeated on the same element. There are six possible attribute types:

CDATA
: CDATA attributes are strings; any text is allowed. Don't confuse CDATA attributes with CDATA sections. In CDATA attributes, markup is recognized; specifically, entity references are expanded.

`ID`
: The value of an ID attribute must be a name [Section 1.5, production 5]. All of the ID values used in a document must be different. IDs uniquely identify individual elements in a document. Elements can have only a single ID attribute.

`IDREF` or `IDREFS`
: An IDREF attribute's value must be the value of a single ID attribute on some element in the document. The value of an IDREFS attribute may contain multiple IDREF values separated by whitespace.

`ENTITY` or `ENTITIES`
: An ENTITY attribute's value must be the name of a single entity (see the discussion of entity declarations below). The value of an ENTITIES attribute may contain multiple ENTITY values separated by whitespace.

`NMTOKEN` or `NMTOKENS`
: Name token attributes are a restricted form of string attribute. In general, an NMTOKEN attribute must consist of a single word [Section 1.5, production 7], but there are no additional constraints on the word, it doesn't have to match another attribute or declaration. The value of an NMTOKENS attribute may contain multiple NMTOKEN values separated by whitespace.

A list of names
: You can specify that the value of an attribute must be taken from a specific list of names. This is frequently called an "enumerated type" because each of the possible values is explicitly enumerated in the declaration. Additionally, you can specify that the names must match a particular notation name (see the "Notation Declarations" section below).

There are four kinds of default values:

`#REQUIRED`
: The attribute must have an explicitly specified value on every occurrence of the element in the document.

`#IMPLIED`
: The attribute value is not required, and no default value is provided. If a value is not specified, the XML processor must proceed without one.

`"value"`
: An attribute can be given any legal value as a default. The attribute value is not required on each element in the document, but if it is not present, it will appear to be the specified default.

`#FIXED "value"`
: An attribute declaration may specify that an attribute has a fixed value. In this case, the attribute is not required, but if it occurs, it must have the specified value. One use for fixed attributes is to associate semantics with an element. A complete discussion is beyond the scope of this article, but you can find several examples of fixed attributes in the XLL specification.*

Entity declarations

Entity declarations [Section 4.3] allow you to associate a name with some other fragment of the document. That construct can be a chunk of regular text, a chunk of the document type declaration, or a reference to an external file containing either text or binary data.

Here are a few typical entity declarations:

```
<!ENTITY ATI
   "ArborText, Inc.">
<!ENTITY boilerplate     SYSTEM "/
   standard/legalnotice.xml">
<!ENTITY ATIlogo         SYSTEM "/
   standard/logo.gif" NDATA GIF87A>
```

* Also known as Part 2 of the "Extensible Markup Language (XML)" spec.

There are three kinds of entities:

Internal entities

The first entity in the preceding example is an internal entity [Section 4.3.1] because the replacement text is stored in the declaration. Using `&ATI;` anywhere in the document inserts “ArborText, Inc.” at that location. Internal entities allow you to define shortcuts for frequently typed text or text that is expected to change, such as the revision status of a document.

Internal entities can include references to other internal entities, but it is an error for them to be recursive.

The XML specification predefines five internal entities:

- < produces the left angle bracket (<)
- > produces the right angle bracket (>)
- & produces the ampersand (&)
- ' produces a single quote character (')
- " produces a double quote character (")

External entities

The second and third entities are external entities [Section 4.3.2].

Using `&boilerplate;` will have the effect of inserting the *contents* of the file */standard/legalnotice.xml* at that location in the document when it is processed. The XML processor will parse the content of that file as if its content had been typed at the location of the entity reference.

The entity **ATIlogo** is also an external entity, but its content is binary. The **ATIlogo** entity can only be used as the value of an ENTITY (or ENTITIES) attribute (on a `graphic` element, perhaps). The XML processor will pass this information along to an application, but it does not attempt to process the content of */standard/logo.gif.*

External entities allow an XML document to refer to an external file. External entities contain either text or binary data. If they contain text, the content of the external file is inserted at the point of reference and parsed as part of the referring document. Binary data is not parsed and may only be referenced in an attribute. Binary data is used to reference figures and other non-XML content in the document.

Parameter entities

Parameter entities can occur only in the document type declaration. A parameter entity is identified by placing `%` (“percent- ”) in front of its name in the declaration. The percent sign is also used in references to parameter entities, instead of the ampersand. Parameter entity references are immediately expanded in the document type declaration and their replacement text is part of the declaration, whereas normal entity references are not expanded.

Notation declarations

Notation declarations [Section 4.6] identify specific types of external binary data. This information is passed to the processing application, which may use it however it wishes to. A typical notation declaration is:

```
<!NOTATION GIF87A SYSTEM "GIF">
```

Do I Need a Document Type Declaration?

As we've seen, XML content can be processed without a declaration. However, there are some instances where the declaration is required:

Authoring environments

Most authoring environments need to read and process document type declarations in order to understand and enforce the content models of the document.

Default attribute values

If an XML document relies on default attribute values, at least part of the declaration must be processed in order to obtain the correct default values.

Whitespace handling

Whitespace handling [Section 2.8] is a subtle issue. Consider the following content fragment:

```
<oldjoke>
<burns>Say <quote>goodnight
    </quote>, Gracie.</burns>
```

Is the whitespace (the new line between `oldjoke` and `burns`) significant? Probably not. But how can you tell? You can only determine if whitespace is significant if you know the content model of the elements in question. In a nutshell, whitespace is significant in mixed content and is insignificant in element content.

The rule for XML processors is that in the absence of a declaration that identifies the content model of an element, all whitespace is significant. If you need precise control over whitespace handling, you must provide a declaration.

In applications where a person composes or edits the data (as opposed to data that may be generated directly from a database, for example), a DTD is probably going to be required if any structure is to be guaranteed.

Including a Document Type Declaration

If present, the document type declaration must be the first thing in the document after optional processing instructions and comments [Section 2.9].

The document type declaration identifies the root element of the document and may contain additional declarations. All XML documents must have a single root element that contains all of the content in the document. Additional declarations may come from an external definition (a DTD), may be included directly in the document, or both:

```
<?XML version="1.0" rmd="internal"?>
<!DOCTYPE chapter SYSTEM "dbook.
    dtd" [
<!ELEMENT ulink (#PCDATA)*>
  <!ATTLIST ulink
     xml-link       CDATA  #FIXED
        "SIMPLE"
     xml-attributes CDATA  #FIXED
        "HREF URL"
     URL            CDATA  #REQUIRED>
]>
<chapter>...</chapter>
```

This example references an external DTD, *dbook.dtd*, and includes element and attribute declarations for the `ulink` element. In this case, `ulink` is being given the semantics of a simple link from the XLL specification.

In order to determine if a document is valid, the XML processor must read the entire document type declaration (both internal and external). But for some applications, validity may not be required, and it may be sufficient for the processor to read only the internal declaration. In the example above, if validity is unimportant and the only reason to read the doctype declaration is to identify the semantics of `ulink`, reading the external definition is not necessary.

You can communicate this information in the required markup declaration [Section 2.10]. The required markup declaration, `rmd="internal"`, `rmd="all"`, or `rmd="none"` occurs in the XML markup declaration. A value of `internal` indicates that only the internal declarations need be processed. A value of `all` indicates that *both* the internal and external declarations must be processed. A value of `none` indicates that the document can be processed without reading either declarations.

If both is specified, the XML processor reads the internal declaration before the external declaration. This is important if the declarations contain duplicate ATTLIST or ENTITY declarations. In XML, the first declaration takes precedence. Duplicate ELEMENT declarations are not allowed.

Validity

Given the preceding discussion of type declarations, it follows that some documents are valid and some are not. There are two categories of XML documents: well-formed and valid.

Well-Formed Documents

A document can only be well-formed [Section 2.2] if it obeys the syntax of XML. A document that includes sequences of markup characters that cannot be parsed, or are invalid, cannot be well-formed.

In addition, the document must meet all of the following conditions (understanding some of these conditions may require experience with SGML):

- The document instance must conform to the grammar of XML documents. In particular, some markup constructs (parameter entity references, for example) are only allowed in specific places. The document is not well-formed if they occur elsewhere, even if the document is well-formed in all other ways.
- The replacement text for all parameter entities referenced inside a markup declaration consists of zero or more complete markup declarations. (No parameter entity used in the document may consist of only part of a markup declaration.)
- No attribute may appear more than once on the same start-tag.
- String attribute values cannot contain references to external entities.
- Non-empty tags must be properly nested.
- Parameter entities must be declared before they are used.
- All entities must be declared except the following: `amp`, `lt`, `gt`, `apos`, and `quot`.
- A binary entity cannot be referenced in the flow of content; it can only be used in an attribute declared as ENTITY or ENTITIES.
- Neither text nor parameter entities can be recursive, directly or indirectly.

By definition, if a document is not well-formed, it is not XML.

Valid Documents

A well-formed document is valid only if it contains a proper document type declaration and if the document obeys the constraints of that declaration (element sequence and nesting is valid, required attributes are provided, attribute values are of the correct type, etc.). The XML specification identifies all of the criteria in detail.

Pulling the Pieces Together

The XML linking specification (XLL), currently under development, introduces a standard linking model for XML. In consideration of space, and the fact that the XLL draft is still developing, what follows is survey of the features of XLL, rather than a detailed description of the specification.

In the parlance of XLL, a link expresses a relationship between resources. A resource is any location (an element identified with an ID or the content of a linking element, for example) that is addressed in a link. The exact nature of the relationship between resources depends on both the application that processes the link and semantic information you supplied.

Some highlights of XLL include the following:

- XLL gives you control over the semantics of the link.
- XLL introduces Extended Links. Extended Links can involve more than two resources.
- XLL introduces Extended Pointers (XPointers). XPointers provide a sophisticated method of locating resources.

Since XML does not have a fixed set of elements, the name of the element cannot be used to locate links. Instead, XML processors identify links by recognizing the `XML-LINK` attribute. Other attributes can be used to provide additional information to the XML processor. An attribute renaming facility exists to work around name collisions in existing applications.

Two of the attributes, `SHOW` and `ACTUATE`, allow you to exert some control over the linking behavior. The `SHOW` attribute determines whether the document that is linked-to is embedded in the current document, replaces the current document, or is displayed in a new window when the link is traversed. `ACTUATE` determines how the link is traversed, either automatically or when selected by the user.

Some applications will require much finer control over linking behaviors. For those applications, standard places are provided where the additional semantics may be expressed.

Simple Links

A Simple Link strongly resembles an HTML `A` link:

```
<LINK XML-LINK="SIMPLE"
    HREF="locator">Link Text</LINK>
```

A Simple Link identifies a link between two resources, one of which is the content of the linking element itself. This is an in-line link.

The *locator* identifies the other resource. The locator may be a URL, a query, or an Extended Pointer.

Extended Links

Extended Links allow you to express relationships between more than two resources:

```
<ELINK XML-LINK="EXTENDED"
    ROLE="ANNOTATION">
<LOCATOR XML-LINK="LOCATOR"
    HREF="text.loc">The Text
    </LOCATOR>
<LOCATOR XML-LINK="LOCATOR"
    HREF="annot1.loc">Annotations
    </LOCATOR>
<LOCATOR XML-LINK="LOCATOR"
    HREF="annot2.loc">More
    Annotations</LOCATOR>
<LOCATOR XML-LINK="LOCATOR"
    HREF="litcrit.loc">Literary
    Criticism</LOCATOR>
<ELINK>
```

This example shows how the relationships between a literary work, annotations, and literary criticism of that work might be expressed. Note that this link is separate from all of the resources involved. The semantics of extended links depend on the application, but another example following the discussion of Extended Pointers will demonstrate how extended links can be used to add links to read-only resources.

Extended Links can be in-line, so that the content of the linking element other than the locator elements participates in the link as a resource—but that is not necessarily the case. The example above is an out-of-line link because it does not use its content as a resource.

Extended Pointers

Cross references with the SGML ID/IDREF mechanism (which is similar to the `#fragment` mechanism in HTML) require that the document being linked-to has defined anchors where links are desired. This may not always be the case, however; sometimes it is not possible to modify the document to which you wish to link.

XML XPointers borrow concepts from HyTime [1] and the Text Encoding Initiative (TEI) [2]. XPointers offer a syntax that allows you to locate a resource by traversing the element tree of the document containing the resource.

For example,

```
child(2,oldjoke)(3,.)
```

locates the third child (whatever it may be) of the second `oldjoke` in the document.

XPointers can span regions of the tree. The XPointer

```
child(2,oldjoke)..child(3,oldjoke)
```

selects the second and third `oldjokes` in the document.

In addition to selecting by elements, XPointers allow for selection by ID, attribute value, and string matching. In this article, the XPointer

```
root()child(3,sect1)string(1,"Here",
    0)..
root()child(3,sect1)string(1,"Here",
    4)
```

selects the first occurrence of the word "Here" in the "What Do XML Documents Look Like?" section of this article. This link can be established by an extended link *without modifying* this document.

Note that an XPointer range can span a structurally invalid section of the document. The XLL specification does not specify how applications should deal with such ranges.

Extended Link Groups

Out-of-line links introduce the possibility that an XML processor may need to process several files in order to correctly display the hypertext document.

Following the annotated text example above, and assuming that the actual text is read-only, the XML processor must load at least the text and the document that contains the extended link.

XLL defines Extended Link Groups for this purpose. The act of loading an Extended Link Group communicates which documents must be loaded to the XML processor. Extended Link Groups can be used recursively; a `STEPS` attribute is provided to limit the depth of recursion.

Style and Substance

HTML browsers are largely hardcoded. A first level heading appears the way it does because the browser recognizes the `H1` tag.

Again, since XML documents have no fixed tag set, this approach will not work. The presentation of an XML document is dependent on a stylesheet.

At the time of this writing, the XSL effort is just getting off the ground. XSL is likely to be focused on DSSSL, the Document Style Semantics and Specification Language [3]. DSSSL is an international standard stylesheet language (ISO/IEC 10179:1996). Some tools already exist which can process XML with DSSSL stylesheets, but none have yet been integrated into browsers.

Other stylesheet languages, like Cascading Style Sheets,* [4] are likely to be supported as well.

Conclusion

In this article, most of the major features of the XML Language have been discussed, and some of the concepts behind XML Link and XML Style have been described. Although some things have been left out in the interest of the big picture (such as character encoding issues), hopefully you now have enough background to pick up and read the XML specifications in this issue without difficulty.

Appendix A: Extended Backus-Naur Form (EBNF)

One of the most significant design improvements in XML is to make it easy to use with modern compiler tools. Part of this improvement involves making it possible to express the syntax of XML in Extended Backus-Naur Form (EBNF) [Section 1.4]. If you've never seen EBNF before, think of it this way:

- EBNF is a set of rules, called "productions."
- Every rule describes a specific fragment of syntax.

* For more information about cascading style sheets, see the article "XML and CSS" (Culshaw, Leventhal, and Maloney) in this issue, as well as "An Introduction to Cascading Style Sheets" by Norman Walsh in the Winter 1997 issue of W3J, *Advancing HTML*.

- A document is valid if it can be reduced to a single, specific rule, with no input left, by repeated application of the rules.

Let's take a simple example that has nothing to do with XML (or the real rules of language):

```
[1] Word       ::= Consonant Vowel+
                   Consonant
[2] Consonant ::= [^aeiou]
[3] Vowel      ::= [aeiou]
```

Rule 1 states that a word is a consonant followed by one or more vowels followed by another consonant. Rule 2 states that a consonant is any letter other than a, e, i, o, or u. Rule 3 states that a vowel is any of the letters a, e, i, o, or u. (The exact syntax of the rules, the meaning of square brackets and other special symbols, is laid out in the XML specification.)

Using the above example, is "red" a `Word`? Yes, for the following reasons:

3. "red" is the letter `r` followed by the letter `e` followed by the letter `d`: `'r' 'e' 'd'`.
4. `r` is a Consonant by rule 2, so "red" is: `Consonant 'e' 'd'`
5. e is a vowel by rule 3, so "red" is: `Consonant Vowel 'd'`.
6. By rule 2 again, "red" is: `Consonant Vowel Consonant` which, by rule 1, is a `Word`.

By the same analysis, "reed", "road", and "xeaiioug" are also words, but "rate" is not. There is no way to match `Consonant Vowel Consonant Vowel` using the EBNF above. XML is defined by an EBNF grammar of about 80 rules. Although the rules are more complex, the same sort of analysis allows an XML parser to determine that `<greeting>Hello World</greeting>` is a syntactically correct XML document while `<greeting]Wrong Bracket!</greeting>` is not.

In very general terms, that's all there is to it. You'll find all the details about EBNF in *Compilers: Principles, Techniques, and Tools* [5] or in any modern compiler text book.

While EBNF isn't an efficient way to represent syntax for human consumption, there are programs that can automatically turn EBNF into a parser. This makes it a particularly efficient way to represent the syntax for a language that will be parsed by a computer. ■

References

1. *ftp://ftp.ornl.gov/pub/sgml/wgs/document/1920.htm*
2. *http://www.uic.edu/orgs/tei/*
3. *http://www.jclark.com/dsssl/*
4. *http://www.w3.org/TR/REC-CSS1-961217*
5. Aho, Alfred V., Ravi Sethi, and Jeffrey D. Ullman, *Compilers, Principles, Techniques, and Tools.* Reading: Addison-Wesley, 1986, rpt. corr. 1988.

About the Author

Norman Walsh
ArborText, Inc.
1000 Victors Way
Ann Arbor, MI 48108
nwalsh@arbortext.com

Norman Walsh is a Senior Application Analyst at ArborText, Inc. ArborText develops industrial stength SGML authoring and publishing tools and distributes these products worldwide. He has also developed a number of Web resources, including The Internet Font Archives, and is the author of *Making TeX Work*, published by O'Reilly & Associates.

Norm telecommutes from beautiful Amherst, Massachusetts where he lives with his wife Deborah, two cats, and several frogs.

XML AND CSS

Stuart Culshaw, Michael Leventhal, and Murray Maloney

Abstract

The simplicity of document creation was a key element in the astonishingly rapid development of the Web. This article describes XML and CSS: the "one-two" punch that will not only bring back that level of simplicity, but also enable the construction of complex applications which are either difficult or impossible using HTML. In this article we outline the steps for using an CSS style sheet in an XML document; we discuss the limitations of CSS in complex applications; and we present a real life example.

HTML provides limited possibilities for the explicit formatting and positioning of text. The mechanisms that are provided—such as the FONT element or the ALIGN attribute—force the page designer to embed presentation-specific information within the document; a fact that makes it difficult to prepare documents for a variety of screen sizes, presentation modalities, and types of audiences. Because these limited features are not sufficient to achieve the formatting results desired by many Web designers, they commonly resort to using tables and various HTML coding "tricks." This presents many negative consequences, particularly because it is so difficult to maintain information content in HTML documents; the content is inextricably interwined with the format-related encoding. More sophisticated formatting capabilities have long been needed to support the many document types, ranging from marketing froufrou to legal documents to scientific journals.

Cascading Style Sheets (CSS) is a style sheet mechanism specifically developed to meet the needs of Web designers and users. CSS provides HTML with far greater control over document presentation in a way that is independent of document content. CSS style sheets can be used to set fonts, colors, whitespace, positioning, backgrounds, and many other presentational aspects of a document. It is also possible for several documents to share the same style sheet, which allows users to maintain consistent presentation within a collection of related documents without having to modify each document separately.

The rationale for XML is discussed at length in other papers in this issue; we will thus restrict our introduction to the observation that, in combination, XML and CSS can once again simplify document creation. XML uses markup to describe the structure and data content of a document, making it easy both for authors to write it and for computer programs to process it. CSS, on the other hand, makes it possible to present that document to the user in a browser. CSS or some type of style sheet mechanism is, in fact, a requisite for browsing XML on the Web. If CSS works well with HTML, it will work wonders with XML.

In this article we will illustrate the use of CSS and XML with two examples. We do not describe the syntax of CSS, but refer the reader to the CSS documentation on the W3C Web site.*

A Thespian Example

The steps in the following sections illustrate the use of a CSS style sheet for an XML document (an extract from the Shakespeare play "Much Ado about Nothing").

* See *http://www.w3.org*. For a user's guide to CSS syntax also see the article by Norman Walsh in the Winter 1997 issue of W3J, *Advancing HTML*.

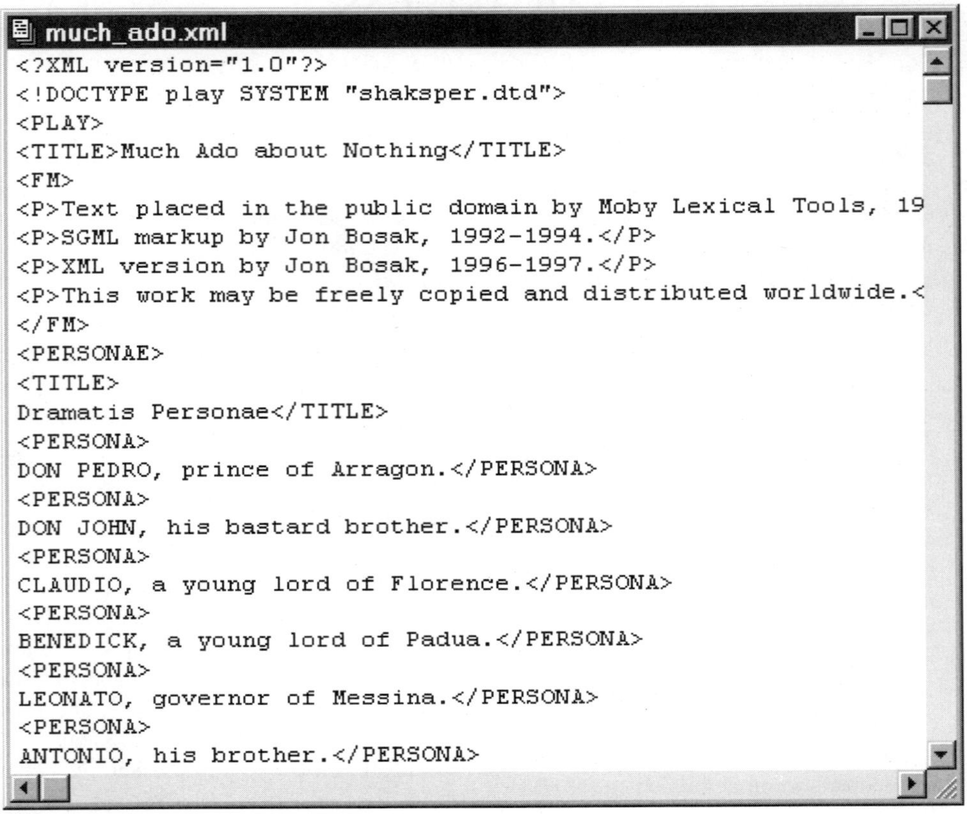

```
<?XML version="1.0"?>
<!DOCTYPE play SYSTEM "shaksper.dtd">
<PLAY>
<TITLE>Much Ado about Nothing</TITLE>
<FM>
<P>Text placed in the public domain by Moby Lexical Tools, 19
<P>SGML markup by Jon Bosak, 1992-1994.</P>
<P>XML version by Jon Bosak, 1996-1997.</P>
<P>This work may be freely copied and distributed worldwide.<
</FM>
<PERSONAE>
<TITLE>
Dramatis Personae</TITLE>
<PERSONA>
DON PEDRO, prince of Arragon.</PERSONA>
<PERSONA>
DON JOHN, his bastard brother.</PERSONA>
<PERSONA>
CLAUDIO, a young lord of Florence.</PERSONA>
<PERSONA>
BENEDICK, a young lord of Padua.</PERSONA>
<PERSONA>
LEONATO, governor of Messina.</PERSONA>
<PERSONA>
ANTONIO, his brother.</PERSONA>
```

Figure 1

Step 1: The Document Source

Figure 1 shows *much_ado.xml*; preparing the document source is the first step in using a CSS style sheet for an XML document.

Step 2: Define Style Sheet Rules

The style rules for a document can be stored either within the document itself, or within a separate text file. In this example, we will save the style sheet as a separate file, *shaksper.css*, so that it can be easily applied to other Shakespeare plays we might like to publish.

You can create the style sheet manually using your favorite text editor, as shown in Example 1.

Alternatively, you can create the style sheet using an editor that supports CSS, such as Grif's Symposia, as shown in Figure 2.

Example 1

```
PLAY { background-color : white }
FM { font-style : italic;
     font-size : 14;
     color : #400040;
     text-align : right }
SPEAKER { font-weight : bold;
```

Example 1 *(continued)*

```
          color : #ff0080 }
LINE { color : #800040;
       left : 15 }
PERSONA { font-style : italic;
          font-size : -1 }
PERSONAE { color : #800040 }
SCNDESCR { margin-top : 30;
           font-size : 18;
           color : #0000a0;
           height : 20 }
STAGEDIR { font-weight : bold;
           font-style : italic;
           height : 20 }
PLAYSUBT { font-weight : bold;
           font-size : 16;
           text-decoration : underline;
           height : 20 }
SPEECH { margin-top : 5 }
```

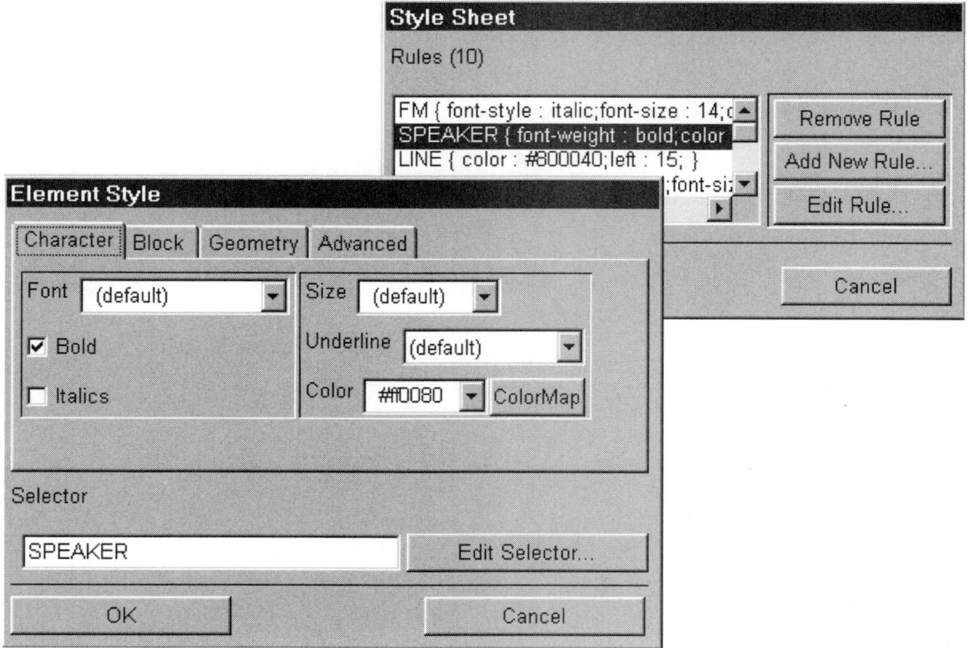

Figure 2

Step 3: Link the Style Sheet to the Document

At the time of writing, there is not yet a standardized method for linking an XML document with a style sheet. This subject forms part of the work, currently in progress by the W3C, that is due to be published in December 1997 as part III of the XML specification: XML-Style.

The method we will use in this example therefore is based on a draft proposal for stylesheet linking in XML which consists of inserting the XML processing instruction `<?XML-stylesheet?>` at the top of the document. The processing instruction has two required attributes `type` and `href` which respectively specify the type of stylesheet and its address. In our example, we thus need to add the following line to our XML document:

```
<?XML-stylesheet type="text/css"
    href="shaksper.css"?>
```

Symposia supports this XML style sheet linking mechanism and inserts the processing instruction for you automatically when you specify an external style sheet using the "Create new Style Sheet/External" command.

Step 4: Publish the Document and its Style Sheet

Once the style sheet is linked to the document, it can be published. When opened in an XML browser (or in Symposia, as shown in Figure 3),

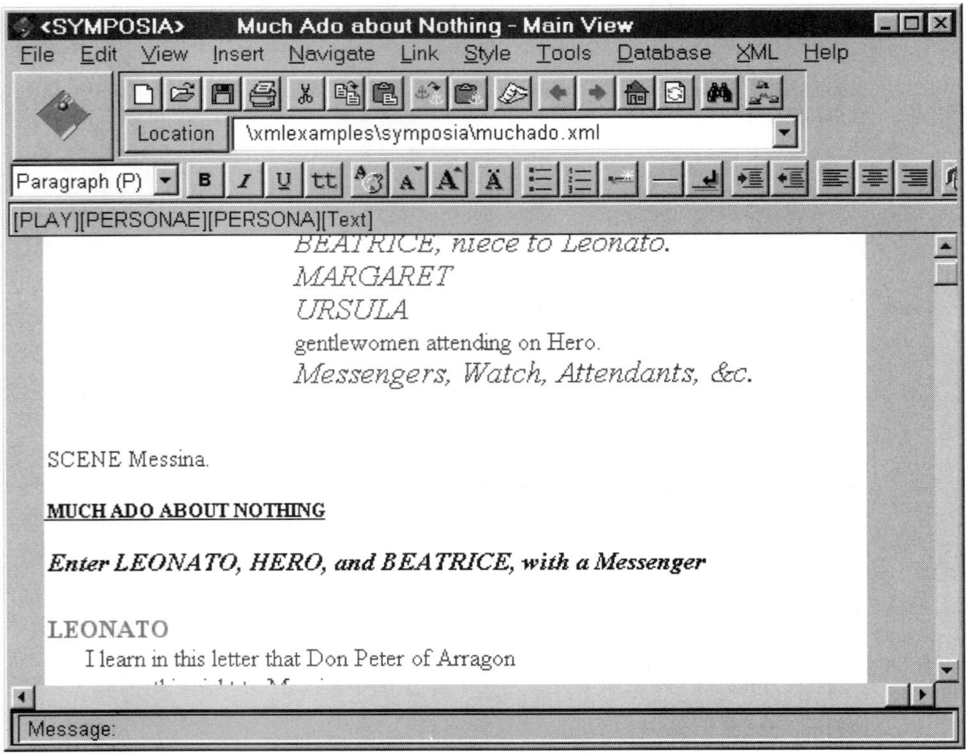

Figure 3

the style rules are applied to the different XML elements in the document.

Limitations of CSS for Complex Applications

Although CSS style sheets can be very effective for improving the presentation of HTML documents, the CSS1 standard has a number of important omissions which can limit the effectiveness of CSS style sheets for more complex applications. The following list, taken from Jon Bosak's presentation at WWW6 on April 11, 1997* describes just a few of the major limitations of the CSS standard:

- CSS cannot grab an item (such as a chapter title) from one place and use it again in another place (such as a page header).
- CSS has no concept of sibling relationships. For example, it is impossible to write a CSS stylesheet that will render every other paragraph in bold.
- CSS is not a programming language; it does not support decision structures and cannot be extended by the stylesheet designer.
- CSS cannot calculate quantities or store variables. This means, at the very least, that it cannot store commonly used parameters in one location that is easy to update.
- CSS cannot generate text (page numbers, etc.)
- CSS uses a simple box-oriented formatting model that works for current Web browsers but will not extend to more advanced applications of the markup, such as multiple column sets.
- CSS is oriented toward Western languages and assumes a horizontal writing direction.

It is for these reasons that the W3C working group responsible for the XML standard is concentrating its efforts on the implementation of a simplified version of the DSSSL standard, DSSSL Online (DSSSL-O). DSSSL-O promises to provide far more layout and document presentation features than CSS, but is a considerably more complex standard and may prove difficult to implement.

What is clear, however, is that the limitations of CSS1 do represent a serious hinderance for its use in the more complex types of application that are possible with XML. As the following section shows, even for a somewhat simple XML application, the CSS standard needs to acquire a certain number of essential features if it is realize its full potential.

A Real Life Example

The following example is taken from a Marketing Contact application which is actually in use at Grif. The Marketing Contact application allows our staff to record information and update information about our business contacts, and to extract reports and find existing records based on specific criteria using a search engine. Though this type of application is often implemented using a database such as Access, a more Web-centric approach would be to create an interface to a database using HTML forms. We choose instead to simply create our database records directly using Symposia. Our search engine is XML-capable so the equivalent of field-specific searches can be performed within XML elements. Among the advantages of this approach is that our application is entirely Intranet-based; and as a result we were neither required to write a line of CGI code, nor to develop HTML or database forms.

The DTD for our application is shown in Example 2.

* "Overview: XML, HTML, and all that." See also Jon Bosak's article in this issue entitled "XML, Java, and the Future of the Web."

Example 2

```
<!XML version="1.0">
<!DocType ContactRec [
<!Element ContactRec (Name, Company, Address,
Product, Contacts)>
<!Element Name(Honorific?, First,
Middle?, Last)>
<!Element Company(JobTitle?, CompanyName)>
<!Element Address(Street+, City, Region?,
PostCode, Country, Phone,
Internet)>
<!Element Product Empty>
<!AttList Product
SGMLEditor(Yes|No) #REQUIRED
SGMLEditorKorean (Yes|No) #REQUIRED
SGMLEditorJapanese (Yes|No) #REQUIRED
ActiveViews(Yes|No) #REQUIRED
SymposiaPro(Yes|No) #REQUIRED
SymposiaDocPlus (Yes|No) #REQUIRED
XMLProducts(Yes|No) #REQUIRED
General(Yes|No) #REQUIRED>
<!Element Contacts (Language, History)>
<!Element Honorific (#PCDATA)>
<!AttList Honorific
Title (Mr|Ms|Mrs|Miss|Dr|Professor|M|Mme|Mlle|SeeContent) "SeeContent">
<!Element First(#PCDATA)>
<!Element Middle(#PCDATA)>
<!Element Last(#PCDATA)>
<!Element JobTitle (#PCDATA)>
<!Element CompanyName (#PCDATA)>
<!Element Street(#PCDATA)>
<!Element City(#PCDATA)>
<!Element Region(#PCDATA)>
<!Element PostCode (#PCDATA)>
<!Element Country(#PCDATA)>
<!Element Phone(DayTime, Fax?)>
<!Element Internet (Email, Web)>
<!Element Language EMPTY>
<!AttList Language
Preference (English|French) "English">
<!Element History(Events+)>
<!Element DayTime(#PCDATA)>
<!Element Fax(#PCDATA)>
<!Element Email(#PCDATA)>
<!Element Web(#PCDATA)>
<!Element Events(Date, Venue, Notes)>
<!Element Date(Day, Month, Year)>
<!Element Venue(#PCDATA)>
<!Element Notes(#PCDATA)>
<!Element Day(#PCDATA)>
<!Element Month(#PCDATA)>
<!Element Year(#PCDATA)>
]>
```

A form-based interface provides many user-friendly features that make data-entry easier for the user, such as the ability to select from a predetermined list of options, or the possibility to select or unselect different options, as appropriate.

To provide an equivalent level of "comfort," we need to provide a predefined document template in which the user need only fill in the required data. Using the DTD as our guide, we can produce a document instance that contains all required document elements. Without a style sheet, however, this template is not of great value. The editor will simply display the document as a list of tags. Users need to know what information to insert where without displaying these tags—the only way we can accomplish this is by using our style sheet.

With the HTML form, it was possible to simply label each input zone with some text. Unfortunately, the CSS standard does not provide a means of displaying predefined text before or after an element. This style sheet feature was left out of CSS1 because of the inherent difficulty of implementing this feature in today's Web browsers (which, of course, by the time you read these words, will already be yesterday's Web browsers). Structure based editor/browsers such as

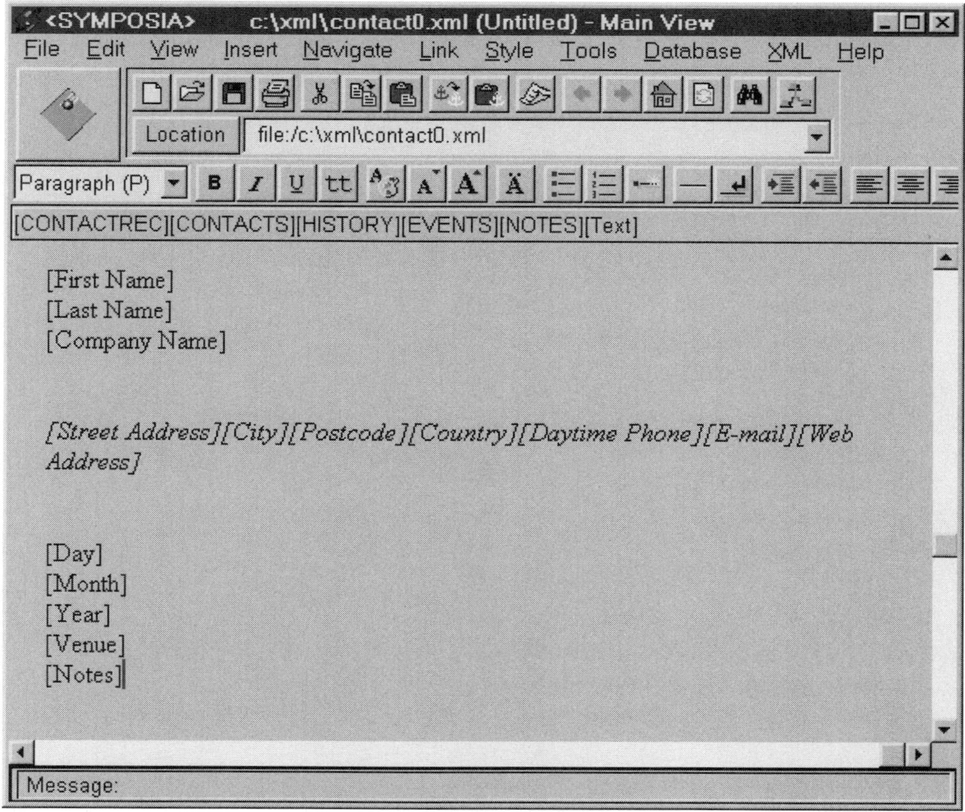

Figure 4

Symposia, or indeed the thoroughbred XML structured editors to come, would have no problem implementing this type of feature, if it were included in the CSS standard.

The only viable solution for the moment seems to be to provide default text content for each data field that is then replaced by the user as he/she enters the information in the page (see Figure 4).

This layout is still not very satisfactory, however. Figure 5 improves the layout of the page using our style sheet to highlight certain elements and group related items together.

While we can achieve quite a pleasing presentation for our data entry screen using the style sheet. However there are two elements in the DTD which we cannot display in this same way: `Product` and `Language`. These two elements are empty and have no text content.

- The `Product` element takes a number of optional attributes to indicate the contact's interest in the company's different products (the value of each attribute is "Yes" or "No," accordingly.
- The `Language` element takes the `Preference` attribute, which can take the values "English" or "French," and for which the default value is "English"—indicating that any communication with or documentation sent to the contact should be in English.

One way around this problem, although not very elegant, would be to specify a background image for each element using the following style rule:

```
Product {background-image:image.gif}
```

Using our authoring tool, we would then be able to select the element by clicking on the image and pull up a list of the element's attributes for modification, as shown in Figure 6.

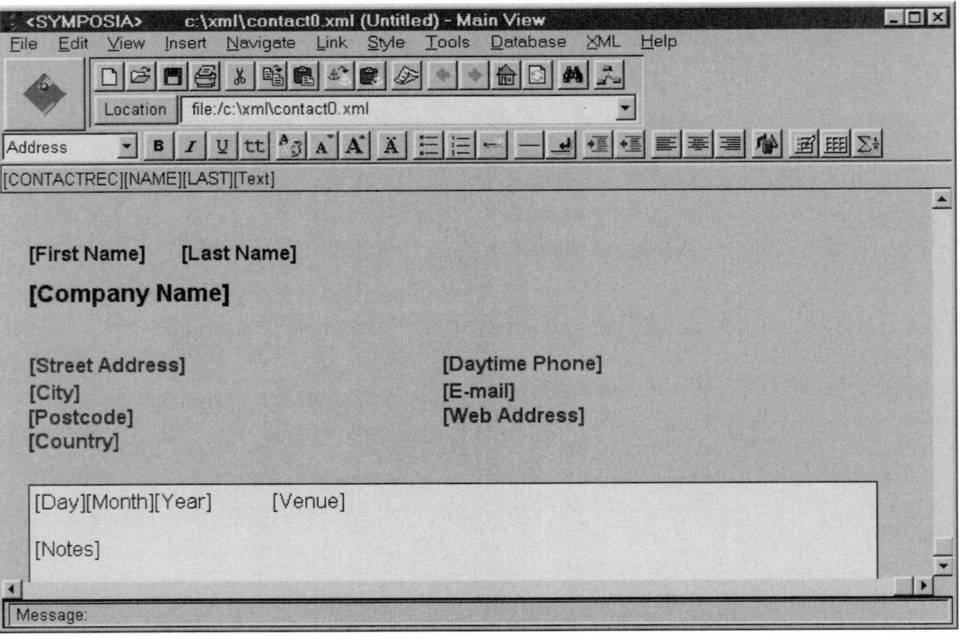

Figure 5

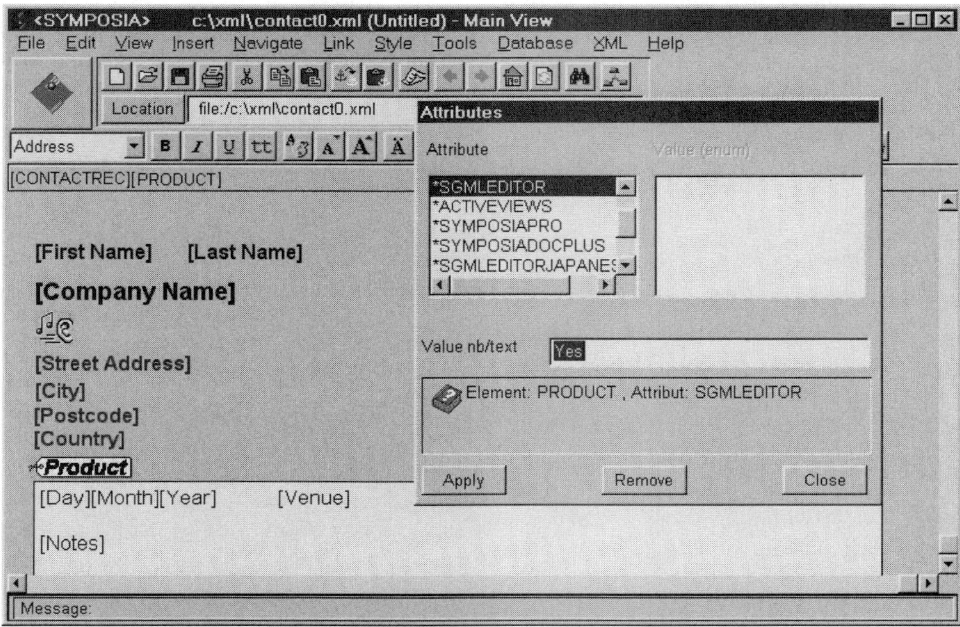

Figure 6

Of course, we are still left with the following problem: using CSS, it is not possible to display the attribute names or values for an element in the document itself. In our example, it would have been nice to be able to pull up the list of attributes for the `Product` element, supply a value for each attribute, then see these changes appear in the document (display some text or an image to indicate which products the contact was interested in, for example). Neither does CSS provide the possibility to apply conditional style rules based on an element's attribute values (one might imagine a different image to be displayed for "Yes" or for "No" values).

Despite the limitations of CSS described here we have found that the language comes close to meeting our needs. This, combined with the fact that CSS is already implemented for HTML in the major Web browsers—and our sense that the simplicity of CSS will appeal to Web designers over more complex (albeit powerful) approaches—leads us to believe that CSS will be the dominant mechanism for displaying XML documents on the Web. ■

About the Authors

Stuart Culshaw
Technical Communication Manager
Grif S.A.,
BP 266,
78053 St Quentin en Yvelines Cedex,
FRANCE
Stuart.Culshaw@grif.fr

Stuart Culshaw is Technical Communication Manager at Grif S.A., a leading SGML and XML software development company. He manages the production of both printed and Web-based documentation for Grif's products and is charged with investigating and evaluating emerging Web technologies and standards.

Born in Morecambe, England in 1970, Stuart joined Grif in 1993 after completing a Bachelor's degree course in European Business Studies. He also holds a Certificate in Technical Writing from the American University of Paris.

Michael Leventhal
Grif, S.A.
Vice-President, Technology
1800 Lake Shore Avenue
Suite 14
Oakland, California 94606
Michael.Leventhal@grif.fr

Michael Leventhal is Vice-President, Technology for GRIF and is responsible for the definition and planning of GRIF's XML products. Before joining GRIF he ran his own consulting company and has worked for Oracle and other Silicon Valley firms in software architecture and development. He has taught an SGML class for U.C. Berkeley Extension and is writing a book on XML and Intranets which will be published by Prentice-Hall next year.

Murray Maloney
Technical Marketing Director
Grif S.A.
671 Cowan Circle
Pickering, Ontario
Canada L1W 3K6
murry@grif.fr

Murray Maloney represents GRIF S.A. as their Technical Marketing Director. A leader in the development of Web standards since 1993, Murray is a founding member of the HTML, XML and CSS working groups, and participates in numerous others. He was previously a technical director with SoftQuad and publishing systems architect and manager with the Santa Cruz Operation (SCO). Murray is a technical advisor to the Yuri Rubinsky Insight Foundation, co-chair of the 8th International World Wide Web Conference to be held in Toronto in 1999. He produced the index to Charles F. Goldfarb's *SGML Handbook* and is co-author, with Yuri Rubinsky, of the recent *SGML on the Web: Small Steps Beyond HTML*.

The Evolution of Web Documents

The Ascent of XML

Dan Connolly, Rohit Khare, Adam Rifkin

Abstract

HTML is the ubiquitous data format for Web pages; most information providers are not even aware that there are other options. But now, with the development of XML, that is about to change. Not only will the choices of data formats become more apparent, but they will become more attractive as well. Although XML succeeds HTML in time, its design is based on SGML, which predates HTML and the Web altogether. SGML was designed to give information managers more flexibility to say what they mean, and XML brings that principle to the Web. Because it allows the development of custom tagsets, we can think of XML as HTML without the "training wheels." In this article, we trace the history and evolution of Web data formats, culminating in XML. We evaluate the relationship of XML, HTML, and SGML, and discuss the impact of XML on the evolution of the Web.

1. World Wide Markup Language

> *The hypertext markup language is an SGML format.*
>
> —Tim Berners-Lee, 1991, in "About HTML"

The idea that structured documents could be exchanged and manipulated if published in a standard, open format dates back to multiple efforts in the 1960s. In one endeavor, a committee of the Graphic Communications Association (GCA) created GenCode to develop generic typesetting codes for clients who used multiple vendors to typeset a variety of data. GenCode allowed them to maintain an integrated set of archives despite the fact that records were set in multiple types.

In another effort, IBM developed the Generalized Markup Language (GML) for its big internal publishing problems from manuals and press releases to legal contracts and project specifications. GML was designed so the same source files could be processed to produce books, reports, and electronic editions.

GML had a "simple" input syntax for typists, including the <> and </> tags we recognize today. Of course, GML also permitted lots of "cheating." Markup minimization allowed typists to elide obvious tags. Though these documents were easy for humans to type and read, they were not well suited for general purpose processing (that is, for computer applications). In fact, because very few document types were required at the time, people wrote special compilers, bound to each particular kind of document, to handle inputting appropriate data formats.

As more document types emerged—each requiring specially suited tagsets—so too did the need for a standard way to publish and manipulate each *Document Type Definition* (DTD). In the early 1980s, representatives of the GenCode and GML communities joined to form the American National Standards Institute (ANSI) committee on Computer Languages for the Processing of Text; their goal was to standardize ways to specify, define, and use markup in documents.

SGML, the Standardized Generalized Markup Language, was published as ISO 8879 in 1986 [17]. Developed for defining and using portable document formats, it was designed to be formal enough to allow proofs of document validity, structured enough to handle complex documents, and extensible enough to support management of large information repositories. While SGML might seem a victim of "design by committee" to the casual observer, it was successful in furnishing an interchange language that could be used to manipulate and exchange text documents.

By the late 1980s, SGML had caught on in organizations such as CERN,* where in a laboratory in Switzerland, a holiday hacker borrowed the funny-looking idiom for his then-new hypertext application. Indeed, Tim Berners-Lee, inventor of the World Wide Web, picked an assortment of markup tags from a sample SGML DTD used at CERN. In NeXUS, the original Web browser and editor, he used tags, style sheets for typesetting, and one more "killer feature": links.

By the time Mosaic took off in 1993, people were stretching the limits of HTML—using it as a hammer to bang nails everywhere. But HTML is not a hammer—even HTML 4.0, released in July 1997 [22], furnishes only a limited tagset—and no single tagset will suffice for all of the kinds of information on the Web.

Starting in 1992, HTML evolved from a somewhat ad-hoc syntax to a conforming SGML application. This did not happen for free, and it involved some rather ugly compromises. However, it was clearly worth the effort. It not only gives the specifications a solid foundation, the intent was that Web tools would implement HTML as a special case of generic SGML and stylesheet support. That way, changes to HTML could be dynamically propagated into the tools by just updating the DTD and stylesheets. This proved to be an idea before its time: the engineering cost was significant and the information providers did not have the necessary experience to take advantage of the extra degrees of freedom.

In 1992, the Web was not ready for a powerful, generic markup language: in its nascent stage, the Web needed one small tagset—suitable for most of its intended documents and simple enough for the authoring community to understand. That small tagset is HTML.

Basing HTML on SGML was the first step in bringing the SGML community to the World Wide Web: at that point, forward-looking companies began to shift their agendas to unite SGML with the Web [24]. Using SGML on the Web is risky. Because SGML has lots of optional features, the sender and receiver have to agree on some set of options. The engineering costs are compounded because the SGML specification does not follow accepted computer-science conventions for the description of languages [18]. For implementers, the specification is hard to read and contains many costly special cases.

The stage is set for XML, the Extensible Markup Language [10], which addresses the engineering complexity of SGML and the limitations of the fixed tag set in HTML.

2. Community-Wide Markup Languages

> *"When I use a word," Humpty Dumpty said, in a rather scornful tone, "it means just what I choose it to mean—neither more nor less."*
>
> —Lewis Carroll,
> *Through the Looking Glass*

For any document to communicate successfully from author to readers, all parties concerned must agree that words *all* choose them to mean. Semantics can only be interpreted within the context of a community. For example, millions of HTML users worldwide agree that `<B>` means bold text, or that `<H1>` is a prominent top-level document heading. The same cannot be said, though, for the date `8-7-97`, which reflects local culture. Or for `<font FACE=Arial>`, which is only usable by Microsoft Windows systems. The larger the community, the weaker the shared

* European Laboratory for Particle Physics.

context; the smaller and more focused the community, the stronger the shared context becomes.

HTML is currently the only common tagset Web users can rely upon. Furthermore, HTML cannot be extended unilaterally, since the shared definition is maintained by a central standardization process that publishes new editions like 2.0, 3.2, and 4.0. Since semantics depend on shared agreements between readers and writers about the state of the world, there is a place for community-specific definitions. XML makes *ontologies* as Document Type Definitions, to decentralize the control of specialized markup languages. The emergence of richly annotated data structures catalyzes new applications for storing, sharing, and processing ideas.

2.1 Semantic Markup

Descriptive markup indicates the role or meaning of some part of a document. While `<H1>` is a generic expression of importance, `<WARNING TYPE=Fire_hazard>` is a much more specific expression. Calling the former "structure" and the latter "semantics" is indeed a matter of semantics, but it seems clear that the more specific the markup, the more meaningful the document and the less potential for confusion.

An ontology codifies the concepts that are noteworthy to a community so that everyone has a common level of understanding upon which future knowledge exchange can proceed. The reverse phenomenon is equally powerful: mastery of the jargon confers membership in the community. In this sense, community recapitulates ontology—but the tools to express private agreements have been late in coming. Communities are mirrored by ontology: when a large community has to use a single ontology, its value is diluted to the least common denominator (as exemplified by HTML itself).

When communities collide, ontological misunderstandings can develop for several reasons. Sometimes it is a matter of context, like the legal interpretation of "profit" according to national accounting and tax rules. Sometimes it is a matter of perception, like "offensive language" in a Platform for Internet Content Selection (PICS) content-rating [23]. Sometimes it is a matter of alternative jargon: "10BaseT cable" to a programmer is "Category 5 twisted pair" to a lineman. Sometimes it is a matter of intentional conflation, like Hollywood "profit," which refers to both the pile of cash in the studio account and the losses recorded in an actor's residuals.

The best remedy is to codify private ontologies that serve to identify the active context of any document. This is the ideal role for a well-tempered DTD. Consider two newspapers with specific in-house styles for bylines, captions, company names, and so on. Where they share stories on a wire service, for example, they can identify it as their story, or convert it according to an industry-wide stylebook. As competing DTDs are shared among the community, semantics are clarified by acclamation [15]. Furthermore, as DTDs themselves are woven into the Web, they can be discovered dynamically, further accelerating the evolution of community ontologies.

2.2 Generating New Markup Languages

> *XML was designed to provide an easy-to-write, easy-to-interpret, and easy-to-implement subset of SGML. It was not designed to provide a "one Markup Language fits all" DTD, or a separate DTD for every tag. It was designed so that certain groups could create their own particular markup languages that meet their needs more quickly, efficiently, and (IMO) logically. It was designed to put an end once and for all to the tag-soup wars propagated by Microsoft and Netscape.*
>
> —Jim Cape, in a post to *comp.infosystems.www.authoring.html* on June 3, 1997

As the Web evolved, people and companies indeed found themselves extending the HTML tagset to perform special tasks. A rich marketplace of server-side-includes and macro-preprocessing extensions to HTML demonstrates that users understand the benefit of using local markup conventions to automate their in-house information management practices. And the cost of "dumbing down" to HTML is becoming more apparent as more organizations go beyond information dissemination to information exchange.

The fundamental problem is that HTML is not unilaterally extensible. A new tag potentially has ambiguous grammar (is it an element or does it need an end-tag?), ambiguous semantics (no metadata about the ontology it is based on), and ambiguous presentation (especially without stylesheet hooks). Instead, investing in SGML offers three critical features:

Extensibility
: Authors can define new elements, containers, and attribute names at will.

Structure
: A DTD can constrain the information model of a document. For example, a Chapter might require a Title element, an Author list, and one or more Paragraphs.

Validation
: Every document can be validated. Furthermore, *well-formedness* can establish conformance to the structure mandated by the DTD.

XML is a simplified (but strict) subset of SGML that maintains the SGML features for extensibility, structure, and validation. XML is a standardized text format designed specifically for transmitting structured data to Web applications. Since XML aims to be easier to learn, use, and implement than full SGML, it will have clear benefits for World Wide Web users. XML makes it easier to define and validate document types, to author and manage SGML-compliant documents, and to transmit and share them across the Web. Its specification is less than a tenth of the size of SGML86's. XML is, in short, a worthy successor in the evolutionary sense.

The "well-formed" versus "valid" distinction is an important one. Since one can always extract and reflect the document structure from the document itself without its DTD, DTD-less documents are already self-describing containers. A DTD simply provides a tool for deciding whether the structure implicit in the body of the document matches the explicit structure (known in the vernacular as "validity"). This phenomenon is very isomorphic to the interface/implementation separation in components; in the XML model, the DTD is the interface and the body is the implementation. We discuss the implications of XML Section 3.1.

The working draft for XML 1.0 provides a complete specification in several parts: the extensible markup language itself [7], methods for associating hypertext linking [8], and forthcoming stylesheet mechanisms for use with XML. From the XML specification, we observe that expressive power, teachability, and ease of implementation were all major design considerations. And although XML is not backward-compatible with existing HTML documents, we note that documents that are HTML 4.0-compliant can easily be converted to XML.

In addition to modifying the syntax and semantics of document tag annotations, XML also changes our linking model by allowing authors to specify different types of document relationships: new linking technology allows the management of bidirectional and multiway links, as well as links to a span of text (within the same or other documents), as a supplement to the single point linking afforded by HTML's existing HREF-style anchors.

2.3 Leveraging Community-Wide Markup

Accepting that community-specific DTDs can represent an ontology and that XML makes it cost-effective to deploy them, the potential of XML-formatted data will catalyze new applications for capturing, distributing, and processing knowledge [19].

Two communities using XML to capture field-specific knowledge have already chalked up early victories: the Chemical Markup Language (CML) [21] and the Mathematical Markup Language (MathML) [16]. Storing and distributing information in XML databases in conjunction with Extensible Linking Language (XLL) can ease data import and data export problems, facilitate aggregation from multiple sources (data warehousing), and enable interactive access to large corpuses.

Web Automation promises the most dramatic leverage, though. Tools like webMethods' Web Interface Definition Language [2] bridge this gap between legacy Web data and structured XML data. WIDL encourages the extraction of information from unstructured data (such as HTML tables and forms) to produce more structured, meaningful XML reports; furthermore, employing WIDL one can synthesize information already stored as structured data into new reports using custom programming, linking, and automated information extrapolation. Manipulating XML-formatted data leverages a cleaner, more rigorous object model for accessing entities within a document, when compared with the Document Object Model's references to windows, frames, history lists, and formats [6].

3. On the Coevolution of HTML and XML

> *We will now discuss in a little more detail the Struggle for Existence.*
>
> —Charles Darwin, *The Origin of the Species*

Now that we have compared the values of HTML for global markup needs and XML for community-specific markup, let's see how all this pans out in practice. How will HTML adapt to the presence of of XML?

It will not be an either-or choice between HTML and XML; you do not have to plan for a Flag Day when your shop stops using HTML and starts using XML. Instead, as HTML tools evolved to support the whole range of XML, your choices will expand with them. Just as the value to information providers is becoming evident, the cost of generic markup is going down because XML is considerably simpler than SGML. In addition, the complimentary piece of infrastructure, stylesheets, is finally being deployed.

If a browser (or editor or other tool) supports stylesheets [12], support for individual tags does not have to be hardcoded. If you decide to add `<part-number>` tags to your documents and specify in a stylesheet that part-numbers should display in bold, a browser with stylesheet support can follow those directions. But, while it's clear how to add a `<part-number>` tag to XML, what about HTML?

3.1 Platforms and Borders: Well-Formed HTML

HTML is built on the platform of SGML. The borders of SGML were originally set by the IETF in 1995, subsequently expanded by W3C in 1996, with HTML 3.2, and again in 1997 with HTML 4.0. But so far, the borders of HTML fit within the borders of SGML.

However, only part of the ground inside the SGML borders is fertile—the XML part. The rest is too expensive to maintain. Although some of HTML is sitting on that infertile ground, it should be a simple task to move a document from that crufty ground to the arable XML territory using the following rules:

1. Match every start-tag with an end-tag.
2. Replace > by /> at the end of empty tags.
3. Quote all your attribute values.
4. Use only lowercase for tag names and attribute names.

By the same token, it should be a simple task to move the HTML specification onto the XML platform. Let's look at those steps a bit more closely.

Consider the following:

```
<p> Some Text <my-markup> More Text.
```

Is `More Text` inside the `my-markup` element or not? The SGML answer is: you have to look in the DTD to see whether `my-markup` is an empty element, or whether it can have content. The XML answer is: don't do that. Make it explicit, one way or another:

```
<p> Some Text <my-empty-thing/>
   More Text.</p>
<p> Some Text <my-container> More
   Text. </my-container> </p>
```

Hence, rule one: match every start-tag with an end-tag. That's right, every `p`, `li`, `dd`, `dt`, `tr`, and `td` start-tag needs a matching end-tag. If you are still using a text editor to write HTML, you can take this as a hint to start looking at direct manipulation authoring tools, or at least text editors with syntax support for this sort of thing.

Rule two says that `br`, `hr`, and `img` elements turn into:

```
<p> a line break: <br />, a
   horizontal rule: <hr />,
and an image: <img src="foo"/> </p>
```

Rule three takes the guesswork out of attribute value syntax. In HTML, quotation is required only in some cases, but it is always allowed. In XML, it is simply required.

Rules one through three only predict the evolution of the specifications, and rule four is especially uncertain. It may turn out that "use only lowercase" is changed to "use only uppercase"—it depends on how HTML adapts to the rules about case sensitivity in XML. XML tag names and attribute names can use characters from a variety of Unicode characters, and matching uppercase and lowercase versions of these characters is not as simple as it is in ASCII. As of this writing, the Working Group has decided to punt on the issue, so that names compare by exact match only.

3.2 Licensed to Tag

According to the official rules, extending HTML is the exclusive privilege of the central authorities. But everybody's doing it in various underground ways: they use `<!--comment conventions-->`, preprocessing extensions with `<if>` `<then>` `<else>` tags, and so on. Even Robin Cover, maintainer of the most comprehensive SGML bibliography on the Web, admits in [11]:

> *An experimental approach is being used in markup—exploiting the behavior of HTML browsers whereby unrecognized tags are simply ignored. If the non-HTML tags are causing problems in your browser, please let me know.*

Once HTML and XML align, there will be legitimate alternatives to all these underground practices. You can add your `<part-number>` and `<abstract>` tags with confidence, knowing that your markup will be supported.

In fact, you have two choices regarding the level of confidence: you can make well-formed documents just by making sure your tags are balanced, there are no missing quotes, etc. A lot of tools check only at this level.

On the other hand, you want that sort of support from your tools, you will have to keep your documents *valid*: you will have to remember to put a `<title>` in every document, an `alt` attribute on every `<img>` element, and so on. In that case, adding tags to a document also requires creating a modified DTD.

For example, you might write:

```
<?XML version="1.0"?>
<!doctype report system "html-
   report.dtd">
<report><title>My Document</title>
<abstract><p>...</p></abstract>
<section><h1>Introduction</h1>
...
</section>
```

where `report-html.dtd` contains:

```
<!entity % html4 system
   "http://www.w3.org/TR/WD-html40-
   970917/sgml/HTML4-strict.dtd">
%html4;
<!element report (title, abstract,
   section*)>
<!element abstract (p*)>
<!element section (h1, (%block;)*)>
```

Then you can validate that the document is not just any old HTML document, but it has a specific technical report structure for consistency with the other technical reports at your site. And you can use stylesheet-based typesetting tools to create professional looking PostScript or Portable Document Format (PDF) renditions.

3.3 Mix and Match, Cut and Paste

Not everyone who wants something different from standard HTML has to write his or her own DTD. Perhaps, in the best of Internet and Web tradition, you can leverage someone else's work. Perhaps you would like to mix elements of HTML with elements of DocBook [3] or a Dublin Core [9] DTD.

Unfortunately, achieving this mixture with DTDs is very awkward. Yet the ability to combine independently developed resources is an essential survival property of technology in a distributed information system. The ability to combine filters and pipes and scripts has kept UNIX alive and kicking long past its expected demise. In his keynote address at Seybold San Francisco [5], Tim Berners-Lee called this powerful notion *"intercreativity."*

Combining DTDs that were developed independently exposes limitations in the design of SGML for things like namespaces, subclassing, and modularity and reuse in general.

There is a great tension between the need for intercreativity and these limitations in SGML DTDs. One strategy under discussion is to introduce qualified names a la Modula, C++, or Java into XML. For example, you might want to enrich your home page by the use of an established set of business card element types. This strategy suggests markup like this:

```
<xml::namespace href="http://bcard.
   org/9801"
   as="bcard" />
<html> <head><title>Dan s Home Page
   and Business Card</title>
   </head>
 <body>
  <bcard::card>
   <h1><bcard::name>Dan Connolly
       </bcard::name><br>
    <bcard::title>Grand
      Poobah</bcard:title></h1>
   <p>Phone: <bcard::phone>555-
      1212</bcard::phone></p>
  </bcard::card>
  <p>...</p>
</body>
</html>
```

This markup is perfectly well-formed, but the strategy does not address DTD validation. Another strategy for mixing and matching elements is to use SGML Architectures [20]. Or perhaps a more radical course of research is needed to rethink the connection between tag names, element names, and element types [4].

3.4 The Future Standardization of XML

> *The language designer should be familiar with many alternative features designed by others, and should have excellent judgment in choosing the best and rejecting any that are mutually inconsistent . . . One thing he should not do is to include untried ideas of his own. His task is consolidation, not innovation.*
>
> —C.A.R. Hoare

If it seems that XML is moving very fast, look again. The community is moving very fast to exploit XML, but the momentum against changes to XML itself is tremendous. XML is not a collection of new ideas; it is a selection of tried-and-true ideas. These ideas are implemented in a host of conforming SGML systems, and employed in truly massive SGML document repositories.

Changes to a technology with this many dependencies are evaluated with utmost care.

XML is essentially just SGML with many of the obscure features thrown out (Appendix A of the specification lists SUBDOC, RANK, and quite a few others). The result is much easier to describe, understand, and implement, despite the fact that every document that conforms to the XML specification also conforms to the SGML specification.

Almost.

In a few cases, the design of SGML has rules that would be difficult to explain in the XML specification. And they prohibit idioms that are quite useful, such as multiple `<!ATTLIST ...>` declarations for the same element type. In these cases, the XML designers have participated in the ongoing ISO revision of SGML. The result is the Web-SGML Technical Corrigendum [14]—a sort of "patch" to the SGML standard.

Every document that conforms to the XML specification does indeed conform to SGML-as-corrected, and the W3C XML Working Group and the ISO Working Group have agreed to keep that constraint in place.

So the wiggle-room in the XML specification is actually quite small. The W3C XML Working Group is considering a few remaining issues, and they release drafts for public review every month or so. The next step in the W3C process, after the Working Group has addressed all the issues they can find, is for the W3C Director to issue the specification as a Proposed Recommendation and call for votes from the W3C membership. Based on the outcome of the votes, the Director will then decide whether the document should become a W3C Recommendation, go back to the Working Group for further review, or be canceled altogether.

Outside the core XML specification, there is much more working room. The XLL specification [8] is maturing, but there are still quite a few outstanding issues. And, work on the eXtensible Stylesheet Language (XSL) is just beginning.

4. The Ascent of XML in the Evolution of Knowledge from Information

Node content must be left free to evolve.

—Tim Berners-Lee, 1991, in "About Document Formats," *http://www.w3.org/DesignIssues/Formats.html*

The World Wide Web Consortium, the driving force behind XML, sees its mission as leading the *evolution* of the Web. In the competitive market of Internet technologies, it is instructive to consider how the Web trounced competing species of protocols. Though it shared several adaptations common to Internet protocols, such as "free software spreads faster," "ASCII systems spread faster than binary ones," and "bad protocols imitate; great protocols steal," it leveraged one unique strategy: *self-description.* The Web can be built upon itself. Universal Resource Identifiers (URIs), machine-readable data formats, and machine-readable specifications can be knit together into an extensible system that assimilates any competitors. In essence, the emergence of XML on the spectrum of Web data formats caps the struggle toward realizing the original vision of the Web by its creators.

The designers of the Web knew that it must adapt to new data formats, so they appropriated the MIME Content Type system. On the other hand, some types were more equal than others: the Web prefers HTML over PDF, Microsoft Word, and myriad others, because of a general trend over the last seven years of Web history from stylistic formatting to structural markup to semantic markup. Each step up in the Ascent of Formats adds momentum to Web applications, from PostScript (opaque, operational, formatting); to *troff* (readable, operational, formatting); to Rich Text Format (RTF) (readable, extensible, formatting); to HTML (readable, declarative, limited descriptive semantics like `<ADDRESS>`); now to XML; and on to intelligent metadata formats such as PICS labels.

The Web itself is becoming a kind of cyborg intelligence: human and machine, harnessed together to generate and manipulate information. If automatability is to be a human right, then machine assistance must eliminate the drudge work involved in exchanging and manipulating knowledge, as indicated by MIT Laboratory for Computer Science Director Michael Dertouzos [13]. As Douglas Adams described [1], the shift from strucutral HTML markup to semantic XML markup is a critical phase in the struggle to *information* space into a universal *knowledge* network. ■

Acknowledgments

This paper is based on our experiences over several years' experience working with the Web community. Particular plaudits go to our colleagues at the World Wide Web Consortium, including Tim Berners-Lee; the teams at MCI Internet Architecture and Caltech Infospheres; and the group at webMethods, especially Charles Allen.

References

1. Adams, Douglas. *The Hitchhiker's Guide to the Galaxy*, Ballantine Books, 1979.
2. Allen, Charles. "Automating the Web with WIDL," *World Wide Web Journal* 2: 4, Autumn 1997. Available at *http://www.webmethods.com/technology/widl.html*
3. Allen, Terry, and Eve Maler. *DocBook Version 3.0 Maintainer's Guide*, O'Reilly and Associates, 1997. Available at *http://www.oreilly.com/davenport/*
4. Akpotsui, E., V. Quint, and C. Roisin. "Type Modelling for Document Transformation in Structured Editing Systems," *Mathematical and Computer Modelling* 25: 4, 1997, pp. 1–19.
5. Berners-Lee, Tim. Keynote Address, Seybold San Francisco, February 1996. Available at *http://www.w3.org/Talks/9602seybold/slide6.htm*
6. Bosak, Jon. "XML, Java, and the Future of the Web," 1997. Available at *http://sunsite.unc.edu/pub/sun-info/standards/xml/why/xmlapps.htm*
7. Bray, Tim, Jean Paoli, and C.M. Sperberg-McQueen. "Extensible Markup Language (XML): Part I Syntax," World Wide Web Consortium Working Draft (Work in Progress), August 1997. Available at *http://www.w3.org/TR/WD-xml-lang.html*
8. Bray, Tim, and Steve DeRose. "Extensible Markup Language (XML): Part II. Linking," World Wide Web Consortium Working Draft (Work in Progress), July 1997. Available at *http://www.w3.org/TR/WD-xml-link.html*
9. Burnard, Lou, Eric Miller, Liam Quin, and C.M. Sperberg-McQueen. "A Syntax for Dublin Core Metadata: Recommendations from the Second Metadata Workshop," 1996. Available at *http://www.uic.edu/~cmsmcq/tech/metadata.syntax.html*
10. Connolly, Dan, and Jon Bosak. "Extensible Markup Language (XML)," W3C Activity Group page, 1997. Available at *http://www.w3.org/XML/*
11. Cover, Robin. "SGML Page: Caveats, Work in Progress," 1997. Available at *http://www.sil.org/sgml/caveats.html*
12. Culshaw, Stuart, Michael Leventhal, and Murray Maloney. "XML and CSS," *World Wide Web Journal*, 2: 4, Autumn 1997. Available at *http://shoal.w3.org/w3j-xml/cssxml/grifcss.htm*
13. Dertouzos, Michael. *What Will Be*, HarperEdge, 1997.
14. Goldfarb, Charles F. Proposed TC for WebSGML Adaptations for SGML, ISO/IEC JTC1/SC18/WG8, WG8 Approved Text, September 1997. Available at *http://www.sgmlsource.com/8879rev/n1929.htm*
15. Hale, Constance. "Wired Style: Principles of English Usage in the Digital Age," Hardwired Publishing, June 1997.
16. Ion, Patrick, and Robert Miner. "Mathematical Markup Language," W3C Working Draft, May 1997. *http://www.w3.org/pub/WWW/TR/WD-math*
17. ISO 8879:1986. ISO 8879, Information Processing—Text and Office Systems—Standard Generalized Markup Language (SGML), 1986.
18. Kaelbling, Michael J. "On Improving SGML," *Electronic Publishing: Origination, Dissemination and Design (EPODD)* 3: 2, May 1990, pp. 93–98.
19. Khare, Rohit, and Adam Rifkin. "XML: A Door to Automated Web Applications," in *IEEE Internet Computing* 1: 4, July/August 1997, pp. 78–87. Available at *http://www.cs.caltech.edu/~adam/papers/xml/x-marks-the-spot.html*
20. Kimber, W. Eliot, and ISOGEN International Corp. "An Approach to Literate Programming With SGML Architectures," July 1997. Available at *http://*

www.isogen.com/papers/litprogarch/litprogarch.html

21. Murray-Rust, Peter. "Chemical Markup Language (CML)," Version 1.0, January 1997. Available at *http://www.venus.co.uk/omf/cml/*
22. Raggett, Dave, Arnaud Le Hors, and Ian Jacobs. "HTML 4.0 Specification," World Wide Web Consortium Working Draft (Work in Progress), September 1997. Available at *http://www.w3.org/TR/WD-html40/*
23. Resnick, Paul, and Jim Miller. "PICS: Internet Access Controls without Censorship," *Communications of the ACM*, Volume 39, 1996, pp. 87–93. Available at *http://www.w3.org/pub/WWW/PICS/iacwcv2.htm*
24. Rubinsky, Yuri, and Murray Maloney. "SGML and the Web: Small Steps Beyond HTML," Charles F. Goldfarb series on Open Information Management, Prentice Hall, 1997.

About the Authors

Dan Connolly
connolly@w3.org

Dan Connolly is the leader of the W3C Architecture Domain. His work on formal systems, computational linguistics, and the development of open, distributed hypermedia systems began at the University of Texas at Austin, where recieved a B.S. in Computer Science in 1990. While developing hypertext production and delivery software in 1992, he began contributing to the World Wide Web project, and in particular, the HTML specification. He presented a draft at the First International World Wide Web Conference in 1994 in Geneva, and edited the draft until it was published as the HTML 2.0 specification, Internet RFC1866, in November 1995. Today he is the chair of the W3C HTML Working Group and a member of the W3C XML Working Group. His research interest is the on the value of formal descriptions of chaotic systems like the Web, especially in the consensus-building process.

Rohit Khare
khare@alumni.caltech.edu

Rohit Khare is a member of the MCI Internet Architecture staff in Boston, MA. He was previously on the technical staff of the World Wide Web Consortium at MIT, where he focused on security and electronic commerce issues. He has been involved in the development of cryptographic software tools and Web-related standards development. Rohit received a B.S. in Engineering and Applied Science and in Economics from California Institute of Technology in 1995. He will enter the Ph.D. program in Computer Science at the University of California, Irvine in Fall 1997.

Adam Rifkin
adam@cs.caltech.edu

Adam Rifkin received his B.S. and M.S. in Computer Science from the College of William and Mary. He is presently pursuing a Ph.D. in computer science at the California Institute of Technology, where he works with the Caltech Infospheres Project on the composition of distributed active objects. His efforts with Infospheres have won best paper awards both at the Fifth IEEE International Symposium on High Performance Distributed Computing in August 1996, and at the Thirtieth Hawaii International Conference on System Sciences in January 1997. He has done Internet consulting and performed research with several organizations, including Canon, Hewlett-Packard, Reprise Records, Griffiss Air Force Base, and the NASA-Langley Research Center.

Embedded Markup Considered Harmful

Theodor Holm Nelson

A new religion, a first-generation religion, starts with a fundamental idea and expands it to fill the universe with visions of Beginnings and Ends—right and wrong, righteousness and sin, good and evil, Hell and Heaven.* It may have strict standards to make sure individuals demonstrate reverent compliance.

A second-generation religion shifts emphasis, because people's concerns have changed—perhaps with new lands to conquer, less worry about sin. The priests adjust the previous fundamental idea to grapple with the new situation. But in this second generation, priests must also show fidelity to the terminology of the earlier generation, framing their new concerns amongst the old ideas wherever possible. Everyone is stuck with the concepts already elucidated.

SGML is a first-generation religion. Its founding idea was to represent nameless fonts and abstracted text blocks at one remove from complete specification, so that the fonts and text blocks could be reformatted by changing a short list of definitions.

This idea was then expanded to fill the universe, becoming a technique for the sequential, hierarchical representation of any data, with embedded tags representing Beginnings and Ends. Great emphasis was put on formal correctness, defining a strict standard for compliance. Originally intended to create order in type-font selection, SGML has been extended and extended to fill the universe, becoming a reference language of sequential attributes and now hypertext links and graphics (HTML). Its believers think SGML can represent anything at all—at least, anything they approve of.

But now we see a change. The second generation of the SGML faith is the HTML religion, whose intention and outlook are entirely different, but which preaches in the robes of the old. A new land has been conquered—the Web. There is great prosperity, as in the time of Solomon, so that sin—formal correctness—is not a worry.

Embedded Markup

I want to discuss what I consider one of the worst mistakes of the current software world, embedded markup; which is, regrettably, the heart of such current standards as SGML and HTML. (There are many other embedded markup systems; an interesting one is RTF. But I will concentrate on the SGML-HTML theology because of its claims and fervor.)

There is no one reason this approach is wrong; I believe it is wrong in almost every respect. But I must be honest and acknowledge my objection as a serious paradigm conflict, or (if you will) religious conflict. In paradigm conflict and religious conflict, there can be no hope of doctrinal victory; the best we can seek is for both sides to understand each other fully and cordially.

SGML's advocates expect, or wish to enforce, a universal linear representation of hierarchial structure.

I believe that if this is a factual claim of appropriateness, it is a delusion; if it is an enforcement, it is an intolerable imposition which drastically cur-

* These days, Heaven takes such forms as "posterity" and "widespread adoption."

tails the representation of non-hierarchical media structure.

I will turn to general problems of the embedded method. I have three extremely different objections to embedded markup. The first is simple; the second is complicated to explain; and the third challenges the claim of generality.

Objection 1: Editing

The SGML approach is a delivery format, not a working format. Editing is outside the paradigm, happens "elsewhere."

If material is to be edited, it generally must be frequently counted to perform the edit operations. *Tags throw off the counts.* This means that while text is being reworked, some *other* representation must be maintained, or complex tricks invoked to maintain counts.* This seems quite wrong.

Objection 2: Transpublishing a Potential Conflict

This topic will take some explaining.

Network electronic publishing offers a unique special-case solution to the copyright problem that has not been generally recognized. I call it *transpublishing*. Let me explain.

In paper publishing, there are two copyright realms: a fortified zone of copyrighted material, defended by its owners and requiring prior negotiation by publishers for quotation and re-use; and an unfortified zone, the open sea of public domain, where anything may be quoted freely—but whose materials tend to be outdated and less desirable for re-use.

Transpublishing makes possible a new realm between these two, where everything may be treated as boilerplate (as with public-domain material), but where publishers relinquish none of their rights and receive revenue exactly proportional to use.

Two different parties have legitimate concerns. Original rightsholders are concerned for their territory of copyrighted material, as defined by law, so that they may maintain and benefit from their hard-won assets. But the public (everybody else, as well as rightsholders in their time off) would like to re-use and republish these materials in different ways.

What if a system could exist which would satisfy all parties—copyright holders and those who would like to quote and republish? What if materials could be quoted without restriction, or size limit, by anyone, without red tape or negotiation—but all publishers would continue to furnish the downloaded copies, and would be exactly rewarded, being paid for each copy?

Transpublication is a unique arrangement—only possible online—which can achieve this win-win solution.†

Transpublishing Defined

Transpublishing means including materials virtually in online documents: the new document pulls material from the old, so the original publisher's system furnishes the quoted material to each user on each download. (So far this only

* Samuel Latt Epstein of Sensemedia, Inc. has pointed out (personal communication to the author) that he learned graphics programming on the Intecolor ISC-8001, ca. 1976, a machine that had a parallel data structure for its screen. 8K of memory was devoted to the text, 8K was devoted to the corresponding bytes of attribute memory. This "made it a snap" to program the screen, he says. The two parallel banks of memory could be manipulated independently, changing the colors without touching the text and vice versa, which greatly simplified (he says) programming both the text and the various graphical effects of those days.

† This has always been the publication model of Project Xanadu, described here in general enough terms to fit both the new and former Xanadu models. The current system is designed for dispersal and distributed processes on the Internet. The transpublishing system contemplated in the old Xanadu work, from 1960 to 1992 [1], planned a Compuserve-like service which (in today's terms) would have been a universal server network under a common system of contracts.

works for pictures, through the `<IMG SRC>` tag in HTML, but we are working on a tag for extracting text quotes.) [2]

Naturally the original rightsholder must give permission for this in advance ("transcopyright"). [3]

Transpublishing turns all participating materials into virtual clip art, freely to be recomposited into new online contexts. Its advantages are special. It provides a bridge to the original (a great benefit to understanding the written intent of the author, and possibly the author's reputation).

Furthermore, with a suitable micropayment system,* transpublishing should provide also a means by which the publisher is paid for each manifestation† thus quoted.

Transpublishing versus Embedded Markup

Embedded markup drastically interferes with transclusive re-use. For one thing, any arbitrary section of an HTML document may not have correct tags (since the tags overlap and extend over potentially long attribute fields). This means HTML-based transclusion cannot be handled by a simple tag, but probably requires some sort of proxy server.

Second—and it has taken a long time to get to this point‡—the quoting author may legitimately want to change fonts and and markup.

This is done all the time in scholarly writing and serious journalism, with phrases like "emphasis mine." It needs to be possible in transpublishing to change emphasis and other attributes by nullifying the original markup. Of course, re-emphasizing through markup *is* an editorial modification, subject to judgment calls and issues of academic etiquette. But the inquiring reader can always follow the bridge of transclusion to see the original as formatted by the author.

There are two markup solutions to make transpublishing work with SGML and HTML.

Alternative method 1: parallel markup

The best alternative is *parallel markup.* I believe that sequential formatted objects are best represented by a format in which the text and the markup are treated as separate parallel members, presumably (but not necessarily) in different files.§

The tags can be like those of SGML, but they are not embedded in the text itself. They are in parallel streams which reference positions in the text data stream. Thus each tag is preceded by a count showing how far the tag is after the *previous* tag. (This incremental counting, rather than stating each tag's distance from the beginning, is to facilitate editing.)

This method has several advantages:

- *Clean data.* The raw text may be counted, scanned, copied, etc. with ease.
- *Pluralism.* Each markup stream is independent, allowing simultaneously different formatting of the same material. (Note that schemes are also possible for markup streams to be combined, but that is outside this discussion.)
- *Editability.* The streams may be edited, though they must be edited in parallel. Operations of insertion, deletion, rearrangement, and transclusion are all easily definable. (However, some attention must be paid

---

* We are working on such a payment system, tentatively named "HyperCoin," with ASCII Corporation of Japan.

† Since a transclusion is technically neither a copy nor an instance, we use the term "manifestation" instead.

‡ Moreover, quoting authors often legitimately change contents, adding bracketed terms and ellipses to clarify a quotation, such as:

> McGillicuddy was seen going down the street, evidently with [the stolen goods under a blanket] . . . but no one challenged him.

However, this becomes two transcluded fields, and thus is a simpler case.

§ This was the design adopted by Project Xanadu about 1968, in order to allow variations of markup on transclusible material. It was superseded by a more complex and general method in our 1981 design [1].

in the design of appropriate editing programs to such features as paired tags defining attribute fields, and when attribute fields are separated and joined, the editing program must behave accordingly.)

- *Transclusion with variation.* The text may be transcluded (re-used by reference as a virtual quotation) in any online document. Transcluding authors may apply their own parallel markup streams.

How can parallel markup be fitted into the SGML model? Easily, as a variant form to be used for various legitimate purposes. Taking an SGML file to a parallel format is in most cases a reversible, non-destructive, non-lossy transformation.

Thus I believe we should call it "the Parallel Representation of SGML," and make it an optional part of the SGML standard.

Alternative method 2: tag override

Where it is inconvenient to break out the tags into a parallel stream—i.e., where they're already stuck or published in the original—we may fall back on the method of tag override. By this I mean simply *treating the original tags as if they are not there*; ignoring them while counting through the contents and furnishing instead a parallel tag stream, as in parallel markup. We do not dislodge the original markup, but simply ignore it.

This is smarmier at the implementation level, losing the benefit of clean counting and requiring a more complex editing apparatus. Otherwise it has the advantages of parallel markup: pluralism, editability, and transclusion with variation.

Note that this is tag *override*, not overload, since no symbol is being redefined.

Objection 3: Structures That Don't Fit

When SGML fanciers say "structure," they mean structure where everything is contained and sequential, with no overlap, no sharing of material in two places, no relations uncontained. SGML advocates I have talked to appear to have the belief that everything is either sequential and hierarchical, or can be represented that way. What is not expresssible sequentially and hierarchically is deemed to be nonexistent, inconceivable, evil, or mistaken.

I believe that embedded structure, enforcing sequence and hierarchy, limits the kinds of structure that can be expressed. The question we must ask is: What is the *real* structure of a thing or a document? (And does it reasonably fit the allowed spectrum of variation within the notational system?)

You can always force structures into other structures and claim that they're undamaged; another way to say this is that if you smash things up it is easier to make them fit. Enforcing sequence and hierarchy simply restricts the possibilities.

Like a TV dinner, embedded markup *nominally* contains everything you could want. "What else could you possibly want?" means "It's not on the menu."

Exactly Representing Thought and Change

My principal long-term concern is the exact representation of human thought, especially that thought put into words and writing. But the sequentiality of words and old-fashioned writing have until now compromised that representation, requiring authors to force sequence on their material, and curtail its interconnections. Designing editorial systems for exact and deep representation is therefore my objective.

This issue creates a very different focus from that of the markup community: the task I see is not merely to represent frozen objects tossed over the transom by an author or management, or format static structures for printout or screen, but to maintain a continuing evolutionary base of material and to track the changes in it.

To find the support functions really needed for creative organization by authors and editors, we must understand the exact representation and presentation of human thought, and be able to track the continuities of structure and change.

This means we must find a stable means of representing structure very different from the sequential and hierarchial—a representation of structure which recognizes the most anarchic and overlapping relations; and the location of identical and corresponding materials in different versions; which recognizes and maintains constancies of structure and data across successive versions, even as addresses of these materials become unpredictably fragmented by editing.

Thus deep version management—knowing locations of shared materials to the byte level—is a vital problem to solve in the design of editing systems. And the same location management is necessary on a much broader scale to support transpublishing.

Embedded markup cannot represent this at all, and merely adds obstacles (impeded data structure) to solving these rich addressing problems.

Three Layers

I believe we should find a very general representational system, a reference model which breaks apart in parallel what is represented by SGML and HTML. This would make the creation of deep editing and version management methods much easier. By handling contents, structure, and special effects separately in such a reference model, the parts can be better understood and worked on, and far more general structures can be represented.

I would propose a three-layer model:*

- A *content layer* to facilitate editing, content linking, and transclusion management.
- A *structure layer*, declarable separately. Users should be able to specify entities, connections and co-presence logic, defined independently of appearance or size or contents; as well as overlay correspondence, links, transclusions, and "hoses" for movable content.
- Finally, a *special-effects-and-primping layer* should allow the declaration of ever-so-many fonts, format blocks, fanfares, and whizbangs, and their assignment to what's in the content and structure layers.

I believe that a parallel system of this kind will soon become necessary because of the degree of entanglement and unmanageability of HTML. But we must learn from the recent past and provide sufficient abstractness and generality.

Conclusion

For editing and transpublishing, there are serious shortcomings to embedded markup. I believe that embedded markup, daily more tangled, will implode and leave HTML as an output format, supplanted by deeper editors and deeper hypermedia forms. In the meantime it is necessary to find other solutions to its shortcomings for transpublishing, especially parallelized tag models.

Few understand the true nature of hypertext and its relation to thought, let alone the vast interconnection of ideas, and the way that most expressions of ideas sever and misrepresent them. Today's popular but trivially-structured Web hypertext has excused people from seeing the real hypertext issues, or being able to create and publish deep complexes of thought.

We greatly need a general structure to represent all forms of interconnection and structure, and changes in both content and structure; and to visualize and re-use variants and alternatives, comparing them in context in order to understand and choose.

Mapping these serious concerns to an SGML-HTML template is not a minor inconvenience but an impossible violation of the problem.

* This has been the Xanadu model since the sixties.

Of course, people always try to fit information into a familiar mold, even when that structure has shown itself inhospitable, unshaped to that information. C. Northcote Parkinson has pointed out [4] that the fullest flowering of a paradigm, at least as seen by its participants—all gaps closed and issues unseen, the people no longer aware that there are any unsatisfied problems—may indicate that the paradigm is near its end. ■

References

1. Theodor Holm Nelson, *Literary Machines*. Mindful Press; latest edition available from Eastgate Systems, Cambridge, Massachusetts.
2. Andrew Pam, "Fine-Grain Transclusion in the Hypertext Markup Language." Available at *www.xanadu.net/xanadu/draft-pam-html-fine-trans-00.txt*
3. Theodor Holm Nelson, "Transcopyright: Dealing with the Dilemma of Digital Copyright." *Educom Review*, vol. 30, Jan/Feb 1997, p. 32.
4. C. Northcote Parkinson, *Parkinson's Law*.

About the Author

Theodor Holm Nelson
ted@xanadu.net

Theodor Holm Nelson, designer and generalist, has been a software designer and theorist since 1960 and a software consultant since 1967. His principal design work includes Project Xanadu and xanalogical systems, the transcopyright system, and the theory of virtuality design. His industry positions include Harcourt Brace & World publishers, Creative Computing Magazine, Datapoint Corporation, and Autodesk, Inc.; his university positions include Vassar College, University of Illinois, Swarthmore College, Strathclyde University, and Keio University.

Mr. Nelson has written several books, the most recent being *The Future of Information* (1997), as well as numerous articles, lectures, and presentations. He is best known for discovering the hypertext concept and for coining various words which have become popular, such as "hypertext," "hypermedia," "cybercrud," "softcopy," "electronic visualization," "dildonics," "technoid," "docuverse," and "transclusion."

He received a B.A. in Philosophy from Swarthmore College in 1959 and an M.A. in Social Relations from Harvard in 1963.

Chemical Markup Language

A Simple Introduction to Structured Documents

Peter Murray-Rust

Abstract

Structured documents in XML are capable of managing complex documents with many separate information components. In this article, we describe the role of the XML-LANG specification in supporting this. Examples are supplied explaining how components can be managed and how documents can be processed, with an emphasis on scientific and technical publishing. We conclude that structured documents are sufficiently powerful to allow complex searches simply through the use of their markup.

Historical Overview

Originally published as an HTML file, this paper was part of the CDROM e-publication ECHET96 ("Electronic Conference on Heterocyclic Chemistry"), run by Henry Rzepa, Chris Leach, and others at Imperial College, London, U.K. The CDROM was sponsored by the Royal Society of Chemistry, who (along with Cambridge, Leeds, and IC) are participants in the CLIC project. This is one of the projects under E-Lib, a U.K.-based program to promote electronic publishing. CLIC makes substantial use of SGML and Chemical Markup Language (CML). As part of this project I have been developing CML, one of the first applications of XML. CML, and its associated software JUMBO, probably represented one of the first complete XML applications (authoring tools, documents, and browser) in any discipline. Although the CML component was essentially a proof-of-concept, it was robust enough to be distributed as a standalone Java-based XML application. A wide variety of examples could therefore be viewed using JUMBO running under a Java-enabled browser.*

The audience for this paper need not be acquainted with SGML or XML; it serves as an introduction to the concept of document structure. As such, we assume no knowledge about markup languages, other than a familiarity with HTML. Though some parts may be trivially obvious to some readers, they may still find it useful as a tutorial aid for their colleagues. It is primarily aimed at those who are interested in authoring or browsing documents with the next generation of markup languages, especially those created with XML. CML [1] is part of the portfolio of the Open Molecule Foundation [2], which is a newly constituted open body to promote interoperability in molecular sciences. The latest versions of JUMBO can be found under the Virtual School of Molecular Sciences [3], which has also recently run a virtual course on Scientific Information Components using Java and XML [4].

The paper alludes to various software tools, but does not cover their operation or implementation. However, with the exception of stylesheets, most of the operations described here for CML have already been implemented as a prototype using the JUMBO browser and processor. The paper does not require any knowledge of chemistry or specific understanding of CML.

Finally, I should emphasize that SGML can be used in many ways; my approach does not necessarily do justice to the most common use, which is the management and publication of complex (mainly textual) documents. Projects in

* An accompanying article by Peter Murray-Rust, "JUMBO: An Object-based XML Browser," is included in this issue as well. The JUMBO paper is more technical, and describes novel work in relating XML document structure to Java classes.

this area often involve many megabytes of data and industrial strength engines. I hope, however, that the principles described here will generally be of use.

Introduction

Two years ago I had never heard of structured documents, and have since come to see them as one of the most effective and cheapest ways to manage information. Though the basic idea is simple, when I first came across it I failed to see its importance. This paper is written as a guide to what is now possible. In particular, it explains XML—the simple new language being developed by a working group (WG) of the W3 Consortium. I have used this language as the basis for a markup language in technical subjects (Technical Markup Language, TecML) and particularly molecular sciences (Chemical Markup Language, CML).

The paper was originally written as a simple structured document, using HTML, although it could have been written in CML. I shall slant it towards those who wish to carry *precise*, possibly *nontextual*, information arranged in (potentially quite complex) *data structures*. While I use the term *document*, this could represent a piece of information without conventional text, such as a molecule. Moreover, documents can have a very close relation to *objects*; if you are comfortable with object-oriented languages you may like to substitute "object" for "document." In practice, XML documents can be directly and automatically transformed into objects, although the reverse may not always be quite so easy.

The markup I describe essentially uses the same syntax as HTML; it is the concepts, rather than the syntax that may be new. Although this paper is written in the context of document delivery over networks, markup is also ideally suited to the management of "traditional" documents. Markup languages are often seen as key tools in making them "future-proof" and interchangeable between applications (interoperability).

The important point about the XML approach is that it has been designed to separate different parts of the problem and to solve them independently. I'll explain these ideas in more detail below, but one example is the distinction between *syntax* (the basic rules for carrying the information components) and *semantics* (what meaning you put on the components and what behavior a machine is expected to perform). This is a much more challenging area than people realize, since human readers don't have problems with it.

One of the great polymaths of this century, J.D. Bernal, inspired the development of information systems in molecular science. In 1962 he urged that the problems of scientific information in crystallography (his own field) and solid state physics should be treated as one in communication engineering. Thirty years later we have most of the tools that are required to *get the best information in the minimum quantity in the shortest time, from the people who are producing the information to the people who want it, whether they know they want it or not.*[*]

Many scientists are unaware of the research during the last thirty years into the management of information.[†] In this review, Schatz shows that previous research in the analysis of complex documents, including hyperlinking, concept analysis, and vocabulary switching between disciplines, is now possible on a production scale. Much of his emphasis is on analysis of conventional documents produced by authors who have no knowledge of markup and who do not use vocabularies (domain ontologies). For that reason, complex systems such as natural language processing (NLP) are required to extract implicit information from the documents, and they rely on having

* Bernal's words, quoted in *Sage*, Maurice Goldsmith, p. 219.

† A recent and valuable review is, "Information Retrieval in Digital Libraries: Bringing Search to the Net," Bruce R. Schatz, *Science*, **275**, pp. 327–334 (1997). (I shall comment on the format of the last sentence shortly.)

appropriate text to analyze. Automatic extraction of numerical and other nontextual information will be much more difficult.

Structure and Markup

We often take for granted the power of the human brain in extracting implicit information from documents. We have been trained over centuries to realize that documents have structure (Table Of Contents [TOCs], Indexes, Chapters with included Sections, and so on). It probably seems "obvious" to you that you are reading the fourth section ("Structure and Markup") in the paper ("A Simple Introduction to Sructured Documents"). The HTML language and rendering tools that you are using to read [the online version] provide a simple but extremely effective set of visual clues; for instance, "Chapter" is set in larger type. However, the logical structure of the document is simply:

```
HTML
  HEAD
    TITLE
  BODY
    H1 (Chapter)
    H2 (Section)
    H3 (Subsection)
    H3
    H2
    P  (Paragraph)
    P
    P
    P
    P
    H2
    P
    P
    P
    H2
    P
    P
    ... and so on ...
    ADDRESS
```

where I have used the convention of indentation to show that one component includes another. This is a common approach in many TOCs, and human readers will implicitly deduce a hierarchy from the above diagram. But a machine could not unless it had sophisticated heuristics, and it would also make mistakes.

The formal structure in this document is quite limited, and that is one of the reasons that HTML has been so successful but also increasingly insufficient. Humans can author documents easily and human readers can supply the implicit structure. But if you look again at the TOC diagram you will see that Chapters do *not* include Sections in a formal manner, nor do Sections include Paragraphs. The first occurrence of `H2` and `H3` is used for the author and affiliation, which is not a "Section."

An information component (an *Element*) *contains* another if the *start-tag* and *end-tag* of the container completely enclose the contained. Thus the HEAD element contains a TITLE element, and the TITLE element contains a string of characters (the SGML/XML term is #PCDATA). There is a formal set of rules in HTML for which elements can contain which other Elements and where they can occur. Thus, it's not *formally* allowed to have TITLE in the BODY of your document. These rules, which are primarily for machines and SGML gurus to read, are combined in a Document Type Definition (DTD).

NOTE

> If you have already come across SGML and been put off for some reason, please don't switch off here. XML has been carefully designed to make it much easier to understand the concepts and there are many fewer terms. For example, you don't even have to have a DTD if you don't want.

This document has an inherent structure in the order of its Elements. Most people would reasonably assume that an `H2` element "belongs to" the preceding `H1`, and that `P` elements belong to the preceding `H2`. It would be quite natural to use phrases like "the second sentence of the second paragraph in the section called Introduction." Although humans can do this easily, it's common to get lost in large documents. The important news is that XML now makes it possible for *machines* to do the same sort of thing with simple rules and complete precision. The Text Encoding Initiative (a large international project to mark up the world's literature) has developed tools for doing this, and they will be available to the XML community.

In HTML there are no formal conventions for what constitutes a Chapter or Section, and no restriction as to what elements can follow others. Therefore, you can't rely on analyzing an arbitrary HTML document in the way I've outlined. This highlights the need for more formal rules, agreements, and guidelines. In XML we are likely to see communities such as users of CML develop their own rules, which they enforce or encourage as they see fit. For example, there is no restriction on what order Elements can occur in a CML document, but there is a requirement that ATOMS can only occur within a MOL (molecule Element). (In CML I use the term "ChemicalElement" to avoid confusion!)

In the Schatz reference that is footnoted earlier, you will probably "know automatically" what the components are. The thing in brackets must be the year, "pp." is short for "pages," the **bold** type must be the volume, and the *italics* are the journal title. But this is not obvious to a machine; trying to write a parser for this is difficult and error-prone. Many different publishing houses have their own conventions. The Royal Society of Chemistry might format this as:

B.R. Schatz, *Science*, 1997, **275**, 327.

Any error in punctuation such as missing periods causes serious problems for a machine, and conversions between different formats will probably involve much manual crafting.

The precise components of the reference, which are well understood and largely agreed within the bibliographic community, are a good example of something that can be enhanced by *markup*. Markup is the process of adding information to a document that is not part of the content but adds information about the structure or elements. Using the Schatz citation as an example, we can write:

```
<BIB>
  <TITLE>
  Information Retrieval in Digital
   Libraries: Bringing Search to
   the Net
  </TITLE>
  <JOURNAL>Science</JOURNAL>
  <AUTHOR>
    <FIRSTNAME>Bruce</FIRSTNAME>
    <INITIAL>R</INITIAL>
    <LASTNAME>Schatz</LASTNAME>
  </AUTHOR>
  <VOLUME>275</VOLUME>
  <YEAR>1997</YEAR>
  <PAGES>327–334</PAGES>
</BIB>
```

A scientist never having seen markup before would implicitly understand this information. The advantage is that it's also straightforward to parse it by machine. If the tags (<...>) and their content are ignored, then the remainder (content) is exactly the same as it was earlier (except for punctuation and rendering). It's often useful to think of markup as invisible annotations on your document. Many modern systems do not mark up the document itself, but provide a separate document with the markup. For example, you may not be allowed to edit a document but can still point to, and comment on, a phrase, section, chapter, etc. This is a feature of hypermedia systems, and one of the goals of XML is to formalize this through the development of linking syntax and semantics in XML-LINK (XLL), but this is outside the scope of this paper.

What is so remarkable about this? *In essence we have made it possible for a machine to capture some of those things that a human takes for granted.*

- *Punctuation and other syntax* are no longer a problem, as there are extremely carefully defined rules in XML. If your markup characters are <...>, how do you actually send < and > characters without them being mistaken for markup? One way is to encode them as `<` and `>`.

- *Character encoding* and other *character entities* have received a huge amount of attention and many *entity sets* have been developed, some by ISO. For example, the copyright symbol (©) is number 169 in ISO-Latin `©`. It also has a symbolic representation (`©`). XML itself has only a very few built-in character entities, but will support Unicode and other approaches to encoding characters. Most *browsers* do not yet support a wide range of *glyphs* for entities, but this is likely to change very rapidly, especially since languages like Java have addressed the problem.
- *The role of information elements is defined.* In the previous example, you can see what the precise components are and what their extent is. Note how the AUTHOR element is divided into three components. What you *do* with this information is the remit of *semantics*, and XML separates *syntax* precisely from semantics in a way that very few other non-SGML systems can do.
- *Documents can be reliably restructured or filtered by machine.* An author might enter the LASTNAME, FIRSTNAME, and INITIAL sequentially, but the machine could be asked to sort them into a different order. This may not appear very important, but to those implementing programs it is an enormous help. If the house style was initials-only, the program could easily turn `Bruce` into `B`.
- *Documents can be transformed, merged, and edited automatically.* This is a great advance in information management. For example, it would be straightforward to write a citation analyzer that found all BIB elements in a document and abstracted parts of them by JOURNAL or YEAR.
- *It's easy to convert from one structured document to another.* The bibliographic example above is not in strict CML, but it's very easy to convert it to CML, *without losing any information*.
- *All information in a document can be precisely identified.* The above example is marked down to the granularity of a single character (the INITIAL). It is conceptually easy to extend this to markup of numbers, formulae, and *parts of things* such as regions in diagrams or atoms in molecules.

Rules, Meta-Languages, and Validity

I started writing Chemical Markup Language because I wanted to transfer molecules precisely using ATOMS, BONDS, and related information. It was always clear that "chemistry" involved more than this and that we needed the tools to encapsulate numeric and other data such as spectra. I looked at a wide variety of journals in the scientific area to see what sort of information was general to all of them, and whether a markup language could be devised which could manage this wide range. It required a meta-language, and this section is an explanation of what that involves.

I'll explain the "meta-" concept using XML and then show how it extends to applications such as TecML. XML, despite its name, is not a language but a *meta-language* (a tool for writing languages). XML is a *set of rules* that enable markup languages to be written; TecML and CML are two such languages. For example, one rule in XML is: *every non-empty element must have a start-tag and an end-tag;* so that the `<AUTHOR>` tag must be balanced by a `</AUTHOR>` tag. This is not a strict requirement of HTML, which uses a more flexible set of rules (but is also harder to parse or read by machine). Another rule is: *all attribute values must occur within quotes (" or ').* Writing a markup language is somewhat analogous to writing a program, and the relation of XML to CML is much the same as C to *hello.c*. We say that CML "is an *application* of XML," or "is written in XML," just as "*hello.c* is written in C." XML is a little stricter than HTML in the syntax it allows, but the benefit is that it's much easier to write browsers and other applications.

XML allows for two sorts of documents: *valid* and *well-formed*. Validity requires an explicit set of rules in a DTD. This is usually a separate file, but part or all can be included in the document itself. An example of a validity criterion in HTML is that `LI` (a ListItem) must occur within a `UL` or `OL` container. Well-formedness is a less strict criterion and requires primarily that the document can be automatically parsed without the DTD. The result can be represented as a tree structure. The bibliographic example above is well-formed, but without a DTD, it may not be valid. It might have been an explicit rule, like "the author must include an element describing the language that the article was written in, such as `<LANGUAGE>EN</LANGUAGE>`"; in this case, the document fragment would be invalid.

The importance of validity will depend on the philosophy of the community using XML. In molecular science all **.cml* documents will be expected to be valid and this is ensured by running them through a *validating parser* such as NXP.* If a browser or other processing application such as a search engine can assume that a certified document was valid (perhaps from a validation stamp) there would be no need to write a validating parser. Being valid doesn't mean the contents are necessarily *sensible*; further processing may be needed for that purpose.

Where, and how, you enforce validity depends on what you are trying to do. If you are providing a form for authors to submit abstracts, you will enforce fairly strict rules. ("It must have one or more AUTHORs, exactly one ADDRESS for correspondence, and the AUTHOR must contain either a FIRSTNAME or INITIALS but not both.") This can be enforced in a DTD. But this would be too restricting for a general scientific document, which need not always have an AUTHOR. The two forces of *precision* and *flexibility* often conflict, but can be reconciled to a large extent by providing different ways of processing documents.

Processing Documents

At this stage it's useful to think about how an XML document might be created and processed. At its simplest level a document can be created with any text editor; this was how the BIB example was written. It can then be processed with the human brain. This isn't a trivial point; there is no fundamental requirement for software at all or any stages of managing XML documents. In practice, however, software adds enormously to the value. CML documents such as those including atomic coordinates only make sense when rendered by computers.

XML documents can be created, processed, and displayed in many ways. The schematic diagram in Figure 1 (which emphasizes the tree structure) shows some of the possible operations.

The lefthand module shows parts of the editing process. Legacy documents can be imported and converted on the fly, and the tree can be edited. There will normally also be a module for editing text. The editor may have access to a DTD and can therefore validate the document as it is created. An important aspect of XML-LINK is that editors should be able to create hyperlinks, either internally or to external files.

The complete document will then be mounted on a server. This will associate it with stylesheets, Java classes, the DTD, entities, and other linked components. The packaged documents are then delivered to the client where the application requires an XML parser. If the client wishes to validate the document the DTD is required.

Many XML applications will then hold the parsed document in memory as a tree (or grove) which can then be further processed. A frequent method will be the delivery of DSSSL stylesheets

* Norbert Mikula's validating XML parser at *http://www.edu.uni-klu.ac.at/~rmikula/NXP*.

with the document (or provided client-side), or other transformation tools (perhaps written in Perl). Alternatively, the components of the document may be associated with Java classes either for display or transformation (as in the JUMBO browser). All of these methods may involve semantic validation (such as "does the document contain sensible information?").

Some of the operations required in processing XML are now explained in more detail:

Authoring
: One of the hardest problems is to write the authoring tools for an SGML/XML system. A good tool has to provide a natural interface for authors, most of whom won't know the principles of markup languages. It may also have to enforce strict and complex rules, possibly after every keystroke. Many current authoring tools are therefore tailored to a limited number of specific applications, one of the most versatile of which is an SGML add-on to Emacs. Sometimes a customer will approach an SGML house and, after agreeing on a DTD, a specific tool will be built. For some common document types—such as military contracts—there is enough communality that commercial tools are available.

Conversion
: In some cases authoring involves conversion of *legacy* documents; if these are well understood, conventional programs can be written in Perl or similar languages. Where the XML documents represent database entries or the output from programs, the authoring process

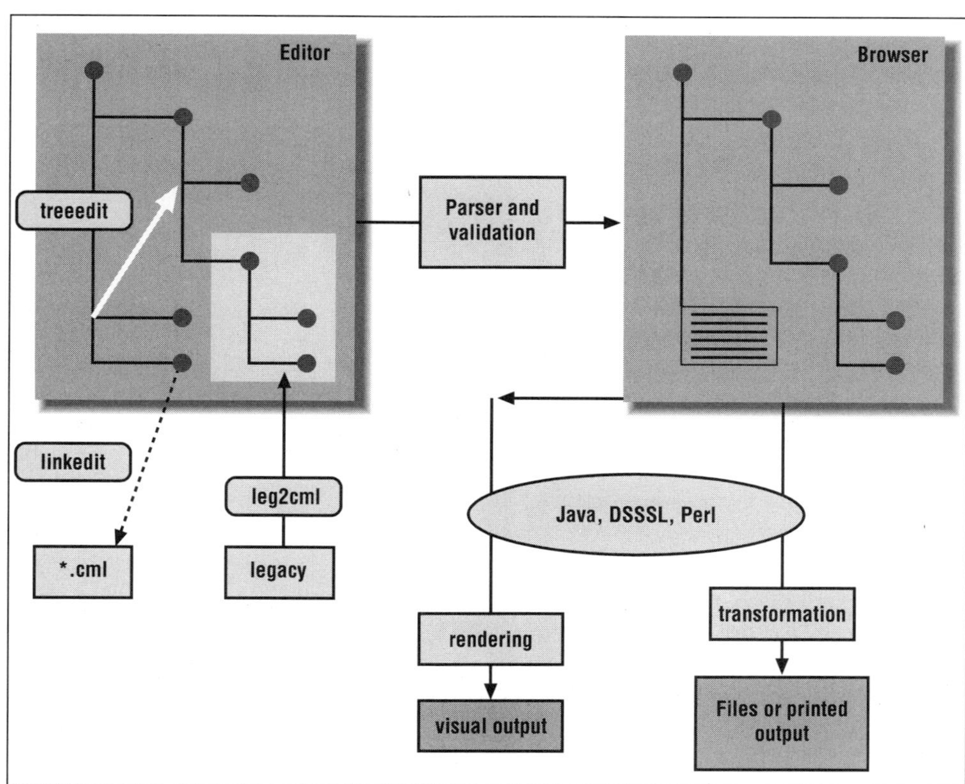

Figure 1 XML document processing

is particularly simple—many CML applications will fall in that category. XML makes it particularly easy to reuse material either by "cut-and-paste" of sections, or preferably through *entities*. Classes written for JUMBO can already convert 15 different types of legacy files into CML.

Editing and merging

Editing and merging affects the structure of the document and therefore may require validation. To write programs that do this on the fly is again difficult; and it may be useful, where possible, to divide documents into "chunks" or *entities*. SGML has a very powerful concept or entities and can describe documents whose components are distributed over a network. For example, if I have an address, it is extremely useful to refer to that chunk by a symbolic name, such as `&pmraddress;`. With appropriate software I can include this at appropriate places and the software will include the full content of the entity. (If the entity contains references to other entities, they are also expanded, and so on.)

The server: assembly and queries

The server has a vital role to play in many XML applications. It is possible to mount sophisticated SGML systems that retrieve document components and assemble them on the fly into XML documents. Alternatively, the components could be retrieved from databases, as with chemical and biological molecules or data, and converted into XML files. Since XML maps onto object storage, it is particularly attractive for those developing object-based systems such as CORBA. Whether the complete document is assembled at the server or the addresses of the fragments are sent to the client will depend on bandwidth, the preference of the community, the availability of software, and many other considerations.

Parsing

Parsing is the process of syntactic analysis and validation. It normally produces a standardized output either on file or in memory. Whether you need to validate documents when you receive them will depend on your community's requirements. For example, if I receive a database entry from a major molecular data center I can rely on its validity, but a publisher getting a hand-edited XML manuscript will probably want to validate it. A validating parser requires that the document be valid against a specified DTD. Finding this DTD normally requires interpretation of the DOCTYPE statement at the head of an XML document. Some authors/servers are prepared to distribute the DTDs when documents are downloaded. While this adds precision in that the correct DTD is used, it can add to the burden of server maintenance and can increase bandwidth. If a community agrees on a DTD, they may find it useful to distribute it with the browsing software. The result of parsing is usually a *parse-tree*. If this is an unfamiliar concept, think of it as a table of contents with every Element corresponding to a chapter or (sub. . .sub) section. Trees are easy to manipulate and display; JUMBO displays the tree as a TOC. There are already two freely available XML parsers written in Java (NXP and Lark)* and I have used both. Lark creates a parse tree in memory that can be subclassed, while NXP produces it on the output stream.

Postprocessing, rendering, and validation

Most documents require at least some postprocessing, and many need a lot. Most users of XML applications will think of "browsers" or "plug-ins" as the obvious tools to use on a document. This will probably be true, but because it's machine processable XML is so powerful that many completely new applications will be developed. An XML document

* See the article entitled "An Introduction to XML Processing with Lark," by Tim Bray.

might consist of an airline reservation and the postprocessor could decide to order a taxi to the airport. A chemical reaction in a CML document could trigger the supply of checmicals and interrogate the safety databases.

Semantics and the postprocessor

An XML document carries no semantics with it, and there has to be an explicit or implicit agreement between the author and reader. Most authors understand roughly the same thing by the TITLE in HTML documents, although they might try and use them in different ways. TITLE is valuable for indexers such as AltaVista, which abstract their content separately from the body of the document. This emphasizes the value of structural markup. However, some widely used element names are ambiguous (`A` is variously used in different DTDs for author, anchor, etc.), and for some, such as LINK, it's unclear what their role is. Clarifying this for each DTD requires *semantics*. Traditionally, semantics have been carried in documentation: if this is not done clearly then implementers may provide different actions for the same Element. The XML project is actively investigating formal automatic ways of delivering semantics, such as stylesheets and Java classes.

Validation at the postprocessor

The DTD/validating-parser cannot deal with some aspects of validation, which must be tackled by a conventional program/application. Common examples of validation are content ("is this number in the allowed range?"), and occurrence counts ("no more than five sections per chapter"). This is likely to need special coding for each application, and will be most important where high precision and low flexibility is the intention.

Stylesheets

Stylesheets are sets of rules that accompany a document.* They can be used to filter or restructure the document ("as in extract all footnotes and put them at the end of a section"). Their most common use is in formatting or providing typesetting instructions ("all subsections must be indented by *x mm* and typeset in this font"). ISO has produced a standard for the creation of stylesheets (DSSSL), which allows their description in Scheme (a derivative of LISP). Stylesheets are generally written to produce a transformed document, rather than to create an object in memory; Java classes are more suitable for this. I expect to see the technologies converge—which is used will depend on the application and the community using it. There are at least four ways that stylesheets might be used; the technology exists for each one. Which overrides which is a matter of politics, not technology.

- *By the author.* If an author wishes to impart a particular style to a document, he can attach or include a stylesheet. This can be invoked at the postprocessor level, unless it has been overridden.
- *By the server.* If an organization such as publishing house is running the server, it may impose a particular style, such as for bibliographic references. XML would give the author the freedom to prepare them in a standard way (e.g., using CML), while the journals could transform this by sending their stylesheets to the reader.
- *By the client software (browser).* The software manufacturer has an interest in providing a common look-and-feel to the display. It reduces training and documentation costs and might provide a competitive market edge.

* For more information on stylesheets, and particularly on W3C's cascading stylesheets, see the article entitled "XML and CSS" (Culshaw, Leventhal, and Maloney) in this issue. Also see the Winter 1997 issue of the W3J for the CSS1 specification as well as an implementation guide to the spec by Norman Walsh.

- *By the reader.* She may have personal preferences concerning the presentation of material, perhaps because of her education. Alternatively, her employer may require a common house style to facilitate training and internal communication.

Java classes

Every Element can be thought of as an object and have methods (or behavior) associated with it. Thus, a LIST object might count and number the items it contains. Most elements will have a `display()` method, which could be implemented differently from object to object. Thus, in JUMBO, `MOLNode.display()` brings up a rotatable screen display of the molecule, while `BIB.display()` displays each citation in a mixture of fonts. As with stylesheets, Java classes can be specified at any of the four places listed above, and the appropriate one downloaded from a Web site if required. One of the problems the XML-WG is tackling and solving is how to locate Java classes. Because Java is a very powerful programming language with full WWW support, it offers almost unlimited scope for XML applications. A document need not be passive, but could awake the client to take a whole series of actions—mailing people, downloading other data, and updating the local database are examples.

Manifests and addressing on the WWW

Most XML "documents" will consist of several physical files or streams, and these may be distributed over more than one server. An important attraction of XML is that common document components such as citations, addresses, boilerplate, etc. can be reused by many authors. Packaging these components is a challenge that the W3C and others are tackling. It involves:

- Methods of locating components. XML uses URLs or their future evolution (such as URNs).
- Labeling a file with its type. XML has provision for NOTATION, which may be linked to a reference URL or a MIME type.
- Creating a manifest of all the components required in a package (perhaps through a Java archive file [**.jar*]).

Attributes

So far I have used only Element names (sometimes called GIs) to carry the markup. XML also provides *attributes* as another way of modulating the element. Attributes occur within start-tags, and well-known examples are `HREF` (in `A`) and `SRC` (in `IMG`):

```
<A HREF="http://www.venus.co.uk/omf/
    cml/">
<IMG SRC="mypicture.gif"
    WIDTH="500" HEIGHT="100">
```

Attributes are semantically free in the same way as Elements, and can be used with stylesheets or Java classes to vary their meaning.

Whether Elements or attributes are used to convey markup is a matter of preference and style, but in general the more flexible the document the more I would recommend attributes. As a point of style, many people suggest that document content should not occur in attributes, but this is not universal. Here are some simple examples of the use of attributes:

- Describing the type of information (e.g., what language the Element is written in)
- Adding information about the document or parts of it (who wrote it, what its origins are)
- Suggestions for rendering, such as recommended sizes for pictures
- Help for the postprocessor (e.g., the word-count in a paragraph)

In XML-LINK attributes are extensively used to provide the target, type, and behavior of links.

Flexibility and Meta-DTDs

As discussed earlier, when developing an XML application, the author has to decide whether precision and standardization is required, or whether it is more important to be flexible. If precision is required, then the DTD will be the primary means of enforcing it, and as a consequence, may become large and complex. It implies that the "standard" is unlikely to change. When new versions are produced, the complete pipeline from authoring to rendering will need to be revised. Because this is a major effort and cost, careful planning of the DTD is necessary.

If flexibility is more important, either because the field is evolving or because it is very broad, a rigid DTD may restrict development. In that case a more general DTD is useful, with flexibility being added through attributes and their values.

In TecML I created an Element type, XVAR, for a scalar variable. Attributes are used to tune the use and properties of XVAR, and it's possible to make it do "almost anything"! For example, it can be given a TYPE such as STRING, FLOAT, DATE, and TITLE. In this way, any number of objects can be precisely described. Here are three examples:

```
<XVAR TYPE="STRING"
    TITLE="Greeting">Hello world!</
    XVAR>
<XVAR TYPE="DATE">2000-01-01</XVAR>
<XVAR TYPE="FLOAT"
    DICTNAME="Melting Point"
    UNITS="Fahrenheit">451</XVAR>
```

The last is particularly important because it uses the concept of *linking* to add semantics. This is an important feature of XML; the precise syntax is being developed in XML-LINK. CML uses DICTNAME to refer to an entry in a specified glossary that defines what `"Melting Point"` is. This entry could have further links to other resources, such as world collections of physical data. Similarly, UNITS is used to specify precisely what scale of temperature is used. Again, this is provided by a glossary in which SI* units are the default.

By using this approach it is possible to describe any scalar variable simply by varying the attributes and their values. Note that the attribute types must be defined in the DTD but their values may either be unlimited or can be restricted to a set of possible values.

NOTE

> In the preceding example the links are implicit; later versions of CML will probably use the explicit links provided by XML-LINK.

The TecML DTD uses very few Element types, and these have been carefully chosen to cover most of the general concepts that arise in technical subjects. They include ARRAY, XLIST (a general tool for data structures such as tables and trees), FIGURE (a diagram), PERSON, BIB, and XNOTATION. (NOTATION is an XML concept which allows non-XML data to be carried in a document, and is therefore a way of including "foreign" file types.) With these simple tools and a wide range of attributes it is possible to mark up most technical scientific publications. There has to be general agreement about the semantics of the markup, of course, but this is a great advance compared with having no markup at all.

Entities and Information Objects

When documents have identifiable components it is often useful to put them into ENTITYs in separate files or resources. For example, although a citation might be used by many documents, only one copy is needed as long as all documents can address it. Chapters in an anthology might all be held as separate entities, allowing each to be edited independently. If the entity is updated (it might be an address, for example) all references to the entity will automatically point to the cor-

* Systèm Internationale: the international standard for scientific units.

rect information. Entities in XML can be referenced through URLs allowing truly global hyperdocuments.

Many documents involve more than one basic discipline. For example, a scientific paper may include text, images, vector graphics, mathematics, molecules, bibliography, and glossaries. All of these are complex objects and most have established SGML conventions. Authors of these documents would like to reuse these existing conventions without having to write their own (very complicated) DTDs. The XML community is actively creating the mechanisms for doing this. If components are mixed within the same document, their *namespaces* must be identified (e.g., "this component obeys the MathML DTD and that one obeys CML"). For example, all the mathematical equations could be held in separate entities, and so could the molecular formulae. This would also support another method of combining components through XML-LINK, where the components are accessed through the **HREF** syntax.

Searching

Realizing the power of structured documents (SD) for carrying information was a revelation for me. In many disciplines, data map far more naturally into a tree structure than into a relational database (RDB). An SD has a concept of sequential information while an RDB does not. The exciting thing is that the new object databases (including the hybrid Object-Relational Databases {ORDBS]) have the exact architecture needed to hold XML-like documents, and suppliers now offer SGML interfaces. (For any particular application, of course, there may be a choice between RDBs and ORDBs.) The attraction of objects over-RDBs is that it is much easier to design the data architecture with objects.

In many cases simply creating well marked-up documents may be all that is required for their use in the databases of the future. The reason for this confident statement is that SDs provide a very rich context for individual Elements. Thus we can ask questions like:

- "Find all MOLECULEs which contain MOLECULEs." (e.g., ligands in proteins)
- "Which DATASET contains one MOLECULE and one SPECTRUM whose attribute TYPE has a value of *nmr*?"
- "Find all references to journals not published by the Royal Society of Chemistry."

Despite their apparent complexity, these can all be managed with standard techniques for searching structured documents. Because of this power, a special language (Structured Document Query Language—SDQL) has been developed and will interoperate with XML. If simple application-specific tools are developed then queries like the following are possible:

- "Find all XVARs whose DICTNAME value is **`Melting Point`**; retrieve the value of the UNITS attribute and use it to convert the content to a floating point number representing a temperature on the Celsius scale. Then include all data with values in the range 150–170."

The XML-LINK specification has borrowed the syntax of extended pointers (XPointers) from the Text Encoding Initiative (TEI). Although primarily intended to access specific components within an XML document, the syntax is quite a powerful query language. The first two queries might be represented as:

```
ROOT,DESCENDANT(1,MOLECULE)
    DESCENDANT(1,MOLECULE)
ROOT,DESCENDANT(DATASET)CHILD(1,MOLE
    CULE)ANCESTOR(1,DATASET)CHILD(1,
    SPECTRUM,TYPE,"nmr")
```

The first finds the first MOLECULE, which is a descendant of the root of the document, and then the first MOLECULE, which is somewhere in the subtree from that. The second is more complex, and requires the MOLECULE and SPECTRUM to be directly contained within the DATASET element. (The details of TEI Xpointers in XML may still undergo slight revision and are not further explained here.)

Summary, and the Next Phase

This document has described only part of what XML can offer to a scientific or publishing community. XML has three phases; only the first has been covered here in any depth. XML-LINK defines a hyperlinking system and XML-STYLE defines how stylesheets will be used. Hyperlinking can range from the simple, unverified link (as in HTML's HREF attribute for Anchors) to a complete database of typed and validated links over thousands of documents. XML-LINK is addressing all of these and has the power to support complex systems.

How will XML develop in practice? A natural impetus will come from those people who already use SGML and see how it could be used over the WWW. It is certainly something that publishers should look at very closely, as it has all the required components—including the likelihood that solutions will interoperate with Java.

XML is the ideal language for the creation and transmission of database entries. The use of entities means it can manage distributed components, it maps well onto objects, and it can manage complex relationships through its linking scheme. Most of the software components are already written.

How would it be used with a browser? Assuming that the bulk of tools are written in Java, we can foresee helper applications or plug-ins, and perhaps there will be more autonomous tools that are capable of independent action. It's an excellent approach to managing legacy documents rather than writing a specific helper for each type.

I hope enough tools will be available for XML to provide the same creative and expressive opportunities as HTML provided in the past. However, it's important to realize that *freely available software is required*—any tools for structured document management, especially in Java, will be extremely welcome. The accompanying paper describes my own contribution through the JUMBO browser. ■

References

1. *http://www.venus.co.uk/omf/cml*
2. *http://www.chic.ac.uk/omf*
3. *http://www.vsms.nottingham.ac.uk/vsms*
4. *http://www.vsms.nottingham.ac.uk/vsms/java*

Additional Resources

1. Robin Cover's SGML Home page: *http://www.si/.org/sgml*
2. FAQ for XML run by Peter Flynn: *http://www.ucc.ie/xml*

About the Author

Peter Murray-Rust
Virtual School of Molecular Sciences
Nottingham University, UK
pazpmr@unix.ccc.nottingham.ac.uk

Peter Murray-Rust is the Director of the Virtual School of Molecular Sciences at the University of Nottingham, where he is participating in a new venture in virtual education and communities. Peter is also a visiting professor at the Crystallography Department at Birkbeck College, where he set up the first multimedia virtual course on the WWW (Principles of Protein Structure).

Peter's research interests in molecular informatics include participation in the Open Molecule Foundation—a virtual community sharing molecular resources; developing the use of Chemical MIME for the electronic transmission of molecular information; creating the first publicly available XML browser, JUMBO; and developing the Virtual HyperGlossary—an exploration of how the world community can create a virtual resource in terminology.

CODIFYING MEDICAL RECORDS IN XML

PHILOSOPHY AND ENGINEERING

Thomas L. Lincoln, MD

Abstract

The following paper was given as a talk at the "XML Mixer" in La Jolla, California in late July '97, before a combined audience of clinicians, computing professionals, and vendors of document processing software. What brought the group together was an ongoing effort to introduce markup technology into the processing of healthcare information in an ISO standard manner, using SGML (Standard Generalized Markup Language) and SGML's strict subset, XML (eXtensible Markup Language). Other speakers spoke more specifically to processing topics, work flow, or business issues in the use of information systems in medicine, but the emphasis here is on some long perceived, but often overlooked problems in the semantics of communication. Both the general and the specific are important ingredients in this area, which indirectly indicates why the document format offers the appropriate middle ground between free text and excessively rigid (but easy to process) data structures.

Introduction

The overriding reason to seek better electronic records and record processing in healthcare is to acquire the ability to use clinical information in ways that will compensate for and move us beyond the cumulative deficiencies of present practice. Some of these deficiencies are the result of the increased complexity of diagnosis and therapy, following the dramatic advances that have been made in both science and technology; others are a consequence of the down-skilling allowed by the increased predictability and reliability of present procedures; and some are due to the change of healthcare focus away from virtuoso medicine toward a production mode of cost-minimization with changed incentives for profit and for care. The danger in the "industrialization" of care through this new direction is that we will arrive at an over-standardized service industry that is little more than a "people processor," and that treats every case as if it were average. By contrast, the potential offered by advanced computing is that we are now in a position to move forward to the much newer concept of mass customization, where information processing provides new means of cost-effective attention to individual needs.

Identifying the Exceptional Cases

The key to effective intervention in healthcare is *triage*—the ability to identify and separate the truly sick from those who are minimally ill, anxious, or merely uncomfortable. Studies have shown that more than 85% of the calls to 911 are not emergencies, and more than 85% of those seen in emergency rooms or clinic settings are not really sick (although these latter may need advice or reassurance.) Thus, the triaging party must be constantly alert in the presence of tedium and much "noise," and must be prepared to respond to exceptions and unusual patterns that are likely to signify serious disease—a personal capacity some have called "a nose for disaster." This capability is not for everyone, but it is markedly reduced wherever examinations are minimized and routines become mindless repetitions.

This problem is not new, nor is it only a problem of healthcare.

Communication from a Linguistic Perspective

All documentation intends communication, whether over space, as with HL7 (Health Level 7, the health content level of the ISO communication standard), or over time, as with a data archive. Most documentation is centered around language, even where images or sound tracks are included. In the latter cases, language is used to interpret them. Language and meaning is a much studied subject outside of medicine with a fruitful history. For example, Susanne K. Langer [1], in an insightful citation, translates and quotes Philipp Wegener [2] as follows:

> All discourse involves two elements, which may be called, respectively, the context (verbal or practical) and the novelty. The novelty is what the speaker is trying to point out or to express. For this purpose he will use any word that serves him. The word may be apt, or it may be ambiguous, or even new; the context, seen or stated, modifies it and determines just what is meant.

The quote is well taken. Meaning must be grasped between the two separate components of context and what is to be specified by naming (i.e., novelty). This has been fruitfully restated in an on-line discussion by Lloyd Harding:

> There seems to be a natural tension between authors (creators of information) and readers (in our particular context—computers). Creators want to be able to say what they need to say. Computers want you to say it in one particular way so it can process the information.

Present Shortcomings

It appears that healthcare informatics has been on the side of the computers, directing most of the effort toward establishing a standard vocabulary for a complete set of specific observations, thereby standardizing the description of novelty and depriving the authors of their initiative. To make what is captured into standard observations that fit neatly into data elements, designed to be retrievable using this same vocabulary, diminishes or even removes the potential balance provided by context. (This includes an assumption that significant change in what is observed and/or documented is sufficiently slow to be ignored.)

What Markup Has to Offer

To my mind, SGML and XML offer a better solution by addressing both the context and the "novelty," in order to arrive at an intended specification. This is not to deny that in healthcare almost all of the context and most of the observations to be made have both a predictable form and a predictable vocabulary, albeit less than stationary. However, it is precisely where the "shoe does not fit" where the key to successful diagnosis and therapeutic management is often made. It is the sick who are the outliers.

Given the ability to include an associative processing function and an intelligent human override, it should be possible to lay out the general descriptive components for markup well enough. For example, in a document such as a classical "History and Physical Examination" (or H&P), the general context is contained in the ritualized and thus more or less standardizable outline (and the sub-outlines contained within it, according to what problems are found). Here Langer points out further:

> Since the context of an expression tells us what is its sense . . . and how . . . it is to be interpreted—it follows that the context itself must always be expressed literally, because it has not, in turn, a context to supplement and define its sense.

Thus, in our domain, the tags for an outline are not only the easiest vocabulary to standardize, but this does not stand in the way of a more dynamic specification of observations and actions. Moreover, these can be further specified and indexed by standard attributes, which can be treated as interpretive caveats. Consider two separate coding schemes which, by virtue of their different objectives, are complimentary:

- SNOMED (Standard Nomenclature of Medicine) codes which are intend to capture the variety of detail within a single diagnosis (such as otitis media) using a multi-factorial interpretive scheme
- ICD (International Classification of Disease) codes, which index disease for epidemiological purposes (and now billing) as aggregates

ICD codes become a means of extracting a complete set of diagnoses, perhaps with an oversort, and SNOMED offers a means of dividing these cases in a useful, analytic manner. Using markup to code a diagnosis both ways we can, in this somewhat more complicated manner, achieve a precision that is much more like an asymptotic relationship than a simple, rigid definition, where the final judgment is left to the user.

With this in mind, the usefulness and purpose of a tagged data base is to increase the descriptive potential in the data in order to better extract different problem-solving relationships for different application programs, each designed to serve the particular interests of one set out of a variety of stakeholders. One conceives of an electronic patient healthcare record that is a compendium of time oriented, marked up documents stored relationally in folders, which can be searched and abstracted into objects designed for these particular applications with their particular objectives.*

Some example objectives are (with considerable overlap):

- Identifying the outlier sick individuals in a clinic practice where most with similar symptoms have minor illnesses
- Adjusting the presentation of information to the problem-solving style of each user
- Determining when a guideline is appropriate and when it should be overridden

It is the neutral enabling property of SGML that is hard for some to see at first exposure. It allows more, by doing less. It does not complete the job, but rather leaves that to another module: the application, and yet another: the judgment of the user. ■

References

1. Langer, Susanne Katherina Knauth. "Philosophy in a new key: A study in the symbolism of reason, rite and art." Cambridge, Mass.: Harvard University Press, 1942.
2. Wegener, Philipp. "Untersuchungen uber die Grundfragen des Sprachlebens" [first published 1885] newly edited, with an introduction by Clemens Knobloch, by Konrad Koerner. Amsterdam; Philadelphia: J. Benjamins Pub. Co., 1991.
3. For an English translation see Abse, D. Wilfred. "Speech and reason. Language disorder in mental disease & a translation of 'The life of speech' [by] Philipp Wegener." Charlottesville, University Press of Virginia, 1971.
4. Harding, Lloyd, *lloyd@bonsai.infoauto.com*, on listserv *sgml-hl7@list.mc.duke.edu*.

About the Author

Thomas L. Lincoln, M.D.
Rom Lincoln, MD
RAND Corporation
1700 Main Street
Santa Monica, CA 90407
lincoln@rand.org

Thomas L. Lincoln, M.D. (Yale Med 1960) took his advanced training in Pathology at Yale and Johns Hopkins before joining the staff of the Institute for Applied Mathematics University of MD, and later the National Institute of General Medical Sciences, NIH. He has been a Senior Scientist at RAND in Santa Monica since 1967. Hav-

* We also refer you to Lincoln Stein's article, "The Electronic Medical Record: Promises and Threats," in the Summer 1997 issue of W3J entitled *Web Security: A Matter of Trust.*

ing retired in 1996 as Emeritus Professor of Research Pathology after 20 years at the University of Southern California, he has just taken a position on the faculty in the School of Biomedical and Health Information Sciences, College of Associated Health Professions, University of Illinois at Chicago. His interests over more than 30 years have been in various aspects of medical computing, with emphasis in the past ten years on health care information systems. This led to work over 20 years with Andersen Consulting, and to a role as reviewer of the NLM IAIMS (Integrated Advanced Information Management Systems) programs. He is a member of the American College of Medical Informatics, American Medical Informatics Association, American Medical Association, IEE, ACM, etc.

XML
Can the Desperate Perl Hacker Do It?

Michael Leventhal

Abstract

Is Perl a suitable language for programming XML? The use of Perl with XML is illustrated in this article with a program that checks to see if an XML document is well-formed. The relative simplicity of the program demonstrates that lightweight Perl programs may be used with XML, although Unicode and the use of entities make it difficult for Perl programmers to handle some XML files.

Perl Meets XML

This article presents a little program written in Perl (4) which checks the well-formedness of an XML document. We'll discuss what well-formedness is exactly in a couple of paragraphs. The main purpose of this article is to show that Perl hackers can do it; that is, that little programs, utility scripts, and CGI stuff, can be hacked in the hacking language of choice, Perl.

Java is all sizzle and sex these days and while proclaiming my liking for Java in the extreme it is not terribly controversial to assert that Java is

- NOT a quick and dirty hacking language
- BEYOND the ken of most people who write computer programs, professional programmers being a minority within this group

I think XML is going to become the ubiquitious standard for the encoding of text, and people a lot smarter than me have already said that—so it stands a reasonable chance of being approximately true. Not only is Perl the pre-eminent, practically uncontested hacking language, but it is doubly pre-eminent in the hacking of text where its regular expression facilities outshine every competitor. People will hack: they will hack text, they will hack text encoding in XML, they will hack in Perl, they will hack XML in Perl. Java will be the language of choice for pristine computer programs and billions of lines of code will be handy-randy shoved into miserable little Perl programs that do all the dirty work.

The Catch: Perl and Unicode

Lovely or unlovely as my proposition of a harmonious coexistence between Java and Perl may be, there is at least one rather important impediment to this vision: Unicode. Perl regular expressions assume 8-bit characters. It is neither terribly difficult to read and write wide characters, nor is it impossible to perform regular expressions on wide character strings, but such acts may prove to be a "royal pain in the butt-inski." You can get away with saying that most 8-bit character files are Unicode—for the time being that is as close to being Unicode as Perl will get. XML, on the other hand, has taken the hard line on Unicode: XML processors must be able to read both UTF-8 and UCS-2 documents and use the Byte Order Mark in UCS-2 to distinguish which is which. It is more or less the case that Perl programs cannot, by this definition, be XML processors. However, the fact that Perl programs cannot be XML processors does not mean that Perl can't and won't be written to do useful things with 8-bit XML documents.

Well-Formedness in a Nutshell

The program described in this article (Example 1) does something useful with XML documents; it checks to see if they are "well-formed." The essential objective in well-formedness checking is to make sure the document can be properly handled by an application that does not use or need the Document Type Definition (DTD). An application that does need to know the DTD would require a different kind of validation—a validity check—to ensure that the document instance follows the grammar expressed in the DTD. The standard requires all XML processors to, at a minimum, check well-formedness. At least one omnipresent application, browsing, is expected to not require anything beyond well-formedness; but it is my guess that in fact most applications will not use the DTD to process XML documents.

"Well-formed" is defined precisely in the XML standard, and more succintly than I could manage, as follows:

> *A textual object is said to be a well-formed XML document if, first, it matches the production labeled document, and if for each entity reference which appears in the document, either the entity has been declared in the document type declaration or the entity name is one of: amp, lt, gt, apos, quot.*
>
> *Matching the document production implies that:*
>
> 1. *It contains one or more elements.*
> 2. *It meets all the well-formedness constraints (WFCs) given in the grammar.*
> 3. *There is exactly one element, called the root, or document element, for which neither the start-tag nor the end-tag is in the content of any other element. For all other elements, if the start-tag is in the content of another element, the end-tag is in the content of the same element. More simply stated, the elements, delimited by start- and end-tags, nest within each other.*
>
> *As a consequence of this, for each non-root element* `C` *in the document, there is one other element* `P` *in the document such that* `C` *is in the content of* `P`*, but is not in the content of any other element that is in the content of* `P`*. Then* `P` *is referred to as the parent of* `C`*, and* `C` *as a child of* `P`*.*

There is a bit more to "matching the document production" than stated; one has to actually look at the document production to get every bit of it. There are various things other than elements that may appear in an XML document, as well as some well-formed conditions to check with respect to their syntax and order.

Caveats

Now I have to admit that I've lied. My program is not a well-formedness checker because I have not done anything with entities. An entity is, well, lots of things—but generally a placeholder for a text or data object that is stored elsewhere. Entities are a good idea in theory since they allow you to store a bit of text that may be used in, say, thousands of files in a single location. When it is time to modify that bit of text this is performed once rather than thousands of times in each file. The idea sounds so good it is hard to believe that entities have proven to be of relatively little use in SGML practice. Among the reasons for this are that other, more robust and complete tools are usually used to manage text fragments outside of SGML's internal mechanisms. Only slightly tongue-in-cheek do we point out the following: had the designers of entities known Perl they would not have invented them in the first place—why bother when you can write a script to replace text in 50,000 files in less than 30 seconds.

Along with text replacement, there are approximately 11 other uses for entities in SGML: fewer in XML than in SGML but still more than the one described in XML, so the entity picture isn't nearly as simple as one may think. Parameter entities, used to modularize DTDs, particularly complicate matters.

One of the goals of XML, as actually stated in the standard is the following:

> *It shall be easy to write programs which process XML documents.*

Of course, this isn't exactly an objective statement. A few more objective criteria have been proposed as modifications of this statement, but no consensus has been reached. To some, "easy" means that a Perl hacker* supplied with enough Jolt cola can write an XML application in a single sitting. To others, it means a computer science graduate student writing an XML parser over the weekend. Another point of view is that the complexity of XML is relatively unimportant in determining whether or not it is easy to write programs. Programs will simply use an XML API that hides the complexity of XML, and applications will be constructed with component architectures such as JavaBeans.

Anyway, my objective is to answer the question—is XML a format that Perl programmers will come to love because of its speed and ease in hacking together applications? The answer is a qualified yes—the two doubtful areas are Unicode and entities.

The following is a list of things I would need to do to handle entities according to the last draft of the XML standard:

1. I must read both the internal and external DTD subsets. I could have entity declarations in either.

   I'm not sure that I'm helped any by the fact that the rules are different for the internal and external subsets. In fact, maybe the fact that they are different just makes it harder. (Internal: No marked sections and "integral" parameter entity declarations.)

   Of course it would help if I could use the declaration `RMD=internal`. But then I would only have a well-formedness checker for documents with `RMD=internal` or `RMD=none`.

2. In view of the above, I must process marked sections in order to correctly interpret the external DTD and possible entity declarations declared within them.

3. I must handle paramter entities. They are used in the declaration of marked sections and also may be used within entity declarations.

4. I must completely expand nested entities to ensure that a general entity isn't recursive, as well as to instantiate it in the document for the document production check.

5. Since it is a WF error to use an entity reference to binary data, I must note which general entities refer to binary data.

After I checked how many cans of Jolt I had in stock, I said forget it.

So here is what my program does do: it checks the document production without expanding entities and without looking at the DTD, either external or internal. It is perfectly adequate for checking the well-formedness of any document with or without entities although the consequences of expanding the entity references are not taken into account.

Real-World Experience

This program started out as an XML transformation engine; I used it to teach XML Web programming to the students in my U.C. Berkeley Extension class. The document is treated as an event stream—each time a start tag, end tag, empty tag, or content is seen, a processing routine is invoked. The name of the processing routine was generated from the tag name and concatenated with the names of ancestor tags to achieve context sensivity. The core program—that is, everything except the processing routines themselves—took thirty lines. Although the processing routine invocation has been removed, most of the program is intact in the `process_element` subroutine (see Example 1). My students, 90% of whom were non-programmers,

* Known to the XML cognoscenti as the DPH, or "Desperate Perl Hacker."

were able to use this framework to write fairly complete CGI programs for transforming XML into HTML; for many it was the first time they had ever written a program in their lives. The program is also used on several Web sites in real-life XML applications.

The original program would catch errors in tag nesting but lacked error reporting and recovery. It would "report" errors by crashing! It did not check for all possible error conditions dicated by the document production. It cost a couple of hundred lines to make the program more complete but it is still a pretty lightweight piece of work.

A point to be gleaned from the above is that the approach used in this program is *useful.* Although it does not process entities and does not handle UCS-2 Unicode documents, it works very well indeed for the projects for which it was intended.

Example 1

```
#!/usr/bin/perl
##########################################################################
# iswf - checks an XML file to see if it is well-formed.                 #
#                                                                        #
#                                                                        #
# iswf < XMLINPUT                                                        #
# writes error messages to STDOUT                                        #
#                                                                        #
# M.Leventhal, Grif, S.A.                                                #
# michael@grif.fr                                                          #
# 1 Sept 1997                                                            #
#                                                                        #
# Notes: based on 07-Aug-97 XML Working draft. Not complete, does no     #
# entity checks, ASCII-only, among other omissions, but catches lots of  #
# stuff.                                                                  #
#                                                                        #
# Unrestricted use is hereby granted as long as the author is credited or #
# discredited as the case may be.                                        #
##########################################################################

# The first two lines cause the entire document is read into the
# $file variable. This spares me certain
# complications which arise from reading it line by line
# and Perl is able to do this sort of thing fairly
# efficiently.

undef($/);
$file = <>;

# I loop through the file, processing each start or end
# tag when it is seen.

while ($file =~ /[^<]*<(\/)?([^>]+)>/) {
  $st_or_et = $1;
  $gi = $2;
  $file = $';

# I recognize the following kinds of objects: XML declaration
# (a particular type of processing instruction), processing
```

Example 1 *(continued)*

```
# instructions, comments, doctype declaration, cdata marked
# sections, and elements. Since the document production has
# order rules I set a flag when a particlar type of object
# has been processed. I invoke a subroutine to process each
# type of object.

 if ($gi =~ /^\?XML/) {
   &process_decl;
   $decl_seen = 1;
 }
 elsif ($gi =~ /^\?/) {
   &process_pi;
   $misc_seen = 1;
 }
 elsif ($gi =~ /^!\-\-/) {
   &process_comment;
   $misc_seen;
 }
 elsif ($gi =~ /^!DOCTYPE/) {
   &process_doctype;
   $doctype_seen = 1;
 }
 elsif ($gi =~ /^\!\[CDATA\[/) {
   &process_cdata;
 }
 else {
   &process_element;
   $element_seen = 1;
 }
}

# There are some checks to catch various errors at the end. I
# make sure I have emptied the stack of all parents and I
# make sure there is no uncontained character data hanging
# around.

&check_empty_stack;
&check_uncontained_pcdata;

# Print a happy message if there are no errors.

&check_error_count;

#--------------------------------------------------------------------#
sub check_error_count {
if ($error_count == 0) {
  print "This document appears to be well-formed.\n"; }
}
#--------------------------------------------------------------------#

# Check to see if the ancestor stack containing all parents up to the
# root is empty.
```

Example 1 *(continued)*

```
sub check_empty_stack {
if ($#ancestors > -1) {
  &print_error_at_context;
}
}
#------------------------------------------------------------------------------#

# Check to see if there is any uncontained PCDATA lying around (white space
# at the end of the document doesn't count). I check also to see that
# a root to the document was found which catches a null file error.

sub check_uncontained_pcdata {
if ($file !~ /^\s*$/ || $ROOT eq "") {
  $error_count++;
  print "\nNot well formed uncontained #PCDATA or null file\n";
}
}
#------------------------------------------------------------------------------#

# Check that the XML declaration is coded properly and in the correct
# position (before any other object in the file and occuring only
# once.)

sub process_decl {
if ($decl_seen || $misc_seen || $doctype_seen || $element_seen) {
  $error_count++;
  print "XML declaration can only be at the head of the document.\n";
}

# No checks are performed on processing instructions but the following
# will be used to store the PI in the $gi variable and advance the
# file pointer.

&process_pi;

# This is slightly lazy since we allow version='1.0". It is quite simple
# to fix just by making an OR of each parameter with either ' ' or " "
# quote marks.

if ($gi !~/\?XML\s+version=[\'\"]1.0[\'\"](\s+encoding=[\'\"][^\'\"]*[\'\"])?
    (\s+RMD=[\'\"](NONE|INTERNAL|ALL)[\'\"])?\s*\?/)
{
  $error_count++;
  print "Format of XML declaration is wrong.\n";
}
}
#------------------------------------------------------------------------------#

# Check that the Doctype statement is in the right position and, otherwise,
# make no attempt to parse its contents, including the root element. The
# root element will determined from the element production itself and
# the "claim" of the Doctype won't be verified.
```

Example 1 *(continued)*

```
sub process_doctype {
if ($doctype_seen || $element_seen) {
  $error_count++;
  print "Doctype can only appear once and must be within prolog.\n";
}
if ($gi =~ /\[/ && $gi !~ /\]$/) {
  $file =~ /\]>/;
  $file = $';
  $gi = $gi.$`.$&;
}
}
#----------------------------------------------------------------------------#

# Performs the well-formed check necessary to verify that CDATA is not
# nested. We will pick up the wrong end of CDATA marker if this is the
# case so the error message is critical.

sub process_cdata {
if ($gi !~ /\]\]$/) {
  $file =~ /\]\]>/;
  $file = $';
  $gi = $gi.$`."]]";
}
$gi =~ /\!\[CDATA\[(.*)\]\]/;
$body = $1;
if ($body =~ /<\!\[CDATA\[/) {
  print "Nested CDATA.\n";
  &print_error_at_context;
}
}
#----------------------------------------------------------------------------#

# Performs the well-formed check of ensuring that '--' is not nested
# in the comment body which would cause problems for SGML processors.

sub process_comment {
if ($gi !~ /\-\-$/) {
  $file =~ /\-\->/;
  $file = $';
  $gi = $gi.$`."--";
}
$gi =~ /\!\-\-((.|\n)*)\-\-/;
$body = $1;
if ($body =~ /\-\-/) {
  $error_count++;
  print "Comment contains --.\n";
}
}
#----------------------------------------------------------------------------#

# This is the main subroutine which handles the ancestor stack (in an
# array) checking the proper nesting of the element part of the document
# production.
```

Example 1 *(continued)*

```
sub process_element {

# Distinguish between empty elements which do not add a parent to the
# ancestor stack and elements which can have content.

if ($gi =~ /\/$/) {
  $xml_empty = 1;
  $gi =~ s/\/$//;

# XML well-formedness says every document must have a container so an
# empty element cannot be the root, even if it is the only element in
# the document.

   if (!$element_seen) {
     print "Empty element <$gi/> cannot be the root.\n";
   }
}
else {
  $xml_empty = 0;
}

# Check to see that attributes are well-formed.

if ($gi =~ /\s/) {
  $gi = $`;
  $attrline = $';
  $attrs = $attrline;

# This time we properly check to see that either ' ' or " " is
# used to surround the attribute values.

  while ($attrs =~ /\s*([^\s=]*)\s*=\s*(("[^"]*")|('[^']*'))/) {

# An end tag may not, of course, have attributes.

      if ($st_or_et eq "\/") {
        print "Attributes may not be placed on end tags.\n";
        &print_error_at_context;
      }
      $attrname = $1;

# Check for a valid attribute name.

      &check_name($attrname);
      $attrs = $';
     }
     $attrs =~ s/\s//g;

# The above regex should have processed all the attributes. If anything
# is left after getting rid of white space it is because the attribute
# expressesion was malformed.
```

Example 1 *(continued)*

```
      if ($attrs ne "") {
        print "Malformed attributes.\n";
        &print_error_at_context;
      }
  }

# If XML is declared case-sensitive the following line should be
# removed. At the moment it isn't so I set everything to lower
# case so we can match start and end tags irrespective of case
# differences.

$gi =~ tr/A-Z/a-z/;
if (!$element_seen) {
  $ROOT = $gi; }

# Check to see that the generic identifier is a well-formed name.

&check_name($gi);

# If I have an end tag I just check the top of the stack, the
# end tag must match the last parent or it is an error. If I
# find an error I have I could either pop or not pop the stack.
# What I want is to perform some manner of error recovery so
# I can continue to report well-formed errors on the rest of
# the document. If I pop the stack and my problem was caused
# by a missing end tag I will end up reporting errors on every
# tag thereafter. If I don't pop the stack and the problem
# was caused by a misspelled end tag name I will also report
# errors on every following tag. I happened to chose the latter.

if ($st_or_et eq "\/") {
  $parent = $ancestors[$#ancestors];
  if ($parent ne $gi) {
    if (@ancestors eq $ROOT) { @ancestors = ""; }
    else {
      &print_error_at_context;
    }
  }
  else {
    pop @ancestors;
  }
}
else {

# This is either an empty tag or a start tag. In the latter case
# push the generic identifier onto the ancestor stack.

   if (!$xml_empty) {
     push (@ancestors, $gi); }
}

}
#----------------------------------------------------------------------------#
```

Example 1 *(continued)*

```
# Skip over processing instructions.

sub process_pi {
if ($gi !~ /\?$/) {
   $file =~ /\?>/;
   $gi = $gi.$`."?";
   $file = $';
}
}
#--------------------------------------------------------------------------#
sub print_error_at_context {

# This routine prints out an error message with the contents of the
# ancestor stack so the context of the error can be identified.

# It would be most helpful to have line numbers. In principle it
# is possible but more difficult since we choose to not process the
# document line by line. We could still count line break characters
# as we scan the document.

# Nesting errors can cause every tag thereafter to generate an error
# so stop at 10.

if ($error_count == 10) {
  print "More than 10 errors ...\n";
  $error_count++;
}
else {
  $error_count++;
  print "Not well formed at context ";

# Just cycle through the ancestor stack.

  foreach $element (@ancestors) {
    print "$first$element";
    $first = "->";
  }
  $first = "";
  print " tag: <$st_or_et$gi $attrline>\n";
}

}
#--------------------------------------------------------------------------#

# Check for a well-formed Name as defined in the Name production.

sub check_name {
local($name) = @_;
```

Example 1 *(continued)*

```
if ($name !~ /^[A-Za-z_:][\w\.\-:]*$/) {
  print "Invalid element or attribute name: $name\n";
  &print_error_at_context;
}
}
#-----------------------------------------------------------------------------#
```

Conclusion

I've been writing Perl programs to process SGML for the last several years, aware of, but blithely undisturbed by, the fact that

1. My SGML files may not have followed all the rules, and
2. My programs could only handle my private SGML variants.

On the other hand, I've rewritten lots of programs over and over again because I did not and could not adhere to a fixed standard. XML is attractive, in principle, because it gives me an attainable target for my Perl programs. And if the promise holds we should start seeing hundreds, maybe thousands, of reusable Perl modules appearing on the Web which will make XML as easy to process as ordinary strings. It will be the ubiquitious text format.

I think the program in Example 1 illustrates that Perl programs can do XML. It would be a blessing for all if those working on the XML standard would simplify entity processing a bit more and fight like the devil against any and all attempts to restuff the relatively Spartan design of XML with padding and fluff from SGML's historical legacy. From the perspective of the Desperate Perl Hacker, XML would do well to simplify a bit more, and cannot afford to add complications of relatively little value. ■

About the Author

Michael Leventhal
Grif, S.A.
Vice-President, Technology
1800 Lake Shore Avenue
Suite 14
Oakland, California 94606
Michael.Leventhal@grif.fr

Michael Leventhal is Vice-President, Technology for GRIF and is responsible for the definition and planning of GRIF's XML products. Before joining GRIF he ran his own consulting company and has worked for Oracle and other Silicon Valley firms in software architecture and development. He has taught an SGML class for U.C. Berkeley Extension and is writing a book on XML and Intranets which will be published by Prentice-Hall next year.

XML

From Bytes to Characters

Bert Bos

Abstract

XML is a syntax for storing hierarchically organized data such as directories, catalogues, user manuals, etc. It can store only textual data, but that is not a severe restriction. This article defines, in some detail, how text is stored in an XML file. It also describes how an XML file is encoded for transportation over the Internet, and upon arrival, decoded again. Under the Internet model for transport of text files, the encoding/decoding may result in a "different" file (i.e., a different sequence of bytes), but retains exactly the same text and structure.

Introduction

An XML file is a simple text file—just like HTML, but unlike a WordPerfect or DBase file, for example. The advantage is that you can usually make sense of an XML file even without XML software, just by viewing it as a text file in WordPad or vi. You can spell-check or *grep* it. The structure of an XML file is so simple that you can write one "by hand"—that is, with any editor or word processor that can write text files. Of course, with specialized XML software, it will probably be easier.

Choosing a text format for XML has a slight cost in efficiency, since every time an XML file is used by a program, it has to be *parsed*: i.e., the linear sequence of characters has to be converted into a complex structure in memory. And since the XML format has been kept human-readable and human-writable to some extent, there are many different ways of writing the same XML document—and the program has to understand them all.

There is also another disadvantage of text format: although most computers have a way of dealing with text files, the files aren't always portable. Here's a common problem: somebody creates text with quote marks or accented letters on one computer and gives it to a friend with a different computer. Suddenly the quotes and accents show up as completely different symbols. The problem can get much worse if you exchange files in different languages: have you ever wondered how the Russians manage to get Cyrillic letters on their screen?

In the following sections I'll show how this problem is handled on the Web and how XML itself has provisions for making it portable. But before that, I'll present a definition of an XML document and its representation as a text file that is somewhat different—more precise—than the way XML is usually described.

XML as a Data Type

You may have noticed that I use the terms XML *file* and XML *document*. XML file refers to the text file, which is a sequence of characters (letters, digits, and other symbols); and XML document refers to the abstract structure, which may be some data structure in memory. An XML document may be the result of parsing an XML file, or it may be constructed directly in memory. It is possible that several different XML files all represent the same document.

On the Web, when you retrieve a document from a server, you get a stream of bytes, which your browser then interprets. In many cases (but not always) the stream of bytes existed as a file on the server's disk. Regardless of whether a file ever existed on the server's disk, I will refer to the stream of bytes—or more precisely the stream of characters represented by those bytes—as the XML file.

The way XML is usually explained starts with a description of XML file syntax, followed by rules for parsing them. I'll start at the other end, by defining XML documents as an (abstract) data structure, and then showing how this data structure is converted to a sequence of characters. In other words, rather than explaining how to *parse* an XML file, I will describe how to *generate* one. We call the latter process *marshaling*.*

Marshaling (a.k.a. "serializing," "pickling" or "flattening") is a term used in the theory of interprocess communication. When two programs need to exchange some data structure, they have to agree on a way to represent the data as a sequence of bytes. That is exactly what is happening when two programs on different machines exchange an XML document. For XML, however, there is also an intermediate representation as a sequence of characters, before the characters are further encoded as bytes.

An XML document is a tree structure. There is a root node, called the root element, and the other nodes are all descendants of the root. All nodes are of one of four types:

- Character
- Processing instruction (PI)
- Comment
- Element

A *character node* contains one character and has no other structure. All characters from the Unicode/ISO-10646 repertoire are allowed. A *processing instruction* node has two fields: a *name* (also called *target*) and a *content,* which is a sequence of characters. A *comment node* has only one field: content, which contains a sequence of characters.

Characters, PIs, and comments have no children, so they are always leaf nodes in an XML document tree. Their parent node is always an element node. In fact, XML states that there must be at least one element in each document, viz., the root node.

Element nodes are much more complex. Not only do they have children, but they also have a *name* (sometimes called a "generic identifier" or GI), and a set of *attributes*. Attributes are keyword-value pairs. Each keyword may occur at most once in an attribute set. The value is again a sequence of characters.

Elements can have zero or more children, and the children are ordered—for example, you can talk about the "seventh child node." This is in contrast to the element's attributes, which are not ordered, but form a set. An element with zero children is called an "empty element."†

An element node may also have a *schema* (also called "doctype" or "namespace"). In XML 1.0, only the root element can have a schema (and it implicitly applies to all elements in the document), but in XML 1.1 all elements can have one.

An XML-based application can store data in all the different types of nodes and in all the fields of each node. XML places no restrictions on what each node or field may be used for, with the exception of the schema field. The schema, if it exists, must be a URL and it must point to something that contains documentation for how an application uses this element and its child nodes. Part of that documentation may be machine read-

* Marshaling, in fact, refers to both the generating and parsing processes, but I'll talk only about the generating step.

† People versed in SGML terminology will notice that I use the term "element" where I should have said "element instance." However, talking about an "instance" presupposes that there is also an "element type" or "element class." In SGML that is indeed the case, but in XML, element typing is optional.

able, allowing an automatic validity check of the element.*

An ADT for XML

This section defines the four types of nodes and their characteristics with mathematical rigor.

An ADT (Abstract Data Type) is a set of mathematical equations that define exactly what information can be stored in a certain data structure. It doesn't show an actual implementation in a computer program, but rather defines the behavior that all implementations must have in common. It relies on set theory. The data type, in this case XML, is regarded as a set. A number of functions are defined on this set to show how it maps back and forth to other well known sets, such as the set of integers and the set of characters.

Because it uses functions, an ADT may look a bit like an API (Application Program Interface), the documentation of a software library. An ADT can indeed be used as a starting point for writing a software library, but for efficiency reasons, the actual functions implemented are often a bit different from the ADT (although they can be expressed in each other). Whereas the primary goal of an ADT is to make the mathematics easy, an API tries to make programming easy (and efficient).

The structure of this ADT is

```
function name : domain -> range
```

Equations that hold for this function are shown here. Variables implicitly have universal scope (i.e., `[forall] X`)

The sets that are used are:

`char[]`
: The set of all sequences of zero or more characters. The square brackets (`[]`) are suggestive of the fact that this is a set consisting of sequences.

`nil`
: The singleton set consisting only of the symbol `nil`.

`error`
: The singleton set consisting only of the symbol `error`.

`Identifier`
: The set of all "names." Names are in fact character sequences with a syntax defined in the XML specification. I'll not define that syntax here, except to note that a name never contains a space or angle bracket characters (< or >).

`boolean`
: The set consisting of the two symbols "true" and "false."

`int`
: The set of whole numbers `{..., -2, -1, 0, 1, 2,...}`

The notation 2^X indicates the *power set* of `X`, i.e., the collection of all possible subsets of `X`.

The ADT for XML is shown in Table 1.

Table 1

```
create : Identifier -> XML
setSchema : XML × URL -> XML
getSchema : XML -> URL + nil
    getSchema(create(S)) = nil
    getSchema(setSchema(X, U)) = U
setAttribute : XML × Identifier × char[] -> XML
```

* XML, in fact, defines a separate language that can be used in the machine-readable part of the documentation. I'll not explain that language in this article.

Table 1 *(continued)*

```
getAttribute : XML × Identifier -> char[] + nil
getAttributes : XML -> 2^Identifier
      getAttribute(create(S), I) = nil
      getAttribute(setAttribute(X, I, S), I) = S
      I1 <> I2 => getAttribute(setAttribute(X, I1, S), I2) = getAttribute(X, I2)
      getAttributes(create(S)) = {}
      getAttributes(setAttribute(X, I, S)) = getAttributes(X) + {I}
      getAttribute(X, I) = getAttribute(setSchema(X, U), I)
      getAttributes(X) = getAttributes(setSchema(X, U))
      getSchema(X) = getSchema(setAttribute(X, I, S))
addNode : XML × XML × char -> XML + error
setNode : XML × int × XML × char -> XML + error
getNode : XML × int -> XML + char + nil
nrNodes : XML -> int
isNode : XML × XML -> boolean
isDescendant : XML × XML -> boolean
isFamily : XML × XML -> boolean
     isNode(X1, X2) <=> E N : getNode(X1, N) = X2
     isDescendant(X1, X2) <=> isNode(X1, X2) | (E X3 : isNode(X3, X2) &
       isDescendant(X1, X3))
     isFamily(X1, X2) <=> X1 = X2 | isDescendant(X1, X2) | isDescendant(X2, X1)
     isFamily(X1, X2) => addNode(X1, X2) = error
     isFamily(X1, X2) => setNode(X1, N, X2) = error
     N < 1 => setNode(X1, N, X2) = error
     N > nrNodes(X1) => setNode(X1, N, X2) = error
     N < 1 => getNode(X, N) = nil
     N > nrNodes(X) => getNode(X, N) = nil
     nrNodes(create(I)) = 0
     ¬isFamily(X1, X2) => nrNodes(addNode(X1, X2)) = nrNodes(X1) + 1
     ¬isFamily(X1, X2) & 0 < N <= nrNodes(X1) => getNode(setNode(X1, N, X2), N)
          = X2
     ¬isFamily(X1, X2) & N = nrNodes(X1) + 1 => getNode(addNode(X1, X2)), N) = X2
     ¬isFamily(X1, X2) => getNode(X1, N) = getNode(addNode(X1, X2), N)
     ¬isFamily(X1, X2) & 0 < M <= nrNodes(X1) & N <> M => getNode(setNode(X1, M,
          X2), N) = getNode(X1, N)
     getNode(setSchema(X1, U), N) = getNode(X1, N)
     getNode(setAttribute(X1, I, S), N) = getNode(X1, N)
     ¬isFamily(X1, X2) => getAttribute(addNode(X1, X2), I) = getAttribute(X1, I)
     ¬isFamily(X1, X2) & 0 < N <= nrNodes(X1) => getAttribute(setNode(X1, N, X2),
          I) = getAttribute(X1, I)
     ¬isFamily(X1, X2) => getAttributes(addNode(X1, X1)) = getAttributes(X1)
     ¬isFamily(X1, X2) & 0 < N <= nrNodes(X1) => getAttributes(setNode(X1, N, X2))
        = getAttributes(X1)
     ¬isFamily(X1, X2) => getSchema(addNode(X1, X2)) = getSchema(X1)
     ¬isFamily(X1, X2) & 0 < N <= nrNodes(X1) => getSchema(setNode(X2, N, X2))
        = getSchema(X1)
getName : XML -> Identifier
     getName(create(I)) = I
     getName(setSchema(X, U)) = getName(X)
     getName(setAttribute(X, I, S)) = getName(X)
     ¬isFamily(X1, X2) => getName(addNode(X1, X2)) = getName(X1)
     ¬isFamily(X1, X2) & 0 < N <= nrNodes(X1) => getName(setNode(X1, N, X2))
        = getName(X1)
```

Table 1 *(continued)*

```
deleteAttribute : XML × Identifier -> XML
     deleteAttribute(create(I1), I2) = create(I1)
     getSchema(deleteAttribute(X, I)) = getSchema(X)
     getAttribute(deleteAttribute(X, I), I) = nil
     getAttributes(deleteAttribute(X, I)) = getAttributes(X) \ {I}
     getNode(deleteAttribute(X, I), N) = getNode(X, N)
     getName(deleteAttribute(X, I)) = getName(X)
popNode : XML -> XML
     popNode(create(I)) = create(I)
     ¬isFamily(X1, X2) => popNode(addNode(X1, X2)) = X1
     ¬isFamily(X1, X2) & 0 < N < nrNodes(X1) => popNode(setNode(X1, N, X2))
          = setNode(popNode(X1), N, X2)
     ¬isFamily(X1, X2) & N = nrNodes(X1) => popNode(setNode(X1, N, X2))
          = popNode(X1)
     nrNodes(X) > 0 => nrNodes(popNode(X)) = nrNodes(X) - 1
     N < nrNodes(X) => getNode(popNode(X), N) = getNode(X, N)
     getSchema(popNode(X)) = getSchema(X)
     getAttribute(popNode(X), I) = getAttribute(X)
     getAttributes(popNode(X)) = getAttributes(X)
     getName(popNode(X)) = getName(X)
```

Linearizing the Tree

The first step in the marshaling process is a conversion from an XML document to an XML file. As I said earlier, there may be several text files that represent the same document, so this process is non-deterministic. Or, expressed differently, the decisions as to what representation to choose may come from elsewhere, such as from considerations of taste or efficiency.

Converting the tree structure to a linear sequence of characters is a recursive process. For each element the same routine is essentially followed. The process starts at the root element.

To linearize an element node, first check if it has a schema—remember that in XML 1.0 only the root element can have a schema. (It is also likely that XML 1.1 will introduce alternative ways to represent a schema, but for now, there is only one.)

If an element has a schema, write the following text to the XML file:

```
<!doctype name "schema">
```

where *name* is the name of the element and *schema* is the schema (a URL). The schema must be quoted and certain characters in it must be escaped: if <, >, &, or " occur in the URL, they must be written as "`<`", "`>`", "`&:`", and "`"`" respectively, or as equivalent escape codes (see the "Character encoding" section). It is also possible to use single quotes ('), in which case any single quote in the URL must be escaped. The section "An XML Marshaling Function" gives the possible variations.

Next, write the name of the element, preceded by <, like this:

```
<name
```

XML restrict the possible names of elements, but all we need to know here is that names never contain < or >, nor do they contain spaces, tabs, or newlines.

If the element has attributes, write all of them as follows (the order of the attributes doesn't matter):

```
name="value"
```

again escaping the characters <, >, & and ". Then write >:

```
>
```

The three steps above produce what is know as a "start tag." Some examples of starts tags are:

```
<p>
<sect n="7" mode="public">
<emph>
```

Next, write all the children recursively. After the children, repeat the name of the element, between </ and >:

```
</name>
```

The reason for this repetition of the name is to make it easier to catch errors that may occur if an XML file is created "by hand," and the author forgets to open or close an element.

A complete linearization of an element "name" with children "first" and "last" may look like this:

```
<name><first
    val="Jan"></first><last
    val="Klaassen"></last></name>
```

To linearize a comment node, simply write the content field, which is a sequence of characters, enclosed in <!-- and -->:

```
<!--content-->
```

Obviously, the --> sequence may not occur in the content. XML doesn't define a rule to escape this occurrence. The expectation is that comments will usually contain text meant for human eyes rather than for processing by a program—so it doesn't really matter how the --> is avoided. A program that *does* want to make use of comments will simply have to define its own rule for escaping them.

To linearize a PI node, write the following sequence:

```
<?name content?>
```

If the characters <, >, or & occur in the content, they must be escaped.[*]

To linearize a character node, simply write the character. The one exception is when it is a <, >, &, or a CR (Carriage Return, ASCII 13), in which case it must be written as "<", ">", "&", or "
" respectively, or as an equivalent escape (see "Character encoding").

Because XML doesn't distinguish CR from LF (Line Feed, ASCII 10), the CR must be escaped. The reason for this is that text editors usually don't allow you to enter one or the other; what the editor creates depends on whether you are on a Mac (where the editor will insert a CR), on UNIX (an LF), or DOS/Windows (a CR+LF pair). XML defines that all three (CR, LF, and CR+LF) actually stand for an LF. This is also the convention used by the standard C I/O library, and similar to many other formats, such as PostScript.

With the above linearization rules, the structure in Figure 1 can be linearized as follows:

```
<doc date="16/8/97"
    author="anonymous"><head><title>
    Title</title
></head><body><!--the body-->body</
    body></doc>
```

Though you might expect that you could write the elements below each other, on separate lines, like this:

```
*    <doc date="16/8/97" author=
               "anonymous">
       <head>
         <title>
           Title
         </title>
       </head>
       <body>
         <!--the body-->
         body
       </body>
     </doc>
```

that is not possible.[†] Of course, there may be applications based on XML in which it *is* possible.

---

* Actually, the June 1977 draft of XML is not clear on this. It says that PIs are normally intended for processing by programs, unlike comments, but it doesn't say explicitly that <, >, and & must be escaped.

† This is based on the XML draft of June 1997. Several people have suggested that the linearization function should be allowed to insert a newline and a number of spaces after a > and before a <, but as of June 1997, that proposal has not been adopted.

One example is MathML, the mathematical markup language in which spaces will likely have no meaning [1].*

An XML Marshaling Function

Table 2 shows a formal definition of the above, using functions. The notation for the functions uses nondeterministic if-statements, borrowed from the programming language Simple, which in turn is based on Dijkstra's guarded commands:

```
if guard1 : stmt1
[] guard2 : stmt2
...
[] guardn : stmtn
fi
```

When evaluating this statement, from among all those `guards` that evaluate to true, one is picked nondeterministically and its statement is executed. The following statement:

```
if guard1 : stmt1
[] guard2 : stmt2
...
[] guardn : stmtn
[> stmt0
fi
```

is an abbreviation for

```
if guard1 : stmt1
[] guard2 : stmt2
...
[] guardn : stmtn
[] ~guard1 & ~guard2 &... & ~guardn
    : stmt0
fi
```

The linearization function in Table 2 makes use of a linearization function for Identifiers, called `writeIdentifier`. We assume that function doesn't produce any characters from the set {<, >, ", ', =, !, ?, <space>, <tab>, <CR>, <LF>} .

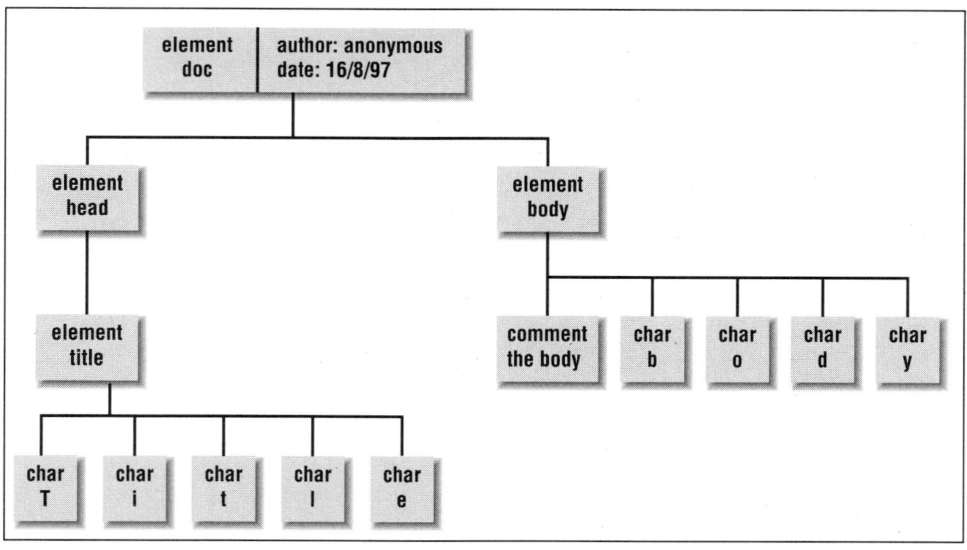

Figure 1

* See the MathML Working Draft included in the "W3C Reports" section.

Table 2

```
import writeIdentifier;
function writeXML(sofar: char[]; X: XML): char[];
  var
    s1, s2, s3, s4, s5: char;
  begin
    s1:= writeSchema(sofar, getSchema(X));
    s2:= s1 + opendelim(sofar + s1) + writeIdentifier(getName(X))
      + writeAttributes(X, getAttributes(X));
    if true :
      s3:= s2 + closedelim();
      s4:= s3 + writeNodes(s3, X, 1);
      s5:= s4 + opendelim(s3 + s4)
    [] nrNodes = 0 :
      s5:= s2 + whitespace(0);
    fi;
    writeXML:= s5 + "/" + writeIdentifier(getName(X)) + closedelim();
  end;

function writeSchema(sofar: char[]; url: char[]): char[];
  begin
    if url <> nil :
      writeSchema:= opendelim(sofar) + "!doctype"
        + whitespace(1) + writeString(url) + closedelim()
    [>
      writeSchema:= ""
    fi
  end;

function whitespace(min: integer): char[];
  begin
    if min <= 0 : whitespace:= ""
    [] true     : whitespace:= " " + whitespace(min - 1)
    [] true     : whitespace:= "" + whitespace(min - 1)
    [] true     : whitespace:= "
    [] true     : whitespace:= "
    fi
  end;

function space(min: integer): char[];
  begin
    if min <= 0 : space:= ""
    [] true     : space:= " " + space(min - 1)
    [] true     : space:= "" + space(min - 1)
    fi
  end;

function opendelim(sofar: char[]): char[];

  begin
    if endsWith(sofar, "
    [] endsWith(sofar, "
    [] endsWith(sofar, "
    [] endsWith(sofar, "
```

Table 2 *(continued)*

```
      [] endsWith(sofar, "
      [] endsWith(sofar, ">
      [] endsWith(sofar, ">
      [] endsWith(sofar, ">
      [] ~endsWith(sofar, "
         & ~endsWith(sofar, "
      [] ~endsWith(sofar, "
         & ~endsWith(sofar, "
      [] ~endsWith(sofar, "
         & ~endsWith(sofar, "
      fi
    end;

  function closedelim(): char[];

    begin
      if true : closedelim:= whitespace(0) + ">"
      [] true : closedelim:= whitespace(0) + ">" + "
      [] true : closedelim:= whitespace(0) + ">" + "
      [] true : closedelim:= whitespace(0) + ">" + "
      fi
    end;

  function writeString(s: char[]): char[];
    begin
    if true : writeString:= "\"" + writeChars(s, 1, "\"") + "\""
    [] true : writeString:= " " + writeChars(s, 1, " ") + " "
    fi
    end;

  function writeChars(s: char[]; start: integer; avoid: char): char[];
    begin
      if start <= length(s) :
        writeChars:= writeChar(s[start], avoid)
          + writeChars(s, start + 1, avoid)
      [>
        writeChars:= ""
    end;

  function writeChar(c, avoid: char): char[];
    begin
      if c = "\"" : writeChar:= """
      [] c = " "  : writeChar:= "&squot;"
      [] c = "<"  : writeChar:= "<"
      [] c = ">"  : writeChar:= ">"
      [] c = "&"  : writeChar:= "&"
      [] c = "
      [] c = "
      [] c = "
      [] true     : writeChar:= "&#" + decimal(ord(c)) + ";"
      [] true     : writeChar:= "&#x" + hexadecimal(ord(c)) + ";"
      [] c <> "<" & c <> "&gt" & c <> "&"
         & c <> "
```

Table 2 *(continued)*

```
    end;

  function writeAttribute(X: XML; names: set of Identifier;
                      name: Identifier): char[];
    begin
      writeAttribute:= whitespace(1) + writeIdentifier(name)
        + whitespace(0) + "=" + writeString(getAttribute(X, name))
        + writeAttributes(X, names - {name})
    end;

  function writeAttributes(X: XML; names: set of Identifier): char[];
    begin
      if names = {} :
        writeAttributes:= ""
      [>
        writeAttributes:= writeAttribute(X, names, getMember(names))
      fi
    end;

  function writeNodes(sofar: char[]; X: XML; n: integer): char[];
    var
      s: char[];
    begin
      if getNode(X, n) isa char :
        s:= writeChar(getNode(X, n));
        writeNodes:= s + writeNodes(s, X, n + 1)
      [] getNode(X, n) isa XML :
        s:= writeXML(sofar, getNode(X, n));
        writeNodes:= s + writeNodes(s, X, n + 1)
      [>
        writeNodes:= ""
      fi
    end;
```

Character Encoding

We have now linearized the XML document. To make it a true marshaling function, however, we have to convert still further, until we reach bytes.

XML could have picked a certain character to byte encoding, but there is a better way. The Internet, and the Web with it, have developed a method for computers to keep using their own character encoding, leaving it to receiving machines (the "clients") to convert text to their own encoding.

The model for exchange of text over the Internet is described in RFC 2130 [2], which was produced after a workshop in February 1996. The model describes various levels at which textual data can be exchanged, the lowest three of which deal with coding characters as numbers (the so-called Coded Character Set), numbers as bytes (Character Encoding Scheme), and with optional further transformations such as compression (Transfer Encoding Syntax).

The model works only if the encoding functions are among the well known ones—in other words, those for which a name has been registered with the Internet Assigned Numbers Authority (IANA).

Most computers in the U.S. use ASCII as the encoding, or ASCII with some extensions. ASCII, as used on the Internet, is both a Coded Character Set and a Character Encoding Scheme. It is a function that assigns bytes to about 100 letters, digits and punctuation marks; one byte for each character. For example, the letter `A` is encoded as the number `65` and then further encoded as the eight bits `01000001`.

Western Europe often uses ISO-8859-1, which encodes about 200 characters, also one byte per character. ISO-8859-1 includes mappings for certain accented characters, which are needed for words like the German süß or the French sucré.

In scripts with more letters, one byte per character is not enough. Japanese, for example, has tens of thousands of characters. Two bytes for each character would have worked, but for various reasons—some historical—many encoding functions are more complicated than that. An example is ISO-2022-JP. The number of bytes needed to encode a character varies, depending on the sequence of characters rather than each individual character.

So, for any computer, an XML file will be encoded with the usual character encoding of that computer (or alternatively, the one chosen by the user). When the file is transferred to another machine, the first machine has to tell the receiving end what encoding is used before it sends the file. This obviously puts some burden on the receiving programs, but this situation is acknowledged on the Internet: there are simply too many programs that produce texts in a given computer's native encoding, as well as too many text files in existence, to be able to switch to a common encoding overnight. Both the IETF and the XML Working Group, however, recommend that new programs use Unicode as the Coded Character Set and UTF-8 as the Character Encoding Scheme. The name "UTF-8" is registered to refer to this combination.

Is it always possible to convert between encodings? In general, no, but XML is a special case. First of all, it is always possible to convert to Unicode, since Unicode contains the characters of all other registered encodings. That's why Unicode has been given a special position in XML.

When characters in an XML document need to be written to an XML file that is encoded with a function that doesn't accept certain characters—say you want to encode Greek characters in ASCII—then XML allows you to escape the Greek characters in such a way that even ASCII can encode them. This works as follows: first find the character in Unicode, then find the *code point* (the character's number) that Unicode assigns to the character, and then write the character with the following escape code:

```
&#code;
```

where *code* is the (decimal) Unicode number. If you prefer hexadecimal numbers, you can also write

```
&#xcode;
```

where *code* is the same number, but in hexadecimal. For example, the Greek lowercase *alpha* can be written as

```
&#945;   or   &#x3B1;
```

This uses only letters that are acceptable in ASCII, and in fact (we're lucky!) in all other character encodings as well.

But there is a problem: though all characters in character nodes, the name and content fields of processing instructions, and the value parts of attributes can be escaped this way, XML doesn't allow these escapes to be used in the name fields of elements and attributes.*

That means that to be sure that an XML file can be parsed on all computers on the Internet, only ASCII characters (in fact, only 66 of them) are safe to use for names, which is somewhat of a limitation. Luckily, the number of computers that can process full Unicode is growing—or perhaps,

* The June 1997 draft doesn't say anything about comment nodes, and is in fact not explicit about processing instructions either.

in the future, XML will be changed to allow character escapes in names. ■

References

1. *http://www.w3.org/TR/WD-math*
2. *ftp://ds.internic.net/rfc/rfc2130.txt*

About the Author

Bert Bos
2004, route des Lucioles—B.P. 93
06902 Sophia Antipolis Cedex
France
bert@w3.org

Bert has a degree in Mathematics from the University of Groningen, The Netherlands (1987), and a Ph.D. from the Faculty of Arts of that same university, on a thesis about a rapid-prototyping language for Graphical User Interfaces (1993). Afterwards, he lead a project called PROSA, aimed at helping scholars in the Humanities make better use of the Internet and the World-Wide Web in particular. He joined W3C in France in October 1995, as coordinator for internationalization.

AN INTRODUCTION TO XML PROCESSING WITH LARK

Tim Bray

Abstract

Lark is a non-validating XML processor implemented in the Java language; it attempts to achieve good trade-offs among compactness, completeness, and performance. This report gives an overview of the motivations for, facilities offered by, and usage of, the Lark processor. This article applies to version 0.92 of Lark, in use in early September 1997.

1. Why Lark?

1.1 Motivations

Lark's creation was driven by the following motivations:

Personal gratification
: Writing language processors is fun, particularly when you have the chance to fix the language.

Desire to learn Java
: It's about time, and Java seems like the appropriate language for the job.

Test compliance with design goals
: In particular, XML Design Principle #4 [1], which states that "It shall be easy to write programs which process XML documents."

Expore the API design space
: There is a chance, while XML is young, to make some real progress in the design of processor APIs. The design of Lark makes very few assumptions about the user interface; thus Lark should be useful as an experimental testbed in this area.

$$$
: Perhaps Lark will turn out to be useful. I have not the slightest desire to start another software company (been there, done that, got the T-shirts), but it would be nice to figure out a way to get paid for the time I've put in writing it.

1.2 Conclusions

Yes, writing Lark was fun. In particular, none of the innocent-looking things in XML turned out, in practice, to be too horribly difficult.

As for Java: <OldFart>well, maybe there's something to this "Object-Oriented" fad.</OldFart> But it ain't fast.

On the design-goal-compliance front, the good news is that if you wanted a program to process XML that you knew was well-formed, you could probably bash it out in Perl (don't know about Java) in a day or so. On the other hand, if you want to build a general purpose tool that does all of XML and provides helpful error messages and a useful API, the nominal week is not nearly enough. The development of Lark has consumed several weeks. I started sketching out Lark at SGML '96 sometime around the 20th of November, and it took into the first week of January. Mind you, in the interim I returned from Boston, bought a house, traveled to Australia to get married and to Saskatchewan for Christmas, and did some other work. As 1997 has worn on, I have put in a day here and there patching missing pieces and tracking changes in the XML spec.

I do think that Lark will be useful for exploring API designs. Of course, none of this will happen unless there are people out there who want to use an XML processor for something or other. Among other things, Lark currently has no user interface at all; while I don't mind editing the

Driver.java file and recompiling to run tests, presumably a UI would be a good thing to have.

As for the financial aspects, I'm kind of gloomy. I think most XML processors are going to be purpose-built for the needs of particular applications, and will thus hide inside them. Which is good; XML's simplicity makes this approach cost-effective. Failing that, processors will be full-dress validating parsers with incremental parsing for authoring support. So I'm not sure that there's all that much need for a standalone processor; but I'd love to be wrong.

Just in case, for the moment I'm going to be giving away all the *.class* files, and some of the Java source code, but not the source code for the two classes with the hard bits. In any case, they're sure to be buggy at this stage, and I wouldn't want to be letting them out of my hands without a bit more polishing. If you can see a way to get a little revenue out of this project, give me a call.

2. Lark Feature Set Overview

2.1 Compactness

Since an XML processor is often going to run on the client and presumably would need to be delivered over the network, it must be compact. At the moment, the total byte count is just just over 40K, which is not too bad. Example 1 shows a snapshot of the *.class* files.

There is some more scope for compression, when some useful facilities appear in the Java class libraries that ought to be there; e.g., a usable symbol table and better Unicode support.

2.2 Performance

At the moment, Lark, running under the Win95 J++ "Jview" application viewer on an underconfigured P100 notebook, runs at about 20K/second. I regard this as totally unacceptable. There are all sorts of glaring inefficiencies in the current implementation, and as soon as I track down a Java profiler I think I can promise much better performance. An XML processor is, after all, not doing very much.

2.3 Completeness

Lark is a processor only; it does not attempt to validate. It does read the internal subset of the DTD; it processes attribute list declarations (to find default values) and entity declarations. Lark does process parameter entities in the internal subset, but only recognizes them at places that a complete markup declaration could start. Lark's internationalization is incomplete; it reads UCS-2, UTF-16, and ASCII, but not UTF-8 (making use of the Byte Order Marks and Encoding Declarations in the appropriate fashion). Aside from that, Lark is relatively full-featured; it implements (I think) everything in the XML spec, and reports violations of well-formedness.

Lark's error-handling is draconian. After encountering the first well-formedness error, no further internal data structures are built or returned to the application. However, Lark does continue pro-

Example 1

```
-rwxrwxrwa   810 Jun 26 15:07 Attribute.class
-rwxrwxrwa  1756 Jun 26 15:07 Element.class
-rwxrwxrwa  1022 Jun 26 15:07 Entity.class
-rwxrwxrwa  1698 Jun 26 15:07 Handler.class
-rwxrwxrwa 32774 Jun 26 15:07 Lark.class
-rwxrwxrwa  1686 Jun 26 15:07 Namer.class
-rwxrwxrwa  1934 Jun 26 15:07 Segment.class
-rwxrwxrwa   855 Jun 26 15:07 Text.class
-rwxrwxrwa   997 Jun 26 15:07 XmlInputStream.class
```

cessing the document looking for more syntax errors (and in fact performing some fairly aggressive heuristics on the tag stack in order to figure out what's going on), and calling `doSyntaxError` application callback (see below) to report further such errors.

2.4 API

Lark presents as a set of Java classes. Those named Element, Attribute, and Entity are obvious in their function. One lesson of this activity is that it may be possible for such classes to be shared independent of the parser architecture; it would be very handy if all XML-processing Java apps used the same Element class, at least as a basis for subclassing.

Those named Lark and Namer have all the "tricky bits" of parsing and text management logic; they are black boxes for the moment.

The class `XmlInputStream` is a place to put logic to get access to streams of Unicode characters in various encodings. It is to be hoped that it can soon be replaced by equivalent functions in the Java base libraries.

The Text and Segment classes do Lark's character data management; details are below.

From an application's point of view, the Lark and Handler classes are central. Handler has methods such as `doPI`, `doSTag`, `doEntityReference`, `doEtag`; the application passes a Handler instance to Lark's `readXML` method, and Lark calls the routines as it recognizes significant objects in the XML document. The base class provides do-nothing methods; the intent is that an application would subclass Handler to provide the appropriate processing semantics.

Along with presenting this event stream to the application, Lark can optionally build a parse tree, and if so doing, can optionally save copies of the XML document's character data, all in parallel with providing the event stream. Lark provides methods to toggle these behaviors. These methods may be used in the Handler callbacks while Lark is running, to build the parse tree or save the text for only a subset of the document.

In building the parse tree, Lark is guaranteed to update only elements which are still open; i.e., for which the end-tag has not been seen. All other sections of the tree, and the entire tree once Lark has hit end-of-file, may be manipulated freely by the application.

An instance of Lark may be initialized with an optional list of element GIs which are to be considered as those of empty elements, whether or not the XML `/>` syntax is used. A typical set might begin: `"HR", "BR", "IMG", ...`.

Another initializer allows a set of entities to be predefined.

Lark also provides the application access to the "entity tree"; there is a method that toggles whether Lark attempts to retrieve and parse external entities.

2.5 Error Handling

Lark makes a serious effort to be robust, by providing useful error messages and continuing to do so after the first error. I tested against a selection of HTML files, most notably *WD-xml.html*, which was produced by my own Perl scripts, and was horrified to find lots of unquoted attribute values and a hideous number of nesting errors, mostly in the HTML tables used to pretty-print the BNF productions. The error handling is good enough that I now use Lark as my primary tool to debug broken XML files.

2.6 Text Segment Management

Probably due to my background in the indexing and search business, Lark pays more attention than is perhaps strictly necessary to the location of objects within the XML file. Lark informs the application of the containing entity and begin/end offsets of each element. A chunk of character data in an element, which may look contiguous to an application, may in fact map to several different byte ranges in different entities, due to the effect of entity references. Also, the use of encodings such as UTF8 may cause the number of bytes of underlying document to differ from the number of bytes that makes up the characters in a chunk of text. Lark represents Text objects as a vector of Segment objects, each of which gives information about the source offset and length, and the number of characters in the segment. If text-saving has not been turned on, the segments contain no character data, but still contain the offset information.

2.7 Entity Handling

Lark does full XML entity handling, and Java provides facilities which make this trivially easy. The application can turn the inclusion of external text entities on and off. Lark makes no use of PUBLIC identifiers, aside from passing them to the Handler in the callback upon recognizing the declaration.

2.8 Concurrency

Lark is thread-safe. Multiple Larks can run in parallel threads, with other threads doing useful processing of under-construction document trees.

3. Lark: Constructors, Methods, and the Handler

3.1 The Handler Class

The Handler class is just a package of methods that act as callback routines for Lark. No arguments are used in constructing a handler.

Handler has a method named *element*, which the internal logic uses to construct a new Element object every time this is required (rather than calling `new Element()` directly). The idea is that this can be subclassed to return, rather than an Element object, a custom-built instance of a subclass of Element.

The first argument of all the other Handler methods is an Entity object, which contains information about the location of the object just encountered and the current state of the entity stack. All of the Handler methods return booleans. If any handler method returnstrue, Lark's **`readXML`** method returns control to whatever called it. In the base Handler class, all the methods return false by default, except for the **`doSyntaxError`** method, which generates a message via `System.err.println()`. Example 2 summa-

Example 2

```
// Detected  Processing Instruction
public boolean doPI(Entity e, String PI)

// Detected a text segment
public boolean doText(Entity ent, Element el, char[] text, int length)

// Doctype declaration; version for SYSTEM-only
public boolean doDoctype(Entity e, String rootID, String externalSubsetID)

// version for no SYSTEM or PUBLIC keyword
public boolean doDoctype(Entity e, String rootID)

// Internal (text) entity declaration
public boolean doInternalEntity(Entity e, String name, char[] value)

// External text entity declaration; external ID is a URL
public boolean doSystemTextEntity(Entity e, String name, String extID)
```

Example 2 *(continued)*

```
// NDATA entity declaration
public boolean doSystemBinaryEntity(Entity e, String name, String extID,
                                    String notation)

// End-tag detected; the element should be complete
public boolean doETag(Entity e, Element element)

// Start tag detected; the element will in general be
//  incomplete, unless element.empty() is true
public boolean doSTag(Entity e, Element element)

// Entity reference detected; e is the containing entity,
//  not the one that was detected
public boolean doEntityReference(Entity e, String name)

// Error condition detected; the entity e will have the
//  current locational information filled in
public boolean doSyntaxError(Entity e, String message)
```

rizes the methods; the names and types of the arguments should make their meaning self-explanatory.

Notes:

- For doPI, the PI argument does not include the opening and closing delimiters, <? and ?>.
- For doText, the length argument is provided because the characters may not occupy the whole text buffer, which is reusable; thus if the application wishes to save the text, it must copy them out and store them.
- If an element contains entity references embedded character data, Lark generates multiple doText calls, one for each text segment thus created. See the discussion of the Text and Segment classes for a fuller explanation of the motivation for and usage of text segments.
- The doInternalEntity, doSystemTextEntity, and doSystemBinaryEntity methods signal the declaration, not the invocation, of these entities.
- If tree building is turned off, the Element object passed by doSTag and doETag is reused; the same one passed in each time. In this scenario, the only function of the Element object is as a container for data fields. When tree building is turned on, each element gets its own object, and they are linked together in the tree.

As noted above, the default Handler class methods all simply return false, except for doSyntaxError, which is as follows:

```
public boolean doSyntaxError(Entity
    e, String message)
{
  System.err.println("Syntax error
        at line " +
      e.lineCount() + ":" +
        e.lineOffset() + ": " +
        message);
    return false;
}
```

3.2 The Lark Class

The Lark class actually does the parsing. It has the following constructors:

```
public Lark() throws Exception
public Lark(String[]
    emptyElementTypes) throws
      Exception
```

```
public Lark(String[] entityNames,
    String[] entityValues) throws
      Exception
public Lark(String[]
    emptyElementTypes,
              String[] entityNames,
              String[]
    entityValues) throws Exception
```

- `emptyElementTypes` is a list of GIs which Lark considers, when encountered, to be empty, whether or not they use the trailing /> XML empty-element syntax. Lark ignores case in GIs, and always reports GIs to the handler in uppercase form.
- `entityNames` and `entityValues` are arrays which respectively give the names and values of entities that Lark is to consider to have

3.3 Controlling Lark's Behavior

Lark has three methods for toggling behaviors:

```
public void buildTree(boolean build)
public void saveText(boolean save)
public void
    processExternalEntities(boolean
    process)
```

- `buildTree` instructs Lark whether or not to build a parse tree of elements as they are encountered. The default behavior is to build no tree. The tree is built downward from the element current at the time of invocation. When that element ends, tree-building stops.
- `saveText` instructs Lark whether or not to save, in the parse tree, all the character data as it is encountered. This behavior cannot be turned on unless the tree-building has been.
- `processExternalEntities` instructs Lark whether or not to read and process the contents of external text entities. The default behavior is not to read and process them.

Each of these methods can be used from within the Handler callbacks; in particular, Lark calls the Handler `doSTag` and `doEntityReference` methods before deciding whether to build the tree, save the text, or read the entity, so a Handler can control this behavior upon notification of the element or entity.

3.4 Initiating Parsing

Lark's `readXML` methods are used to initiate parsing. There are three as shown in Example 3.

In each case, the caller must provide a Handler (or more likely an instance of a class subclassed from Handler). Lark can read from an `Xml-InputStream` (subclassed from `BufferedIn-putStream`—see below) or from a byte array. Perhaps Lark should also be able to read from a character array.

As noted above, Lark returns from `readXML` whenever one of the Handler methods returns true; in which case it maintains the parsing state and `readXML` can be reinvoked. It also returns when it encounters end of input on the document entity.

The Element object returned by `readXML` is not meaningful if tree-building has not been turned

Example 3

```
// no input stream provided - assume current state is valid
public Element readXML(Handler handler)
  throws java.io.IOException

// XmlInputStream provided - assume it s new
public Element readXML(Handler handler, XmlInputStream input)
   throws java.io.IOException

// byte-buffer provided - make an inputstream and put it on stack
public Element readXML(Handler handler, byte[] buffer)
   throws java.io.IOException
```

Example 4

```
class Attribute
{
  String mName;
  Text   mValue;

  // Constructor
  Attribute(String name, String value)

  public String name() { return mName; }
  public void setName(String name) { mName = name; }
  public String value() { return mValue; }
  public void setValue(String value)  { mValue = value; }
}
```

on. If tree-building has been turned on, it is topmost node in the tree built by Lark—this may not be the node for the root element if tree-building was not turned on until later in the tree.

4. The XmlInputStream Class

XmlInputStream is a subclass of BufferedInputStream. It adds one additional method:

```
public int getXmlChar() throws
    IOException
```

This is intended to retrieve enough bytes from the BufferedInputStream to constitute one Unicode character, and return it. Obviously, the logic is highly dependent on the input encoding.

XmlInputStream has all the same constructors as BufferedInputStream, plus one extra:

```
XmlInputStream(char[] charBuf)
```

This allows getXmlChar() to work out of a character array. Lark uses this facility to support internal text entities.

It is remarkable that Java's built-in BufferedInputStream has no getCharacter() method; with any luck, this oversight will soon be corrected, allowing XmlInputStream to be retired. Java does have facilities for reading characters from a DataInputStream, but their design makes them unusable by XML (or by any other application I can think of). Or perhaps I just didn't understand the documentation.

5. Elements, Attributes, and Entities

The types in Example 4 are self-explanatory, contain essentially no nontrivial logic, and are designed for general use in XML applications. Attribute contains a name and a value, and trivial methods for getting and setting them.

Element is more complex. Readers are urged to look at the source code, which is heavily commented. A few fields and methods of special interest are excerpted in Example 5.

Example 5

```
public class Element
{
  Attribute[] mAttrs;    // Attributes
  String mType;

  // Children are a Vector because they might be Elements
  //  and they might be Text objects
  Vector mChildren = new Vector();

  // Parent element.  null does not mean this is the root,
```

Example 5 *(continued)*

```
  //  it just means this is where Lark started constructing
  //  the tree.
  Element mParent;

  public String type();

  public Attribute[] allAttributes()
  public void setAllAttributes(Attribute[] attributes)

  // get & set attribute by name
  public Attribute attribute(String name)
  public void setAttribute(String name, String value)

  public Vector children()
  public Element parent()
}
```

Note that Lark only creates one String object for each unique element type. This means that the String objects returned by the `type()` method may be simply compared for equality to establish whether two elements are the same type.

The Entity class's fields are shown in Example 6: it has only trivial get and set methods for these fields.

Note that Entities differ from Elements in one important respect: Lark always constructs the Entity tree.

6. Text Handling and Segmentation

The Text object exists mostly to serve as an abstraction layer in front of objects which present as Strings, but may be stored in a segmented fashion. This supports lazy evaluation, the String being (expensively) constructed only when it is requested. Example 7 shows the complete source code.

The Segment class is much more complex, and tries to provide a means of storing information

Example 6

```
  // locational info
  int mOffset;
  int mLineCount;
  int mLineOffset; // how far into this line

  // not true for internal entities
  boolean mTextIsReal;

  XmlInputStream mInput; // read characters for this entity
  String mDescription;   // metadata
  Entity mParent;        // entity tree; null means doc entity
```

about character data, and optionally the character data itself, efficiently while keeping track of source offset information. Its implementation, particularly the constructors, is fairly complex, but the methods that an application might use are straightforward:

```
public Entity entity()
public int sourceOffset()
public int sourceLength()
public int dataOffset()
public int dataLength()
public String string()
```

7. To-Do List

- Fix up `XmlInputStream` so it can read UTF-8 as well as ASCII.
- Find a profiler and make Lark faster.
- Make an applet-ized version of Lark.
- Add an Entity member to the Element class.
- If any signs of interest in Lark develop, formalize the test suite and config management.

Example 7

```
class Text
{
  // This is a Text object, which can appear in the Children()
  //  of an element.  The text itself is actually stored in a
  //  Vector of Segments; this object really only exists to
  //  provide a nice singular object to sit in the parse
  //  tree, and to avoid recalculating the String value
  //  of a multi-segment object.
  Vector mSegments = new Vector();
  String mString;

  public void addSegment(Segment segment)
  {
    mSegments.addElement(segment);
    mString = null; // invalidate string
  }
  public Vector segments() { return mSegments; }


  // construct string only on request
  public String string()
  {
    int i;
    Segment seg;
    if (mString == null)
    {
      mString = new String();
      for (i = 0; i < mSegments.size(); i++)
      {
        // there must be a better way
        seg = (Segment) mSegments.elementAt(i);
        mString = mString.concat(seg.string());
      }
    }
    return mString;
  }
}
```

8. How to Get Lark

All of the classes, and all the source code except Lark, Namer, `XmlInputStream`, are at [2]. ■

References

1. *http://www.textuality.com/sgml-erb/dd-1996-oool.htm*
2. *http://www.textuality.com/Lark/lark.tar.gz*

About the Author

Tim Bray
321–3495 Cambie Street
Vancouver, B.C., Canada V5Z 4R3
tbray@textuality.com

Tim Bray is a Canadian. He entered the software profession in 1981; after on-the-job training from Digital and GTE, he became manager of the New Oxford English Dictionary Project at the University of Waterloo in 1986. He co-founded Open Text Corporation in 1989, and started an independent consulting practice under the name Textuality in 1996. He is a Seybold Fellow, editor of the *Gilbane Report*, and co-editor of the World Wide Web Consortium's "Extensible Markup Language Specification."

Building XML Parsers for Microsoft's IE4

Jean Paoli, David Schach, Chris Lovett, Andrew Layman, Istvan Cseri

Abstract

Microsoft cofounded the XML working group at the W3C in July 96 and actively participated in the definition of the standard. This article describes why Microsoft implemented its first XML application and how it led to the development of two XML parsers shipping in Internet Explorer 4.0, one written in C++ and the other in Java. We describe the importance of designing an object model API and our vision of XML as a universal, open data format for the Internet.

Motivation

Our First Application: Active Channels for Internet Explorer 4.0

Conventional Web use waits for a user to request a page before sending it. That is known as the "pull" mode. A powerful alternative exists, however, called "push" or "webcasting," in which pages are sent to a user in advance, based on automatic matching of pages to the user's interests. Webcasting provides each user with automatic delivery and offline access to the information and Web sites that he uses most often.

To bring this idea to reality, in February 1997 the Internet Explorer team needed a standard way of describing sites and pages. The first broadly popular form of Web "metadata" (so called because it describes data about other data) is the Channel Definition Format, or CDF [1]. This allows a Web site to post a description of itself in a standard form. Having done so, it is no longer just a site; it is also an "Active Channel."

A channel is a set of related Web pages. Channel Definition Format files include the following characteristics:

- A minimal CDF file contains a list of URLs pointing to the pages that make up the content of the channel.
- A more advanced CDF file can include title and abstract information describing individual items, a schedule for updates, and a hierarchical organization of the channel's offerings.
- A CDF file must be easy to create and not require changes to existing HTML pages.

In looking for a suitable technology on which to build channels, the Internet Explorer team found that XML and Active Channels are a perfect fit. XML is excellent for metadata, since many of its rules are similar to the widely known HTML language rules; yet it has more facilities for structure and extensibility. This gave the IE team the assurance that parsers would be easy to implement and the format would be broadly usable.

CDF is an application of XML that deals with the particulars of Web metadata. CDF consists of a vocabulary of terms that are related to Web sites and their Active Channel content. Technically, the terms are used as "Elements" and "attributes," and CDF defines how they can be used together to expand a Web site into a webcasting channel (see Example 1).

A Universal, Open Data Format for the Internet

At the same time as the metadata CDF work was proceeding, members of the Internet Explorer team and others in Microsoft started to understand the broad need for a universal, open data format for the Internet. The opportunities are very exciting.

The Web has created an opportunity to communicate with anyone, anywhere. Fully realizing this potential depends on widespread use of standards—as with the telephone, this communication depends on numerous layers of interoperating technology. One such important layer is visual display and user interface, exemplified by standards such as HTML, GIF, and ECMAScript (previously JavaScript). These standards allow a page to be created once, yet displayed at different times by many receivers.

Although visual and user interface standards are a necessary layer, they are insufficient for representing *access medium* to text and pictures. There are no standards for intelligent search, data exchange, adaptive presentation, and presonalization. The Internet must go beyond setting an information *access* and *display* standard; it must set an information *understanding* standard—a standard way of representing data so that software can better search, move, display, and otherwise manipulate information currently hidden in contextual obscurity. HTML cannot fulfill these needs because it is a format that describes how a Web page should *look*, rather than one that represents *data*. For example:

- HTML does not provide a standard way for a doctor to send a prescription to a pharmacist.
- HTML does not enable a medical laboratory to publish statistical information in a format that any receiver can analyze.
- HTML does not describe an electronic payment in a form that any recipient can decode and process.
- HTML does not provide a standard way to search legal libraries to find, for example, all litigation documents about a certain topic.
- HTML does not specify how information in a company catalog can be transmitted, such that a salesman can work offline, show the catalog to clients, take orders, then upload those orders in a standard format.

In short, while HTML provides rich facilities for display, it does not provide any standards-based way to manage as *data*.

A standard for data representation will expand the Internet in much the same way that the HTML standard did for display a few years ago. The data standard will be the vehicle for business transactions, publication of personal preference profiles, automated collaboration, and database sharing. Payments, medical histories, pharmaceutical research data, semi-conductor part sheets,

Example 1

```
<?XML version="1.0" RMD="NONE" ?>
<!DOCTYPE Channel SYSTEM
"http://www.microsoft.com/standards/channels.dtd">
<CHANNEL>
    <SCHEDULE>
        <INTERVALTIME HOUR="2"/>
        <LATESTTIME MIN="30"/>
    </SCHEDULE>
    <TITLE>Internet Explorer News</TITLE>
    <ITEM HREF="http://www.microsoft.com/ie/new/666784.htm">
        <ABSTRACT> The latest news on Internet Explorer. </ABSTRACT>
        <TITLE> Latest support for CDF </TITLE>
    </ITEM>
</CHANNEL>
```

and purchase orders will all be written in this format. It will open up a wide variety of new uses, all based on a standard representation for moving structured data around the Web as easily as we move HTML pages today. That data standard is XML.

XML: A Standard Format for Data

XML provides a data standard that can encode the content, semantics, and schemata for a range of cases, from simple to complex. XML can encode the representation for the following:

- An ordinary document
- A structured record, such as a appointment record or purchase order
- An object with data and methods (for example, the persistent form of a Java object or ActiveX control)
- A data record, such as the result set of a query
- Meta-content about a Web site (such as CDF)
- Graphical presentation (such as an application's user interface)
- Standard schema entities and types
- *All* the links between information and people on the Web

Benefits of XML

As a universal standard for the expression of data, XML offers many advantages to organizations, software developers, Web sites, and ultimately to end-users.

For software developers building Web applications and line-of-business Intranet software, XML provides a powerful, flexible format for expressing data—whether as a wire format for sending data between client and server, a transfer format for sharing data between applications, or a persistent storage format on disk. Because structured data in XML can include a self-describing schema, XML promises interoperability between applications that manipulate structured data independent of the underlying semantics.

For example, because XML enables publishers to supplement their Web sites with metadata such as CDF, users can receive "pushed" content as structured channels. XML can also provide a means for embedding arbitrary data and annotations within HTML, extending the possibilities for Web-based applications based on HTML and scripts.

For end-users, XML promises to provide a much richer set of Web applications for browsing, communication, and collaboration. The growing use of XML will improve Web-browsing applications for viewing, filtering, and manipulating information on the Internet.

As collaboration on the Web spreads to more businesses, customer services will eventually migrate from phone lines and storefronts to Web sites. The majority of these Intranet and Internet business applications will involve manipulation or transfer of data and database records, such as purchase orders, invoices, customer information, appointments, maps, and so forth. XML promises a revolution in the richness of end-user possibilities on the Web because it enables such a wide array of business applications to be implemented on the Internet.

Microsoft XML Parsers

Our long-term goal of XML is that it function as a data format that anyone can use to build a range of Web applications. To achieve this goal, we decided to write an XML parser and make it freely available. The result of these efforts was two XML parsers—one in C++ and the other in Java—both of which are included as part of Microsoft Internet Explorer 4.0. The parsers were written in parallel, but with somewhat different design goals.

The Microsoft XML parser in C++ (MSXML in C++) was written to perform as an integral part of

Internet Explorer 4.0. Consequently, its design was oriented toward the following:

- Fast parsing speed
- Low memory usage
- Asynchronous parsing during download
- Strong international support

In other words, this is a performance parser. Although much effort was spent on wringing the most efficiency from the code, all non-essential features were eliminated. For example, MSXML in C++ is a non-validating parser.

In contrast to the XML parser in C++, the goals of the Microsoft XML parser in Java (MSXML in Java) included the following:

- To be a reference implementation
- To be a full validating parser
- To be cross-platform
- To promote widespread acceptance of the XML standard
- To experiment with leading edge XML standards efforts, like DOM and namespaces

For this reason, the Java parser is fully validating, it implements the latest proposed features (such as namespaces), and the source code is freely available.

With some minor exceptions (such as no current support for conditional sections), Microsoft's XML parsers completely implement the W3C Working Draft of the XML specification dated June 30, 1997.*

MSXML in Java shipped in the spring of 1997 and is available from *http://www.microsoft.com/standards/xml/xmlparse.htm*. Both MSXML in C++ and MSXML in Java are shipping with IE40.

Object Model

Once parsed, an XML document is manipulated through an object model (or API). To really help make XML the standard format for data over the Web, we felt that a standard object model was crucial; one that was simple, scriptable, minimal, and consistent with the Document Object Model (DOM) Working Group.† We are currently working with the W3C to standardize the XML object model. The object model is language neutral, which means it is equally accessible from all programming languages. To keep the object model independent of the parsers, it was designed prior to implementing them. The idea was to completely separate the parser implementation from the XML data structures. Having the parser use the object model ensured that problems with the object model would be flushed out during development.

Document object

The object model is very simple. It models the XML document as a tree structure using only three classes of objects:

- A Document
- An Element
- A Collection

The Document object represents an entire XML document. This object holds the Element tree and document information such as the document type, version and character encoding. The Element object is used for representing the nodes in the tree, and the Collection object is used to represent the child Elements of a given node.

Element object

All XML data is stored in a tree of Element objects. Container Elements are non-leaf nodes. Empty Elements, text, as well as comments and

* The latest version of this draft was in fact August 7, 1997, and is published as the "Extensible Markup Language (XML)" specification in the "W3C Reports" section of this issue.

† The "Document Object Model (DOM)" specification is in this issue's "W3C Reports" section.

processing instructions are stored as leaf nodes in the tree. An Element's type is revealed by the *type* property. Currently, the following types are returned:

ELEMENT
: For container and empty XML Elements

TEXT
: For PCDATA and CDATA

COMMENT
: For comments

OTHER
: Processing instructions

We considered using a different object in the object model for each of these types rather than a single object with a type property, but decided that multiple objects complicated the object model. This was particularly the case when navigating the Element tree and for untyped languages like JavaScript and VBScript.

The other important properties of the Element object are:

tagName
: The name (or GI) for objects of type ELEMENT (otherwise an empty string)

parent
: The parent Element of this object in the tree.

text
: The text for objects of type TEXT or COMMENT (otherwise an empty string)

children
: A collection of the objects contained by this object. This collection is empty for all other types besides Element

Finally, the Element class provides a basic set of methods for setting, getting, and removing attribute values as well as adding and removing child Elements.

Element collections

Element collections are used to walk the XML tree. An Element collection has one property, the length, which is the number of Elements in the collection. Child Elements are fetched via the item method, which returns either an Element by index, or by name. When more than one Element has the same name, the item method returns a new collection with all of the child Elements with that name.

The object model for the C++ parser is written using Microsoft's component object model architecture (COM). As a result, it is language neutral and equally accessible from JavaScript and VBScript as well as C++ and Java. For example, once a Document object is created, loading a document involves setting the document's URL. The following JavaScript code fragment shows how to load an XML document from an HTML page using the C++ parser:

```
myXMLDoc = new
    ActiveXObject("msxml");
myXMLDoc.URL = "http://www.
    somecompany.com/somedata.xml;"
```

Using the Java parser and the XML DSO applet that is shipping with IE 4, you can load an XML document as follows:

```
<APPLET class=com.ms.xml.dso.XMLDSO.
    class width=0 height=0
    id=xmldso>
<PARAM NAME=URL VALUE="http://www.
    somecompany.com/somedata.xml">
</APPLET>
```

Then you can access the Document object via script as follows:

```
var doc = xmldso.getDocument();
```

While the object model is minimal, it is functionally complete. We expect that it will evolve over time.

For more information about Microsoft's XML object model see [2] and [3].

Technical Details

Simplicity of design

The Microsoft XML parsers are simple. This is by design. They are implemented as hand-coded, recursive-descent parsers. This has a couple of benefits:

- First, the minimal syntax of XML makes a parser generator unnecessary: a hand-coded parser works just fine.
- Second, recursive-descent parsers are both easy to write and easier to understand.

This latter point is especially important since the source code for MSXML in Java is available to the public on the Microsoft Web site. We want it to be a reference implementation that can be understood by any Java programmer. (Another reason parser generating tools are not used is that the language has many lexical Elements that are unlimited in length; we do not want to test a parser generator's buffer size limits.)

Character encodings

Although XML parsers are required only to read UTF-8 and UCS-2 encodings, the Microsoft's XML parsers handle many more encodings, such as `shift-jis`, `euc-jp`, and `big5`. In fact, the C++ parser supports the same set of character encodings as IE40, and the Java parser supports all the encodings supported by the Java VM. The recursive-descent parsers are isolated from these different encodings by input readers that convert everything to Unicode. While this increases memory usage for European languages, it simplifies string processing overall.

Storage of Element and Attribute names

Because Element and Attribute names tend to repeat, they are stored as *atoms* so that only one copy of each string is stored. This also speeds up string comparisons because atom objects can be compared for equality very quickly, without comparing the characters in the strings. This technique amortizes some of the cost of checking for `NameChar` characters and converting Unicode characters to uppercase.

Object model implementation

The Java parser builds the Element tree using the object model. When it creates new Elements it uses an Element class factory that is passed in by the creator of the parser. The parsers come with a default object model implementation that is fully functional; however, clients with special needs can write their own class factory that creates custom objects. This makes it easy for programs that want to use XML but still need to process legacy data structures.

The Java parser does not parse asynchronously, it could be run on a separate thread. The C++ parser parses asynchronously by running on a fiber. The object model was designed so that asynchronous parsing can be implemented transparently to the programmer. Because all properties and methods are function calls, the object model can block the caller when attempting to access a node in the tree that isn't completely downloaded.

Entities and other language features

The Java parser also implements DTD validation, full Entity handling, and the namespace proposal. We found that DTD validation was relatively easy. The XML spec was clear and pointers to algorithms for implementing validation were helpful, but we found that supporting validation does seem to impact the overall performance of the parser.

Correct entity handling was actually quite subtle—especially when we were trying to figure out how to expose entity references in the Object Model. The problem is that some clients of the Object Model (like JavaScript's) prefer the entities to be fully expanded and thereby essentially invisible to their scripts. Other clients of the Object Model (like an authoring tool), on the other hand, want to actually know where the entities are, how to edit them, and so on. We decided that entity references should be simple leaf nodes in the tree of type ENTITYREF that point to the full entity definition in the DTD and also decided to provide helper functions like `getText()` for those clients who just want the fully expanded text. Parameter entities in the DTD are more difficult. Currently parameter entities are expanded by the parser and not represented in the Object Model. It is not clear whether we can ever represent parameter entities in the Object Model or in fact we'd even want to.

Namespaces were relatively simple since we already had an atomized Name object in the Java parser to represent all tag and attribute names in the document. We simply added a namespace field to these Name objects, support for parsing the name space declarations, and we were done.

The parsers are small and fast. MSXML in C++ with full international character support is less than 100K and the MSXML Java Parser is 127K.

Using the Object Model to Process XML Data

To illustrate how the Object Model can be used to do interesting things we will show you a small example based on the CDF data we saw earlier in Example 1. Example 2 shows how to walk the

Example 2

```
<script>
function GetInterval()
   {
// Fetch the CDF file and extract the INTERVALTIME element
       var doc = new ActiveXObject("msxml");
       doc.URL = Resolve("cdf.xml");
// First extract the SCHEDULE node
        var s = doc.root.children.item("SCHEDULE");
// Then the INTERVALTIME
        var t = s.children.item("INTERVALTIME");
// Then the HOUR attribute
        var h = t.getAttribute("HOUR");
        return h;
    }
    function DisplayTime(hour)
    {
// Display this with an appropriate message in a popup window
        var w = window.open("","NextShow",
            "resizable,width=400,height=100");
        w.document.open();
        w.document.write("<body bgcolor=yellow>");
        w.document.write( "<h2>The next show is in " +
            hour + " hours !</h4>" );
        w.document.write("</body>");
        w.document.close();
    }
    function Resolve(relurl)
    {
// This is a useful little function that I use to resolve a URL relative to the
current document location
        var url = document.location.toString();
        var base = url.substring(0,url.lastIndexOf("/"));
```

Example 2 *(continued)*

```
        var href = base + "/" + relurl;
        return href;
    }
</script>
// A button that invokes the above scripts
<input type=button value="When ?"
    onclick="DisplayTime(GetInterval());">
```

XML Object Model to find out the INTERVAL-TIME of the scheduled event.

Notice that the `GetInterval()` method uses a small fixed set of objects and methods to manipulate the XML data that is independent of display-oriented things like HTML. As long as the CDF DTD (or schema) stays relatively fixed, this script code will work on any CDF file. In other words, this is robust enough to build Web-based business applications.

Conclusion

When we choose XML to encode CDF files, we were a little bit anxious. XML was just created—even though Microsoft co-created the W3C XML Working Groups in July 1996, it was as new to us as anyone else. In addition, launching "channels"—by using the first broad, public application of metadata—by using an untried standard was risky. A few months later (as of this writing in August 1997), we know that we have made the right choice.

The flexibility and ease of use of a text format for representing and exchanging structured information has been demonstrated. CDF is now widely used by industry's leading content providers, Web and Java authoring tool vendors, and "push" developers (such as PointCast, AirMedia, and BackWeb). Multiple tools have been developed to produce CDF files. Because it is simple text-based format, tools are easily developed to generate and process it. XML helped make CDF successful.

Now a set of XML enabling technologies, including C++ and Java parsers with their Object Models, are shipping in Internet Explorer 4.0. Because IE 4.0 will be integrated into Windows 98, there will be an XML parser on each desktop—another step toward the vision of making structured data an integral part of the Web.

At Microsoft, we strongly believe that XML is the standard, extensible, universal data format for the Internet. It is simple and easily authored. It is based on international standards that have been tested for many years. It is enormously extensible. It is flexible enough to allow representation of an incredibly wide range of information, and it also allows this information to be self-describing, so that structured data expressed in XML may be manipulated by software that doesn't have previous knowledge of the underlying meaning behind the data. XML provides a file format for representing data and can be extended to contain a description of its own structure. It is a means of formatting data and also a mechanism for extending and annotating standard HTML.

With its powerful expressiveness and flexibility, XML promises to add structure to data on the Internet, bringing the Web one step closer to realizing the potential for universal communication with anyone, anywhere. ■

References

1. *http://www.w3.org/Submission/1997/2/*
2. *http://www.microsoft.com/msdn/sdk/inetsdk/help/inet5017.htm*
3. *http://www.microsoft.com/standards/xml/default.htm*

About the Authors

Jean Paoli
1 Microsoft Way
Redmond, WA 98052-6399
jeanpa@microsoft.com

Jean Paoli is a Product Manager in the Internet Explorer 4.0 team where he manages the XML and databinding effort. Prior to joining Microsoft in May 1996, he was the technical director of GRIF S.A., a leader in the creation of SGML authoring tools. Jean has a strong background in SGML and designed for important corporations a lot of systems where SGML, in its approach of structuring and storing information, ensured the long life and easy exchangeability of the data. Jean is a co-editor of the XML standard and co-created with Jon Bosak (and others) the W3C XML working group in July 1996.

Andrew Layman
1 Microsoft Way
Redmond, WA 98052-6399
AndrewL@microsoft.com

Andrew Layman is a Senior Program Manager at Microsoft where he works on Internet and database technologies. Prior to joining Microsoft in 1992, he was a Vice President of Symantec Corporation and original author of the Time Line project management program.

Istvan Cseri
1 Microsoft Way
Redmond, WA 98052-6399
istvanc@microsoft.com

Istvan Cseri is the technical architect of the XML project at Microsoft. Istvan designed the Java XML parser and is one of the co-authors of the Proposal for Extensible Style Language (XSL), which was recently submitted to the W3C. Istvan has a strong background in object oriented frameworks and user interfaces. Prior to join Microsoft, Istvan was at Borland where he was one of the designers and developpers of Quattro Pro for Windows.

Chris Lovett
1 Microsoft Way
Redmond, WA 98052-6399
clovett@microsoft.com

Chris is one of the developer leads on the XML project at Microsoft. He has been working mostly on the Java XML parser reference release. He joined Microsoft in May of this year from a silicon valley startup company where he was working on CD ROM quality multimedia delivery over the web. Chris has a strong background in networking, communications and user interface work from his former work at Taligent and IBM's Santa Teresa Labs.

David Schach
1 Microsoft Way
Redmond, WA 98052-6399
davidsch@microsoft.com

David Schach is a developer lead on XML in the Internet Explorer Group. He collaborated on the XML Object Model design and wrote the Microsoft XML Parser in C++. Currently, he is working on using XML as a style sheet language and is a co-author of Proposal for Extensible Style Language (XSL), which was recently submitted to the W3C. He has master's degree in computer science from the University of Pennsylvania and joined Microsoft in 1994.

JUMBO

An Object-Based XML Browser

Peter Murray-Rust

Abstract

JUMBO (Java Universal Markup Language) is an object-oriented XML browser/editor and transformation tool, written in Java. It has been developed as a development tool to explore the emerging XML-LANG and XML-LINK specifications, and implements most of the current proposals. Its emphasis is on the management of structured documents; specifically their interpretation as trees. It provides behavior for ELEMENTs by providing Java classes for rendering or transformation. It is particularly aimed at nontextual applications where ELEMENTs (such as those in technical disciplines) require complex processing. JUMBO also implements much of the current XML-LINK spec, including TEI extended pointers and simple aspects of EXTENDED XML-LINKs.*

Introduction

The management and "publication" of information in scientific disciplines such as molecular science is difficult; current approaches involve a large number of incompatible legacy files. Because HTML was not developed for managing nontextual information, its success has further highlighted this problem—one that can be solved only by offering specific, machine-dependent plug-ins for each legacy type. What is required is a single information architecture, independent of platform, and easily extensible. I have developed such a system: Chemical Markup Language (CML), with a generic core Technical Markup Language (TecML), originally using SGML. To distribute and process this requires the following package of components:

`sgmls`
: James Clark's validating parser [1]. This is excellent software, but it is not trivial to distribute SGML systems to a community with no SGML experience. (Most applications require an SGML declaration, a CATALOG, a DTD, possibly some entity sets.) Moreover, a different **.exe* is needed for each platform.

`CoST`
: Joe English's rewrite of the original CoST for transforming and searching the output of sgmls. [2] CoST is an excellent tel-based tool, but again has to be distributed as an **.exe*.

`costwish`
: I wrote a series of tcl/tk-based scripts to render the output of CoST and to package the SGML environment for non-SGML users. This was successful for UNIX systems, but foundered on the difficulties of a simple port of tk to a Windows-based environment.

`costwish` was successful in that a virtual collaborator was able to use it for a novel application—the tree-structured display of Chomskian analysis of sentence structure. However, it was clear that the absence of platform-independent graphics and the difficulty of packaging SGML applications made this too complex for general use.

This problem has become radically simpler over the last 12 months through the development of two new technologies, which interoperate extremely easily. Both are designed for use over the Inter- and Intranets, and to be platform independent.

* Throughout this document you'll see references to XML-LANG and XML-LINK. XML-LANG is currently referred to as "XML," while XML-LINK is now "XLL."

Java

A platform-independent object-oriented language supporting graphics at GUI level. Of particular importance is its availability under modern browsers such as Netscape and Microsoft Explorer, which now come with a Java Virtual Machine. This means that installation effort of Java applications can be effectively made nil.* Although Java is often promoted as a language for distributing graphical APPLETs, it is also a clean, powerful, easy, fully object-oriented language. Unlike C++ it comes with a very large library of classes that provide functions for textual management, WWW operations, and much more.

XML

XML is described at length in this volume. One particular feature that is valuable for CML, is that it is much simpler than SGML—XML applications should hold few terrors for experienced HTML developers. The SGML declaration is not required, and many applications can dispense with the DTD. This eliminates many of the newcomer's problems to SGML applications and makes packaging documents much easier. Very importantly, since XML is now catching the imagination of the world, the incentive for authors and implementers to learn it will be much greater. We can expect shrink-wrapped tools on which particular applications like CML can be built.

Rationale for JUMBO

The traditional SGML market is very heavily based on processing textual documents, although there are many examples (such as technical manuals) where non-textual objects (diagrams, parts, etc.) occur. Most SGML applications involve customizing tools for a particular purpose and are often site-specific (i.e., for a particular customer). In general, an SGML application usually has a defined "purpose." Because CML covers a much wider range of object types (see Table 1), it needs software that is generic, abstract,, graphically oriented, and freely available. The simplest solution was to port the ideas from `costwish` to Java.

The port coincided with the development of XML-LANG, and offered an opportunity to redesign SGML browsing software from scratch. (TecML and CML are now fully conformant DTDs of XML.) The fundamental design decision was that XML elements should be closely linked to Java classes. Since JUMBO was designed to deal with any DTD, there must be a mechanism to locate classes appropriate for it. For any DTD in the DOCTYPE statement, a class should be available that loads the appropriate classes for that DTD. JUMBO also anticipates that a document may refer to more than one DTD and has a mechanism for hierarchical loading of classes for DTDs. Thus, CML requires the loading of TecML classes, and TecML (which uses HTML2.0) loads classes related to that.

Technical Markup Language

Although the main motivation for CML was to manage molecular data, much of the material is generic to a wide range of scientific disciplines. After browsing publications from a wide range of journals I compiled Table 1. To support this I developed a generic scientific language, TecML, and wrote a number of tcl and Java-based classes for it. As XML continues to develop, however, standard tools may support some of these components, and I hope that much of TecML may be eventually become redundant.

* Earlier this year JUMBO was packaged on a CDROM for the chemical community, and many of the readers had never even heard of Java.

Table 1

Component	*TecML ELEMENT*	*XML/WWW Solutions*
Text	(X)HTML	HTML, TEI, DocBook, 12083
hyperlinks	Hardcoded, XML-LINK	XML-LINK various
Structured graphics	FIGURE	CGM, VRML
Images (i.e., pixel maps)	FIGURE	NOTATION (e.g. GIF)
Typed fields	XVAR	XML-TYPE?
Typed arrays	ARRAY	
Generic container	XLIST	
Graphs	XLIST+ARRAY children	CGM?
Tables	XLIST+children	HTML? CALS?
Bibliography	BIB	
Terminology/Glossary	TERMENTRY	MARTIF/ISO1260?
Person	PERSON	
Parsable Mathematics		MathML
Molecules	CML, MOL, etc	
Relationships	Hardcoded, XML-LINK	XML-LINK EXTENDED

NOTE

The X- prefixes were used to avoid clashes with elements within HTML and other DTDs that might be used. When XML solves the syntax and semantics of namespaces these will change to `ElementTypes` such as `TecML::VAR`, `TecML::LIST`, and so on. When and where the qualifying namespace is required is yet to be decided by the XML-WG.

At an early stage I decided to limit the number of `ElementTypes` in TecML to about 15, roughly mirroring those in Table 1 along with a few extra subelements. A few categories such as mathematics were deferred—I am delighted that MathML* has been developed in XML and can support mathematics semantics (i.e., equations and expressions can be parsed and manipulated by symbolic packages such as Mathematica). The small number of `ElementTypes` avoids namespace clashes and allows authors to introduce new concepts without having to rewrite the DTD. Flexibility is achieved by widespread use of attributes. For example, to describe a Melting Point we could write:

```
<MELTING_POINT>23.4</MELTING_POINT>
```

Using this code, the number of `ElementTypes` could soon reach millions. TecML describes all scalar quantities like the one above with a single `ElementType` and qualifying attributes, such as the following:

```
<XVAR CONVENTION="http://www.
    learned.soc/physics"
    DICTNAME="mpt" UNITS="Celsius"
    TYPE="Float">23.4</XVAR>
```

TYPE is hardcoded in TecML and can take values of Float, Integer, String, Date and Pointer. It may yet be made obsolete by the XML-TYPE proposal from Tim Bray and others. UNITS is hardlinked to a glossary of scientific units distributed with TecML. CONVENTION and DICTNAME locate

* See also the paper entitled "HTML Math: Mathematical Markup Language Working Draft" in the "W3C Reports" section by Robert Miner and Patrick Ion.

the glossary and entry within it, ideally provided by an institution of repute and stability such as a learned society.

The preceding example makes it clear that hyperlinking is a powerful means of resolving semantics. It is also the simplest way of avoiding namespace collisions in TecML documents. Thus, equations can be constructed in MathML, stored in separate files, and linked through XML-LINK's `HREF` rather than being included in the document directly or indirectly (by entities).

Basics of JUMBO

JUMBO has been developed as a prototype XML engine primarily aimed at:

- Providing a prototyping tool for XML developers.
- Exploring non-textual uses of XML.
- Specifically, but not exclusively, supporting Molecular Science.
- Resolving semantics through hyperlinking to documents or Java methods.

At the time of this writing, JUMBO has tracked most of the draft specifications of XML-LANG and XML-LINK.

JUMBO is built from components; the applications it can be configured for are not limited. At present it consists of the following parts:

An XML parser

The built-in parser is simplistic. JUMBO will also interoperate with Lark,* NXP or ESIS input. When the Xapi-J interface (from John Tigue) [3] is stable, it will be implemented so that JUMBO is layered on top of the parsing machinery; this will enable different parsers to be switched under user control.

A TableOfContents/Tree tool

JUMBO's main emphasis is on Structured Documents, and most instances are presented as TOCs. The TOC allows:

- Control of presentation through PIs (automatic or user-activated)
- Flexible display of ELEMENT tree (toggling visibility)
- Editing of tree (move, delete, add Elements, including partial DTD-based validation)
- Attribute display and editing
- Element-based Help based on Java inheritance
- Flexible URL-based navigation to next hyperlinked instance (implementing XML: EMBED/REPLACE/NEW and AUTO/USER)
- Lookup of DOCTYPE and automatic downloading of ELEMENT-specific Java classes
- ELEMENT-specific icons leading to `display()` when clicked
- Resolution of semantics by links to VirtualHyperGlossary entries
- TEI searches based on XML-LINK
- Save contents as XML, HTML GIF or customised format (through Java)

Generic Java class Downloader

Applications as Java classes, including TechnicalMarkupLanguage and ChemicalMarkupLanguage

Inside JUMBO

JUMBO has over 300 classes, the most important of which are `SGMLTree`, `SGMLNode`, and `SGMLAttribute`.† Objects are created from the result of parsing either via a stream or from a parsed object in memory. At present JUMBO is limited to objects that will fit in the space available in the Java Virtual Machine. Node is nor-

* For more information about Lark, see "An Introduction to XML Processing with Lark," by Tim Bray.
† These names predate XML and will be revised! They are abbreviated to Tree, etc. below.

mally subclassed for each element type—an example is `MOLNode` (see Figure 2). When the document is parsed, a DTD-specific class (e.g., CMLDTD.class) is required to decide what subclass type is required for each `ElementType` (GI). If none is found, the methods default to those of Node.

If the following example (which has no DTD) is processed by JUMBO the display can be expanded to Figure 1.

```
<?XML VERSION="1.0"?>
<FOO>
<BAR TITLE="I am a bar" ID="bar1">
<PLUGH>
This is an ASCII string contained
    as a child of PLUGH
</PLUGH>
<BAR TITLE="younger sibling of
    PLUGH">
A BAR can contain other BAR
    elements.
</BAR>
</BAR>
</FOO>
```

JUMBO "guesses" a reasonable title from the TITLE attribute, the content or the `ElementType`. The small circular icons are the default; when clicked they `display()` a textual `debug()` of the Node.

Each subclassed Node may have a `drawIcon()` and a `display()` method. When the class-specific icon is clicked the appropriate `display()` is automatically used. Figure 2 shows a datafile for the three-dimensional structure of a protein molecule, which contains a mixture of textual and nontextual records. Despite the input being published as a "flat file," the JUMBO conversion program can create a highly structured TOC (see the left of the diagram). Different `ElementTypes` can have different icons. Thus, clicking on "D-T-G" (a protein sequence Element) displays the top window, while clicking on an inverted V-shaped ball-and-stick icon displays one of the bottom two windows. The textual records (as in the "Annotation") Node can also be displayed. Note that Nodes labeled "HELIX" etc. use the default SGMLNode `display()` method.

TecML supports tables, which can contain objects or pointers to objects. In Figure 3 the table contains links to MOLNodes in OBJECT column which, when clicked, `display()` their contents.

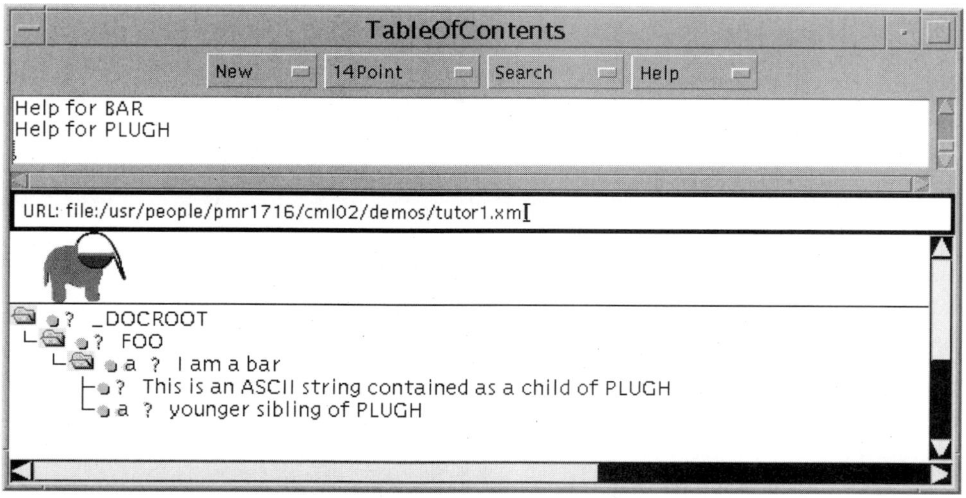

Figure 1

XML-LINK

In early versions of CML and its related classes a lot of semantics were hardcoded. Some of these can now be seen as generic and potentially manageable by the XML-LINK tools. One common use of XML-LINK is to assemble objects into a common display such as EMBEDding them in text. Early versions of JUMBO supported some experimental rendering but since this is a useful generic operation for browsers I have delayed further implementation.

Many technical documents and data have relationships (often implicit) between components. Single Element-based classes cannot support these, but linking through XML-LINK may provide generic support. The mapping ("Assign-

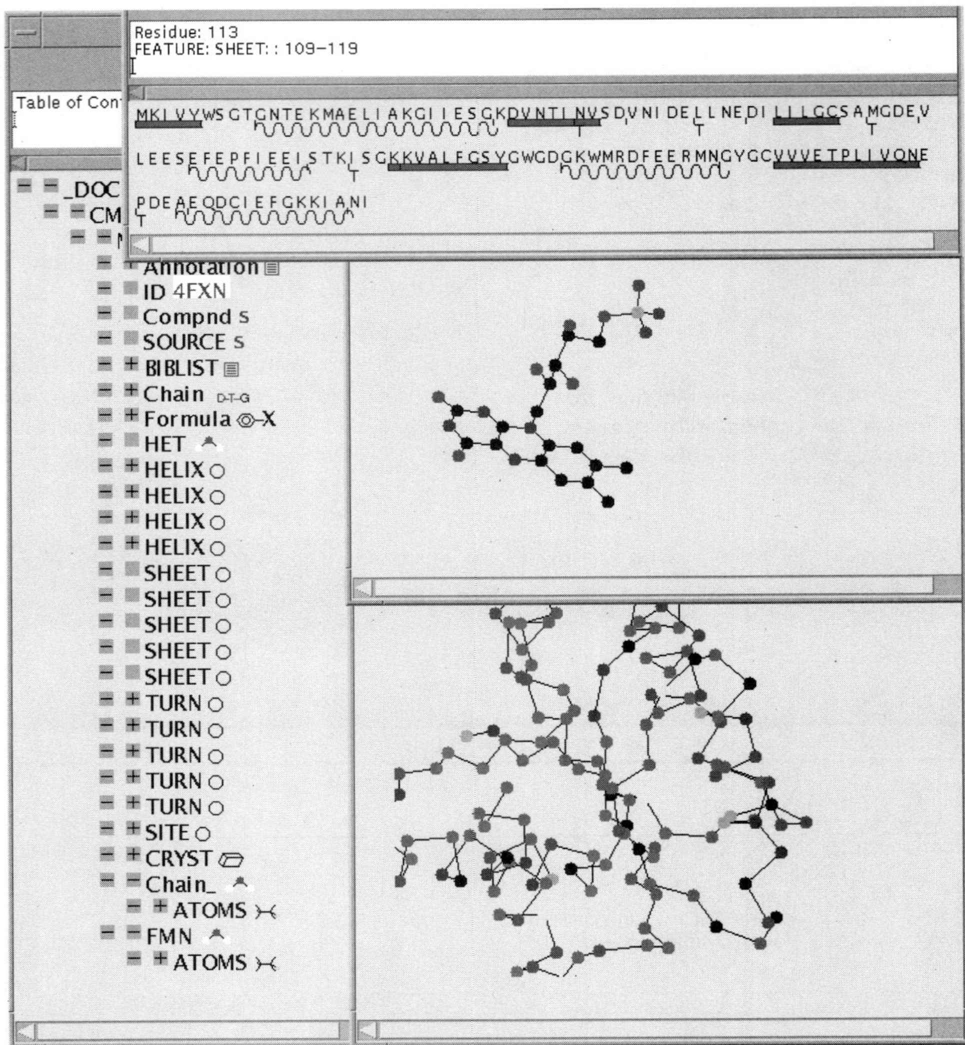

Figure 2

ments") of atoms in a molecule to peaks in a spectrum is shown in Figure 4. This is particularly simple since there is a 1:1 correspondence—for each bar in the spectrum there is an atom. An assignment is thus a link between the two and could be representated as:

```
<RELATION XML-LINK="EXTENDED"
    TITLE="Peak1">
<XVAR XML-LINK="LOCATOR"
    HREF="ATOM(3)"
    BEHAVIOR="highlight">
<XVAR XML-LINK="LOCATOR"
    HREF="LINE(17)"
    BEHAVIOR="highlight">
</RELATION>
```

Clicking on `Peak1` sends signals to the children of the RELATION to display themselves and to highlight the particular feature. As different peaks are clicked, the highlights are updated in both windows. If it is possible to catalogue a variety of such behaviors, XML-LINK can provide very powerful support.

How to Use JUMBO

JUMBO can be used in several modes:

- *As a standalone Java application* (see Figure 5). This simply requires the user to install a Java interpreter. (Note that XML-LINK is used to transmit the effect of clicking the `???` icon (near `Pyrrole`) to display the groups of atoms in the molecule). In this mode JUMBO can read and write local files and also connect to servers. Here's an example:

```
java jumbo.sgml.SGMLTree myfile.xml
```

- *Applets downloaded from a server* to a traditional Java-enabled browser. The XML document is referenced inside an APPLET element in a **.html* document:

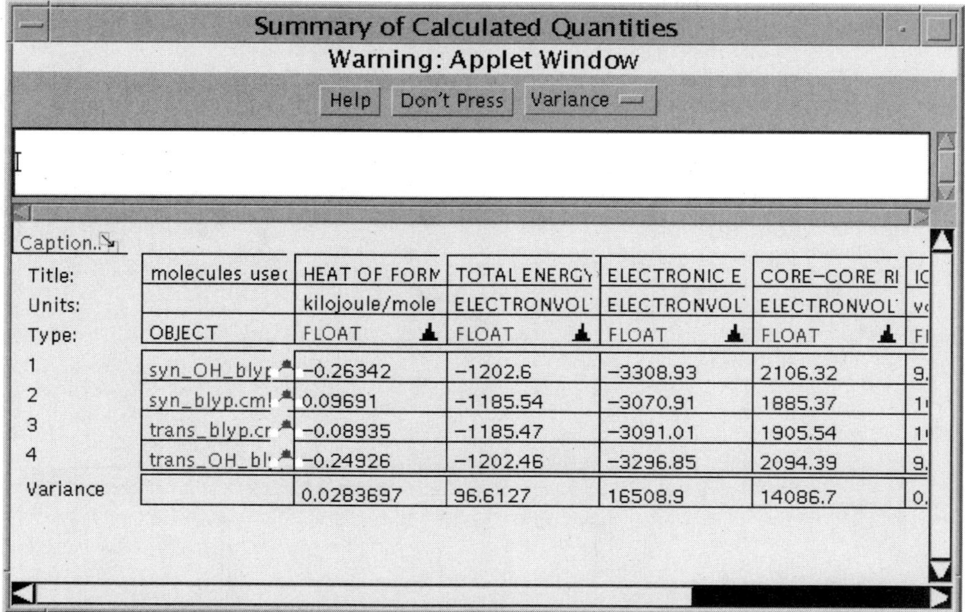

Figure 3

```
<APPLET CODE="jumbo.sgml.SGMLTree.
    class"><PARAM NAME="commandline"
VALUE="myfile.xml"></APPLET>
```

- *Locally,* within a Java-enabled browser, with the classes under the document tree.

The last two bullet items are very convenient since many modern browsers support Java.

Extending JUMBO

JUMBO is distributed as a set of classes. Since Java is designed for extensibility, developers can modify its function without needing source code. The most common way to extend JUMBO will be to create a set of classes for a new DTD. In specialized cases (e.g., molecules) this requires one class per element. Where many Elements share common features, however, they can inherit methods. It should be straightforward to extend JUMBO to support stylesheets.

Recently Javasoft published a vastly improved set of classes (Swing [4]) for creating GUIs. Some of these support generic tree functionality and its display, and this is an obvious way to make JUMBO more robust and efficient.

Using JUMBO, TecML/CML, and VHG

JUMBO was developed as reusable code and is available for collaboration. Use of JUMBO for molecular purposes is likely to be in conjunction with the Open Molecule Foundation. CML and TecML will soon be published in the chemical community and others on CDROM (including Java-based demos).

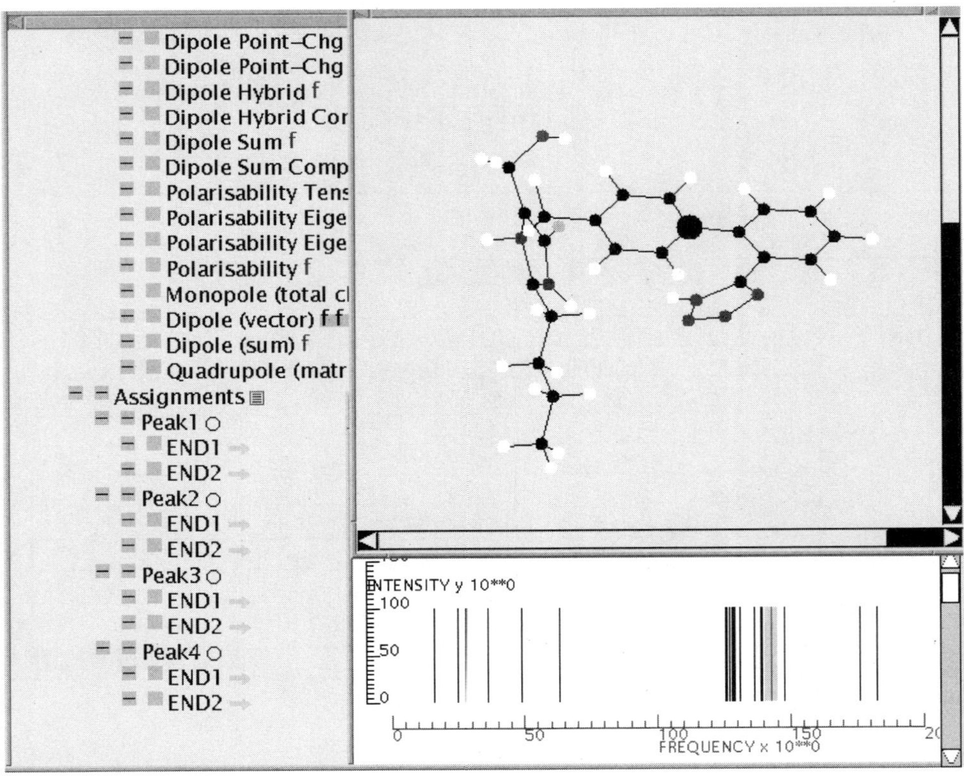

Figure 4

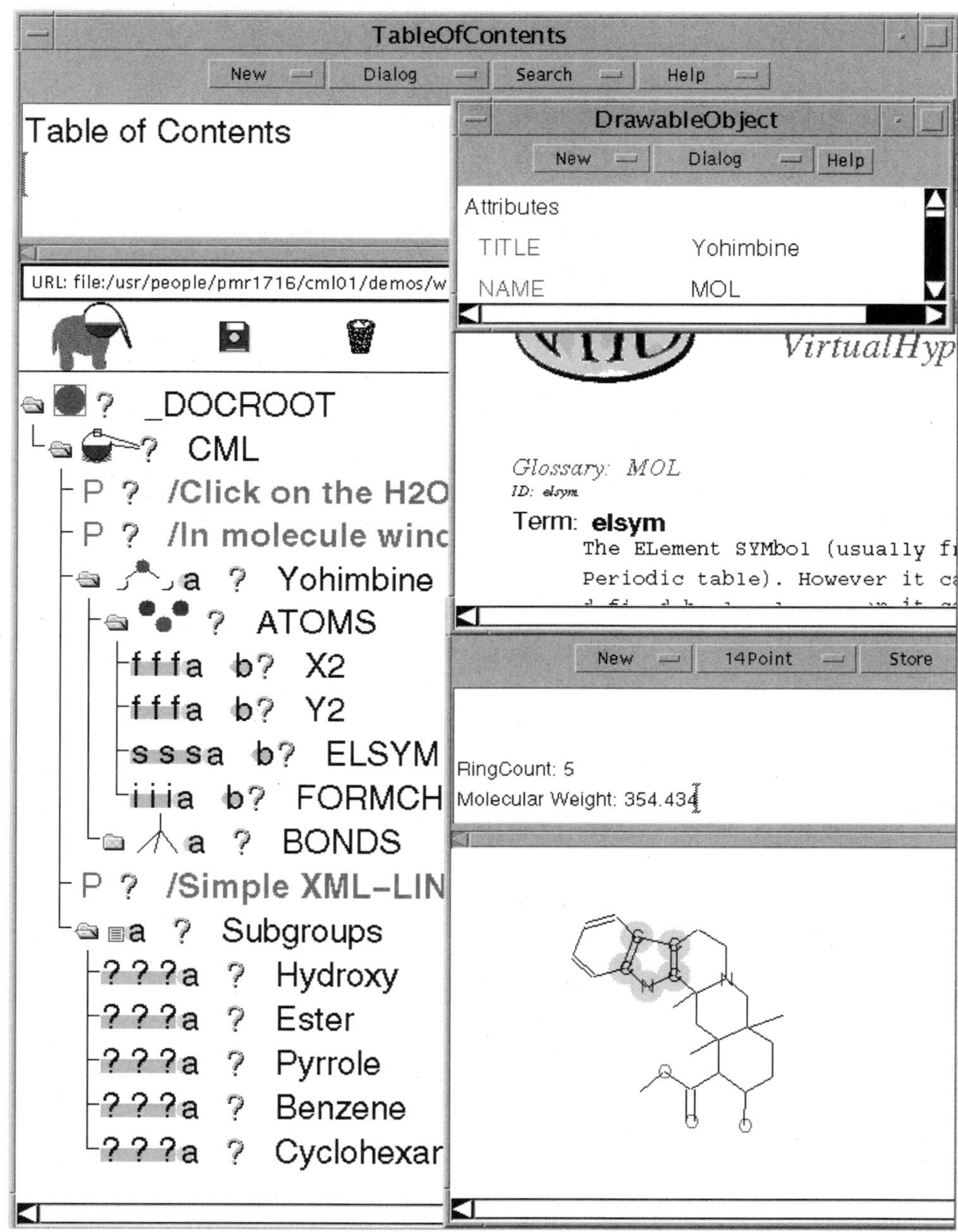

Figure 5

JUMBO and CML rely heavily on adding semantics through hyperlinks to glossaries (as in the "melting point" example above). To systematize the format and creation, we have developed the Virtual HyperGlossary project [5]. The project is communicating with providers of high-quality terminological content to create stable, curated XML-based glossaries to which XML documents can be linked. The glossaries have a simple syntax based either on TecML or ISO12200 (MARTIF). In either case they use attribute values from ISO12620 data categories. Hierarchy (superordinate concepts) and other entailment (e.g., "related term") are provided through XML-LINKs. There is support for ADMINistrative details and for VirtualHyperMarkup (the linking of documents to glossaries). XML's addressing and naming schemes allow for distributed glossary servers. ■

Acknowledgments

The OMF has supported the creation of this demo, and many of them (especially Henry Rzepa, Richard Kinder, Andrew Payne and Adam Precious) have given me encouragement. I am particularly grateful to Jon Bosak for his virtual encouragement and presentation of a JUMBO demo at WWW6. Lesley West has partnered me in the creation of the Virtual HyperGlossary.

References

1. *http://www.jclark.com*
2. *http://www.art.com/~joe/cost/index.html*
3. *http://www.datachannel.com/*
4. *http://www.javasoft.com*
5. *http://www.venus.co.uk/vhg*

Additional Resources

1. TecML and CML: *http//www.venus.co.uk/omf/cml/*
2. JUMBO *code/DTDs/examples/tutorials* are at *http://www.vsms.nottingham.ac.uk/vsms/java/jumbo*
3. The VHG is at *http://www.venus.co.uk/vhg/*
4. The OMF is at *http://www.ch.ic.ac.uk/omf/*

About the Author

Peter Murray-Rust
Virtual School of Molecular Sciences
Nottingham University, UK
pazpmr@unix.ccc.nottingham.ac.uk

Peter Murray-Rust is the Director of the Virtual School of Molecular Sciences at the University of Nottingham, where he is participating in a new venture in virtual education and communities. Peter is also a visiting professor at the Crystallography Department at Birkbeck College, where he set up the first multimedia virtual course on the WWW (Principles of Protein Structure).

Peter's research interests in molecular informatics include participation in the Open Molecule Foundation—a virtual community sharing molecular resources; developing the use of Chemical MIME for the electronic transmission of molecular information; creating the first publicly available XML browser, JUMBO; and developing the Virtual HyperGlossary—an exploration of how the world community can create a virtual resource in terminology.

CAPTURING THE STATE OF DISTRIBUTED SYSTEMS WITH XML

Rohit Khare, Adam Rifkin

Abstract

This paper discusses the challenges of capturing the state of distributed systems across time, space, and communities, and looks to XML as an effective solution. First, when recording a data structure for future reuse, XML format storage is self-descriptive enough to extract its schema and verify its validity. Second, when transferring data structures between different machines, XML's link model in conjunction with Web transport protocols reduces the burden of marshaling entire data sets. Third, when sharing collaborative data structures between disparate communities, it is easier to compose new systems and convert data definitions to the degree that XML documents are adopted for the World Wide Web. Just as previous generations of distributed system architectures emphasized relational databases or object-request brokers, the Web generation has good reason to adopt XML as its common archiving tool, because XML's sheer generic power has value in knowledge representation across time, space, and communities.

1. Distributing Data Across Time, Space, and Communities

Twenty-four thousand miles of adventures reduced to six letters. A journey across eleven flight segments, seven countries, three carriers, and one planet—and all that the airline flight reservation center can be moved to speak is the cryptic code "NQSS5A." A Passenger-Name Record (PNR) is the quintessential digital age artifact, unlocking yet more data stored in tickets, tariff filings, baggage claim checks, catering orders, security profiles, credit records, and myriad other components of this half-real, half-virtual distributed system called an airline.

Throughout a PNR's lifecycle, from the first call to a travel agent to the final posting of frequent-flier miles, these complex data structures face three challenges: to be distributed across time, to both past and future readers; to be distributed across space, to other machines; and to be distributed across communities, to other organizations and applications. The first challenge calls for a stable data format, since itineraries have to be updated consistently by reservationists, ticket agents, gate agents, flight crews, database engineers, accountants, and others. In the second case, there needs to be a stable grain of exchange, to share records and commit transactions between a bevy of information systems. Finally, to communicate across organizations, there have to be common definitions: agreements between airlines, hotels, rental car agencies, travel agents, and passengers about the interpretation of dates, locations, flights, prices, and so on.

In each of these situations, system designers can leverage several strategies to manage distributed data cost-effectively. File formats, for example, must be machine-readable, but can be more future-proof if they are also human-readable and use self-describing schema. When packaging related objects together to exchange with other machines, finer-grained marshaling strategies are more flexible than integrating systems through a handful of fixed report formats. Finally, industry-wide coordination has been notoriously difficult to design by committee. Instead of fixing protocols and data dictionaries, the best strategy may be to collaborate through conventional "documents"—for example, purchase orders instead of Electronic Data Interchange (EDI) records.

All too commonly, the actual decisions of system designers fall short against these measures. Proprietary, underdocumented, binary file formats are not merely quick hacks; they are strategic decisions to lock in users. Concurrent systems almost immediately retreat to a unified system image, so instead of marshaling only relevant data, the entire database needs to be shared. The result is horrifying: black-box legacy systems that are rarely shared within a community, much less among suppliers, vendors, and other outside users.

In this paper, we argue that the Extensible Markup Language (XML) [3][*] and its companion Extensible Linking Language (XLL) [4] can together provide an effective solution for capturing the state of distributed systems, particularly on the World Wide Web. XML was designed to provide a subset of the Standardized General Markup Language (SGML) that is easy to write, interpret, and implement.[†] Since XML allows extensible markup while preserving rigorous validation, we advocate storing information in XML, sharing it according to XLL's link model, and weaving XML-enhanced data structures into Web documents.

2. Capturing State

The airline system is constantly in motion, but suppose it were possible to hold back the rush of transactions momentarily to take a global snapshot. The resulting tower of storage media would be almost useless to re-animate the system a few years hence. The bits can surely be preserved, but the file formats slowly fade into gibberish as the applications evolve. Worse, the applications might not evolve at all: that hasty decision to use a slightly more compact two-digit year field may come crashing down decades hence (to the tune of $600 billion in North America alone, according to an oft-quoted Gartner Group study).

The point of reducing some complex multidimensional data structure to a bitstream is ultimately to allow some future user to reconstitute that same data structure and manipulate it accurately. The key is enforcing a schema for these transformations. In this section, we will explore the tensions that lead to brittle data formats (Section 2.1), three strategies for future-proofing data formats (Section 2.2), and how XML-based data formats execute those strategies (Section 2.3).

2.1 Data Archaeology

"Data Archaeologist" smacks of postmodernism gone awry, but the business of rummaging through now-forgotten tapes of healthcare records or satellite observations for archival data is already a viable industry. Even mission-critical systems can remain underdocumented as a result. The tendency toward proprietary schema and binary encodings also increases the fragility of file formats. There are several seductive reasons why designers argue that extensible, self-describing formats are not cost-effective, including the following:

- *"We have been using our house style for generations!"*
- *"That format is too bloated and inefficient to parse!"*
- *"The tools are too immature!"*
- *"Besides, that data isn't for outside consumption . . ."*

Paradoxically, the quest for "high-fidelity" archiving tools that directly map data structure in memory to the bit stream leads to more brittle, less flexible formats. Object systems that helpfully default to recording all instance data force file formats to evolve as rapidly as the code. Separate versions of an application cannot exchange files without littering the parsing logic with evidence

* Both of these specifications are included in the "W3C Reports" section of this issue.

† For more information regarding the relationships of SGML and XML, see the article "The Evolution of Web Documents: The Ascent of XML" (Connolly, Khare, and Rifkin) in this issue.

of previous generations' data structures. The archives generated by operating system or language tools are often inextensible: there is no way to gently add new fields to a record, much less to indicate if comprehension is optional or mandatory.

Type-equivalence problems in a language can spread to the archives, too, like the impedance mismatch between Java's (and its Serialization's) `int` type and `Integer` class [14]. Each system establishes its own set of canonical primitives such as character, string, integer, and float, and its own encodings, leading to yet more conversion challenges—both on the wire level (for example, COM [6]) and on the interface level [19]. Abstract Syntax Notation (ASN.1) [13] encoding rules, for example, specify the type, length, and value of each datum in the stream—as well as the type, length, and value of the type and length.

Human-readable formats have their own traps. Many UNIX system databases, for example, embrace the need for extensibility, manual editability, and to include comments [17]. Each of the many column-separated flat-file databases for users, groups, email aliases, and so on are still cryptic, not automatically validatable, and are not self-documenting. As the system grows, some databases need to be replaced wholesale by incompatible binary forms updated by distributed directory protocols.

In short, data storage formats are difficult to "future-proof." It takes care and effort to design extensible, editable, scalable, and correct formats, as well as the parsers, generators, and Application Programming Interfaces (APIs) that implement it. Instead, designers face immediate concerns about:

Inertia
: Applications and programmers each have habits for recording state, sometimes dating back to the particular layout of punch cards or drum memory. There may also be resistance to formats "Not Invented Here."

Efficiency
: A primary rationalization is that accommodating extensibility and human-readablity wastes parsing effort and storage space. However, the further into the future this data will be used, the cheaper these resources and the more valuable flexibility will become.

Tools
: Tools can be the root of the two earlier objections. The archiving tools already support the *status quo*, and new tools to support a more future-proof format are immature or expensive. ASN.1 parsers, for example, are too resource-intensive for small smart cards.

Openness
: Sometimes file formats are exempt from any analysis because that data is expected to be used only within the context of this system. Each open interface to the state of the system *increases* the complexity of the overall design, after all.

Underdocumentation, though, is still a greater flaw than whether the file format is technically well-suited to the task or not. Without preserving a description of the data—much less self-descriptive data—there can be no communication across time to future readers and writers of that data.

2.2 Describing Formats with Metadata

We posit three strategic requirements for future-proof data formats:

Machine-readable formats
: Ultimately, computers have to manipulate these bitstreams, so consider the space, speed, and accuracy of the parsers and generators; and to a lesser extent, the size of the bitstream.

Human-readable formats
: The flexibility of human-readable and human-editable formats requires robust error handling and simpler document structure.

Self-descriptive formats

It is not enough merely to use a rigorous schema for the data contained within a bitstream; the actual stream should include enough information to extract out the schema, and to validate its contents.

The natural tension between these three strategies inspires a delicate balancing act: mechanical logic and human fuzziness can only be reconciled in a format that can be dynamically learned by each.

Successfully *machine-readable formats* are measured by the logic required to extract and manipulate them. Rigorous enforcement of syntax rules simplifies parsing logic at the expense of robust error handling. Direct projection of the data-representation in memory simplifies parsing and generation at the expense of human-readability and cross-platform support. For example, capturing numeric data in binary form is simple and potentially compact, but unreadable and dependent on the endianness of the CPU architecture. Mission-specific grammars can be more compact than adapting general purpose encodings (e.g., ASN.1). Turing-complete formats, representing state as executable program text, inflate parser and generator size while reducing the fidelity of the data manipulation. For example, an airline ticket as PostScript requires executing a large program and even then ending up with strokes and arcs instead of cities and flights.

Successfully *human-readable formats*, by contrast, are measured by the cognitive effort to extract and manipulate information [18]. In this case, flexible enforcement of syntax rules makes it easier to edit and read. Data representations need to be translated to accessible forms, potentially at the expense of fidelity. For example, integers can be represented accurately in decimal, but inaccuracies can crop up for floating-point. Data presentations also need to be accessible: a Portable Network Graphics (PNG) picture is "human-readable" when presented as an image. A spreadsheet presented as a table, though, loses the equations and symbolic logic behind the numbers in the process. The benefit of all of these tradeoffs is increased reusability, which will increase the viability and investment in maintaining that format. Conversely, when human-readability is reduced to an afterthought as a companion "import/export" format, the canonical binary format may still not become future-proof.

Successfully *self-describing formats* are measured by how much can be discovered dynamically about their mechanical structure and semantics. The first test is simple identification. The file should contain some type signature, perhaps even a revision number, or at least a filename extension—enough to characterize the format. Leveraging that identity to define the provenance of the data and its definitions is the next step. A typical Unix system configuration file, for example, at least refers to the section of the manual that defines its entries. The third test is whether that definition is sufficient to dynamically extract and manipulate the information within both structural and presentational guides. These kinds of metadata can future-proof a format, preserving machine-readability *and* human-readability.

2.3 Capturing Database Schema as DTDs

XML strikes an appealing balance among the three strategic goals laid out in Section 2.2. The very constraints applied to SGML in specifying XML make it well-suited to dynamically generating new data formats.

First, each specific XML-based file format is based on a separate, explicit Document Type Definition (DTD). Each DTD defines the names of new tags, their structure, and their content model. More to the point, XML files are required to disclose their respective DTDs in their headers, or include the entire DTD within the XML file itself, neatly enforcing self-description. The DTD functions analogously to an Interface Definition Language (IDL) specification or a relational database schema.

Second, XML parsers can validate files with or without the DTD. The implicit grammar rules define a hybrid machine- and human-readable text format that can represent numbers, strings, and even escaped binary content. The tools themselves can be built small and run quickly, as described elsewhere in this issue. The resulting files are probably larger than alternative formats, but XML markup should compress effectively for tightly constrained environments. XML-formatted metadata can also be stored alongside legacy files as appropriate.

Furthermore, using XML unlocks other opportunities. DTDs can be cascaded to represent compound data types [5]. A `TravelAuthorization` record, for example, could combine an `Itinerary` record and an `EmployeeAccount`. DTDs can also be hosted on the Web, allowing users to dynamically learn about new formats. Style sheets can be applied to the tagged XML data, garnering all of the formatting abilities that application entails.

3. Exchanging State

Although an airline system could be simulated as one massively centralized application, it is distributed across multiple subsystems for scale and redundancy (by multiplying the number of parallel instances) and to manage complexity (by dividing the problem). The flight dispatcher is an example of the latter: as the delays propagate across the country each day, it decides to schedule or scrub flights and allocate planes. Each decision to fly is based on a number of factors: the reservations for each flight, to estimate the size of the plane; the fares at stake, to determine profitability; and the itineraries of each passenger, to predict missed connections. The PNR database has all that information and more: seat assignments, VIP status flags, baggage claims . . . so much data that the challenge becomes how to select and transfer just the relevant portions.

While every system needs to ensure that its input and output formats can withstand the test of time, distributed systems need to share knowledge between different physical locations at the same time. Protocols must be established for excerpting relevant parts of the workload and shipping data between subsystems, either across a network of separate computers or using interprocess communication within the same computer. In this section, we explain some of the tradeoffs of marshaling data (Section 3.1), a strategy to use the network to defer marshaling decisions (Section 3. 2), and how the Extensible Link Language improves upon the Web's hypertext semantics to match (Section 3.3).

3.1 Distributed Systems with Centralized Data

The simplest way to cope with the complexity of data flowing back and forth intermittently in varying packages is not to; "distributed" does not imply "decentralized." Instead of deciding how to export part of an interlinked data structure and how often, it can be considered cost-effective to either unify the entire state of the system in a central relational database [11], or partition that whole state between isolated subsystems.

Consider the challenge of exchanging state between the flight dispatcher and another critical resource, the crew dispatcher. Once a flight has been scheduled onto a plane, it still needs pilots and attendants certified to operate that plane in that departure city. It is an especially complex space-time chess game because people, unlike planes, need to return home soon. Optimization algorithms manipulate all of these records simultaneously, producing a complex, connected graph of Employees, Flights, and Planes in memory. The results need to be shared with yet other subsystems in operations and human resources: reports summarizing the activity of each Plane and Employee.

To "pickle" the state of a Plane, we can write down its particulars, but then there are pointers to the several Flights it will take that day which in turn point to several crews. Extracting that report requires marking all the records that plane depends on, then cutting that subgraph out of the larger database by replacing pointers with internal references in the archive. Of course, it is not just a simple spreading tree: pickling an Employee requires enumerating the Flights and Planes it is linked to, and the recursive, tangled mess could easily expand to encompass the entire database.

The system designer has to break this cycle, literally. Decisions must be made either to include a linked record in the archive, or else to replace the pointer with a symbolic name. For example, the daily roster for a Plane can terminate by recording only the Employee name and ID, eliding other details that can be reconstructed by dereferencing that ID. The Employee schedule need only list Flight numbers, rather than include the full details of the flight's passengers, meals, and revenue.

In the geography of distributed systems, distance is (the inverse of) bandwidth, which constrains both the size and frequency of messages. Designers also have to enforce policies about how often to update the system. At one extreme, all data can be stored in atomically small records in one high-performance database. Even if that database is hosted on several computers running in parallel, it is essentially a centralized philosophy at work. It can be made to scale: today's airline reservation systems pool dozens of mainframes in a massive hardened data centers into some of the highest throughput transaction networks in the world. At the other extreme, all related data can be isolated within one system that emits a batch-processed summary of the entire set every so often.

3.2 Linking Instead of Marshaling

Marshaling is an expensive strategy because the perogative always lies with the sender. First, the sender has to decide the marshaling policy for each data structure when the application is written. Second, at runtime, the marshaling process has to mark all of the records to be written and resolve all of the internal pointers before the first byte hits the wire.

The Web solves this problem rather differently. A page can include many subsidiary resources, some of which load other subparts in turn. Different pages can also share common resources. Web servers do not transmit a single neat package, though: each resource is transferred in a separate HTTP request-response pair [10].

The key observation is that the links between resources already have names. Instead of pointers that can only be interpreted in the sender's context (like memory addresses), relative and absolute Uniform Resource Locators [1] can be interpreted by any recipient. Instead of expensive marshaling burdens on the server (writer), the client (reader) can incrementally fetch the desired resources as needed.

Separating each transaction does not necessarily compromise consistency. At first it might seem that since each resource is exchanged at a different point in time, the entire set could change in the middle. That race condition can be prevented by incorporating state into the URL (for example, a version indicator a la Web Distributed Authoring and Versioning (WebDAV) [20]) or into the protocol (for example, an HTTP Cookie [16]).

Separating each transaction can hamper performance, though. HTTP's strictly synchronous model implies a round-trip delay for each resource, even if the sender already knows what dependent resources should be marshaled together. HTTP caching or the future evolution of HTTP to allow "push" responses can both address this limitation.

Neither of these engineering concerns dilute the lesson of linking with names, since URLs are designed to assimilate new naming schemes and access protocols. The strategy of linking resources together with names defers both of the costs associated with marshaling: the perogative to drill down shifts to the recipient, and the sender does not have to map out an entire report.

3.3 Leveraging the XML Link Model

XML-formatted data is particularly well suited to this strategy because of the rich new linking model in the complementary XLL specification. The W3C Generic SGML activity charter, for example, is aimed at protocols supporting interactive access to structured documents that fetch just a single definition from a dictionary (instead of retrieving the entire dictionary). In another example, the addressing model that allows source documents to select any span of elements in another SGML or XML document can also serve the needs of distributed system designers accessing one baggage record out of a manifest.

XLL can indicate whether each linked resource should be interpreted within the same context or a new one (the SHOW axis) and suggests whether to access it in parallel or in series (the ACTUATE axis).

Since the actual link address format is just a URL, it can point at any named span in the target document. Fragment identifiers like `document#label` behave just as they do for HTML. First, they load and parse the entire document, and then they search for the anchor element the original author so labeled. Unlike HTML, though, URLs referring to XML documents can use an extended pointer (XPTR) syntax developed by the Text Encoding Initiative (TEI). An XPTR identifier such as `document|ID(label),CHILD(2,*)` points to the second element below the labeled anchor; there are many other operators for navigating the parse tree, counting characters, matching strings, and indicating spans. XLL deliberately leaves it unspecified who dereferences an XPTR identifier, so the dictionary server can indeed return only matching definitions.

The latter development is perhaps the most significant for XML's future as an archiving format. Portions of the state within a structure can be named, linked to, and even excerpted without modifying the source. Even state-of-the-art object-oriented serialization services for Objective-C and Java can only archive an entire stream all at once [9] [14]. XML's well-formedness requirements produce structured documents that can be correctly manipulated, even without the entire contents of the document at hand.

4. Sharing Meaning

The airline system does an admirable job of abstraction for its passengers, hiding almost all of the machinations discussed in the previous two sections. For the traveler, black-box reuse means the only interface necessary is to specify the origin, destination, time, and then pay the fare. Black-box reuse also means that when a traveler submits an expense report, the only documentation left is the mere *image* of a ticket stub. A PNR unlocks no data for an outsider.

The information to fill out an expense report certainly exists within the airline's databases. That information was even collated into a self-contained document. When that ticket changed hands from agent to passenger, though, it was ripped out of context. The point of preparing a report should be to come to enough ontological agreement to allow an outsider to reconstitute its context, and hence its meaning. In this section, we explore the challenges of interorganizational collaboration (Section 4.1), document-centered integration strategy (Section 4.2), and how XML-enhanced documents can provide a usable face to structured data (Section 4.3).

4.1 Coordinating Tasks Across Organizations

A traveler planning a meeting of his clients has to make air, car, and hotel arrangements and obtain consensus from his clients for a schedule. Ideally, once reservations have been made, the traveler would like to link all these affairs together. For example, if the flight is delayed, each participant's calendar will show an alternate meeting time. Or, if the meeting is rescheduled to two days, the travel arrangements are extended to match. In reality, these four systems (air, car, hotel, and company meeting) are so loosely coupled that there is a vibrant market for a fifth organization: the travel agency.

This is not a technology problem. It is not a matter of wiring up all the players with email and Web sites. It is an *ontological* problem where no two vocabulary sets quite line up. For example, if a meeting slips from the afternoon to the next morning, it is one extra hotel "night" (which are calculated as solar days), and zero extra car rental "days" (calculated as 24-hour blocks) and possibly even a more expensive airline ticket (if the fare had a "maximum-stay" limit, which would be measured in the *originating* timezone).

Understanding these varying bits of jargon for marking time confers membership in each industry. Organizations can be defined by their language: *ontology recapitulates community.* Coordinating tasks across organizations ineluctably requires adapting to local conventions. It also requires prying information out of the several distributed systems: each of the travel plans hide behind an opaque reservation code, to say nothing of the chaos in calendaring standards.

4.2 Collaborating Through Documents

The best remedy to conflicting speech is yet more speech. The conventional practice for forestalling such confusion is to "put it in writing" through legal contracts and other trust agreements [15]. From the Warsaw Convention fine print on luggage loss liability limits to credit card charge slips, business proceeds by paperwork. Such documents have two roles in brokering interorganizational collaboration: the document itself becomes the concrete face of the task, and it defines its own ontology for the task.

Consider a bank check. Legally, a demand deposit account can be used with a signed napkin, but the U.S. Federal Reserve's clearance policies set out the physical dimensions, layout, and magnetic-ink encoding of a check. As the check moves from bank to bank, there is no confusion as to the exact interpretation of accounts, amounts, and dates, because the check incorporates its own legal conventions. At another end of the spectrum, a forty-thousand page New Drug Application to the U.S. Food and Drug Administration still has the same roles. The application is the one artifact that represents years of negotiations, carefully logged. The application sets out its own drug-specific scientific terms and tests, negotiated by both sides' analysts.

Documents in cyberspace assume the same roles: embodying the user interface to a task and defining its terms. The document metaphor has a long pedigree in user interface research, far predating the web. Taligent, arguably the most sophisticated mulituser collaborative document toolkit to date, strongly endorsed the convergence of application-as-document and "collaborative places" [8]. Concurrent documents views were assembled from active components consulting a shared structured storage model while interaction could pass from user to user. While such peer-to-peer collaboration may be several generations ahead of current Web client technology, server-based coordination of Web pages with forms and active content is a sufficient simulacrum. The broader lesson is that an intelligent "purchase order" document can be a more usable representation of the collaborative process than a traditional application. Web technology accelerates the development cycle by dramatically lowering the threshold for creating document interfaces. A form and a CGI interface to the Shipping Department can put a business online faster than an army of EDI consultants, because the Web's markup format is so accessible.

The logic embedded in a collaborative document also defines the ontology for that task. Within a community, understanding the semantics of a document is a matter of identifying its format (Section 2.2). An outsider has to understand the ontology behind the format, well enough perhaps to translate it into locally-meaningful terms. A calendar developer has to build a lot of shared context with an airline reservation structure to extract facts like "the user will be on a plane and inaccessible during each flight; during a flight, the calendar's time zone should be reset; and the user will not be available for meetings at the office." On the other hand, instead of waiting for an industrywide or international standards process to deliberate over the canonical meaning of "place" and "time," developers can at least knit one-to-one mappings. Popular ontologies can emerge organically, like well-trodden paths in a field.

4.3 Weaving XML into the Web

XML promises to realize the vision of interorganizational collaboration through Web documents. As discussed in Section 2.3, XML will "let a thousand DTDs bloom," making it cost-effective to capture community-specific semantics in XML-formatted data. Several further developments, taken together, will enable XML to assume the roles discussed above: including XML-formatted data structures in HTML documents; building usable interfaces using forms and style sheets; naming and locating DTDs on the Web; and automated processing and conversion of XML-formatted data.

Electronic commerce on the Web is already big business [15], but its HTML form-based infrastructure is not enough to "become the concrete face of the task." For example, two sites selling books and flowers will both inevitably ask for a shipping address. But without a structured container for addresses, there is no way to automatically fill in the order page at either site, much less use a shared address format. As XML-savvy tools become more popular, Web developers will be able to publish and receive XML street addresses within HTML Web pages [7]. Forms extensions could specify the DTD of input data. Style sheets will format the appearance of embedded data structures.

The technology to manipulate the ontology of XML documents is a little further off. The key is XML's hooks for identifying DTDs. The Formal Public Identifier for a document type can now be associated with a URL. XML processing tools could expect to dereference that address and not only discover a DTD file, but also metadata about the meaning of each tag, default style sheets, and possibly even mobile code resources for manipulating such data. With this kind of documentation, automated translation tools might be able to associate an airline's `<location>` tag, which refers to airport codes with an atlas's latitude and longitude entries.

In the interim, several exciting tools are already focusing on this vision. webMethods' Web Interface Definition Language (WIDL)* can extract structured data from HTML and XML web pages, invoke processing on Web servers using forms, and collate reports harvested from multiple sites in a single format. Many developers have rallied to the motto "XML gives Java something to chew on,"† referring to the synergy of XML and mobile code embedded in Web pages together. All of these trends are narrowing the gap between human-readable and machine-readable documents.

5. Knowledge Representation Across Time, Space, and Communities

In this paper, we have spoken of distributing data across time, space, and community as though they are impossible chasms. We believe they are. The arrow of time points opposite to the arrow of memory. Separation in space is separation in time; thus, latency compels brevity. The gulf between communities is the root of communication.

We have tried to set forth the challenges facing distributed system designers in this context. We argue that XML can effectively future-proof data formats, exchange data structures, and enhance

---

* See the article "Automating the Web with WIDL," by Charles Allen in this issue.

† As quoted from Jon Bosak's article, "XML, Java, and the Future of the Web" in this issue, and also available at *http://sunsite.unc.edu/pub/sun-info/standards/xml/why/xmlapps.htm.*

Web documents into robust platforms for system integration. It is not the first, last, or universal solution, but it does accelerate the continuing evolution of the Web. As the Web assimilates "the universe of all network-accessible information" [2], and as XML adds the metadata to define that universe, at some point information transubstantiates into knowledge.

A modern airline can no more take flight without its information systems than without jet fuel. At some point, the distributed system no longer models reality; it *becomes* reality. As David Gelernter predicted in his 1991 book, when the image in the machine corresponds to the real world, in both directions, we have built a *Mirror World* [12]. Today, these only exist in limited domains at vast expense: transportation systems, telecommunications systems, military operations. Soon, to the degree that the Web continues to evolve toward richer data representation, and proprietary systems gain Web interfaces, XML will mediate the recreation of reality in cyberspace. ■

Acknowledgments

This paper is based on our experiences over several years working with the Web community. Particular plaudits go to our colleagues at the World Wide Web Consortium, including Dan Connolly and Tim Berners-Lee; and the teams at MCI Internet Architecture and Caltech Infospheres. We also thank Ron Resnick, Mark Baker, and Doug Lea for their helpful comments.

References

1. Berners-Lee, Tim, Larry Masinter, and Mark McCahill. Uniform Resource Locators (URL), RFC 1738, December 1994. Available at *http://www.w3.org/Addressing/rfc1738.txt*
2. Berners-Lee, Tim. "WWW: Past, Present, and Future," *IEEE Computer* 29: 10, October 1996.
3. Bray, Tim, Jean Paoli, and C.M. Sperberg-McQueen. "Extensible Markup Language (XML): Part I. Syntax," World Wide Web Consortium Working Draft (Work in Progress), August 1997. Available at *http://www.w3.org/TR/WD-xml-lang.html*
4. Bray, Tim, and Steve DeRose. "Extensible Markup Language (XML): Part II. Linking," World Wide Web Consortium Working Draft (Work in Progress), July 1997. Available at *http://www.w3.org/TR/WD-xml-link.html*
5. Bray, Tim. "Adding Strong Data Typing to SGML and XML," May 1997. Available at *http://www.textuality.com/xml/typing.html*
6. Chappell, David. *Understanding ActiveX and OLE*, Microsoft Press, 1996.
7. Connolly, Dan, Rohit Khare, and Adam Rifkin. "The Evolution of Web Documents: The Ascent of XML," *World Wide Web Journal* 2: 4, Autumn 1997. Available at *http://www.cs.caltech.edu/~adam/papers/xml/ascent-of-xml.html*
8. Cotter, Sean, and Mike Potel. *Inside Taligent Technology*, Addison-Wesley, 1995. Available at *http://www.taligent.com/itt.html*
9. Cox, Brad, and Andrew Novobilski. *Object-Oriented Programming: An Evolutionary Approach*, Second Edition, Addison-Wesley, 1991.
10. Fielding, Roy, Jim Gettys, Jeff Mogul, Henrik Frystyk, and Tim Berners-Lee. "Hypertext Transfer Protocol—HTTP/1.1," RFC 2068, January 1997. Available at *http://www.w3.org/Protocols/rfc2068/rfc2068*
11. Flemming, Candace, and Barbara Vonhalle. *Handbook of Relational Database Design*, Addison-Wesley, 1988.
12. Gelernter, David. *Mirror Worlds: The Day Software Puts the Universe in a Shoebox . . . How it Will Happen and What it Will Mean*, Oxford University Press, 1991.
13. ISO 8825:1987. "Information Processing Systems—Open Systems Interconnection—Specification of Basic Encoding Rules for Abstract Syntax Notation One (ASN.1)," 1987.
14. Javasoft Java RMI Team. "Java Remote Method Invocation and Object Serialization Specification," Sun Microsystems, 1997. Available at *http://www.javasoft.com/products/jdk/rmi/index.html*
15. Khare, Rohit, and Adam Rifkin. "Weaving a Web of Trust," *World Wide Web Journal* 2: 3, Summer 1997, pp. 77–112. Available at *http://www.cs.caltech.edu/~adam/papers/trust.html*
16. Kristol, David, and Lou Montulli. "HTTP State Management Mechanism, RFC 2109" (Work in Progress), February 1997. Available at *http://www.internic.net/rfc/rfc2109.txt*
17. Leffler, Samuel J., Marshall Kirk McKusick, Michael J. Karels. *The Design and Implementation of*

the 4.3Bsd Unix Operating System, Addison-Wesley, 1989.

18. Schriver, Karen A. *Dynamics in Document Design: Creating Texts for Readers*, John Wiley and Sons, 1997.
19. Siegel, Jon. *Corba Fundamentals and Programming*, John Wiley and Sons, 1996.
20. Slein, J.A., F. Vitali, E. Jim Whitehead Jr., and D.G. Durand. "Requirements for Distributed Authoring and Versioning on the World Wide Web," Internet Draft (Work in Progress), May 1997. Available at *ftp://ietf.org/internet-drafts/draft-ietf-webdav-requirements-00.txt*

About the Authors

Rohit Khare
khare@alumni.caltech.edu

Rohit Khare is a member of the MCI Internet Architecture staff in Boston, MA. He was previously on the technical staff of the World Wide Web Consortium at MIT, where he focused on security and electronic commerce issues. He has been involved in the development of cryptographic software tools and Web-related standards development. Rohit received a B.S. in Engineering and Applied Science and in Economics from California Institute of Technology in 1995. He will enter the Ph.D. program in Computer Science at the University of California, Irvine in Fall 1997.

Adam Rifkin
adam@cs.caltech.edu

Adam Rifkin received his B.S. and M.S. in Computer Science from the College of William and Mary. He is presently pursuing a Ph.D. in computer science at the California Institute of Technology, where he works with the Caltech Infospheres Project on the composition of distributed active objects. His efforts with Infospheres have won best paper awards both at the Fifth IEEE International Symposium on High Performance Distributed Computing in August 1996, and at the Thirtieth Hawaii International Conference on System Sciences in January 1997. He has done Internet consulting and performed research with several organizations, including Canon, Hewlett-Packard, Reprise Records, Griffiss Air Force Base, and the NASA-Langley Research Center.

XML, JAVA, AND THE FUTURE OF THE WEB

Jon Bosak

Introduction

The extraordinary growth of the World Wide Web has been fueled by the ability it gives authors to easily and cheaply distribute electronic documents to an international audience. As Web documents have become larger and more complex, however, Web content providers have begun to experience the limitations of a medium that does not provide the extensibility, structure, and data checking needed for large-scale commercial publishing. The ability of Java applets to embed powerful data manipulation capabilities in Web clients makes even clearer the limitations of current methods for the transmittal of document data.

To address the requirements of commercial Web publishing and enable the further expansion of Web technology into new domains of distributed document processing, the World Wide Web Consortium has developed an Extensible Markup Language (XML) for applications that require functionality beyond the current Hypertext Markup Language (HTML). This paper describes the XML effort and discusses new kinds of Java-based Web applications made possible by XML.*

Background: HTML and SGML

Most documents on the Web are stored and transmitted in HTML. HTML is a simple language well suited for hypertext, multimedia, and the display of small and reasonably simple documents. HTML is based on SGML (Standard Generalized Markup Language, ISO 8879), a standard system for defining and using document formats.

SGML allows documents to describe their own grammar—that is, to specify the tag set used in the document and the structural relationships that those tags represent. HTML applications are applications that hardwire a small set of tags in conformance with a single SGML specification. Freezing a small set of tags allows users to leave the language specification out of the document and makes it much easier to build applications, but this ease comes at the cost of severely limiting HTML in several important respects, chief among which are extensibility, structure, and validation.

- *Extensibility*. HTML does not allow users to specify their own tags or attributes in order to parameterize or otherwise semantically qualify their data.
- *Structure*. HTML does not support the specification of deep structures needed to represent database schemas or object-oriented hierarchies.
- *Validation*. HTML does not support the kind of language specification that allows consuming applications to check data for structural validity on importation.

In contrast to HTML stands generic SGML. A generic SGML application is one that supports SGML language specifications of arbitrary complexity and makes possible the qualities of extensibility, structure, and validation missing from HTML. SGML makes it possible to define your own formats for your own documents, to handle large and complex documents, and to manage large information repositories. However, full SGML contains many optional features that are

* This paper, first published on the Web on November 17, 1996 [1], was revised March 10, 1997 [2] and is here presented in a form edited for the *World Wide Web Journal*.

not needed for Web applications and has proven to have a cost/benefit ratio unattractive to current vendors of Web browsers.

The XML Effort

The World Wide Web Consortium (W3C) has created an SGML Working Group to build a set of specifications to make it easy and straightforward to use the beneficial features of SGML on the Web. See the W3C SGML/XML Activity page [3] for the current status of this effort. The goal of the W3C SGML activity is to enable the delivery of self-describing data structures of arbitrary depth and complexity to applications that require such structures.

The first phase of this effort is the specification of a simplified subset of SGML specially designed for Web applications. This subset, called XML (Extensible Markup Language), retains the key SGML advantages of extensibility, structure, and validation in a language that is designed to be vastly easier to learn, use, and implement than full SGML.

XML differs from HTML in three major respects:

1. Information providers can define new tag and attribute names at will.
2. Document structures can be nested to any level of complexity.
3. Any XML document can contain an optional description of its grammar for use by applications that need to perform structural validation.

XML has been designed for maximum expressive power, maximum teachability, and maximum ease of implementation. The language is not backward-compatible with existing HTML documents, but documents conforming to the W3C HTML 3.2 specification can easily be converted to XML, as can generic SGML documents and documents generated from databases.

The first working draft of XML was announced November 1996 at the SGML 96 Conference. A major revision of the draft was announced at the Sixth World Wide Web Conference in April 1997. XML 1.0 is currently scheduled for recommendation to the W3C Advisory Council during October 1997. See the W3C XML page [3] for links to the latest draft.

Web Applications of XML

The applications that will drive the acceptance of XML are those that cannot be accomplished within the the limitations of HTML. These applications can be divided into four broad categories:

1. Applications that require the Web client to mediate between two or more heterogeneous databases.
2. Applications that attempt to distribute a significant proportion of the processing load from the Web server to the Web client.
3. Applications that require the Web client to present different views of the same data to different users.
4. Applications in which intelligent Web agents attempt to tailor information discovery to the needs of individual users.

The alternative to XML for these applications is proprietary code embedded as "script elements" in HTML documents and delivered in conjunction with proprietary browser plug-ins or Java applets. XML derives from a philosophy that data belongs to its creators and that content providers are best served by a data format that does not bind them to particular script languages, authoring tools, and delivery engines but provides a standardized, vendor-independent, level playing field upon which different authoring and delivery tools may freely complete.

Database Interchange: The Universal Hub

A paradigmatic example of this first category of XML applications is the information tracking system for a home health care agency.

Home health care is a major component of America's multibillion-dollar medical industry that continues to increase in importance as the health care burden is shifted from hospitals to home care settings. Information management is critical to this industry in order to meet the record-keeping requirements of the federal agencies and health maintenance organizations that pay for patient care.

The typical patient entering a home health care agency is represented to the information system by a large collection of paper-based historical materials in the form of patient medical histories and billing data from a variety of doctors, hospitals, pharmacies, and insurance companies. The biggest task in getting the patient into the system is the manual entry of this material into the agency's database.

The coming of the Web has given the medical informatics community the hope that an electronic means can be found to alleviate this burden.* Unfortunately, existing Web applications represent fundamentally insufficient models for an adequate solution. Hospitals have begun to offer the agencies a solution that goes something like this:

1. Log into the hospital's Web site.
2. Become an authorized user.
3. Access the patient's medical records using a Web browser.
4. Print out the records from the browser.
5. Manually key in the data from the printouts.

The knowledgeable reader may smile at this "solution," but in fact this is not a joke; this is an actual proposal from a large American hospital known for its early adoption of advanced medical information systems.

A slightly more sophisticated version of this "solution" envisions the operator reading the patient data from the Web browser and keying it directly into the agency's online forms-based interface in a separate window instead of making a printout first. The only difference between this version and the previous one is that it saves the paper that would have been needed for the printout. It does nothing to address the root of the problem. A real solution would look more like this:

1. Log into the hospital's Web site.
2. Become an authorized user.
3. Access the patient's medical records in a Web-based interface that represents the records for that patient with a folder icon.
4. Drag the folder from the Web application over to the internal database application.
5. Drop it into the database.

However, this solution is not possible within the limitations of HTML, for three reasons.

- The HTML tag set is too limited to represent or differentiate between the multitude of database fields in the mixture of documents making up the patient's medical history.
- HTML is incapable of representing the variety of structures in those documents.
- HTML lacks any mechanism for checking the data for structural validity before the receiving application attempts to import it into the target database.

One technically feasible way to implement seamless interchange of patient care records is simply to require all hospitals and health care agencies to use a single standard system dictated by the government (such an approach has actually been suggested). In an environment where hospitals are going out of business on a daily basis and many health care agencies are in deep financial

* For more information we refer you to Lincoln Stein's article, "Electronic Medical Records: Promises and Threats," in the Summer 1997 issue of the W3J entitled *Web Security: A Matter of Trust.*

difficulty, however, a scheme that *en masse* is hardly practical.

The other way to enable interchange between heterogeneous systems is to adopt a single industry-wide interchange format that serves as the single output format for all exporting systems and the single input format for all importing systems. This is, in fact, the purpose for which SGML was initially designed, and XML simply carries on this tradition.

A number of industries, including the aerospace, automotive, telecommunications, and computer software industries, have been using hub languages to perform data interchange for years, and by this time the process is well understood. Typically, the major players in an industry form a standards consortium tasked with defining a Document Type Definition, which is the way in which the tag set and grammar of a markup language are defined. This DTD can then be sent with documents that have been marked up in the industry standard language using off-the-shelf editing tools, and any standard application on the receiving end can validate and process them.

The XML solution is system-independent, vendor-independent, and proven by over a decade of SGML implementation experience. XML merely extends this proven approach to document interchange over the Web. Interestingly, the same day on which the first XML 1.0 draft was released also saw the formal announcement of an SGML initiative within HL7, the standards organization for health care IS vendors, to develop a Health Care Markup Language designed to solve exactly the kind of problem described in this example.

Previous vertical-industry efforts have shown that capturing data in a rich markup often has benefits beyond the immediate requirements of data exchange. In a well-designed standardized patient data system, for example, specific information originally gathered in the course of a routine physical exam and tagged <allergies>, <drug-reactions>, and so on would instantly be available to alert the staff of an emergency room that an unconscious patient from a distant city was allergic to penicillin. The ability of XML to define tags specific to an area of application is critical to this scenario, because the otherwise unqualified word "penicillin" in the thousands of pages of a patient's entire medical history could not trigger the recognition that the same word inside an <allergies> element could trigger.

The health care example is relevant not only because of the scope of the problem and the enormous sums of money involved but also because it is paradigmatic of a very wide range of future Web applications—any in which Web clients (or Java applications running on those clients) are expected to mediate the lossless exchange of complex data between systems that use different forms of data representation in a way that can be standardized across an industry or other interest group. Some random examples of such applications are:

- Legal publishing
- The government drug approval process
- Collaborative CAD/CAM efforts
- Collaborative calendar management across different systems
- Any corporate network application that works across databases, especially where policies must be enforced: purchase orders, expense requests, etc.
- Exchange of information between players in any broker-organized business: insurance, securities, banking, etc.

Distributed Processing: Giving Java Something to Do

A paradigmatic example of this second category of XML applications is the data delivery system designed by the semiconductor industry.

Each major semiconductor manufacturer maintains several terabytes of technical data on all of the ICs that it produces. To enable interchange of this data, an industry consortium (the Pinnacles Group) was formed several years ago by Intel,

National Semiconductor, Philips, Texas Instruments, and Hitachi to design an industry-specific SGML markup language. The consortium finished that specification in 1995, and its member companies are now well into the implementation phase of the process.

One might think that the rise in popularity of HTML would cause the Pinnacles members to reconsider their decision, but in fact the limitations of HTML have convinced them that their original strategy was the correct one. Their initial idea was that the richly parameterized data stream made possible by the industry-specific SGML markup would enable intelligent applications not merely to display semiconductor data sheets as readable documents but actually to drive design processes. It is now recognized that this approach is a perfect fit with the concept of distributed Java applets, and the vision of the near future is one in which engineers can access a manufacturer's Web site and download not only viewable data on particular integrated circuits but also a Java applet that allows them to model those circuits in various combinations.

The semiconductor application is a good demonstration of the advantages of XML because:

1. It requires industry-specific markup that cannot be implemented within the confines of the fixed HTML tag set.

2. It requires that the data representation be platform- and vendor-independent so that data from a variety of sources can be used to drive a variety of distributed applications (some of which may be provided by third parties, generating a subindustry of providers of tools that can work with the standardized data stream).

3. Its utility rests ultimately in the fact that a computation-intensive process (modeling circuits for hours at a time) that would otherwise entail an enormous, extended resource hit on the server has been changed into a brief interaction with the server followed by an extended interaction with the user's own Web client. This aspect has been summed up in the slogan "XML gives Java something to do."

Note that validation, while sometimes important, does not always play the crucial role in this category of applications that it does in applications where data must be checked for structural integrity before entering a database. To make processing as efficient as possible, XML has been designed so that validation is optional in applications where it is not needed.

As with the health-care example, the semiconductor application is notable not merely for the sheer size of the market it represents but also because it is paradigmatic of an enormous range of future Java-based Web applications -- virtually any application in which standardized data is expected to be manipulated in interesting ways on the client. Perhaps the most obvious examples of such applications are the following:

- Design applications where the designer would otherwise use server cycles to consider various alternatives: electronics, engineering, architecture, menu planning, etc.

- Scheduling applications where a customer would otherwise use server cycles to entertain various possibilities: airlines, trains, buses, and subways; restaurants, movies, plays, and concerts. This is what Easy Saabre and Ticketron will look like a few years from now as the economies of distributed Java-based processing become evident.

- Commercial applications that allow consumers to explore alternatives by supplying different shopping criteria: real estate, automobiles, appliances, etc.

- The entire spectrum of educational applications, a small subset of which are the ones we call "online help."

- The entire spectrum of customer-support applications, ranging from lawn-mower maintenance through technical support for computers.

A harbinger of applications to come in the last category is the Solution Exchange Standard, an SGML markup language announced in June 1996 by a consortium of over 60 hardware, software, and communications companies to facilitate the exchange of technical support information among vendors, system integrators, and corporate help desks. In the words of the announcement:

> The standard has been designed to be flexible. It is independent of any platform, vendor or application, so it can be used to exchange solution information without regard to the system it is coming from or going to. [. . .] Additionally, the standard has been designed to have a long lifetime. SGML offers room for growth and extensibility, so the standard can easily accommodate rapidly changing support environments.

Such applications, which the XML subset is specifically designed to address, will grow in importance as consumers come to expect interoperability among their data-manipulating applets and information providers confront the realities of trying to support computation-intensive tasks directly on their Web servers.

View Selection: Letting the User Decide

A third variety of XML applications are those in which users may wish to switch between different views of the data without requiring that the data be downloaded again in a different form from the Web server.

One early application in this category will be dynamic tables of contents. It is possible now, using Web servers built on object-oriented databases, to present the user with a table of contents into a large collection of data that can be expanded with a mouse click to "open up" a portion of the TOC and reveal more detailed levels of the document structure. Dynamic TOCs of this kind can be generated at run time directly from the hierarchical structure of the document. Unfortunately, the Web latency built into every expansion or contraction of the TOC makes this process sluggish in many user environments. A much better solution is to download the entire structured TOC to the client rather than just individual server-generated views of the TOC. Then the user can expand, contract, and move about in the TOC supported by a much faster process running directly on the client.

A group at Sun actually implemented a form of this solution as part of a Java-based HTML help browser, but the limitations of HTML required the team to come up with a couple of clever workarounds. In this application, a TOC was constructed by hand (the lack of structure in ordinary HTML makes it impossible to reliably generate a TOC directly from the document) using nonstandard tags invented for the purpose, and then the TOC piece was wrapped in a comment within an HTML page to hide the nonstandard markup from Web browsers. A Java applet downloaded with the HTML document interpreted the hidden markup and provided the client-based TOC behavior.

In practice, this application worked very well and testified both to the ingenuity of its designers and to the validity of the basic concept. But in an XML environment, neither the manual creation of the TOC nor its concealment would have been necessary. Instead, standard XML editors would have been used to create structured content from which a structured TOC could be generated at run time and downloaded to browsers that would automatically create and display the TOC using either a downloaded Java applet or a standard set of JavaHelp class libraries.

The ability to capture and transmit semantic and structural data made possible by XML greatly expands the range of possibilities for client-side manipulation of the way data appears to the user. For example:

- A technical manual that covers both the Sparc and x86 versions of the Solaris operating system can be made to appear like a manual for Sparc only, or a manual for x86 only, just by clicking a preferences switch.

- An installation sheet that carries warnings in multiple languages can be made to show just the ones in the language selected by the user.
- A document containing many annotations can be switched from a mode that shows only the text, to a mode that shows only the annotations, to a mode that shows both, just by making a menu selection.
- A phone book sorted by last name can instantly be changed into a phone book sorted by first name.

This list only hints at the possible uses that creative Web designers will find for richly structured data delivered in a standardized way to Web clients.

Web Agents: Data That Knows About Me

A future domain for XML applications will arise when intelligent Web agents begin to make larger demands for structured data than can easily be conveyed by HTML. Perhaps the earliest applications in this category will be those in which user preferences must be represented in a standard way to mass media providers. The key requirements for such applications have been summed up by Matthew Fuchs of Disney Imagineering: "Information needs to know about itself, and information needs to know about me."

Consider a personalized TV guide for the fabled 500-channel cable TV system. A personalized TV guide that works across the entire spectrum of possible providers requires not only that the user's preferences and other characteristics (educational level, interest, profession, age, visual acuity) be specified in a standard, vendor-independent manner—obviously a job for an industry-standard markup system—but also that the programs themselves be described in a way that allows agents to intelligently select the ones most likely to be of interest to the user. This second requirement can be met only by a standardized system that uses many specialized tags to convey specific attributes of a particular program offering (subject category, audience category, leading actors, length, date made, critical rating, specialized content, language, etc.). Exactly the same requirements would apply to customized newspapers and many

While such applications still lie over the horizon, it is obvious that they will play an increasingly important role in our lives and that their implementation will require XML-like data in order to function interoperably and thereby allow intelligent Web agents to compete effectively in an open market.

NOTE

XML-based metadata initiatives, which began after this paper was written have given an early demonstration of the validity of this approach.

Advanced Linking and Stylesheet Mechanisms

Outside XML as such, but an integral part of the W3C SGML effort, are powerful linking and stylesheet mechanisms that go beyond current HTML-based methods just as XML goes beyond HTML.

Linking

Despite its name and all of the publicity that has surrounded HTML, this so-called "hypertext markup language" actually implements just a tiny amount of the functionality that has historically been associated with the concept of hypertext systems. Only the simplest form of linking is supported—unidirectional links to hardcoded locations. This is a far cry from the systems that were built and proven during the 1970s and 1980s.

In a true hypertext system of the kind envisioned for the XML effort, there will be standardized syntax for all of the classic hypertext linking mechanisms:

- Location-independent naming
- Bidirectional links
- Links that can be specified and managed outside of documents to which they apply
- N-ary hyperlinks (e.g., rings, multiple windows)
- Aggregate links (multiple sources)
- Transclusion (the link target document appears to be part of the link source document)
- Attributes on links (link types)

The first draft of a specification for basic standardized hypertext mechanisms to be used in conjunction with XML was released at the Sixth World Wide Web Conference in April, 1997.*

Stylesheets

The current CSS (cascading style sheets) effort provides a style mechanism well suited to the relatively low-level demands of HTML but incapable of supporting the greatly expanded range of rendering techniques made possible by extensible structured markup. The counterpart to XML is a stylesheet programming language that is:

- Freely extensible so that stylesheet designers can define an unlimited number of treatments for an unlimited variety of tags.
- Turing-complete so that stylesheet designers can arbitrarily extend the available procedures.
- Based on a standard syntax to minimize the learning curve.
- Able to address the entire tree structure of an XML document in structural terms, so that context relationships between elements in a document can be expressed to any level of complexity.
- Completely internationalized so that left-to-right, right-to-left, and top-to-bottom scripts can all be dealt with, even if mixed in a single document
- Provided with a sophisticated rendering model that allows the specification of professional page layout features such as multiple column sets, rotated text areas, and float zones
- Defined in a way that allows partial rendering in order to enable efficient delivery of documents over the Web.

Such a language already exists in a new international standard called the Document Style Semantics and Specification Language (DSSSL, ISO/IEC 10179). Published in April, 1996, DSSSL is the stylesheet language of the future for XML documents. An initial specification of a DSSSL subset for use with XML applications has already been published [4]. This specification will be further developed as part of the XML activity.†

Conclusion

HTML functions well as a markup for the publication of simple documents and as a transportation envelope for downloadable scripts. However, the need to support the much greater information requirements of standardized Java applications will necessitate the development of a standard, extensible, structured language and similarly expanded linking and stylesheet mechanisms. The W3C SGML effort is actively developing a set of specifications that will allow these objectives to be met within an open standards environment. ■

References

1. *http://sunsite.unc.edu/pub/sun-info/standards/xml/why/xmlapps.961117.htm*

* This specification, now called XLL, can be obtained through the W3C XML page.

† The stylesheet portion of the XML activity is now known as XSL. A proposal for implementing XSL is at [5].

2. *http://sunsite.unc.edu/pub/sun-info/standards/xml/why/xmlapps.htm*
3. *http://www.w3.org/XML/*
4. *http://sunsite.unc.edu/pub/sun-info/standards/dsssl/dssslo/dssslo.htm*
5. *http://www.w3.org/Submission/1997/13/*

Acknowledgments

The author would like to thank his colleagues in the Davenport Group for early contributions to the beginnings of this document. The example applications were clarified and expanded with the help of participants in the workshop "Internet Applications of SGML and DSSSL" held at the GCA Information and Technology Week in Seattle on August 23, 1996. Special thanks are due to Tim Bray, Kurt Conrad, Steve DeRose, Matt Fuchs, and Murray Maloney for their outstanding contributions to the workshop.

About the Author

Jon Bosak
Sun Microsystems
901 San Antonio Road, MPK17-101
Palo Alto, CA 94303
bosak@eng.sun.com

Jon Bosak is SunSoft's Online Information Technology Architect. He is chairman of the W3C XML Working Group and a member of the W3C HTML Coordination Group. He is also Sun's representative to ISO/IEC JTC1/SC18/WG8, the international standards group responsible for SGML, HyTime, and DSSSL, and is Sun's representative to its U.S. national counterpart, NCITS V1. He is a founding member of SGML Open and was for several years a sponsor of the Davenport Group, which maintains the industry-standard DocBook markup language for software documentation.

Mr. Bosak originated the SGML-based Web strategy used for the distribution of Solaris documentation. Before joining Sun, he was responsible for the SGML-based delivery system used by Novell to put its documentation on CDs and later on the World Wide Web.

WIDL

Application Integration with XML

Charles Allen

Abstract

The problem of direct access to Web data from within business applications has until recently been largely ignored. The Web Interface Definition Language (WIDL) is an application of the Extensible Markup Language (XML) which allows the resources of the World Wide Web to be described as functional interfaces that can be accessed by remote systems over standard Web protocols. WIDL provides a practical and cost-effective means for diverse systems to be rapidly integrated across corporate intranets, extranets, and the Internet.

Overview

The explosive growth of the World Wide Web is providing millions of end-users access to ever-increasing volumes of information. The resources of legacy systems, relational databases, and multi-tier applications have all been made available to the Web browser, which has been transformed from an occasionally informative accessory into an essential business tool for organizations large and small.

While the Web has achieved the extraordinary feat of providing ubiquitous accessibility to end-users, it has in many cases reinforced manual inefficiencies in business processes as repetitive tasks are required to transcribe or copy and paste data from browser windows into desktop and corporate applications. This is as true of Web data provided by remote business units and external (i.e., partner or supplier) organizations as it is of Web data accessible from both public and subscription based Web sites.

Business units that have previously been unable to agree on middleware and data interchange standards are (by default) agreeing on HTTP and HTML as data communication and presentation standards. Because of the overwhelming focus on the browser, almost all Web applications require interaction with a human user. The problem of direct access to Web data from within business applications has been largely ignored, as has the possibility of using the Web as a platform for automated information exchange between organizations. The debut of XML is set to change all this, and in the process spark a major Web revolution: Web Automation (see Figure 1).

XML enables the creation of Web documents that preserve data structure and include "machine-readable" hooks to enable intelligent processing by client applications. It is not necessary, however, for Web content to exist as XML in order for XML to be used today to automate the Web. The use of XML to deliver metadata about existing Web resources can provide sufficient information to empower non-browser applications to automate interactions with Web servers.

XML metadata defining interfaces to Web-enabled applications can provide the basis for a common API across legacy systems, databases, and middleware infrastructures, effectively transforming the Web from an access medium into an integration platform.

Web Automation

Imagine everything a browser can do: sign-on to a secure Web site; query that site for data; download the results; upload a response. Now imagine that your business applications can do the same thing, automatically, without human intervention and without using a browser. This is the power of Web Automation.

The benefits of Web Automation are numerous:

- Competitive intelligence—aggregate product pricing data, news reports
- Application integration—leverage investments in Web data and infrastructure
- Implement robust ecommerce solutions without expense and difficulty of EDI or CORBA
- Realize a 100% Web-based alternative to EDI
- Put Web site functionality in the heart of customers' and suppliers' IT infrastructures

The incredible diversity of Web resources presents significant challenges for the automation of arbitrary tasks on the Web.

A robust infrastructure for Web Automation needs to provide:

- Full interaction with HTML forms
- An ability to handle both HTTP Authentication and Cookies
- Both on-demand and scheduled extraction of targeted Web data
- Aggregation of data from a number of Web sources
- Chaining of services across multiple Web sites
- An ability to integrate easily with traditional application development languages and environments
- A framework for managing change in both the locations and structures of Web documents

webMethods has defined the Web Interface Definition Language (WIDL) as an application of XML to lay the foundation for Web Automation.

WIDL

The goal of the Web Interface Definition Language is to enable automation of all interactions with HTML/XML documents and forms, providing a general method of representing request/response interactions over standard Web protocols, and allowing the Web to be utilized as a universal integration platform.

Where XML supports the creation of Web content that preserves data structure, and promises Web

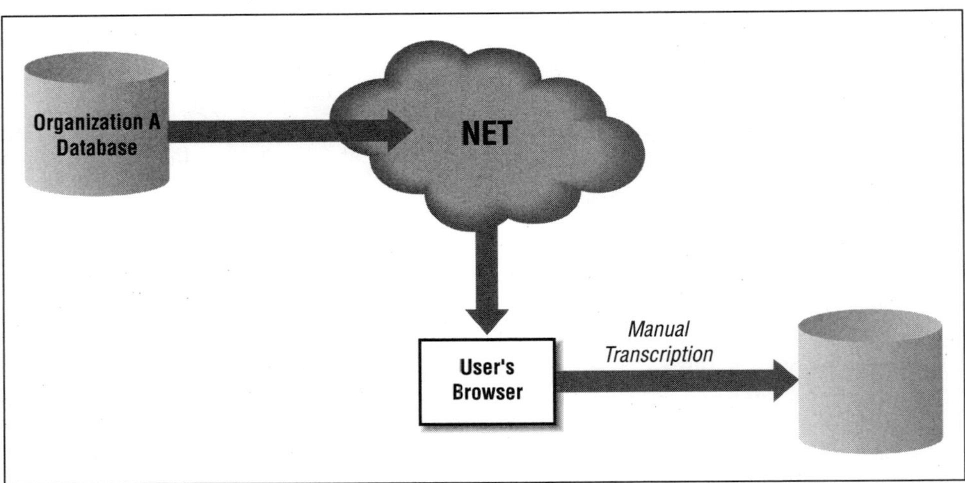

Figure 1 The need for Web Automation

documents that are "machine-readable," WIDL is an application of XML that defines interfaces and services within and across HTML, XML, and text documents. As shown in Figure 2, services defined by WIDL map existing Web content into program variables, allowing the resources of the Web to be made available, without modification, in formats well-suited to integration with diverse business systems.

WIDL brings to the Web many of the features of IDL concepts that have been implemented in distributed computing and transaction processing platforms, including DCE and CORBA. A major part of the value of DCE and CORBA is that they can define services offered by applications in an abstract but highly usable fashion. WIDL describes and automates interactions with services hosted by Web servers on intranets, extranets and the Internet; it provides a standard integration platform and a universal API for all Web-enabled systems.

A service defined by WIDL is equivalent to a function call in standard programming languages. At the highest level, WIDL files are collections of services. WIDL defines the locations (URLs) of each service, input parameters to be submitted (via GET or POST methods) to each service, and output parameters to be returned by each service.

WIDL provides the following features:

- A browser is not required to drive Web applications
- Service definitions are dynamically interpreted and can thus be centrally managed
- Client applications are insulated from changes in service locations and data extraction methods
- Developers are insulated from network programming concerns
- Application resources can be integrated across firewalls and proxies

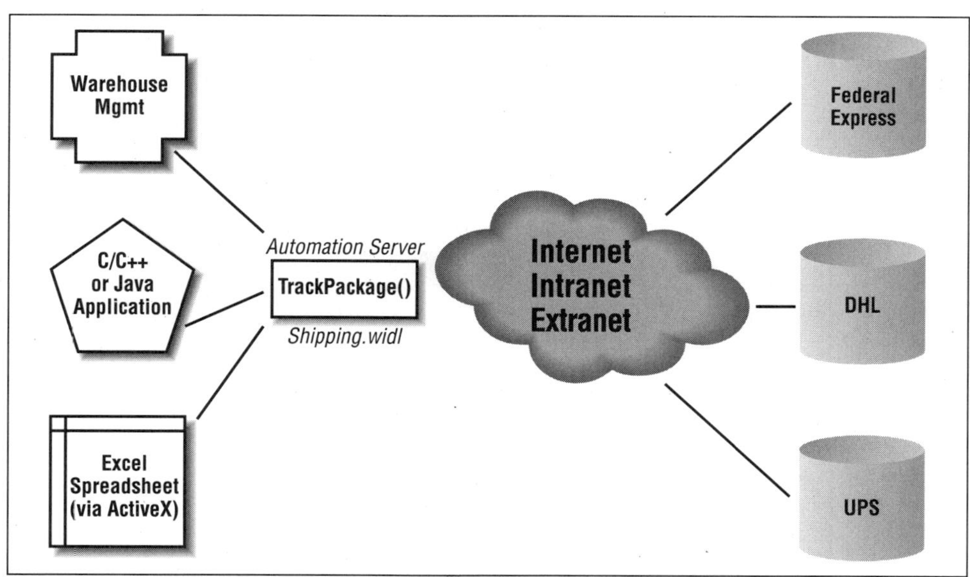

Figure 2 WIDL allows Web resources such as package tracking services to be accessed directly from business applications

WIDL can be used to describe interfaces and services for:

- Static documents (HTML, XML, and plain text files)
- HTML forms
- URL directory structures

WIDL also has the ability to specify conditions for successful processing and error messages to be returned to calling programs. Conditions further enable services to be defined that span multiple documents.

Applications of WIDL

The success of the Web has exposed the advantages of distributed information systems to a global audience. Around the world, IT organizations, regardless of industry, are searching for ways to connect the Internet with new or existing applications, to use Web technology to reduce development, deployment, and maintenance costs.

Using HTML, XML, and HTTP as corporate standards glue, application integration requires only that target systems be Web-enabled. There are hundreds of products in the market today which Web-enable existing systems, from mainframes to client/server applications. The use of standard Web technologies empowers various IT departments to make independent technology selections. This has the effect of lowering both the technical and "political" barriers that have typically derailed cross-organizational integration projects.

The use of proprietary middleware infrastructures to integrate applications requires not only that the same software product be purchased by both organizations and successfully installed in both target hardware environments, but also that both target applications be tailored to support the middleware API. This type of investment can be disastrous if one company spends six months designing a CORBA-based business system only to discover that one of their business units or business partners is unable to install CORBA because it conflicts with their existing infrastructure. Conflicts can arise because of hardware or software incompatibilities, or simply because of difficulties in acquiring appropriate development resources.

A number of analysts have already warned that proprietary ecommerce platforms could lock suppliers into relationships by forcing them to integrate their systems with one infrastructure for business-to-business integration, making it costly for them to switch to or integrate with other partners who have selected alternate ecommerce platforms. Buyer-supplier integration issues involve many-to-many relationships, and demand a standard platform for functional integration and data exchange.

Here is a brief overview of the types of applications that WIDL enables:

Manufacturers and distributors

- Access supplier and competitor ecommerce systems automatically to check pricing and availability
- Load product data (spec sheets) from supplier Web sites
- Place orders automatically (i.e., when inventory drops below predetermined levels)
- Integrate package tracking functionality for enhanced customer service

Human resources

- Automated update of new employee information into multiple internal systems
- Automated aggregation of benefits information from healthcare and insurance providers

Governments

- Kiosk systems that aggregate data and integrate services across departments or state and local offices

Shipping and delivery services

- Multi-carrier package tracking and shipment ordering

- Access to currency rates, Customs regulations, etc.

Shipping companies were early leaders in bringing widely applicable functionality to the Web. Web-based package tracking services provide important logistics information to organizations large and small.

Many organizations employ people for the sole purpose of manually tracking packages to ensure customer satisfaction and to collect refunds for packages that are delivered late. Integrating package tracking functionality directly into warehouse management and customer service systems is a huge benefit, boosting productivity and enabling more efficient use of resources.

Using WIDL, the web-based package tracking services of numerous shipping companies can be described as common application interfaces, to be integrated with various internal systems. In almost all cases, programmatic interfaces to different package tracking services are identical, which means that WIDL can impose consistency in the representation of functionality across systems.

Example 1 illustrates the use of WIDL to define a package tracking service for Federal Express. Note that the WIDL specifies a "Shipping" template. This indicates that there is a general class of shipping services, and that this particular WIDL is one implementation of the shipping interface.

The FedexShipping interface in Example 1 contains one service (`TrackPackage`) which takes three input parameters (`TrackingNum`, `DestCountry`, `ShipDate`) and returns three output parameters (`disposition`, `deliveredOn`, `deliveredTo`). The WIDL definition describing the `TrackPackage` service is stored in an ASCII file, which is utilized by client programs at runtime to determine both the location of the service (URL) and the structure of documents that contain the desired data. Client programs access WIDL definitions from local files, naming services such as LDAP, HTTP servers, or other URL access schemes (see Figure 3).

Unlike the way CORBA and DCE IDL are normally used, WIDL is interpreted at runtime. As a

Example 1 The WIDL Representation of a Package Tracking Service

```
<WIDL NAME="FedexShipping" Template="Shipping"
      BASEURL="http://www.fedex.com" VERSION="2.0">

<SERVICE NAME="TrackPackage" METHOD="GET"
         URL="/cgi-bin/track_it"
         INPUT="TrackInput" OUTPUT="TrackOutput" />

<BINDING NAME="TrackInput" TYPE="INPUT">
   <VARIABLE NAME="TrackingNum" TYPE="String" FORMNAME="trk_num" />
   <VARIABLE NAME="DestCountry" TYPE="String" FORMNAME="dest_cntry" />
   <VARIABLE NAME="ShipDate" TYPE="String" FORMNAME="ship_date" />
</BINDING>

<BINDING NAME="TrackOutput" TYPE="OUTPUT">
   <CONDITION TYPE="FAILURE" REFERENCE="doc.title[0].text"
              MATCH="FedEx Warning Form"
              REASONREF="doc.p[0].text['&.*']" />
   <CONDITION TYPE="SUCCESS" REFERENCE="doc.title[0].text"
              MATCH="FedEx Airbill:*"
              REASONREF="doc.p[1].value" />
```

Example 1 The WIDL Representation of a Package Tracking Service *(continued)*

```
   <VARIABLE NAME="disposition" TYPE="String"
             REFERENCE="doc.h[3].value" MASK="$*" />
   <VARIABLE NAME="deliveredOn" TYPE="String"
             REFERENCE="doc.h[5].value" MASK="%%%$*" />
   <VARIABLE NAME="deliveredTo" TYPE="String"
             REFERENCE="doc.h[7].value" MASK="*:" />
</BINDING>

</WIDL>
```

result, Service, Condition, and Variable definitions within WIDL files can be administered without requiring modification of client code. This usage model supports application-to-application linkages that are far more robust and maintainable than if they were coded by hand.

One of WIDL's most significant benefits is its ability to insulate client programs from changes in the format and location of Web documents. As long as the parameters of services do not change, Service URLs, object references in variables, regions, and conditions can all be modified without affecting applications that utilize WIDL to access Web resources.

There are three models for WIDL management:

- Client side—where WIDL files are colocated with a client program
- Naming service—where WIDL definitions are returned from directory services, i.e., LDAP
- Server side—where WIDL files are referenced by, colocated with, or embedded within Web documents

WIDL does not require that existing Web resources be modified in any way. Flexible management models allow organizations to describe and integrate Web sites that are beyond their control, as well as to provide their business partners with interfaces to services that are controlled. The ability to seamlessly migrate from independent to shared management eases the transition from informal to formal business-to-business integration.

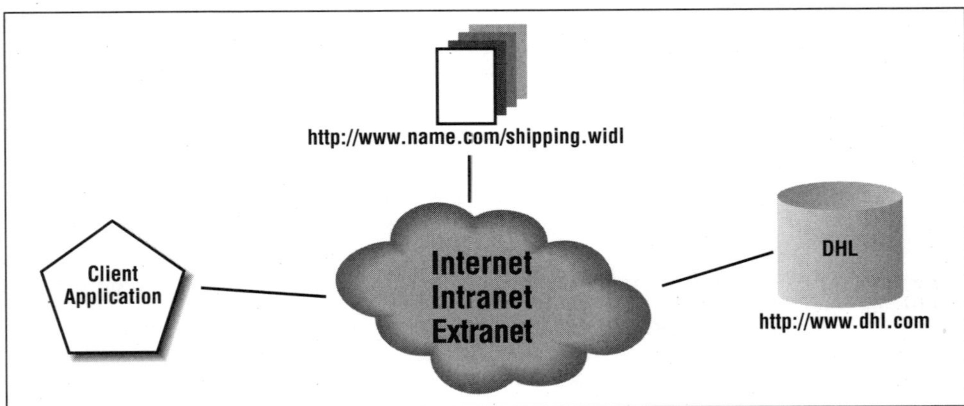

Figure 3 WIDL files can be centrally managed with a well known URL or via a directory service such as LDAP

Elements of WIDL

The Web Interface Definition Language (WIDL) consists of six XML tags:

- <WIDL> defines an interface, which can contain multiple services and bindings
- <SERVICE/> defines a service, which consists of input and output bindings
- <BINDING> defines a binding, which specifies input and output variables, as well as conditions for successful completion of a service
- <VARIABLE/> defines input, output, and internal variables used by a service to submit HTTP requests, and to extract data from HTML/XML documents
- <CONDITION/> defines success and failure conditions for the binding of output variables; specifies error messages to be returned upon service failure; enables alternate bindings attempts and the chaining of services
- <REGION/> defines a region within an HTML/XML document; useful for extracting regular result sets which vary in size, such as the output of a search engine, or news stories

The complete WIDL DTD is included in Appendix A. In the next sections the attributes of each element of WIDL are presented and discussed by way of example.

<WIDL>

<WIDL> is the parent element for the Web Interface Definition Language; it defines an interface. Interfaces are groupings of related services and bindings. The following are attributes of the <WIDL> element:

NAME

Required. Establishes a name for an interface. The interface name is used in conjunction with a service name for naming or directory services.

VERSION

Optional. Specifies the version of WIDL. webMethods first implemented WIDL as HTML extensions. Experience with customers since late 1996 resulted in WIDL 2.0, an application of XML that is capable of automating complex interactions across multiple Web servers.

TEMPLATE

Optional. WIDL enables common interfaces to services provided by multiple sites. Templates allow the specification of interfaces, implementations of which may be available from multiple sources. A shipping template defines a functional interface for shipping services; various implementations can be provided for FederalExpress, UPS, and DHL.

BASEURL

Optional. BASEURL is similar to the <BASE HREF=""> statement in HTML. Some of the services within a given WIDL may be hosted from the same Base URL. If BASEURL is defined, the URL for various services can be defined relative to BASEURL. This feature is useful for replicated sites which can be addressed by changing only the BASEURL, instead of the URL for each service.

OBJMODEL

Optional. Specifies an object model to be used for extracting data elements from HTML and XML documents. Object models are the result of parsing HTML or XML documents. The use of object models is central to the functionality of WIDL. Object references are used in <VARIABLE/>, <CONDITION/> and <REGION/> elements. For this reason, the object model will be briefly discussed before proceeding with the description of the element definitions that constitute WIDL.

Object model

Many of the features of WIDL require a capability to reliably extract specific data elements from Web documents and map them to output parameters.

Two candidate technologies for data extraction are pattern matching and parsing. Pattern matching extracts data based on regular expressions, and is well suited to raw text files and poorly constructed HTML documents. There is a lot of bad HTML in the world! Parsing, on the other hand, recovers document structure and exposes relationships between document objects, enabling elements of a document to be accessed with an object model.

Using an object model, an absolute reference to an element of an HTML document might be specified:

```
doc.p[0].text
```

This reference would retrieve the text of the first paragraph of a given document.

From both a development and an administrative point of view, pattern matching is more labor intensive for establishing and maintaining relationships between data elements and program variables. Regular expressions are difficult to construct and prone to breakage as document structures change. For instance, the addition of formatting tags around data elements in HTML documents could easily derail the search for a pattern. An object model, on the other hand, can see through many such changes.

Patterns must also be carefully constructed to avoid unintentional matching. In complex cases, patterns must be nested within patterns. The process of mapping patterns to a number of output parameters can easily become unmanageable.

It is possible to achieve the best of both worlds by using pattern matching when necessary to match against the attributes of elements accessible via an Object Model. Using a hybrid model of pattern matching within parsed elements provides for the extraction of target information from preformatted text regions or text files.

This reference would retrieve the text of the first paragraph that contains `'Currency:'` within a given document.

Various object models for working with HTML documents have been specified. The W3C has established a working group to define a standard Document Object Model (DOM). The WIDL specification allows for multiple object models. In implementing WIDL, we discovered many functional requirements not currently addressed by existing object models. These requirements will be demonstrated in various examples later in this article.

We now continue with a discussion of the attributes of the elements of the WIDL.

<SERVICE/>

The `<SERVICE/>` element describes a Web service, such as those provided by CGI scripts, or via NSAPI, ISAPI, or other back-end Web server programs. Services take a set of input parameters, perform some processing, then return a dynamically generated HTML, XML or text document.

The attributes of the `<SERVICE/>` element map an abstract service name into a service's actual URL, specify the HTTP method to be used to access the service, and designate "bindings" for input and output parameters.

NAME

Required. Establishes a name for a service. The service name is used in conjunction with an interface for naming or directory services.

URL

Required. Specifies the Uniform Resource Locator for the target document. A service URL can be either a fully qualified URL or a partial URL that is relative to the BASEURL provided as an attribute of the `<WIDL>` element.

METHOD

Required. Specifies the HTTP method (GET or POST) to be used to access the service.

INPUT

Required. Designates the <BINDING> to be used to define the input parameters for programs that call the service. The specified name must be that of a <BINDING> contained within the same <WIDL> as the service.

OUTPUT

Required. Designates the <BINDING> to be used to define the output parameters for programs that call the service. The specified name must be that of a <BINDING> contained within the same <WIDL> as the service.

AUTHUSER

Optional. Establishes the username for HTTP authentication.

AUTHPASS

Optional. Establishes the password for HTTP authentication.

TIMEOUT

Optional. Amount of time before service times out.

RETRIES

Optional. Number of times to retry the service before failing.

Typically the username/password combination is set independent of service definitions in WIDL. The AUTHUSER and AUTHPASS attributes allow a username and password to be defined outside of a calling program. This is useful in cases where multiple client programs use the same service.

<BINDING>

The <BINDING> element defines input and output variables for a service. Input bindings describe the data provided to a Web resource, and are analogous to the input fields in an HTML form. For a static HTML document no input variables are required. Output bindings describe which data elements are to be mapped from the output document returned as a result of accessing the Web resource with the given input variables. In most cases an output binding will map only a subset of the available elements in the output document.

NAME

Required. Identifies the binding for reference by service definitions and other binding definitions.

TYPE

Required. Specifies whether a binding defines input or output parameters.

<VARIABLE/>

The <VARIABLE/> element is used to describe both input and output binding parameters; different attributes are used depending on the type of parameter being described.

Common attributes are:

NAME

Required. Identifies the variable to calling programs.

VALUE

Optional. Designates a value to be assigned to the variable in HTTP transactions. For input variables this has the effect of rendering the variable invisible to calling programs; i.e., the specified value is submitted to the Web service without requiring an input from calling programs. For output variables this has the effect of hard-coding the value returned when the service is invoked.

USAGE

Optional. The default usage of variables is for specification of input and output parameters. Variables can also be used internally within WIDL, as well as to pass header information (i.e., USER-AGENT or REFERER) in an HTTP request. The USAGE attribute will be explored in Examples 2 and 3, which follow this <VARIABLE/> element overview.

TYPE
: Required. Specifies both the data type and dimension of the variable.

The following attributes are specific to input variables:

FORMNAME
: Optional. Specifies the variable name to be submitted via GET or POST methods. Obscure back-end variables can be given names that are more meaningful in the context of the service described by WIDL. Used in conjunction with WIDL Templates, FORMNAME permits the mapping of a single variable name across multiple service implementations. In the package tracking service in Example 1, the FORMNAME differs from the variable name. It is also possible to set `FORMNAME=""` to pass only the variable's value to the back-end program.

OPTIONS
: Optional. Captures the options of list boxes, check boxes, and radio buttons. Useful for validating inputs prior to submitting input parameters to a service and for transforming input criteria into formats acceptable to back-end programs. For example, an options list could be used to translate a meaningful input of "full" to the "f" acceptable to a back-end program.

The following attributes are specific to output variables:

REFERENCE
: Optional. Specifies an object reference to extract data from the HTML, XML, or text document returned as the result of a service invocation.

MASK
: Optional. Masks permit the use of pattern matching and token collecting to easily strip away unwanted labels and other text surrounding target data items.

NULLOK
: Optional. Overrides the implicit condition that all output variables return a non-null value.

Apart from the "default" behavior of variables defined in input bindings, there are two other usage models supported by WIDL: "internal" and "header." The USAGE attribute can define service inputs in place of or in addition to those required by a Web service's HTML form.

Internal variables enable variable substitution within input and output bindings. For instance, using internal variables, a portion of a service's URL or a pattern for matching within an object reference can be specified as a variable that is part of an input binding.

Header variables allow HTTP header information to be included as part of a service request. This is useful in many situations, including the passing of referrer information where required by back-end systems.

In Example 2, an auto loan service is defined for a site that uses a directory structure to organize

Example 2 Using Internal Variables to Parameterize Directory Structures

```
<WIDL NAME=autoLoan VERSION=2.0>

<SERVICE NAME=AutoLoan METHOD=GET
         URL="http://www.bankrate.com/autobytel/abt%state%a.htm"
         INPUT="AutoLoanInput" OUTPUT="AutoLoanOutput" />

<BINDING NAME=AutoLoanInput TYPE=INPUT>
   <Variable NAME=state TYPE=String FORMNAME="state" USAGE="INTERNAL" />
</BINDING>
```

Example 2 Using Internal Variables to Parameterize Directory Structures *(continued)*

```
<BINDING NAME="AutoLoanOutput" TYPE="OUTPUT">
   <CONDITION TYPE="Failure" REASONTEXT="State not found" />
   <VARIABLE NAME="state" TYPE="String"
             REFERENCE="doc.table[4].tr[1].th[0].text" />
   <VARIABLE NAME="avgNew" TYPE="String"
             REFERENCE="doc.table[4].tr[2].td[1].text" />
   <VARIABLE NAME="highNew" TYPE="String"
             REFERENCE="doc.table[4].tr[2].td[2].text" />
   <VARIABLE NAME="lowNew" TYPE="String"
             REFERENCE="doc.table[4].tr[2].td[3].text" />
   <VARIABLE NAME="avgUsed" TYPE="String"
             REFERENCE="doc.table[4].tr[3].td[1].text" />
   <VARIABLE NAME="highUsed" TYPE="String"
             REFERENCE="doc.table[4].tr[3].td[2].text" />
   <VARIABLE NAME="lowUsed" TYPE="String"
             REFERENCE="doc.table[4].tr[3].td[3].text" />
</BINDING>

</WIDL>
```

loan information for various states. Rather than using CGI scripts to access a database of high, low, and average loan rates, unique URLs which contain a state abbreviation as part of target document names are linked from a pick list. The use of internal variables enables the parameterization of a portion of the URL. In this fashion, WIDL is able to define an input binding even though no HTML forms are present to query the user for information. The input binding specifies a variable "state" that is referenced in the URL attribute of the service definition as `%state%`. At runtime the value passed into the "state" variable is used to complete the service URL.

Because the `AutoLoan` service uses a variable to complete the URL to access a static document, an invalid input parameter results in an invalid URL. The `<CONDITION/>` statement in the output binding traps the document not found condition and returns a sensible error message to client programs.

Internal variables can also be used within object references that use pattern matching to index into the object tree.

Example 3 uses the currency exchange service provided by the Federal Reserve Bank to illustrate the use of internal variables to interactively query a single static document.

Example 3 Using Internal Variables to Input Criteria in Object References

```
<WIDL NAME="FederalReserve" TEMPLATE="Currency"
      BASEURL="http://www.ny.frb.org/" VERSION="2.0">

<SERVICE NAME="ExchangeRate" METHOD="GET"
         URL="/pihome/mktrates/forex12.shtml"
         INPUT="currencyInput" OUTPUT="currencyOutput" />

<BINDING NAME="currencyInput" TYPE="INPUT">
   <VARIABLE NAME="Currency" TYPE="String"
             FORMNAME="CURRENCY" USAGE="INTERNAL" />
</BINDING>
```

```
<BINDING NAME="currencyOutput" TYPE="OUTPUT">
   <CONDITION TYPE="FAILURE" REASONTEXT="Currency not found" />
   <VARIABLE NAME="rate" TYPE="String"
             REFERENCE="doc.pre[0].line['*%Currency%*'].text[53-65]" />
</BINDING>

</WIDL>
```

In this example currency rates for a number of countries are provided in a single document. The object reference for the `'rate'` variable in the output binding uses an internal variable `'Currency'` as part of the pattern that is matched to discover the current exchange rate.

The object reference used in this example also demonstrates two additional text manipulation features of the object model developed by webMethods. The `.line[]` construct allows access to individual lines of both preformatted text and text that has been formatted with the `<br>` line-break element. This greatly simplifies pattern matching expressions within object references.

The Federal Reserve Currency Exchange service returns rate information in a column from character position `53` to character position `65`. This range of characters is specified by qualifying the `.text[53-65]` attribute of the line matching the input criteria.

<CONDITION/>

The `<CONDITION/>` element is used in output bindings to specify success and failure conditions for the extraction of data to be returned to calling programs. Conditions enable branching logic within service definitions; they are used to attempt alternate bindings when initial bindings fail and to initiate service chains, whereby the output variables from one service are passed into the input bindings of a second service. Conditions also define error messages returned to calling programs when services fail.

TYPE

Required. Specifies whether a condition is checking for the "Success" or the "Failure" of a binding attempt.

Any variable that returns a NULL value will cause the entire binding to fail, unless the NULLOK attribute of that variable has been set to true. Conditions can catch the success or failure of either a specific object reference or of an entire binding. In the case where a condition initiates a service chain, it is important that all variables bind properly.

REFERENCE

Optional. Specifies an object reference which extracts data from the HTML or XML document returned as the result of a service invocation. The REFERENCE attribute for conditions is equivalent to the REFERENCE attribute used in variable definitions.

MATCH

Required. Specifies a text pattern that will be compared with the object property referenced by the REFERENCE attribute.

REBIND

Optional. Specifies an alternate output binding. Typically a failure condition indicates that the document returned cannot be bound properly. REBIND redirects the binding attempt. This is useful in situations where the documents returned by a service are dependent upon the input criteria that was submitted. For example, a retail Web site may return a different document structure for an SKU depending on whether the item requested is a shirt, a tie, or trousers. The use of REBIND allows a conditions to determine the appropriate binding for extracting the desired data.

SERVICE
: Optional. Specifies a service to invoke with the results of an output binding. Aside from the obvious benefit of chaining services to further automate the tasks that can be encapsulated for client programs, there are many cases when target documents can only be retrieved after visiting several Web pages in succession. In some instances cookies are issues by an entry page that must be visited prior to interacting with HTML forms, in others URLs are dynamically generated from databases for specific user identities.

REASONTEXT
: Optional. The text to be returned as an error message when a service fails.

REASONREF
: Optional. Reference to an element's attribute to be returned as an error message when a service fails.

WAIT
: Optional. Amount of time to wait before retrying retrieval of a document after a server has returned a 'service busy' error.

RETRIES
: Optional. Number of times to retry the service before failing.

Example 4 illustrates the use of conditions to specify alternate bindings. Alternate bindings can be used when documents returned by services are dependent upon the inputs submitted to the service. In some rare cases, such as the `StockMarketInfo` service defined in this example, a service occasionally returns different document formats for no apparent reason. Conditions and rebinding handle any such situations.

Example 5 illustrates the use of conditions to specify a service chain. Service chains pass the name-value pairs of an output binding into the input binding of the service specified by a `<CONDITION/>` statement. Any name-value pairs matching the variables of the chained service's

Example 4 Conditions Initiate Alternate Attempts for Extracting Output Values

```
<WIDL NAME="Yahoo" VERSION="2.0">

<SERVICE NAME="StockMarketInfo" METHOD ="GET"
         URL="http://quote.yahoo.com/" OUTPUT ="marketOut">

<BINDING NAME="marketOut" TYPE="Output">
   <CONDITION Type="Failure" REBIND="marketOut2" />
   <VARIABLE TYPE="String[][]" NAME="info"
             REFERENCE="doc.table[0].tr[0].td[].text" />
   <VARIABLE TYPE="String[]" NAME="links"
             REFERENCE="doc.table[0].tr[0].a[].href" />
</BINDING>

<BINDING NAME="marketOut2" TYPE="Output">
   <VARIABLE TYPE="String[][]" NAME="info"
             REFERENCE="doc.table[1].tr[0].td[].td[].text" />
   <VARIABLE TYPE="String[]" NAME="links"
             REFERENCE="doc.table[1].tr[0].a[].href" />
</BINDING>

</WIDL>
```

input binding will be used as input parameters. In this example, the **productSearch** service returns a URL when it successfully finds a product matching the search criteria. The success condition on the **ProductSearchOutput** binding causes the **ExtractPrices** service to be called. Because the output binding of **productSearch** matches the input binding of **ExtractPrices**, the variables are passed from one service into the other.

It is important to note that the **ExtractPrices** service can be called independent of the **productSearch** service, and that the **ExtractPrices** service specifies **productURL** as an internal variable. The output variables from the **productSearch** service are not available to the **ExtractPrices** service except in the case where they have been passed via an input binding.

Service chains make it possible to interact with "shopping cart" services, where multiple service calls are required to add items, followed by a service call to submit an order.

<REGION/>

The **<REGION/>** element is used in output bindings to define targeted subregions of a document. This is useful in services that return variable arrays of information in structures that can be located between well known elements of a page.

Example 5 Conditions Initiate Service Chains

```
<WIDL NAME="EddieBaeur" VERSION=2.0>

<SERVICE NAME="ProductSearch" METHOD=GET
         URL="http://www.ebauer.com/eb/ShopEB/prod_search_results.asp"
         INPUT="productSearchInput" OUTPUT="productSearchOutput" />

<BINDING NAME="productSearchInput" TYPE="INPUT">
     <VARIABLE NAME="searchstring" FORMNAME="searchstring"
  </BINDING>

  <BINDING NAME="productSearchOutput" TYPE="OUTPUT">
     <CONDITION TYPE="Failure" REFERENCE="doc.p['*Sorry*'].text"
                MATCH="*Sorry*" REASONREF="doc.p['*Sorry*'].text" />
     <CONDITION TYPE="Success" SERVICE="ExtractPrices" />
     <VARIABLE NAME="productURL" TYPE="String"
               REFERENCE="doc.table[0].tr[1].td[3].a[0].href" />
  </BINDING>

  <SERVICE NAME="ExtractPrices" METHOD=GET URL="%productUrl%"
           INPUT="ExtractPricesInput" OUTPUT="ExtractPricesOutput" />

  <BINDING NAME="ExtractPricesInput" TYPE="INPUT">
     <VARIABLE NAME="productUrl" TYPE="String" USAGE="INTERNAL" />
  </BINDING>

  <BINDING NAME="ExtractPricesOutput" TYPE="OUTPUT">
     <VARIABLE NAME="Price" TYPE="String"
               REFERENCE="doc.table[1].strong[0].value['*$$']" />
  </BINDING>

  </WIDL>
```

Regions are critical for poorly designed documents where it is otherwise impossible to differentiate between desired data elements (for instance, story links on a news page) and elements that also match the search criteria.

NAME
: Required. Specifies the name for a region. This name can then be used as the root of an object reference. For instance, a region named `foo` can be used in object references such as:

```
foo.p[0].text
```

START
: Required. An object reference that determines the beginning of a region.

END
: Required. An object reference that determines the end of a region.

Example 6 demonstrates the use of regions in a news service, where the number of news stories varies day to day. Regions permit the extraction of data elements relative to other features of a document. The `tops` region begins with a text object that matches the pattern `'Last Updated'` and ends with an object that matches `'For more*'`.

Variable references into the `tops` region collect arrays of anchors and anchor text, regardless of the fact that the sizes of the arrays change throughout the day. The object references within `tops` are vastly simplified by the processing already provided by the region definition:

```
tops.a[].text
tops.a[].href
```

It is also worth noting that the news service in Example 6 has no input binding. Input bindings are not required for service definitions.

Object References

The default object model used by WIDL provides object references for accessing elements and properties of HTML and XML documents. This model is based on the JavaScript page object model, but without the JavaScript method definitions.

Using the default object model, all elements of HTML and XML documents can be addressed in the following ways:

- *By name,* if the target element has a non-empty name attribute. For example, the value of an HTML element `<a name="foo">` can be referenced:
  `doc.foo.value`

By absolute indexing, where each array of elements has a zero-based integer index, i.e.:

```
doc.headings[0].text
doc.p[1].text
```

By relative indexing, which directs the binding algorithm to search the VALUE attributes of each element in the array, until a match is found. The match must be complete, which requires the use of wildcard metacharacters for partial string matches. Note that the search will return the first matching element, if any:

```
doc.tr['*pattern*'].td[1].text
```

By region indexing, which directs the binding algorithm to search only within a region of a document:

```
myregion.a[2].href
```

By attribute matching, which directs the binding algorithm to search an object's attributes until a match is found. Attribute matching is done with parenthesis instead of square brackets:

```
doc.a(name='foo').href
```

The following properties are available for all objects:

`.text/.txt`
: Returns the text of a container

`.value/.val`
: Returns the value of a container

`.source/.src`
: Returns the source of a container

`.index/.idx`
: Returns the index of a container

`.reference/.ref`
: Returns the fully qualified object reference

Attributes of HTML containers take precedence over properties, which have alternate accessors.

`.text/.txt` and `.value/.val` are equivalent except when a document element has an identically named attribute.

Putting WIDL to Work

WIDL files can be hand-coded or developed interactively with command line or graphical tools, which provide aids for determining object references used in `<VARIABLE/>`, `<CONDITION/>`, and `<REGION/>` declarations.

Once a WIDL file has been created, its use depends upon the implementation of products that can process and understand WIDL services. A Web integration platform based on WIDL needs to provide:

- A mechanism for retrieving WIDL files, either from a local file system, a directory service such as LDAP, or a URL
- An HTML and XML parser, and text pattern matching capabilities, providing an object model for accessing elements of Web documents
- HTTP and HTTPS support, to initiate requests and receive Web documents

Apart from these requirements, a WIDL processor could be delivered as a Java class or a Windows DLL, for integration directly with client applications, or as a standalone server with middleware interfaces, allowing thin-client access to Web automation functionality.

Generating Code

The primary purpose of WIDL is integration with corporate business applications. In much the same way that DCE or CORBA IDL is used to generate code fragments, or "stubs," to be included in development projects, WIDL provides the necessary ingredients for generating Java, JavaScript, C/C++, and even Visual Basic client code.

webMethods has developed a suite of Web Automation products for the development and management of WIDL files, as well as the generation of client code from WIDL files. Client stubs, which we affectionately call "Weblets," present developers with local function calls, and encapsulate all the methods required to invoke a service that has been defined by a WIDL file.

Example 6 Regions Permit the Extraction of Data Elements

```
<WIDL NAME="News" VERSION="2.0">

<SERVICE NAME="Techweb" METHOD="GET"
         URL="http://www.techweb.com/" OUTPUT="techwebOut">

<BINDING NAME="techwebOut" TYPE="OUTPUT">
   <REGION NAME="tops" START="doc.font['Last?Updated*']"
                        END="doc.b['For?more*']" />
   <VARIABLE NAME="service" TYPE="String" VALUE="TECHWEB Top Stories" />
   <VARIABLE NAME="url" TYPE="String" REFERENCE="doc.url" />
   <VARIABLE NAME=stories TYPE="String[]" REFERENCE="tops.a[].text" />
   <VARIABLE NAME="links" TYPE="String[]" REFERENCE="tops.a[].href" />
</BINDING>

</WIDL>
```

Example 7 features a Java class generated from the package tracking WIDL presented earlier in Example 1. This class demonstrates the following methods that are part of the API that webMethods has developed for processing WIDL:

- `Context`
- `loadDocument`
- `invokeService`
- `getVariable`

After declaring the variables that will be used by the `PackageTracking` class, a handle `c` to a new `Context` of the webMethods Web automation runtime is created. All API calls are then made against this handle.

`loadDocument` loads and parses the specified WIDL file, in this case `Shipping.widl`. Loading the WIDL defines the services of the Shipping interface to the runtime. `invokeService` actually submits the input parameters to the `TrackPackage` service, which makes the appropriate HTTP request and returns either a result set which contains the bound output variables or an error message specified by a `<CONDITION/>` statement within the `<SERVICE/>` definition. `getVariable` is then used to extract the values of the output variables and to assign them to class variables.

Example 7 Java Stub

```
import watt.api.*;

public class TrackPackage extends Object
{
      public String TrackingNum;
      public String disposition;
      public String deliveredOn;

      public String deliveredTo;

      public TrackPackage(String TrackingNum)

throws IOException, WattException, WattServiceException

      {
              String args[][] = {
              {"TrackingNum", TrackingNum},
              {"DestCountry", DestCountry},
              {"ShipDate", ShipDate}
              };

              Context c = new <I>Context</I>();

              c.loadDocument("Shipping.widl");
              Result r = c.invokeService("FedexShipping",
                                        "TrackPackage", args);

              disposition = r.<I>getVariable</I>("disposition");
              deliveredOn = r.<I>getVariable</I>("deliveredOn");
              deliveredTo = r.<I>getVariable</I>("deliveredTo");
      }
}
```

Within the Java application, the package tracking service looks like a simple instantiation of the TrackPackage class:

```
TrackPackage p = new
    TrackPackage("12345678");
```

In short, an application makes a call to a local function that has been generated by WIDL. The local function encapsulates the API calls to the WIDL processor. The WIDL processor:

- Loads the WIDL file from a local or remote file system
- Passes the function's input parameters as an HTTP request
- Parses the retrieved document to extract target data items
- Executes any conditional logic for error checking or service chaining
- Returns the extrated data into the output parameters of the calling function

Generated Java classes can be incorporated in standalone Java applications, Java Applets, JavaScript routines, or server-side Java "Servlets." Generated C/C++ encapsulating Web services can be deployed as DLLs, shared libraries, or standalone executables. webMethods implementation, the Web Automation Platform, provides Java classes, a shared library, a Windows DLL and an Active/X control to support Visual Basic modules which can be embedded in spreadsheets and other Microsoft Office applications.

Conclusion

Web technology is strong on interactivity but low on automation. The primary applications of the Web, including Push and Agent technologies, are almost exclusively focused on end users. Data that is being made available in HTML format is effectively inaccessible to business applications other than the Web browser.

On corporate intranets and extranets, the Web browser has enabled access to business systems, but has in many cases reinforced manual inefficiencies as data must be transcribed from browser windows into other application interfaces.

Electronic commerce on the Web is typically driven manually via a browser. In order to achieve business-to-business integration, organizations have resorted to proprietary protocols. The many-to-many nature of Web commerce demands a standard for automated integration.

Interactions normally performed manually in a browser, such as entering information into an HTML form, submitting the form, and retrieving HTML documents, can be automated by capturing details such as input parameters, service URLs, and data extraction methods for output parameters. Mechanisms for condition processing can also be provided to enable robust error handling.

The Web Interface Definition Language (WIDL) is an application of the Extensible Markup Language (XML), which allows the resources of the World Wide Web to be described as functional interfaces that can be accessed by remote systems over standard Web protocols. WIDL transforms the Web into a standards-based integration platform, providing a practical and cost-effective infrastructure for business-to-business electronic commerce over Web. ■

Appendix A

Example 8 shows the WIDL DTD in its entirety.

Example 8 The WIDL DTD

```
<bigger><<!ELEMENT WIDL ( SERVICE | BINDING )* >
<<!ATTLIST WIDL
    NAME        CDATA #IMPLIED
    VERSION (1.0 | 2.0 | ...) "2.0"
```

Example 8 The WIDL DTD *(continued)*

```
     TEMPLATE   CDATA #IMPLIED
     BASEURL    CDATA #IMPLIED
     OBJMODEL (wmobj | ...) "wmobj"

<<!ELEMENT SERVICE EMPTY>
<<!ATTLIST SERVICE
     NAME       CDATA #REQUIRED
     URL        CDATA #REQUIRED
     METHOD (Get | Post) "Get"
     INPUT      CDATA #IMPLIED
     OUTPUT     CDATA #IMPLIED
     AUTHUSER   CDATA #IMPLIED
     AUTHPASS   CDATA #IMPLIED
     TIMEOUT    CDATA #IMPLIED
     RETRIES    CDATA #IMPLIED

<<!ELEMENT BINDING ( VARIABLE | CONDITION | REGION )* > <<!ATTLIST BINDING
     NAME       CDATA #REQUIRED
     TYPE (Input | Output) "Output"

<<!ELEMENT VARIABLE EMPTY>
<<!ATTLIST VARIABLE
     NAME       CDATA #REQUIRED
     FORMNAME   CDATA #IMPLIED
     TYPE (String | String[] | String[][]) "String"
     USAGE (Default | Header | Internal) "Function"
     REFERENCE  CDATA #IMPLIED
     VALUE      CDATA #IMPLIED
     MASK       CDATA #IMPLIED
     NULLOK          #BOOLEAN

<<!ELEMENT CONDITION EMPTY>
<<!ATTLIST CONDITION
     TYPE (Success | Failure | Retry) "Success"
     REF        CDATA #REQUIRED
     MATCH      CDATA #REQUIRED
     REBIND     CDATA #IMPLIED
     SERVICE    CDATA #IMPLIED
     REASONREF  CDATA #IMPLIED
     REASONTEXT CDATA #IMPLIED
     WAIT       CDATA #IMPLIED
     RETRIES    CDATA #IMPLIED

<<!ELEMENT REGION EMPTY>
<<!ATTLIST REGION
     NAME       CDATA #REQUIRED
     START      CDATA #REQUIRED
     END        CDATA #REQUIRED

</bigger>
```

About the Author

Charles Allen
3975 University Drive
Suite 360
Fairfax, VA 22030
(703) 352-8345
charles@webMethods.com

Charles Allen is VP of Product Management for webMethods, Inc., the leading provider of Web Automation and integration solutions for the Global 2000. Prior to joining webMethods, Mr. Allen was a founding member of Open Environment Corporation. Most recently he was responsible for technology acquisitions and joint ventures in the Asia/Pacific region. An inveterate communicator, Mr. Allen has presented extensively on the Web and distributed systems technology at events around the world.

More Titles from O'Reilly

World Wide Web Journal *Volume 1*

Fourth International World Wide Web Conference Proceedings

A publication of O'Reilly & Associates and the World Wide Web Consortium (W3C)
Winter 1995/96
748 pages, ISBN 1-56592-169-0

The *World Wide Web Journal* is a quarterly publication that provides timely, in-depth coverage of research developments on the World Wide Web. This issue contains the Conference Proceeding papers that were chosen for the 4th International World Wide Web Conference.

Key Specifications of the World Wide Web

A publication of O'Reilly & Associates and the World Wide Web Consortium (W3C)
Spring 1996
356 pages, ISBN 1-56592-190-9

This issue of the *World Wide Web Journal* collects in a single volume the key specifications that describe the architecture of the World Wide Web and how it works. It includes the specifications for HTML, HTTP, and URLs, plus the emerging standards for PNG, PICS, PEP, and CSS. A valuable reference for webmasters, application programmers, and technical managers.

The Web After Five Years

A publication of O'Reilly & Associates and the World Wide Web Consortium (W3C)
Summer 1996
226 pages, ISBN 1-56592-210-7

This issue reflects "The Web After Five Years" through an interview with Tim Berners-Lee, selections from the MIT/W3C Workshop on Web Demographics and Internet Survey Methodology, and papers from the Fifth International World Wide Web Conference. Also includes technical proposals from the W3C, lively debates on the size of the Web, the impact of advertising on caching, and ethical guidelines for using such data.

Building an Industrial Strength Web

A publication of O'Reilly & Associates and the World Wide Web Consortium (W3C)
Fall 1996
244 pages, ISBN 1-56592-211-5

Issue four focuses on the infrastructure needed to create and maintain an "Industrial Strength Web," from network protocols to application design. It includes the first standard versions of core Web protocols: HTTP/1.1, Digest Authentication, State Management (Cookies), and PICS. This issue also provides guides to the specs highlighting new features, papers explaining modifications to 1.1 (sticky and compressed headers), extensibility, support for collaborative authoring, and using distributed objects.

World Wide Web Journal *Volume 2*

Advancing HTML: Style and Substance

A publication of O'Reilly & Associates and the World Wide Web Consortium (W3C)
Winter 1996/97
254 pages, ISBN 1-56592-264-6

This issue is a guide to the specifications and tools that buttress the user interface to the World Wide Web: the technologies that make the Web come alive on the screen, on paper, in Braille, and on the phone. It includes the HTML 3.2 spec and a corresponding user guide, the CSS1 (cascading style sheets) spec and a corresponding user guide, a report on Amaya, an overview of GIF animation, a look at how JavaScript can customize HTML, papers on web accessibility, usability engineering, and multimedia design. We also take a look behind the scenes at the members of the HTML editorial review board, and their challenges in developing 3.2.

Scripting Languages: Automating the Web

A publication of O'Reilly & Associates and the World Wide Web Consortium (W3C)
Spring 1997
By Lincoln Stein, Clint Wong, Ron Petrusha, Shishir Gundavaram, et al.
244 pages, 1-56592-265-4

The informality, ease, and rapid development cycle of scripting languages make them well suited to the constant change common to most web sites. This issue of the *World Wide Web Journal*, *Scripting Languages: Automating the Web*, guides developers and users in choosing and deploying scripting solutions such as JavaScript, Perl, VB, Python, and Win-CGI. It also includes discussion of web database connectivity with scripting languages, CGI programming, and an in-depth interview with Perl developers Larry Wall and Tom Christiansen.

Web Security: A Matter of Trust

A publication of O'Reilly & Associates and the World Wide Web Consortium (W3C)
Summer 1997
By C. Bradford Biddle, Simson Garfinkel, John Gilmore, Rohit Khare, Cricket Liu, Lincoln Stein, et al.
282 pages, ISBN 1-56592-329-4

This collection of timely, in-depth articles frames web security as a matter of ***trust*** rather than ***cryptography***. It covers W3C's Digital Signature Initiative (DSI), which breaks new ground in this area by binding machine-readable labels to public key signatures. Other topics include medical records privacy issues, signature legality, trust in Internet information systems, electronic commerce, tips and tricks for secure web programming, and an interview with Christine Varney, FTC Commissioner and specialist in Internet-related commerce issues.

XML: Principles, Tools, and Techniques

A publication of O'Reilly & Associates and the World Wide Web Consortium (W3C)
Fall 1997
By Dan Connolly (Guest Editor)
250 pages (est.), ISBN 1-56592-349-9

XML, a landmark in the evolution of Internet information systems, allows authors to say what they mean, rather than merely how to say it. The shift to XML will unleash a diverse range of new applications, ranging from mathematical equation structures to new browser and client tools. This issue of the *Web Journal*, by guest editor Dan Connolly, is your first look at the technical specifications and early applications of a new data format that will rock every aspect of the Web, including markup, linking, and exchange.

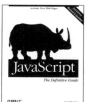

Information Architecture for the World Wide Web

By Louis Rosenfeld & Peter Morville
1st Edition November 1997 (est.)
200 pages (est.), ISBN 1-56592-282-4

Information Architecture for the World Wide Web is about applying the principles of architecture and library science to web site design. With this book, you learn how to design web sites and intranets that support growth, management, and ease of use. This book is for webmasters, designers, and anyone else involved in building a web site.

Learning VBScript

By Paul Lomax
1st Edition July 1997
616 pages, includes CD-ROM
ISBN 1-56592-247-6

This definitive guide shows web developers how to take full advantage of client-side scripting with the VBScript language. In addition to basic language features, it covers the Internet Explorer object model and discusses techniques for client-side scripting, like adding ActiveX controls to a web page or validating data before sending it to the server. Includes CD-ROM with over 170 code samples.

Web Client Programming with Perl

By Clinton Wong
1st Edition March 1997
228 pages, ISBN 1-56592-214-X

Web Client Programming with Perl shows you how to extend scripting skills to the Web. This book teaches you the basics of how browsers communicate with servers and how to write your own customized web clients to automate common tasks. It is intended for those who are motivated to develop software that offers a more flexible and dynamic response than a standard web browser.

Building Your Own WebSite

By Susan B. Peck & Stephen Arrants
1st Edition July 1996
514 pages, ISBN 1-56592-232-8

This is a hands-on reference for Windows® 95 and Windows NT™ users who want to host a site on the Web or on a corporate intranet. This step-by-step guide will have you creating live web pages in minutes. You'll also learn how to connect your web to information in other Windows applications, such as word processing documents and databases. The book is packed with examples and tutorials on every aspect of web management, and it includes the highly acclaimed WebSite™ 1.1 server software on CD-ROM.

Designing for the Web: Getting Started in a New Medium

By Jennifer Niederst
with Edie Freedman
1st Edition April 1996
180 pages, ISBN 1-56592-165-8

Designing for the Web gives you the basics you need to hit the ground running. Although geared toward designers, it covers information and techniques useful to anyone who wants to put graphics online. It explains how to work with HTML documents from a designer's point of view, outlines special problems with presenting information online, and walks through incorporating images into web pages, with emphasis on resolution and improving efficienc

Perl

Perl Resource Kit—UNIX Edition

By Larry Wall, Clay Irving, Nate Patwardhan, Ellen Siever & Brian Jepson
1st Edition November 1997 (est.)
1700 pages (est.)
ISBN 1-56592-370-7

The *Perl Resource Kit* is the most comprehesive collection of documentation and commercially enhanced software tools yet published for Perl programmers. The UNIX edition, the first in a series, is the definitive Perl distribution for webmasters, programmers, and system administrators.

Software tools on the Kit's CD include:

- A Java/Perl back-end to the Perl compiler, written by Larry Wall, creator of Perl
- Snapshot of the freeware Perl archives on CPAN, with an Install program and a web-aware interface for identifying more recent online CPAN tools

This new Java/Perl tool allows programmers to write Java classes with Perl implementations (innards), and run the code through a compiler back-end to produce Java byte-code. Using this new tool, programmers can exploit Java's wide availability on the browser (as well as on the server), while using Perl for the things that it does better than Java (such as string processing).

The Kit also includes four tutorial and reference books that contain systematic documentation for the most important Perl extension modules, as well as documentation for the commercially enhanced and supported tools on the CD. The books in the Kit are not available elsewhere or separatelyand include:

- *Perl Module Programmer's Guide*, by Clay Irving and Nate Patwardhan.
- *Perl Module Reference Manual* (two volumes), compiled and edited by Ellen Siever and David Futato.
- *Perl Utilities*, by Brian Jepson.

The *Perl Resource Kit* is the first comprehensive tutorialand reference documentation for hundreds of essential third-party Perl extension modules used for creating CGI applications and more. It features commercially enhanced Perl utilities specially developed for the Kit by Perl's creator, Larry Wall. And, it is all brought to you by the premier publisher of Perl and UNIX books and documentation, O'Reilly & Associates.

Programming Perl, 2nd Edition

By Larry Wall, Tom Christiansen & Randal L. Schwartz
2nd Edition September 1996
670 pages, ISBN 1-56592-149-6

Programming Perl, second edition, is the authoritative guide to Perl version 5, the scripting utility that has established itself as the programming tool of choice for the World Wide Web, UNIX system administration, and a vast range of other applications. Version 5 of Perl includes object-oriented programming facilities. The book is coauthored by Larry Wall, the creator of Perl.

Perl is a language for easily manipulating text, files, and processes. It provides a more concise and readable way to do many jobs that were formerly accomplished (with difficulty) by programming with C or one of the shells. Perl is likely to be available wherever you choose to work.And if it isn't, you can get it and install it easily and free of charge.

This heavily revised second edition of *Programming Perl* contains a full explanation of the features in Perl version 5.003. Contents include:

- An introduction to Perl
- Explanations of the language and its syntax
- Perl functions
- Perl library modules
- The use of references in Perl
- How to use Perl's object-oriented features
- Invocation options for Perl itself, and also for the utilities that come with Perl

Perl 5 Desktop Reference

By Johan Vromans
1st Edition February 1996
46 pages, ISBN 1-56592-187-9

This is the standard quick-reference guide for the Perl programming language. It provides a complete overview of the language, from variables to input and output, from flow control to regular expressions, from functions to document formats—all packed into a convenient, carry-around booklet. Updated to cover Perl version 5.003.

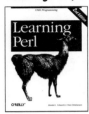

Web Server Administration

UNIX Web Server Administration

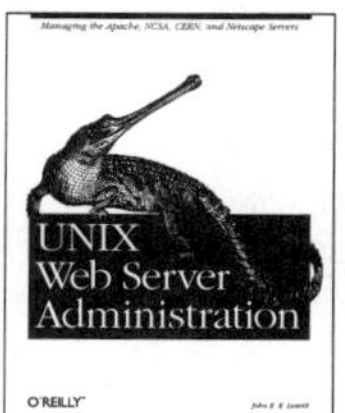

By John Leavitt
1st Edition December 1997 (est.)
350 pages (est.), ISBN 1-56592-217-4

The web server is one of the most crucial services a company can offer. *UNIX Web Server Administration* is a book for web administrators. It covers installation, customization, log analysis, multihoming, security, long-term maintenance, and performance tuning of the Apache, NCSA, CERN, and Netscape web servers.

Managing USENET

By David Lawrence & Henry Spencer
1st Edition October 1997 (est.)
400 pages (est.), ISBN 1-56592-198-4

USENET, also called Netnews, is the world's largest discussion forum, and it is doubling in size every year. This book, written by two of the foremost authorities on USENET administration, contains everything you need to know to administer a Netnews system. It covers C News and INN, explains the basics of starting a Netnews system, and offers guidelines to help ensure that your system is capable of handling news volume today—and in the future.

Web Security & Commerce

By Simson Garfinkel with Gene Spafford
1st Edition June 1997
506 pages, ISBN 1-56592-269-7

Learn how to minimize the risks of the Web with this comprehensive guide. It covers browser vulnerabilities, privacy concerns, issues with Java, JavaScript, ActiveX, and plug-ins, digital certificates, cryptography, web server security, blocking software, censorship technology, and relevant civil and criminal issues.

Apache: The Definitive Guide

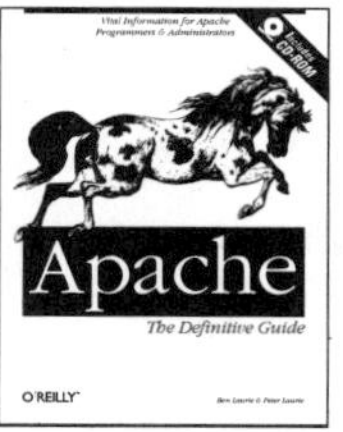

By Ben Laurie & Peter Laurie
1st Edition March 1997
274 pages, includes CD-ROM
ISBN 1-56592-250-6

Despite all the media attention to Netscape, Apache is far and away the most widely used web server platform in the world. This book, written and reviewed by key members of the Apache Group, is the only complete guide on the market today that describes how to obtain, set up, and secure the Apache software. Includes CD-ROM with Apache sources and demo sites discussed in the book.

Managing Internet Information Services

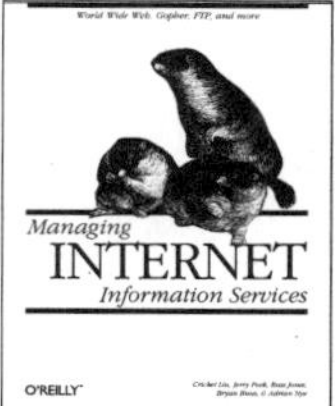

By Cricket Liu, Jerry Peek, Russ Jones,
Bryan Buus & Adrian Nye
1st Edition December 1994
668 pages, ISBN 1-56592-062-7

This comprehensive guide describes how to set up information services and make them available over the Internet. It discusses why a company would want to offer Internet services, provides complete coverage of all popular services, and tells how to select which ones to provide. Most of the book describes how to set up Gopher, World Wide Web, FTP, and WAIS servers and email services.

Java Programming

Java in a Nutshell, DELUXE EDITION

By David Flanagan, et al.
1st Edition June 1997
628 pages, includes CD-ROM and book,
ISBN 1-56592-304-9

Java in a Nutshell, Deluxe Edition, brings together on CD-ROM five volumes for Java developers and programmers, linking related info across books. *Exploring Java, 2nd Edition*, covers Java basics. *Java Language Reference, 2nd Edition*, *Java Fundamental Classes Reference*, and *Java AWT Reference* provide a definitive set of documentation on the Java language and the Java 1.1 core API. *Java in a Nutshell, 2nd Edition*, our bestselling quick reference, is included both on the CD-ROM and in a companion desktop edition. This deluxe library is an indispensable resource for anyone doing serious programming with Java 1.1.

Exploring Java, Second Edition

By Pat Niemeyer & Josh Peck
2nd Edition September 1997 (est.)
628 pages (est.)
ISBN 1-56592-271-9

Whether you're just migrating to Java or working steadily in the forefront of Java development, this book, fully revised for Java 1.1, gives a clear, systematic overview of the language. It covers the essentials of hot topics like Beans and RMI, as well as writing applets and other applications, such as networking programs, content and protocol handlers, and security managers.

Java Language Reference, Second Edition

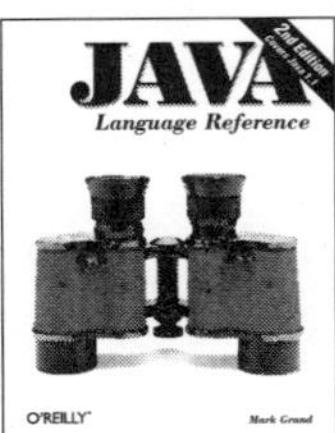

By Mark Grand
2nd Edition July 1997
492 pages, ISBN 1-56592-326-X

This book helps you understand the subtle nuances of Java—from the definition of data types to the syntax of expressions and control structures—so you can ensure your programs run exactly as expected. The second edition covers the new language features that have been added in Java 1.1, such as inner classes, class literals, and instance initializers.

Java Fundamental Classes Reference

By Mark Grand &
Jonathan Knudsen
1st Edition May 1997
1114 pages, ISBN 1-56592-241-7

The *Java Fundamental Classes Reference* provides complete reference documentation on the core Java 1.1 classes that comprise the *java.lang*, *java.io*, *java.net*, *java.util*, *java.text*, *java.math*, *java.lang.reflect*, and *java.util.zip* packages. Part of O'Reilly's Java documentation series, this edition describes Version 1.1 of the Java Development Kit. It includes easy-to-use reference material and provides lots of sample code to help you learn by example.

Java AWT Reference

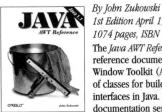

By John Zukowski
1st Edition April 1997
1074 pages, ISBN 1-56592-240-9

The *Java AWT Reference* provides complete reference documentation on the Abstract Window Toolkit (AWT), a large collection of classes for building graphical user interfaces in Java. Part of O'Reilly's Java documentation series, this edition describes both Version 1.0.2 and Version 1.1 of the Java Development Kit, includes easy-to-use reference material on every AWT class, and provides lots of sample code.

Java in a Nutshell, Second Edition

By David Flanagan
2nd Edition May 1997
628 pages, ISBN 1-56592-262-X

The bestselling Java book just got better. Newly updated, it now describes all the classes in the Java 1.1 API, with the exception of the still-evolving Enterprise APIs. And it still has all the great features that have made this the Java book most often recommended on the Internet: practical, real-world examples and compact reference information. It's the only quick reference you'll need.

Java Programming *continued*

Java Distributed Computing

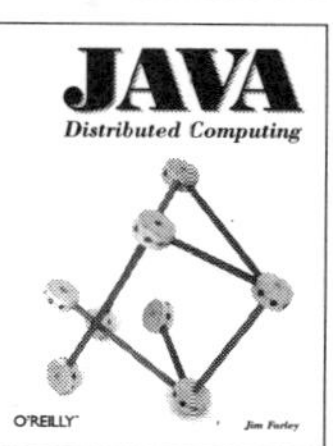

By Jim Farley
1st Edition November 1997 (est.)
350 pages (est.), ISBN 1-56592-206-9

Java Distributed Computing offers a general introduction to distributed computing, meaning programs that run on two or more systems. It focuses primarily on how to structure and write distributed applications and, therefore, discusses issues like designing protocols, security, working with databases, and dealing with low bandwidth situations.

Java Examples in a Nutshell

By David Flanagan
1st Edition September 1997 (est.)
400 pages (est.), ISBN 1-56592-371-5

Java Examples in a Nutshell is chock full of practical, real-world Java programming examples. The author of the bestselling *Java in a Nutshell* has created an entire book of example programs that you can learn from and modify for your own use. If you learn best "by example," this companion volume to *Java in a Nutshell* is the book for you.

Netscape IFC in a Nutshell

By Dean Petrich with David Flanagan
1st Edition August 1997
370 pages, ISBN 1-56592-343-X

This desktop quick reference and programmer's guide is all the documentation programmers need to start creating highly customizable graphical user interfaces with the Internet Foundation Classes (IFC), Version 1.1. The IFC is a Java class library freely available from Netscape. It is also bundled with Communicator, making it the preferred development environment for the Navigator 4.0 web browser. Master the IFC now for a head start on the forthcoming Java Foundation Classes (JFC).

Developing Java Beans

By Robert Englander
1st Edition June 1997
316 pages, ISBN 1-56592-289-1

Developing Java Beans is a complete introduction to Java's component architecture. It describes how to write Beans, which are software components that can be used in visual programming environments. This book discusses event adapters, serialization, introspection, property editors, and customizers, and shows how to use Beans within ActiveX controls.

Java Virtual Machine

By Jon Meyer & Troy Downing
1st Edition March 1997
452 pages, includes diskette
ISBN 1-56592-194-1

This book is a comprehensive programming guide for the Java Virtual Machine (JVM). It gives readers a strong overview and reference of the JVM so that they may create their own implementations of the JVM or write their own compilers that create Java object code. A Java assembler is provided with the book, so the examples can all be compiled and executed.

Database Programming with JDBC and Java

By George Reese
1st Edition June 1997
240 pages, ISBN 1-56592-270-0

Database Programming with JDBC and Java describes the standard Java interfaces that make portable,object-oriented access to relational databases possible and offers a robust model for writing applications that are easy to maintain. It introduces the JDBC and RMI packages and includes a set of patterns that separate the functions of the Java application and facilitate the growth and maintenance of your application.

Java Network Programming

By Elliotte Rusty Harold
1st Edition February 1997
442 pages, ISBN 1-56592-227-1

The network is the soul of Java. Most of what is new and exciting about Java centers around the potential for new kinds of dynamic, networked applications. *Java Network Programming* teaches you to work with Sockets, write network clients and servers, and gives you an advanced look at the new areas like multicasting, using the server API, and RMI. Covers Java 1.1.

Java Threads

By Scott Oaks and Henry Wong
1st Edition January 1997
268 pages, ISBN 1-56592-216-6

With this book, you'll learn how to take full advantage of Java's thread facilities: where to use threads to increase efficiency, how to use them effectively, and how to avoid common mistakes like deadlock and race conditions. Covers Java 1.1.

How to stay in touch with O'Reilly

1. Visit Our Award-Winning Web Site

http://www.oreilly.com/

★"Top 100 Sites on the Web" —*PC Magazine*
★"Top 5% Web sites" —*Point Communications*
★"3-Star site" —*The McKinley Group*

Our web site contains a library of comprehensiveproduct information (including book excerpts and tables of contents), downloadable software, background articles, interviews with technology leaders, links to relevant sites, book cover art, and more. File us in your Bookmarks or Hotlist!

2. Join Our Email Mailing Lists

New Product Releases

To receive automatic email with brief descriptions of all new O'Reilly products as they are released, send email to:
listproc@online.oreilly.com
Put the following information in the first line of your message (*not* in the Subject field):
subscribe oreilly-news "Your Name" of "Your Organization" (for example: subscribe oreilly-news Kris Webber of Fine Enterprises)

O'Reilly Events

If you'd also like us to send information about trade show events, special promotions, and other O'Reilly events, send email to: **listproc@online.oreilly.com**
Put the following information in the first line of your message (*not* in the Subject field):
subscribe oreilly-events "Your Name" of "Your Organization"

3. Get Examples from Our Books via FTP

There are two ways to access an archive of example files from our books:

Regular FTP

- ftp to:
  ftp.oreilly.com
  (login: anonymous
  password: your email address)
- Point your web browser to:
  ftp://ftp.oreilly.com/

FTPMAIL

- Send an email message to:
  ftpmail@online.oreilly.com
  (Write "help" in the message body)

4. Visit Our Gopher Site

- Connect your gopher to:
  gopher.oreilly.com
- Point your web browser to:
  gopher://gopher.oreilly.com/
- Telnet to:
  gopher.oreilly.com
  login: gopher

5. Contact Us via Email

order@oreilly.com
To place a book or software order online. Good for North American and international customers.

subscriptions@oreilly.com
To place an order for any of our newsletters or periodicals.

books@oreilly.com
General questions about any of our books.

software@oreilly.com
For general questions and product information about our software. Check out O'Reilly Software Online at **http://software.oreilly.com/** for software and technical support information. Registered O'Reilly software users send your questions to: **website-support@oreilly.com**

cs@oreilly.com
For answers to problems regarding your order or our products.

booktech@oreilly.com
For book content technical questions or corrections.

proposals@oreilly.com
To submit new book or software proposals to our editors and product managers.

international@oreilly.com
For information about our international distributors or translation queries. For a list of our distributors outside of North America check out:
http://www.oreilly.com/www/order/country.html

O'Reilly & Associates, Inc.
101 Morris Street, Sebastopol, CA 95472 USA
TEL 707-829-0515 or 800-998-9938
(6am to 5pm PST)
FAX 707-829-0104

Titles from O'Reilly

Please note that upcoming titles are displayed in italic.

WebProgramming

Apache: The Definitive Guide
Building Your Own Web Conferences
Building Your Own Website
CGI Programming for the World Wide Web
Designing for the Web
HTML: The Definitive Guide, 2nd Ed.
JavaScript: The Definitive Guide, 2nd Ed.
Learning Perl
Programming Perl, 2nd Ed.
Mastering Regular Expressions
WebMaster in a Nutshell
Web Security & Commerce
Web Client Programming with Perl
World Wide Web Journal

Using the Internet

Smileys
The Future Does Not Compute
The Whole Internet User's Guide & Catalog
The Whole Internet for Win 95
Using Email Effectively
Bandits on the Information Superhighway

Java Series

Exploring Java
Java AWT Reference
Java Fundamental Classes Reference
Java in a Nutshell
Java Language Reference, 2nd Edition
Java Network Programming
Java Threads
Java Virtual Machine

Software

WebSite™ 1.1
WebSite Professional™
Building Your Own Web Conferences
WebBoard™
PolyForm™
Statisphere™

Songline Guides

NetActivism
Net Law
NetLearning
Net Lessons
NetResearch
NetSuccess
NetTravel

System Administration

Building Internet Firewalls
Computer Crime: A Crimefighter's Handbook
Computer Security Basics
DNS and BIND, 2nd Ed.
Essential System Administration, 2nd Ed.
Getting Connected: The Internet at 56K and Up
Linux Network Administrator's Guide
Managing Internet Information Services
Managing NFS and NIS
Networking Personal Computers with TCP/IP
Practical UNIX & Internet Security, 2nd Ed.
PGP: Pretty Good Privacy
sendmail, 2nd Ed.
sendmail Desktop Reference
System Performance Tuning
TCP/IP Network Administration
termcap & terminfo
Using & Managing UUCP
Volume 8: X Window System Administrator's Guide
Web Security & Commerce

UNIX

Exploring Expect
Learning VBScript
Learning GNU Emacs, 2nd Ed.
Learning the bash Shell
Learning the Korn Shell
Learning the UNIX Operating System
Learning the vi Editor
Linux in a Nutshell
Making TeX Work
Linux Multimedia Guide
Running Linux, 2nd Ed.
SCO UNIX in a Nutshell
sed & awk, 2nd Edition
Tcl/Tk Tools
UNIX in a Nutshell: System V Edition
UNIX Power Tools
Using csh & tsch
When You Can't Find Your UNIX System Administrator
Writing GNU Emacs Extensions

Web Review Studio Series

Gif Animation Studio
Shockwave Studio

Windows

Dictionary of PC Hardware and Data Communications Terms
Inside the Windows 95 Registry
Inside the Windows 95 File System
Windows Annoyances
Windows NT File System Internals
Windows NT in a Nutshell

Programming

Advanced Oracle PL/SQL Programming
Applying RCS and SCCS
C++: The Core Language
Checking C Programs with lint
DCE Security Programming
Distributing Applications Across DCE & Windows NT
Encyclopedia of Graphics File Formats, 2nd Ed.
Guide to Writing DCE Applications
lex & yacc
Managing Projects with make
Mastering Oracle Power Objects
Oracle Design: The Definitive Guide
Oracle Performance Tuning, 2nd Ed.
Oracle PL/SQL Programming
Porting UNIX Software
POSIX Programmer's Guide
POSIX.4: Programming for the Real World
Power Programming with RPC
Practical C Programming
Practical C++ Programming
Programming Python
Programming with curses
Programming with GNU Software
Pthreads Programming
Software Portability with imake, 2nd Ed.
Understanding DCE
Understanding Japanese Information Processing
UNIX Systems Programming for SVR4

Berkeley 4.4 Software Distribution

4.4BSD System Manager's Manual
4.4BSD User's Reference Manual
4.4BSD User's Supplementary Documents
4.4BSD Programmer's Reference Manual
4.4BSD Programmer's Supplementary Documents
X Programming
Vol. 0: X Protocol Reference Manual
Vol. 1: Xlib Programming Manual
Vol. 2: Xlib Reference Manual
Vol. 3M: X Window System User's Guide, Motif Edition
Vol. 4M: X Toolkit Intrinsics Programming Manual, Motif Edition
Vol. 5: X Toolkit Intrinsics Reference Manual
Vol. 6A: Motif Programming Manual
Vol. 6B: Motif Reference Manual
Vol. 6C: Motif Tools
Vol. 8 : X Window System Administrator's Guide
Programmer's Supplement for Release 6
X User Tools
The X Window System in a Nutshell

Career & Business

Building a Successful Software Business
The Computer User's Survival Guide
Love Your Job!
Electronic Publishing on CD-ROM

Travel

Travelers' Tales: Brazil
Travelers' Tales: Food
Travelers' Tales: France
Travelers' Tales: Gutsy Women
Travelers' Tales: India
Travelers' Tales: Mexico
Travelers' Tales: Paris
Travelers' Tales: San Francisco
Travelers' Tales: Spain
Travelers' Tales: Thailand
Travelers' Tales: A Woman's World

International Distributors

UK, Europe, Middle East and Northern Africa *(except France, Germany, Switzerland, & Austria)*

INQUIRIES
International Thomson Publishing Europe
Berkshire House
168-173 High Holborn
London WC1V 7AA, United Kingdom
Telephone: 44-171-497-1422
Fax: 44-171-497-1426
Email: itpint@itps.co.uk

ORDERS
International Thomson Publishing Services, Ltd.
Cheriton House, North Way
Andover, Hampshire SP10 5BE, United Kingdom
Telephone: 44-264-342-832 (UK orders)
Telephone: 44-264-342-806 (outside UK)
Fax: 44-264-364418 (UK orders)
Fax: 44-264-342761 (outside UK)
UK & Eire orders: itpuk@itps.co.uk
International orders: itpint@itps.co.uk

France

Editions Eyrolles
61 bd Saint-Germain
75240 Paris Cedex 05
France
Fax: 33-01-44-41-11-44

FRENCH LANGUAGE BOOKS
All countries except Canada
Phone: 33-01-44-41-46-16
Email: geodif@eyrolles.com

ENGLISH LANGUAGE BOOKS
Phone: 33-01-44-41-11-87
Email: distribution@eyrolles.com

Australia

WoodsLane Pty. Ltd.
7/5 Vuko Place, Warriewood NSW 2102
P.O. Box 935, Mona Vale NSW 2103
Australia
Telephone: 61-2-9970-5111
Fax: 61-2-9970-5002
Email: info@woodslane.com.au

Germany, Switzerland, and Austria

INQUIRIES
O'Reilly Verlag
Balthasarstr. 81
D-50670 Köln
Germany
Telephone: 49-221-97-31-60-0
Fax: 49-221-97-31-60-8
Email: anfragen@oreilly.de

ORDERS
International Thomson Publishing
Königswinterer Straße 418
53227 Bonn, Germany
Telephone: 49-228-97024 0
Fax: 49-228-441342
Email: order@oreilly.de

Asia *(except Japan & India)*

INQUIRIES
International Thomson Publishing Asia
60 Albert Street #15-01
Albert Complex
Singapore 189969
Telephone: 65-336-6411
Fax: 65-336-7411

ORDERS
Telephone: 65-336-6411
Fax: 65-334-1617
thomson@signet.com.sg

New Zealand

WoodsLane New Zealand Ltd.
21 Cooks Street (P.O. Box 575)
Wanganui, New Zealand
Telephone: 64-6-347-6543
Fax: 64-6-345-4840
Email: info@woodslane.com.au

Japan

O'Reilly Japan, Inc.
Kiyoshige Building 2F
12-Banchi, Sanei-cho
Shinjuku-ku
Tokyo 160 Japan
Telephone: 81-3-3356-5227
Fax: 81-3-3356-5261
Email: kenji@oreilly.com

India

Computer Bookshop (India) PVT. LTD.
190 Dr. D.N. Road, Fort
Bombay 400 001
India
Telephone: 91-22-207-0989
Fax: 91-22-262-3551
Email: cbsbom@giasbm01.vsnl.net.in

The Americas

O'Reilly & Associates, Inc.
101 Morris Street
Sebastopol, CA 95472 U.S.A.
Telephone: 707-829-0515
Telephone: 800-998-9938 (U.S. & Canada)
Fax: 707-829-0104
Email: order@oreilly.com

Southern Africa

International Thomson Publishing Southern Africa
Building 18, Constantia Park
138 Sixteenth Road
P.O. Box 2459
Halfway House, 1685 South Africa
Telephone: 27-11-805-4819
Fax: 27-11-805-3648

PLEASE TEAR OUT THE BOOKMARK AND POSTCARD ALONG THE PERFERATIONS AND ENJOY!

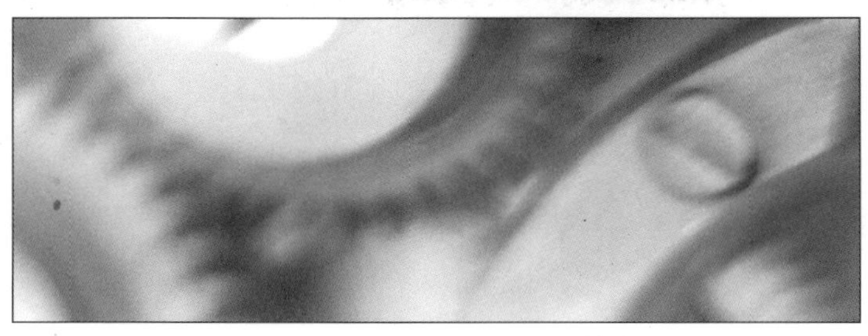

O'REILLY™

O'Reilly & Associates, Inc.
101 Morris Street
Sebastopol, CA 95472-9902
1-800-998-9938

Visit us online at:
http://www.oreilly.com/
orders@oreilly.com

WORLD WIDE WEB JOURNAL

SUBSCRIBE NOW!

☛ **To order a subscription to the *World Wide Web Journal*, complete this card and drop it in the mailbox, or**

CALL: (800) 998-9938 (US and Canada, Weekdays 6 a.m.- 5 p.m. pst) **FAX:** (707) 829-0104 **EMAIL:** subscriptions@oreilly.com

For more information about the *World Wide Web Journal*, point your Web browser to **http://www.w3j.com/**

Name ____________________ Company/Organization ____________________

Address ____________________

City ____________ State ____________ Zip/Postal Code ____________ Country ____________

Telephone ____________ Fax ____________ Internet or other email address (specify network) ____________

☛ **Your subscription will start with the next available issue. Prices subject to change.**

❑ $99.95 USA Regular Subscriptions ❑ $119.95 Canada & Mexico ❑ $149.95 International

☛ **Charge it!** ❑ Visa ❑ MasterCard ❑ American Express ❑ Discover Card

Account Number ____________________ Exp. Date ____________

Name as it appears on card ____________________ Signature ____________________

WWJL

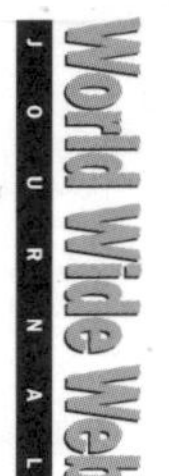

The *World Wide Web Journal*, published quarterly by O'Reilly & Associates, Inc, records the work of the World Wide Web Consortium (W3C), and publishes timely, state-of-the-art articles from the wider Web community.

Visit us online at:
http://www.w3j.com/

The *World Wide Web Journal*, published quarterly by O'Reilly & Associates, Inc, records the work of the World Wide Web Consortium (W3C), and publishes timely, state-of-the-art articles from the wider Web community.

Visit us online at:
http://www.w3j.com/

PLACE
STAMP
HERE

NO POSTAGE
NECESSARY IF
MAILED IN THE
UNITED STATES

BUSINESS REPLY MAIL

FIRST CLASS MAIL PERMIT NO. 80 SEBASTOPOL, CA

Postage will be paid by addressee

O'Reilly & Associates, Inc.
101 Morris Street
Sebastopol, CA 95472-9902
Attn: Subscriptions